The Evolution of Carbon Markets

Carbon markets are developing and expanding around the world, but how and to what extent is their design shaped by learning and interaction between them? How do these markets function, and what is the role of design?

Carrying out a ground-breaking analysis of their design and diffusion, this book covers all the major carbon market systems and processes around the world: the EU, RGGI, California, Tokyo, New Zealand, Australia, China, South Korea and Kazakhstan. It offers a systematic, in-depth discussion and comparison of the key design features in these systems with expert contributors exploring how, and to what extent, these features have been shaped by central policy diffusion mechanisms and domestic politics.

By focusing on the specific design features of the instruments used, this volume makes important contributions to diffusion theory, highlighting how ETS diffusion processes more often have resulted in design divergence than convergence, and discussing the implications of this finding for the vision of linked systems in the post-Paris era. It will be of significant interest to a broad audience interested in the emergence, evolution, functioning and interaction of carbon markets.

Jørgen Wettestad is research professor at the Fridtjof Nansen Institute in Oslo, Norway. He has published several books and numerous articles on international and EU environmental policy, with particular attention to emissions trading. His most recent books are *Rescuing EU Emissions Trading: The Climate Policy Flagship* (Palgrave 2016, together with Torbjørg Jevnaker) and *EU Climate Policy: Industry, Policy Interaction and External Environment* (Ashgate 2013, together with Elin L. Boasson). He has been a visiting scholar at IIASA, Austria, and the Institute for International Studies, Berkeley, CA. He has also led and participated in several EU-funded projects, participated in numerous international research projects and been programme director at the Fridtjof Nansen Institute for a long period. Wettestad serves regularly as peer reviewer for international journals and national research councils and has been editorial board member of the journal *Climate Policy* since 2001.

Lars H. Gulbrandsen is research professor and the deputy director at the Fridtjof Nansen Institute in Oslo, Norway, where he also served as director of the research programme on Global Environmental Governance and Law (2000–16). His main research interests are within the fields of global environmental politics and international political economy, with a particular focus on climate and energy policy, eco-labelling and certification, private regulation and corporate social responsibility. He holds a PhD in political science from the University of Oslo and an MSc from the London School of Economics and has been a visiting scholar at the Kennedy School of Government, Harvard University. Gulbrandsen participates in several international and national research projects, serves regularly as peer reviewer for international journals and national research councils and is editorial board member of the journal *Global Environmental Politics*.

Transforming Environmental Politics and Policy

Series Editors: Timothy Doyle, Keele University, UK and University of Adelaide, Australia and Philip Catney, Keele University, UK

The theory and practice of environmental politics and policy are rapidly emerging as key areas of intense concern in the first, third and industrializing worlds. People of diverse nationalities, religions and cultures wrestle daily with environment and development issues central to human and non-human survival on the planet Earth. Air, Water, Earth, Fire. These central elements mix together in so many ways, spinning off new constellations of issues, ideas and actions, gathering under a multitude of banners: energy security, food sovereignty, climate change, genetic modification, environmental justice and sustainability, population growth, water quality and access, air pollution, mal-distribution and over-consumption of scarce resources, the rights of the non-human, the welfare of future citizens-the list goes on.

What is much needed in green debates is for theoretical discussions to be rooted in policy outcomes and service delivery. So, while still engaging in the theoretical realm, this series also seeks to provide a 'real world' policy-making dimension. Politics and policy making is interpreted widely here to include the territories, discourses, instruments and domains of political parties, non-governmental organizations, protest movements, corporations, international regimes, and transnational networks.

From the local to the global-and back again-this series explores environmental politics and policy within countries and cultures, researching the ways in which green issues cross North-South and East-West divides. The 'Transforming Environmental Politics and Policy' series exposes the exciting ways in which environmental politics and policy can transform political relationships, in all their forms.

For a full list of titles in this series, please visit - https://www.routledge.com/politics/series/ASHSER-1371

Recent titles

US Climate Change Policy
Christopher J. Bailey

Community Gardening as Social Action
Claire Nettle

Energy, Governance and Security in Thailand and Myanmar (Burma)
A Critical Approach to Environmental Politics in the South
Adam Simpson

Global Environmental Governance, Civil Society and Wildlife
Birdsong After the Storm
Margi Prideaux

The Evolution of Carbon Markets

Design and Diffusion

Edited by Jørgen Wettestad and Lars H. Gulbrandsen

Routledge
Taylor & Francis Group
LONDON AND NEW YORK

First published 2018 by Routledge

2 Park Square, Milton Park, Abingdon, Oxfordshire OX14 4RN
52 Vanderbilt Avenue, New York, NY 10017

Routledge is an imprint of the Taylor & Francis Group, an informa business

First issued in paperback 2019

British Library Cataloguing-in-Publication Data
A catalogue record for this book is available from the British Library

Library of Congress Cataloging-in-Publication Data
Names: Wettestad, Jørgen, 1955– editor. | Gulbrandsen, Lars H., editor.
Title: The evolution of carbon markets : design and diffusion / edited by Jørgen Wettestad and Lars H. Gulbrandsen.
Description: Abingdon, Oxon ; New York, NY : Routledge, [2018] | Series: Transforming environmental politics and policy | Includes bibliographical references and index.
Identifiers: LCCN 2017033216 | ISBN 9780415785426 (hardback) | ISBN 9781315228266 (e-book)
Subjects: LCSH: Emissions trading—Case studies. | Carbon taxes—Case studies.
Classification: LCC HC79.P55 E96 2018 | DDC 363.738/747—dc23
LC record available at https://lccn.loc.gov/2017033216

ISBN: 978-0-415-78542-6 (hbk)
ISBN: 978-0-367-26446-8 (pbk)

Typeset in Times New Roman
by Apex CoVantage, LLC

Contents

Figures

Tables

Contributors

Steinar Andresen is a research professor at the Fridtjof Nansen Institute, Norway.

Ian Bailey is a professor at the School of Geography, Earth and Environmental Sciences, Plymouth University, UK.

Guri Bang is research director at CICERO – Center for International Climate and Environmental Research, Norway.

Katja Biedenkopf is an assistant professor at Leuven International and European Studies, Leuven University, Belgium.

Christoph Böhringer is a professor at the Department of Economics, University of Oldenburg, Germany.

Lars H. Gulbrandsen is a research professor and the deputy director at the Fridtjof Nansen Institute, Norway.

Nichola Harmer is a lecturer at the School of Geography, Earth and Environmental Sciences, Plymouth University, UK.

Gørild Heggelund is a senior research fellow at the Fridtjof Nansen Institute, Norway.

Masahiko Iguchi is an associate professor at the Department of International Relations, Kyoto Sangyo University, Japan.

Tor Håkon Jackson Inderberg is a senior research fellow at the Fridtjof Nansen Institute, Norway.

Torbjørg Jevnaker is a research fellow at the Fridtjof Nansen Institute, Norway.

Solveig Lygre is a former master student at the Fridtjof Nansen Institute, Norway.

Duan Maosheng is an associate professor at the Institute of Energy, Environment and Economy, Tsinghua University, China.

Knut Einar Rosendahl is a professor at the School of Economics and Business, Norwegian University of Life Sciences, Norway.

François Sammut is a director at Carbon Limits, Norway.

Iselin Stensdal is a research fellow at the Fridtjof Nansen Institute, Norway.

Arild Underdal is a professor at the Department of Political Science, University of Oslo, Norway.

David G. Victor is a professor at the School of Global Policy and Strategy, University of California at San Diego, US.

Tang Weiqi is deputy director at the Center for Energy Economics and Strategy Studies at Fudan University and analyst at CIB Research, China.

Jørgen Wettestad is a research professor at the Fridtjof Nansen Institute, Norway.

Preface

The first ideas for this project were developed in 2013, through work at the Fridtjof Nansen Institute (FNI) on a project proposal on emissions trading. Fascinated by the proliferation of emissions trading systems around the world, we became interested in how they diffuse across jurisdictions, and with what design outcomes. In particular, we wanted to learn more about the causal role of international diffusion in shaping the design of emissions trading systems.

In late 2013, KLIMAFORSK, a large-scale research programme on climate change under the Research Council of Norway, awarded a three-year grant to fund our proposed project. This book is based on work conducted as part of that project, which was called 'Designing Effective Emissions Trading: The Contribution of International Diffusion' (ETS DIFFUSION). Additional funding came from the FNI and the research programme CICEP (Strategic Challenges in International Climate and Energy Policy), allowing us to cover more cases than envisioned in the initial project proposal.

This book is the result of a journey that brought together more than a dozen researchers with a shared interest in climate politics and, more specifically, in emissions trading as a climate policy instrument. It could not have been written without the dedication and commitment of the entire project group, all of whom have participated as contributing authors. In addition to providing in-depth knowledge about almost all emissions trading systems that are, or have been, operational around the world, they have contributed significantly to developing our analytical framework and comparative analysis through discussions and comments at several project meetings. We thank them for their hard work and insightful contributions – it was indeed a pleasure to work together. We are especially grateful to Arild Underdal and David Victor for their key contributions to the theory framework (Chapter 2) and the comparative analysis (Chapter 13), as well as for their thoughtful comments on the introduction (Chapter 1). Discussions with Arild and David, on phone from California and other parts of the world, have also been a great source of inspiration.

All case studies have been reviewed by the editors and other members of the project group in several rounds. In that sense, too, this has truly been a collaborative project, resulting, we hope, in a tightly integrated book. As editors, we have urged all authors to follow the same methodology, research design and case-study structure, all leading up to what we believe are solid conclusions. We are grateful to Harro van Asselt for reviewing all the case-study chapters as well as the conceptual and comparative chapters. His insightful and detailed comments helped us improve the manuscript considerably. Our work has also benefited from discussions at a 2016 ETS workshop in Leuven, Belgium, as part of the EU-funded INOGOV project, at the 2016 Berlin Conference on Global Environmental Change and at several International Studies Association annual conventions over the last few years. Special thanks to Matthew J. Hoffmann, Robert O. Keohane and Sebastian Oberthür for providing critical and helpful comments on the research presented.

Susan Høivik provided invaluable and encouraging assistance with language polishing and editing. We thank her for her great efforts to improve the language and style of the book. Ida Folkestad Soltvedt has done an excellent job of final editing and formatting the entire manuscript. Finally, Rob Sorsby and Claire Maloney at Routledge have provided timely and encouraging assistance with the publishing process.

Working on this project has truly been exiting, from start to finish. We hope that you, the readers, will enjoy the outcome just as much as we have enjoyed producing it.

Jørgen Wettestad and Lars H. Gulbrandsen
Lysaker, Norway
June 2017

1 Introduction

Jørgen Wettestad and Lars H. Gulbrandsen

The emergence of emissions trading

Global climate change caused by anthropogenic sources – greenhouse gas emissions from human activity – is widely seen as a 'malign' or 'wicked' problem (Miles et al. 2002; Jordan and Huitema 2014).[1] The problem is a by-product of multiple necessary societal activities all around the globe, such as burning fossil fuels for electricity, heat and transportation; industrial production; and agriculture. The actors involved are numerous, and policy-makers struggle to find the best 'cures' and policy responses. Essentially, what is required is a broader low-carbon transformation – meaning significant transition costs. It is widely acknowledged that such a low-carbon transition is needed, but wealth and energy systems vary considerably, and with mitigation and transition costs unevenly distributed among and within countries. This helps explain why the idea of flexible policy measures, based on economic incentives, has emerged. Carbon pricing is seen by many as a better way of addressing the multifarious policy challenges at hand than more rigid command-and-control measures (see e.g. Stern 2006).

Taxes belong to this category of carbon-pricing instruments. But taxes have a long history of being politically difficult to implement. Enter emissions trading, which is favoured by many in industry who worry about compliance costs and is tolerable to many in the environmental community who are keen to see an absolute cap on emissions. A fundamental reason for the growing interest from governments as well as industries and other stakeholders is that emissions trading systems (ETS) leave governments in control of total emission levels in the ETS sectors and the basic rules for market transactions – while stakeholders are free to determine how many emissions permits to buy or sell. This instrument uniquely combines elements of political governance and 'steering' with flexibility. But it is also complex, and has in practice run into various problems, to which we return throughout this book.

This volume examines the proliferation of emissions trading, which has increasingly been adopted as a response to the 'super-wicked' climate problem. As some systems are frontrunners while others have taken up ETS more recently, it is crucial to understand interaction and learning among the various systems. In particular, we are interested in the *diffusion* of emissions trading across jurisdictions. In international relations theory, policy diffusion has been understood as 'interdependent, but uncoordinated, decision making' in which one jurisdiction unilaterally adopts a policy or practice pursued by another jurisdiction (Elkins and Simmons 2005: 35). As explained in the following, the key focus of this book is *the role of policy diffusion for ETS design outcomes around the globe*.

According to the Elkins/Simmons definition, diffusion is a process generally seen as leading to *convergence*, as jurisdictions adopt similar policies or practices. This expectation of convergence is understandable because earlier work, including that of Elkins and Simmons, examined processes in which there were strong incentives for convergence. However, the ETS experience has entailed fewer such pressures, as we will show. Hence, we adopt a broader understanding of diffusion that allows for *divergence*. While such an understanding of diffusion might constitute 'concept stretching' (Sartori 1970), we maintain that our interpretation is consistent with definitions framed in terms that allow also for divergence.

Specifically, we adopt the definition proposed by Simmons et al. (2006: 787): 'international policy diffusion occurs when government policy decisions in one country are systematically conditioned by prior policy choices made in another country (sometimes mediated by the behaviour of international organizations or even private actors or organizations)'. Our broad understanding of diffusion processes is also better suited for the ETS experience and our focus on domestic political factors as mediating variables. That focus on domestic politics is the central explanation why our study finds more divergence in ETS design than earlier studies of diffusion have found.[2]

An important point of departure and reference for other systems is undoubtedly the EU ETS, adopted in 2003 and operational since 2005. In 2008, after the overhaul of the ETS for the third trading period (2013–20), the leader of the European Commission's environment department at the time, Stavros Dimas, triumphantly declared: 'the [EU] ETS is going to be the prototype for the world to imitate' (ENDS Europe 2008).

But for proponents of carbon trading, the post-2008 era has definitely been a mixed experience (see Mehling 2012; Calel 2013; IETA 2016; World Bank 2016; ICAP 2016). The EU has experienced increasing problems, with a growing surplus of allowances and a low carbon price, caused not least by recessionary pressures. Furthermore, the growth of renewables has further lowered demand for allowances, highlighting the importance of smooth interactions with other policy instruments and of placing carbon trading systems in a broader political, social and cultural context.

Around the globe, other significant systems have started operating, like that in California, which covers the world's seventh biggest economy. Of particular interest and importance is the turn to emissions trading in China, the world's biggest greenhouse gas (GHG) emitter (some 10 billion tons CO_2 per year). Seven subnational pilot systems have been established, and a national system, twice as large as the EU ETS, is to be introduced in 2017. There are also interesting developments elsewhere – such as smaller systems established in countries as diverse as Kazakhstan, Switzerland and South Korea, as well as countries such as Thailand, Brazil and Mexico now considering the introduction of emissions trading (see e.g. ICAP 2016). The December 2015 climate summit in Paris showed and offered further support to the increasing interest in carbon pricing worldwide. About half of the world's countries signed pledges to the summit to reduce their emissions by means of carbon trade (ICAP 2016: 3).

The proliferation of emissions trading is indeed a fascinating development, and this volume builds upon and complements a rapidly increasing body of knowledge. Briefly summing up, there is valuable knowledge on several individual markets, particularly the EU and the Chinese pilots (see Skjærseth and Wettestad 2008; Zhang 2015; Wettestad and Jevnaker 2016; Goron and Cassisa 2017). As to more general markets and systems overviews, several useful mapping exercises have been conducted (e.g. EDF/IETA 2016; IETA 2016; ICAP 2016), including interesting anecdotal evidence (PMR/ICAP 2016). In addition, there are more general discussions of carbon markets (e.g. Meckling 2011; Stephan and Lane 2015; Rosenzweig 2016; Weishaar 2016), also highlighting the differing 'cultures' (Knox-Hayes 2016). Paterson et al. (2014) and Van Asselt (2016) are valuable contributions to the more specific issue of ETS diffusion.

Still, important research gaps need to be addressed. First, despite numerous helpful mapping exercises, there has been little systematic, in-depth, comparative research on ETS *design*. Second, there are several ETS systems that have hardly been examined in the academic literature; examples here are Kazakhstan, New Zealand and South Korea. Third, regarding ETS policy diffusion, most research has focused on diffusion of the ETS instrument per se, not specific design features (see Voss 2007; Betsill and Hoffman 2011; Meckling 2011; Paterson et al. 2014). Fourth, there has been little systematic research on how domestic politics and institutions act as mediating variables of international diffusion influences.

This volume provides in-depth studies of how policy diffusion has influenced ETS design in most of the systems operational today. We pay particular attention to design convergence and divergence across systems and the relationship between diffusion mechanisms, domestic politics and such outcomes. This examination can help us understand the emergence and evolution of ETS around the world, how these systems spread and ultimately the mechanisms and processes that influence their design and operation. Hence, we contribute both to policy diffusion theory and to lessons about ETS design with a clear policy relevance, not least in the aftermath of the Paris 2015 summit.

Research questions

The problems experienced by the EU ETS and other systems – in particular too many allowances handed out and too low carbon prices – have put the spotlight on the question of design: how to design systems that will yield a stable and reasonably high carbon price and at the same time will interact well with other policy instruments in fulfilling the overriding goal of achieving emissions reductions cost-effectively (see Klinsky et al. 2012). There is a substantial literature on 'clean' or 'optimal' cap-and-trade systems, but relatively little on how political and economic interests as well as other policy instruments affect the design and operation of these systems (but see e.g. Stephan and Lane 2015 and Knox-Hayes 2016). Furthermore, as systems develop at different speeds, with frontrunners and more recent adopters, the question of interaction among systems becomes increasingly pertinent. Such a focus on inter-system communication and learning creates links to rich and extensive debates in political science on how to conceptualize and understand policy diffusion (for overview of this debate and key references, see Chapter 2).

As noted, most ETS research has focused on the diffusion of systems for emissions trading as such, not on specific design characteristics. Further, studies dealing with the spread of particular design features have focused on similarities across systems – policy *convergence* – not differences across systems – policy *divergence* (Paterson et al. 2014). Similarly, Shipan and Volden (2012: 788) have observed that while much of the literature on policy diffusion focuses on the adoption stage, less is known about how the policy instruments that diffuse globally change over time. Hence, they argue, 'Extending the policy diffusion literature beyond initial policy adoptions is warranted and long overdue' (Shipan and Volden 2012: 793). Both convergence and divergence may be expected to occur as policy instruments evolve over time. Indeed, it has been observed that full convergence is not a necessary or even a likely outcome of diffusion because norms, ideas and practices often change in form and content as they diffuse (Gilardi 2013; Klingler-Vidra and Schleifer 2014: 264).

In this book, we examine diffusion as a causal mechanism and the link between diffusion mechanisms and design outcomes. The examination of specific diffusion mechanisms can help organize process tracing within the cases examined. In particular, it is possible to test if the chain of events and path dependencies one uncovers are consistent with one's expectations based on a specific diffusion mechanism (see George and Bennett 2005).

Our focus in this book is on the design of ETS. The topic is important because more governments are looking to such market instruments in their search for ways of making deeper cuts in emissions. Design will have a big impact on whether these systems actually work as intended – and whether they perform in ways that align with the goals of important interest groups. Moreover, the extent to which they converge or diverge will shape whether different national systems can be linked into a more interconnected global system – an approach many analysts have been advocating for decades (e.g. Bodansky et al. 2015; Ranson and Stavins 2014).

Against this backdrop, in this book we examine the following overarching research questions:

- What are main ETS design similarities and differences in existing systems across the globe?
- To what extent and how can policy diffusion explain these similarities and differences?
- How can domestic politics serve as a mediating variable through which international diffusion processes affect design outcomes?

In addressing the first research question, we single out eight specific design attributes for further scrutiny in all case studies. As elaborated in Chapter 2, these design characteristics are:

- Type of system (e.g. cap-and-trade or baseline and credit)
- Ambitiousness (e.g. level of targets to achieve emissions reductions)
- Allocation method (free allocation or auctioning)
- Coverage (inclusion of sectors and gases in the system)
- Offset and linking rules (e.g. types of domestic offsets or credits based on the Clean Development Mechanism – CDM)
- Monitoring, reporting and verification (MRV) and compliance rules
- Price-management mechanisms (focused on quantity or price)
- Rules for earmarking of auctioning revenues.

We systematically map and compare these design features to see if there are any *patterns* in terms of similarities and differences across systems.

The second research question addresses a major research gap in the literature on emissions trading: the role of *policy diffusion* in shaping ETS design. In examining the extent to which and how policy diffusion affects ETS design, the chapters of this book focus on mechanisms and pathways of international policy diffusion. We identify four main types of diffusion mechanisms in the literature – coercion, competition, learning and emulation – and investigate the various diffusion mechanisms at play in the cases examined here. The intention is to explain not only what mechanisms are involved, but also where and how they lead to convergence or divergence.

Our third research question concerns the kind of outcomes likely to be produced by different diffusion mechanisms in a given setting. *ETS systems* as such do not respond to external impulses or learn from experience – that is what governments and other actors do. Consequently, we also provide substantial information about the role of various internal and domestic policy drivers in the different jurisdictions, including the role of governments and governmental agencies, parliaments, industries, environmental organizations, consultants and researchers and international organizations. Chapter 2 elaborates the possible role of those drivers, with attention to how domestic institutions and politics come into play at the stage of policy adoption and also the implementation stage.

We describe outcomes in terms of two rough dichotomies: whether ETS design outcomes *converge* or *diverge*, and whether there is movement *upwards* or *downwards* in design outcomes. Regarding the first dichotomy, our point of departure for this study is that policy diffusion can result in both converging and diverging designs. Likely outcomes on the second dichotomy can be roughly described as whether we see upwards change – towards more ambitious, more demanding systems design – or downwards change – towards less ambitious, less demanding systems design. These two dimensions are important for policy analysts, but also offer important insights for practical policy. Better understanding of convergence or divergence can help reveal the opportunities for linkages among systems over time. Insights into stringency and effectiveness help shape realistic expectations as to the emissions cuts possible under the trading mechanism.

In terms of empirical coverage, this volume is unique, providing in-depth examination of almost all systems actually in operation worldwide: the EU ETS, the Regional Greenhouse Gas Initiative (RGGI), California, Tokyo, New Zealand, Australia, China, South Korea and Kazakhstan.[3] We are aware there are other trading schemes scheduled or under consideration that could have been examined too.[4] Here we focus on *the key systems that have been operational* for some time, since actual operation often reveals important diffusion dynamics and political influences not evident in the planning or early construction phases, and systems that have been operational but are *currently on hold* (Australia and Kazakhstan).

In addressing the three overarching research questions, this volume makes an original contribution to the already substantial literatures on policy diffusion and emissions trading. Our approach to identifying and operationalizing the processes of diffusion differs substantially from most of the literature on diffusion, especially that of American political scientists, because we envision causal processes that allow for (perhaps even encourage) divergence. Indeed, unlike nearly all the literature on diffusion, we find that divergence is more evident across these systems than is convergence. While this book is principally empirical in focus, to theorists we recommend paying closer attention to the forces that can lead to convergence in broad policy goals (e.g. adoption of an emission trading system) but to divergence in nearly all the factors of implementation that affect how those policy goals are put into practice.[5]

Carbon markets: a brief overview of their emergence and design

The idea of using markets in the context of environmental policy started in the US in the late 1960s and 1970s, with the 'Project 88' network of US economists and policy-makers as an important milestone in the more specific context of climate change (see Calel 2013 for an overview of this early history; also Voss 2007; Mehling 2012; and Paterson et al. 2014). In Europe, a similar idea was presented by Michael Grubby in the late 1980s (Grubb 1989). However, the 1992 UN Framework Convention on Climate Change had little to say on the market concept. In 1995, the US launched the first major ETS, restricted to air pollutants (SO_2 and NOx).

The idea of carbon markets and flexible mechanisms was also pushed by the US in the process leading up to the 1997 Kyoto Protocol, which ended up including three flexible mechanisms: the Clean Development Mechanism (CDM) directed at developing countries: Joint Implementation (JI), directed at Eastern Europe and Russia; and international emissions trading, providing Northern/Western Annex I countries with additional options for reducing emissions. Some firms organized themselves to push hard for market-based strategies, on the assumption that they would prove less expensive than direct regulation. BP, in particular, became a highly visible advocate for climate policy and also used its own internal emissions trading system to demonstrate that trade was feasible and effective (Victor and House 2006).

Spurred by the Kyoto Protocol and the failure to get an internal carbon tax adopted, the EU made an about-turn in 1998 and set about designing an EU ETS, with companies (the term used was 'installations') in the member-states as prime units. The EU ETS Directive was adopted in 2003, establishing the main design rules for a pilot phase 2005–7 and the subsequent Kyoto commitment phase 2008–12. As the EU was an international frontrunner and uncertainty was high among stakeholders, the initial design was a generally 'decentralized' one, granting considerable power to member-states over implementation of the system, and with permits ('allowances') handed out for free. The power sector and several energy-intensive industries were key target groups. To provide additional flexibility, the 2004 EU Linking Directive opened up for using CDM credits in the pilot phase, as well as JI credits from 2008. The EU ETS started operating in 2005.

At this point, Norway launched a national ETS aimed at linking up to the EU ETS. In Japan, a voluntary ETS was launched. There were also further developments in the US, with the Chicago Climate Exchange established in 2003 and a memorandum on the establishment of an East Coast Regional Greenhouse Gas Initiative adopted in 2005. RGGI focused only on the power sector, and auctions started in 2008; its design was notable for including price-management mechanisms (in the form of a price floor and ceiling) and the use of auctioning to distribute allowances.

On the US West Coast, the 2006 Global Warming Act required the California Air Resources Board to develop a Scoping Plan and explore the possibility of an ETS. This was followed in 2007 by the launch of the Western Climate Initiative (WCI), which came to include British Columbia, Manitoba, Ontario, Quebec and California. California Governor Schwarzenegger was also central in launching the International Carbon Action Partnership (ICAP) in 2007, together with the EU and others. The establishment of ICAP was illustrative of the growing organizational density within the field of international carbon trading.

In the Asia/Pacific region, a Tokyo Strategy/Plan was launched in 2007, including an ETS, showing a subnational dynamic at work also in Japan. In Australia, a climate policy assessment process was started (the Garnaut Process) which included discussion of an ETS; and in New Zealand, an ETS was launched in 2008, with a rather unique 'trading without cap' design and broad coverage. In Europe, Switzerland launched a voluntary ETS in 2008. Moreover, in that year, the EU adopted significantly altered ETS rules for the 2013–20 phase, with greater centralization and a gradual turn to more auctioning as main pillars.

In 2009, the EU also launched a goal of an Organisation for Economic Co-operation and Development (OECD)-wide carbon market by 2015, to be 'even broader' by 2020. The first formal ETS link was established, with linkage between the EU ETS and Norway and the two other European Economic Area members Lichtenstein and Iceland. The EU envisioned a transatlantic carbon market, related to the work underway in the US on a national carbon market. However, this US bill (Waxman-Markey) was stopped in 2010, and the EU had to look for linking partners elsewhere. A Carbon Pricing Mechanism (ACPM) was launched in Australia, and the EU started to look in this direction.

A potentially very important development came in 2010: China's National Development and Reform Commission (NDRC) designated 13 low-carbon zones and made reference to emissions trading. A dialogue on emissions trading was started with the EU. A milestone was reached already in 2011, when the China NDRC and State Council announced ETS pilots in five cities and two provinces, to be followed by a national market. Regional action continued in the US, with the California ETS launched in 2012, including a complex price-floor system.

However, 2013 proved to be a mixed year for carbon markets: Tony Abbott became PM in Australia and halted the ETS process there. The EU ETS carbon price was sagging, and the crisis came to a head when the European Parliament voted down a temporary postponement of the auctioning of some allowances ('backloading') in the spring of 2013. On the other hand, an ETS was launched in Kazakhstan. And not least, the Chinese ETS pilot projects started operating, with similarities as well as differences in their designs.

More positive events happened for carbon markets in 2014, with the European Commission's launch of a proposal for a price-stabilizing mechanism: the Market Stability Reserve (MSR), adopted in May 2015. In Asia, 2015 saw the launching of a South Korean ETS, and in 2016 China announced that a national ETS would be launched. The Paris UN summit in December 2015 resulted in the adoption of a bottom-up, pledge-and-review framework from 2020 on, with several elements interpreted as positive for carbon markets.

Then came another mixed year for carbon trading, 2016. Plans for the launch of a Chinese national ETS in 2017 became more specific, an ETS twice as big as the EU ETS. But the EU ETS again experienced falling carbon prices, and Kazakhstan put its own system on hold.

Thus, the evolution of carbon markets has been somewhat of a rollercoaster ride, with the ebb and tide of several 'market waves'. Key developments are presented and discussed in the subsequent chapters of this book.

Structure of the book

Chapter 2 presents our analytical framework. This chapter begins with a discussion of the dependent variable ETS design, with eight specific attributes. This is followed by examinations of the focused causal mechanisms related to policy diffusion (learning, emulation, coercion and competition), the role of domestic institutions and politics as mediating variables, and five specific expectations about policy diffusion and design outcomes. Next, we briefly discuss alternative explanations for the spread of emissions trading, including 'parallel play', and interplay between emissions trading and other climate policy instruments. The chapter ends with a brief discussion of our methodological approach and data.

Chapter 3 examines the international frontrunner EU ETS, which is so far the largest carbon market in the world and an important provider of experience in how to design a carbon market. The EU ETS has been assigned a cornerstone position in a more complex EU climate policy mix. However, the system has encountered problems, with a volatile and generally low carbon price. This makes further scrutiny of its design and the main shaping factors especially pertinent.

Moving across the Atlantic, the next two chapters examine two frontrunner systems in the United States. Chapter 4 focuses on the first subnational carbon market in the US, the Regional Greenhouse Gas Initiative on the East Coast. RGGI targets only power producers. Further, RGGI is, as yet, the only ETS in the world which auctions all allowances; it has both a price floor and ceiling. RGGI administrators have learned from previous US ETS experience and from the EU ETS.

In Chapter 5, the spotlight is on the other main subnational carbon market in the United States – in California, the seventh-largest economy in the world. This case shows an interesting gap between an official cornerstone position in the policy mix and the reality of a less prominent 'backstop' function – whereby the ETS primarily 'sweeps up' emissions not adequately addressed by other policy instruments. System designers have learned from others and also inspired others as regards emissions trading, linking up with the Quebec ETS in 2015.

Chapter 6 moves across the Pacific to examine the Tokyo ETS, the main subnational system in Japan. It has unique coverage of large-scale office buildings and factories and has at times seen very high carbon prices. Although the role of policy diffusion is rather limited, lessons from the EU ETS contributed to shaping the design of Tokyo system regarding allocation mechanism. Otherwise, domestic factors shaped much of the design features of the Tokyo ETS.

The next two chapters put the spotlight on experimentation with emissions trading in Oceania. Chapter 7 discusses the New Zealand ETS, a system with some unique design elements, including the lack of a specific cap, a strong focus on land-use emissions (especially forestry) and the as yet unfilled intention to include biological emissions from agriculture. The system's design included some lesson-drawing from the EU ETS and Australia, but with a clear focus on evaluating the implications for the competitiveness of New Zealand's open trading economy.

The focus in Chapter 8 is on Australia and the processes of introducing an ETS there. Those efforts unfolded in several phases and became heavily politicized because of competitiveness concerns and strong industry lobbying. However, they also included negotiations on a link to the EU ETS and some adjustments to the Australian system. This process was halted in 2013 by the then prime minister, Tony Abbott, and the scheme was finally repealed in 2014.

Chapter 9 focuses on an important ETS newcomer in Asia: South Korea, a substantial emitter. Its ETS features very broad coverage of sectors and gases, with centrally steered adjustment of allowance quantity and hence price management. South Korea's ETS had among the highest carbon prices globally in early 2016 (more than EUR 20). Although domestic factors provide the main explanations for the adoption and design of the ETS, South Korea has also learned from the experiences of other jurisdictions, the EU in particular.

In Chapter 10, the authors examine emissions trading in Kazakhstan – a big country and significant emitter, with an ETS that was put in place very quickly, due to high-level political pressure. However, the fast-tracked nature of the implementation process did not provide sufficient notification to the donor community to mobilize much-needed technical support until the pilot phase was completed. Implementation of a fully operational system has been postponed because of industry resistance and unresolved legal and technical issues. Among other things, the rush did not allow time for establishing a proper MRV system.

Chapter 11 examines the emergence and evolution of emissions trading in China – the biggest GHG emitter globally. The turn to ETS in China is a fascinating process which has involved introducing a fundamentally decentralized market instrument in a centrally governed society with a tradition of top-down 'command and control' policies. Seven pilot systems were introduced from 2013 onwards, and a nationwide system, twice as large as the EU ETS, is to be introduced in 2017. China has been assisted by various external actors, including the EU, other countries and international organizations such as the World Bank.

Chapter 12 complements the China picture with a comparison of the potential effects of emissions trading in China and in the EU, based on economic modelling. The aim is to quantify the potential effects of national ETS design with respect to effectiveness (reductions in CO_2 emissions) and economic efficiency (economic welfare costs of emission reductions). Four design properties are in focus: ambition level, sectoral coverage, allocation method and access to offsets. Special attention is paid to the potential effects on emissions at the national and the sectoral levels, as well as carbon prices and the economic costs of reducing emissions.

Chapter 13 rounds off the volume with a more comprehensive cross-case analysis. We begin with a discussion of central factors that have shaped the turn to emissions trading in the systems studied here. Then we turn to the key design question, providing first an overview of central design similarities and differences among the systems and the role of policy diffusion in shaping those design outcomes. Next, we examine our five expectations about the relationship among policy diffusion mechanisms, domestic politics and design outcomes in light of the empirical evidences. We wrap up the chapter with some concluding reflections, including implications for further research and future prospects for carbon markets and their role in the follow-up of the Paris Agreement.

Notes

1 Our warm thanks to Arild Underdal and David Victor for important and helpful inputs and comments to this chapter.
2 We thank Bob Keohane for pressing us to clarify this point.
3 Main systems in operation that we do not cover are those in Saitama, Switzerland, Ontario and Quebec. See ICAP 2016.
4 This includes Brazil, Mexico, Ukraine, Thailand and Vietnam. See ICAP 2016.
5 Thanks to David Victor for clarifying this point.

References

Betsill, M. and M. J. Hoffman. 2011. The contours of 'cap and trade': The evolution of Emissions Trading Systems for greenhouse gases. *Review of Policy Research* 28 (1), 83–106.

Bodansky, D. M., S. A. Hoedl, G. E. Metcalf and R. N. Stavins. 2015. Facilitating linkage of climate policies through the Paris outcome. *Climate Policy* 15, 1–17.

Calel, R. 2013. Carbon markets: A historical overview. *WIREs Climate Change* 4 (March/April), 107–119.

EDF/IETA. 2016. *The World's Carbon Markets: A Case Study Guide to Emissions Trading.* Washington/Geneva: EDF/IETA.

Elkins, Z. and B. Simmons. 2005. On waves, clusters and diffusion: A conceptual framework, *Annals of the American Academy of Political and Social Science* 598, 33–51.

ENDS Europe. 2008. Global carbon market 'unlikely by 2020'. 25 February.

George, A. L. and A. Bennett. 2005. *Case Studies and Theory Development in the Social Sciences*. Cambridge, MA: MIT Press.

Gilardi, F. 2013. Transnational diffusion: Norms, ideas, and policies. In *Handbook of International Relations*, edited by W. Carlsnaes, T. Risse and B. A. Simmons, 453–477. London: Sage.

Goron, C. and C. Cassisa. 2017. Regulatory institutions and market-based climate policy in China. *Global Environmental Politics* 17 (1), 99–120.

Grubby, M. 1989. *The Greenhouse Effect; Negotiating Targets*. London: The Royal Institute of International Affairs.

ICAP. 2016. *Emissions Trading Worldwide: International Carbon Action Partnership Status Report 2016*. Berlin: International Carbon Action Partnership (ICAP).

IETA. 2016. *Bridging the Ambition Gap – The Rise, Reach and Power of Carbon Markets, Greenhouse Gas Market 2016/17 Report*. Geneva: IETA.

Jordan, A. and D. Huitema. 2014. Policy innovation in a changing climate: Sources, patterns and effects. *Global Environmental Change* 29, 387–394.

Klingler-Vidra, R. and P. Schleifer. 2014. Convergence more or less: Why do practices vary as they diffuse? *International Studies Review* 16 (2), 264–274.

Klinsky, S., M. Mehling and A. Tuerk. 2012. Beyond déjà vu: Opportunities for policy learning from emissions trading in developed countries. *Carbon Climate Law Review* 4, 291–305.

Knox-Hayes, J. 2016. *The Cultures of Markets*. Oxford: Oxford University Press.

Meckling, J. 2011. *Carbon Coalitions: Business, Climate Politics, and the Rise of Emissions Trading*. Cambridge, MA: MIT Press.

Mehling, M. 2012. Between twilight and renaissance: Changing prospects for the carbon market. *Carbon Climate Law Review* 4, 277–290.

Miles, E. L., A. Underdal, S. Andresen, J. Wettestad, J. B. Skjærseth and E. M. Carlin. 2002. *Environmental Regime Effectiveness: Confronting Theory with Evidence*. Cambridge, MA: MIT Press.

Paterson, M., M. Hoffman, M. Betsill and S. Berntstein. 2014. The micro foundations of policy diffusion toward complex global governance: An analysis of the transnational carbon emission trading network. *Comparative Political Studies* 47 (3), 420–449.

PMR/ICAP. 2016. *Emissions Trading in Practice: A Handbook on Design and Implementation*. Washington: The World Bank.

Ranson, M. and R. Stavins. 2014. Linkage of greenhouse gas emissions trading systems: Learning from experience. *Climate Policy* 14, 1–17.

Rosenzweig, R. H. 2016. *Global Climate Change Policy and Carbon Markets – Transition to a New Era*. London: Palgrave Macmillan.

Sartori, G. 1970. Concept misinformation in comparative politics. *The American Political Science Review* 64 (4), 1033–1053.

Shipan, C. R. and C. Volden. 2012. Policy diffusion: Seven lessons for scholars and practitioners. *Public Administration Review* 72 (6), 788–796.

Simmons, B. A., F. Dobbin and G. Garrett. 2006. Introduction: the international diffusion of liberalism, *International Organization* 60 (4), 781–810.

Skjærseth, J. B. and J. Wettestad. 2008. *EU Emissions Trading – Initiation, Decision-making and Implementation*. Aldershot: Ashgate.

Stephan, B. and R. Lane (eds.). 2015. *The Politics of Carbon Markets*. New York: Routledge.

Stern, J. 2006. *The Stern Review on the Economics of Climate Change, Report*. London: Government of the United Kingdom.

van Asselt, H. 2016. The design and implementation of greenhouse gas emissions trading. In *The Oxford Handbook of International Climate Change Law*, edited by C. P. Carlarne, K. R. Gray and R. G. Tarasofsky, 332–356. Oxford: Oxford University Press.

Victor, D. G. and J. C. House. 2006. BP's emissions trading system. *Energy Policy* 34 (15) (October), 2100–2112.

Voss, J. P. 2007. Innovation processes in governance: The case of 'emissions trading' as a new policy instrument. *Science and Public Policy* 34 (5), 329–343.

Weishaar, S. (ed.). 2016. *Research Handbook on Emissions Trading*. Cheltenham: Edward Elgar.

Wettestad, J. and T. Jevnaker. 2016. *Rescuing EU Emissions Trading – The Climate Policy Flagship*. Basingstoke: Palgrave Pivot.

World Bank. 2016. *State and Trends of Carbon Pricing 2016*. Washington, DC: World Bank.

Zhang, Z. 2015. Carbon emissions trading in China: The evolution from pilots to a nation-wide scheme. *Climate Policy* 15, 104–126.

2 Theory and method

Lars H. Gulbrandsen, Arild Underdal, David G. Victor and Jørgen Wettestad

Introduction

In this chapter, we examine the deeper theoretical motivations and foundations for the studies presented in this book, along with the methodology that has guided our research.

The first section defines our *dependent* variable: the design of emissions trading systems (ETS). In the second section, we define the key *explanatory* variables – the forces that explain convergence and divergence in ETS design – in three steps. We begin by examining diffusion mechanisms and the relationship between these mechanisms and policy outcomes. Next, we discuss how domestic political factors operate as intervening variables. The fundamental driving forces that may explain international policy diffusion are refracted through various interest groups and institutions that have considerable influence on the policy choices of individual governments. The explanatory and intervening variables can also help explain path dependence in design choices – when early choices are made, they create interest groups and various rigidities that may impede rapid change in the future. We end this section by formulating five broad expectations about policy diffusion and design outcomes.

The third section briefly presents some alternative explanations to policy diffusion as a causal driving mechanism and discusses the interplay between emissions trading and other policy instruments. The final section presents methodological issues, case selection and empirical coverage.

The dependent variable: ETS design

Our principal research question concerns the causal role of international diffusion in shaping the design of emissions trading systems. Although we operate with a single dependent variable, in practice 'design' has many dimensions because such trading systems can be highly complex markets in which the details have a considerable impact on outcomes.

As noted in Chapter 1, we hold that design properties influence whether an ETS is *effective* (brings about a higher and more stable carbon price, with subsequent reductions in greenhouse gas, GHG, emissions) and *efficient* (achieves such reductions at minimal, or at least lower, costs). A highly effective and efficient design is a benchmark for analysis – but, in the real world, political processes and institutional decision-making will often yield design properties that are far from optimal. In particular, efficiency may suffer when interest groups that prize factors other than economic efficiency have considerable influence on political decision-making – as is frequently the case (see e.g. Victor 2014).

Drawing on studies such as those of Skjærseth and Wettestad (2008), Weishaar (2014), van Asselt (2016) and PMR/ICAP (2016), we identified *eight key design properties* that, together, broadly characterize the design of a trading system – as summarized in the following.[1] We have focused on properties of central substantive importance for the effectiveness and efficiency of trading systems. For instance, take the design property 'sectors and gases covered'. Other things being equal, a system that covers most of a country's economy and most of its greenhouse gas emissions can achieve more mitigation at lower cost than a system limited to one marginal sector or gas can achieve. In the real world, however, systems vary greatly in terms of their sectoral and gas coverage.

In developing this list of eight properties we faced a strategic dilemma between *a priori* selecting a few presumably critical properties for intensive study or casting the net wider to reduce the risk of premature closure. We began with a wide net of eight main design features and asked the case-study author teams to examine whether important design choices were made on each of the eight:

- Type of system: here we include the following key elements: 1) the distinction between baseline-and-credit and cap-and-trade systems. Systems of the latter type establish an ex ante total amount of allowances (the cap), whereas the former do not have such a pre-determined ceiling, but distribute allowances ex-post; 2) the length of trading periods; 3) the existence of specific mechanisms to allow additional flexibility within or between phases (such as 'banking', i.e. saving allowances from one phase/period to another, and 'borrowing', i.e. using allowances for a subsequent trading period for compliance in the current period); and 4) the governance level (e.g. national vs sub-national or supra-national systems).
- Ambition level: this concerns the level of the cap and the emissions cuts aimed for within a given period, as well as any specific role assigned to the ETS for achieving the target(s). The level of the cap is a strong precursor of the fundamental scarcity of allowances created, which in turn shapes the carbon price and the incentive effects of the ETS in question.
- Sectors, gases and emissions covered: as to sectors, a basic distinction here is between energy-producing and energy-consuming/energy-intensive sectors/industries. Other relevant sectors include transport, agriculture and forestry. With gases, a key distinction is between systems which target only CO_2 and those that include other greenhouse gases as well. Finally, there is a distinction to be made between systems that cover only 'direct emissions' (from production) or include also 'indirect emissions' (from consumption of goods, such as electricity).

- Allocation mechanism(s): here, the basic distinction is between allocation by market (auctioning) and allocation for free, based on historical emissions ('grandfathering') or some type of benchmarking (as to the best-performing companies in the sector).
- External offsetting and linking: this concerns the external outreach and visions for the system – such as 1) rules for allowing companies/installations to use credits/allowances produced by activities not formally covered by the ETS in question for compliance purposes (whether national or international, such as CDM credits, and including specific priorities given to particular countries/sectors – or, conversely, specific prohibitions); and 2) formal provisions for linking up to other systems further down the line.
- MRV (monitoring, reporting and verification) and enforcement: this pertains to the rules and institutions for conducting MRV tasks and reacting to cases of non-compliance.
- Price or quantity-focused management mechanisms: these features concern the rules and possible institutions established to stabilize the carbon price (such as price floors/ceilings or quantity-focused measures like allowance reserves).
- Revenue earmarking: in systems where auctioning is a significant means of distributing allowances, this concerns possible rules for earmarking auctioning revenues for specific activities or sectors, whether within or outside the field of climate mitigation or adaptation.

Awareness of these design properties helped the case-study author teams structure their cases and facilitated comparative cross-case analysis. All the case studies in this book examine these eight design features, making it possible to compare the cases systematically for each design feature (see Chapter 13). However, we also realize that, with a limited number of cases, a dependent variable with eight distinct properties is unwieldy and poorly suited for generating propositions that can be tested empirically. Thus, in order to generate propositions about the causal role of diffusion for ETS design, we reduced the list of eight design features to three broader categories of features.

The most basic category includes the *general idea* of emissions trading: the idea of using market mechanisms (as distinct from regulation by directive) to (re) allocate emissions permits within a framework of existing targets and rules. At this level, ETS can be regarded as a distinct 'species' of policy instruments, and attention is directed primarily to similarities and not differences.

Our second main category of design features includes *the main policy components* of the scheme – ambition level, sectors, gases and emission sources covered, main allocation mechanism(s) and price management. These components are designed to fit a specific economy and society and may therefore be expected to vary significantly from one jurisdiction to another.

The third category includes *technicalities* of varying complexity: rules and provisions specifying the operational aspects of the system. In some respects, the substantive focus and contents of these rules and provisions will reflect the main policy components of a given ETS system, but their chief function is 'technical': they specify managerial operations and procedures intended to enhance the effectiveness and efficiency of the system in question.

The distinction between main policy components and specific technicalities will sometimes be fuzzy, so applying it to any given case may not always be easy. A brief illustration may indicate how we conceive of this distinction. In a system where the (initial) allocation of emissions permits is to take place through auctioning, we consider the core mechanism of auctioning to be a *main policy component*, whereas the subordinate rules specifying exactly how to conduct the process of auctioning belong to the category of *technicalities*. We formulate and explain our propositions in the third sub-section that follows.

Explaining patterns of policy diffusion

Diffusion mechanisms and outcomes

Policy diffusion has been defined as a particular type of 'interdependent, but uncoordinated, decision making' in which a party unilaterally adopts a policy or practice initiated and pursued by others (Elkins and Simmons 2005: 35). Thus defined, diffusion differs from cooperation by not being based on an explicit exchange of (conditional) commitments: the adopting party recognizes that a relationship of interdependence exists and takes an interest in other emissions trading systems but designs its own system through unilateral decisions and with no functional links to other systems. In this sense, there is a strong overlap with tacit cooperation (cooperation based on signalling and expectation rather than codification) as against formal cooperation (Downs and Rocke 1990).

It also differs from 'parallel play' – a concept developed in psychology and education research to describe how young children play 'alongside each other, in similar activities, without obvious communication or interaction'.[2] Also in politics, 'parallel play' is most likely to occur at an early stage and for policy options that are not well known. In the area of climate change, emissions trading systems offer an interesting opportunity to test whether ideas of diffusion versus parallel play are at work because the ETS idea has relatively clear origins (first with early systems for trading lead and sulphur and other pollutants in the US; then with Europe adopting the largest ETS applied to greenhouse gases). After much discussion, ETS has become well established today as an important regulatory option. Governments contemplating adopting such a system often seek advice from 'frontrunners' but go on to implement ETS in their own distinctly separate (unconnected) systems.

According to the Elkins and Simmons definition, diffusion is a process that has generally been seen as leading to *convergence*, as 'policies and institutions [. . .] spread across different contexts' (Börzel and Risse 2012: 1; see also Holzinger et al. 2008; Paterson et al. 2014; Solingen and Börzel 2014). This expectation of convergence is understandable because earlier work, including by Elkins and Simmons, examined processes in which there were strong incentives for convergence.

If there are clear leaders, then followers will follow; moreover, if policies are adopted in the context of internationally fungible goods and services, there may be strong market pressures for convergence – for example, in securities regulation and accounting standards, where divergence can rapidly lead to commercial disadvantage. By contrast, the ETS experience will reveal fewer such pressures, as we will show.

Some definitions are framed in terms that allow also for *divergence*. Simmons et al. (2006: 787) propose that 'international policy diffusion occurs when government policy decisions in one country are systematically conditioned by prior policy choices made in another country (sometimes mediated by the behaviour of international organizations or even private actors or organizations)'. Both definitions refer to observed patterns, but for our purposes a definition that explicitly includes adjustments to national or local circumstances will be more useful. Hence, in this book we adopt the broader definition of Simmons et al.

Drawing on the literature on policy diffusion, we distinguish between two main triggers for convergence or divergence, operating through different causal mechanisms (see Finnemore and Sikkink 1998; Elkins and Simmons 2005; Simmons et al. 2006; Shipan and Volden 2008, 2012). The first main trigger concerns cognitive or normative influence – *ideas* – that can be understood in constitutive terms (notably, internalization or socialization). Diffusion may take the form of more or less sophisticated *learning* that can involve correcting design flaws in response to the perceived failures of another system (Gilardi 2013; Underdal et al. 2015). 'Learning' here is a matter of voluntary and active engagement in acquiring and perhaps further developing new knowledge and innovative ideas that can help governments and other actors improve problem diagnostics and treatment.

Learning may be fairly simplistic, limited to diffusion in the form of direct copying of policies or practices pursued by more prestigious peers (*emulation*). However, learning will often be a far more sophisticated process, involving careful probing and efforts to correct choices made in other system(s) – either because they are inappropriate to the jurisdiction at hand or have demonstrably failed. This function is particularly relevant in early stages where potential adopters have little or no experience with the policy in question. Learning – sophisticated learning in particular – has been shown to contribute positively to international diffusion of, for instance, norms protecting essential human rights (Finnemore and Sikkink 1998).[3]

The conditions for learning seem to depend heavily on the institutional infrastructure – notably, the density of transnational and intergovernmental networks – through which parties 'connect' and gain useful information about events in other jurisdictions (see e.g. Kinne 2013). In a study of the global spread of liberal economic ideas and policies, Simmons and Elkins (2004: 187) report that 'broad cultural orientation' – including a shared religious identity – stands out as 'a central explanation for policy diffusion'. This finding seems to apply particularly to diffusion by learning: broadly defined, cultural affinity may well enhance a party's interest in ideas developed or measures taken by its 'cultural peers' (see also Holzinger et al. 2008). Political scientists have studied the mechanisms for learning and the role of institutions in learning in many ways – as in the rich early literature on epistemic communities of technical experts, as well as the literature on transnational networks of bureaucrats (Haas 1990; Slaughter 2005).

The second main trigger involves *material consequences* (incentives) and operates through the mechanism of adaptation to altered conditions. This mechanism directs attention to *coercion* and *competition* stemming from growing political and economic interdependencies between economies and the related impact of these interdependencies on the payoff structures associated with the pursuit of various policies (Gilardi 2013; Underdal et al. 2015). It is important to pay attention to economic interdependency relationships and the extent to which decision-makers and industries see policy differences as an impediment to effective low-carbon policy-making.

More specifically, *coercion* refers to the imposition of certain policies or practices by international organizations and powerful states, typically through conditionality requirements (Simmons and Elkins 2004). 'Conditionality' means that, in order to gain access to certain (material) benefits, a state must adhere to given policy requirements. One example is the way international financial institutions like the World Bank and the International Monetary Fund use their legal status to tie their financial assistance to neoliberal economic reforms that must be enacted by recipient governments. Another example is how the EU makes accession conditional on wide-ranging reforms and transposition of EU legislation in applicant countries (Gilardi 2013). As these examples indicate, coercion often reflects an asymmetrical distribution of power, where the stronger party can rely on legal provisions or effective control over important goods to bring about compliance by the weaker party.

Competition has been defined as 'the process whereby policy makers anticipate or react to the behavior of other countries in order to attract or retain economic resources' (Gilardi 2013: 10). For competition to qualify as a *policy* diffusion mechanism, there must be a policy or practice that spreads from a source jurisdiction to another jurisdiction. The classic example is tax competition, where the decision to lower taxes to help attract investments is conditional on the policies of other countries (Swank 2006). Whereas tax competition often results in a 'race to the bottom', competition could in other settings generate a 'race to the top', as described in the 'California effect' identified by Vogel (1995, 1997). Vogel found that stricter automobile emissions standards in California in the 1970s and 1990s compelled US producers to upgrade cars sold elsewhere in the country to Californian standards, as well as forced other US states to ratchet up their automobile emission standards (Vogel 1997).

Similarly, the environmental standards of voluntary certification schemes have converged upwards in markets where such schemes compete for consumer recognition and trust (Gulbrandsen 2010; Overdevest 2010). In the domain of emissions trading, functionally equivalent mechanisms are still absent or weak, but progress in linking (national) systems could generate incentives similar to those found in the US automobile market.

Firms that find themselves disproportionately disadvantaged, facing substantial compliance costs that many of their competitors are exempt from, are likely to support national, regional or global regulation that can harmonize environmental standards and level the playing field within and across sectors. Conversely, firms that benefit significantly from advantageous (national) regulations will be likely to defend the existing system. Early political science research on regional integration (see e.g. Haas 1964) recognized that competition among states over offering industry and business the most favourable terms could lead to collectively suboptimal outcomes. With reference to Europe in particular, Haas and many others found some degree of *political* integration to be an important condition for facilitating economic development and building stable peace.

As noted, we focus on the causal role of diffusion at the level of specific design properties – that is, how the ETS in each of the jurisdictions studied is implemented. That requires a small set of general outcome categories. Previous research provides two rather crude but useful dichotomies: whether policies and practices *converge* or *diverge* (see e.g. Gilardi 2013; Klingler-Vidra and Schleifer 2014), and whether there is movement *upwards*, i.e. towards arrangements that are more effective and efficient, or *downwards*, generating, at worst, a race to the bottom (Elkins et al. 2006; Gilardi 2013). These two dimensions may be combined, as indicated in Table 2.1.

Convergence upwards is what most supporters of emissions trading hope to see because carbon markets could then be harmonized and perhaps linked globally. *Divergence upwards* is what most supporters of emissions trading expect to see. In the climate-change setting, this type of outcome can be found in the 'bottom-up' approach that led to the Paris Agreement. *Convergence downwards* is the less desirable outcome described by Gresham's law.[4] This may involve withdrawal from an existing agreement (e.g. the Kyoto Protocol) or an earlier pledge.

Table 2.1 Main categories of diffusion outcomes, examples

	Convergence	*Divergence*
Upwards	Technological innovation. Harmonization of rules and regulations within an existing institution.	Sophisticated learning, enabling more accurate differentiation to varying circumstances.
Downwards	Supply-side market competition, e.g. price cuts 'forcing' other suppliers to reciprocate. Negotiations: ambitious leaders giving in and accepting a weaker deal.	Pivotal and disappointed parties responding to negotiation deadlock by withdrawing from the process and/or an existing agreement and focusing squarely on own national interests.

Divergence downwards is a race-to-the-bottom situation, with several unambitious yet different ETS emerging in various jurisdictions.

Domestic political factors as mediating variables

Students of international policy diffusion recognize that, by limiting their attention to relational variables, they may well miss important aspects of the diffusion process. Since domestic institutions and politics come into play at both the policy adoption and implementation stages, international diffusion is likely to be mediated by domestic (or local) institutions and political processes in different jurisdictions. Seeing domestic influences as mediating factors, we expect the domestic context to be an important determinant for the adaptation of policies. For example, domestic lobbying by agents representing industry sectors is likely to influence ETS design outcomes in the recipient state. Domestic institutions can act as 'filters' through which external practices and impulses pass (Falkner and Gupta 2009): certain design features might be refined, adjusted or rejected in the domestic policy process.

But domestic institutions and political processes can also have a more active role, adding issues and creating issue linkages (Sebenius 1983; Hovi and Skodvin 2008) so that new and innovative design features emerge through domestic 'mediation' of external ideas and impulses. Domestic influences may result in the modification or rejection of certain design features, as well as the creation of new ones.

We operate with four broad sets of domestic political factors for explaining both policy convergence and divergence as possible outcomes of diffusion processes. The first set concerns *the role of governments and party politics* in diffusion processes. It is well documented that political parties and politics matter when it comes to the prioritization of certain policy areas or to the direction of policy-making (see e.g. Knill et al. 2012; Biesenbender and Tosun 2014: 427). For example, countries with similar scores on national mitigation and damage cost variables may pursue quite different climate-change policies (Harrison and Sundstrom 2010: 3; Bang et al. 2015: 8), indicating that domestic politics and priorities shape mitigation policies. Changes in government, political parties, party manifestos and party constellations can thus be expected to influence policy accommodation within the domestic system.

In line with a standard political economy approach, the second set of domestic factors refers to the mobilization and relative power of interest groups. When the costs of a given policy or practice are concentrated to specific subgroups of society while the benefits are widely distributed, such subgroups will often achieve 'disproportionally' high influence (Olson 1965; Wilson 1973; Underdal 1998). Emissions trading systems typically entail concentrated costs and dispersed benefits because they target selected emitters (like utilities, energy-intensive industries, other industries). Affected industries and utilities can generally be expected to resist costly ETS design features and use the political opportunity structure to lobby for modification or rejection of such features. Differing industry structures and economic interests across countries can result in variation in the domestic accommodation of international policy influences.

The third set of domestic factors concerns the role of institutions in influencing which politically organized interests get a voice in policy design. We will examine the opportunities that formal and informal policy-making procedures provide for actors to influence policy outcomes (see Deutsch 1966). Two types of domestic actors are of particular importance here: *veto players* (Tsebelis 2002) and *winning (advocacy) coalitions* (Sabatier 1988). To be adopted, a certain policy or practice must steer clear of potential veto players and attract the support of at least one winning coalition. Affected interest groups – industry and trade associations, for example – may be involved on both sides.

Last, the scope of policy innovation and upgrading may be heavily constrained by *path dependencies* and *lock-in effects* generated by previous policy programmes. Our fourth set of domestic factors is whether such path dependencies and lock-in effects have influenced ETS design. Path dependencies can create lock-in effects that constrain and influence policy choices (Pierson 1993). Importantly, the timing and sequence of choices governing the development of a policy can constrain and impact future choices and political processes. Pierson (2000) argues that 'increasing returns' is a key feature of path dependency: over time, policy choices become more stable and increasingly difficult to change.

However, the analysis of path dependencies resulting from existing policies should remain open to the potentially disruptive effects of exogenous shocks, events or crises and the related opening or closing of windows of opportunity (see Kingdon 1984; Baumgartner and Jones 1993). A campaign to discard or alter existing policies may be greatly boosted by the disruptive effects of (exogenous) shocks. For instance, it is impossible to understand the dynamics of recent EU ETS reform without acknowledging the financial crisis and its effects in contributing to building up a large surplus of allowances (and downward pressure on the carbon price). Shocks may occur early, perhaps spurring interest in ETS, or at a later stage when systems are up and running, perhaps leading policy-makers and participants to focus attention on the immediate crisis.

Expectations about policy diffusion and design outcomes

In seeking to explain the forces that may lead to variation in our dependent variable we have examined various diffusion mechanisms and domestic political factors that may lead to convergence or divergence in ETS design, on the assumption that major practical design elements condition levels of ETS efficiency and effectiveness. Let us now present five hypotheses we have used to help guide this study, returning to the three broader categories of design features discussed earlier.

First, we expect that *interest in emissions trading* will increase when the policy instruments already in use are considered insufficient or ineffective *and* emissions trading in other jurisdictions is deemed successful. At least two main sources of motivation may be identified. One is widespread (and growing) dissatisfaction with the regulatory scheme currently in use. Such dissatisfaction is likely to generate a search for better solutions, not necessarily involving emissions trading. The second source of motivation is found in what policy-makers and stakeholders perceive to be a well-functioning ETS in operation somewhere else – particularly if that system has been developed and adopted by a close partner (Simmons et al. 2006). Alone, neither condition is sufficient for diffusion to take place. However, dissatisfaction with one's own scheme, combined with enthusiasm about achievements attributed to another ETS system, is likely to boost interest in testing the mechanism of emissions trading at home.

Second, the diffusion of *general principles* and *operational technicalities* can be expected to entail fewer and less radical adjustments than in the case of *main policy components*. Because the idea of relying on market mechanisms to allocate emissions permits seems to have a common interpretation, the general principles of emissions trading can be expected to diffuse with few changes across jurisdictions. By contrast, main policy components seem likely to undergo significant change as governments and domestic stakeholders seek to protect and advance their interests (see prior discussion). Changes made in these policy components may well have consequences for operating procedures and other technicalities, but the reverse order of influence seems unlikely. And, just as with the general principles of emissions trading, we generally expect the diffusion of operational technicalities to involve fewer and less radical changes than in the case of main policy components. *Ceteris paribus*, we may assume that the more similar the economies and societies involved, the fewer and less radical adjustments a country adopting a 'new' policy instrument (here: emissions trading) will want to make (see e.g. Simmons et al. 2006; Holzinger et al. 2011). This assumption applies equally to all the design properties of an ETS.

Third, we expect general principles and operational technicalities to spread primarily through *learning or emulation*, whereas main policy components will be designed mainly in response to *competition* in international or domestic markets. The basis for this expectation is the finding that, in most instances, more than one diffusion mechanism is involved when different policies and practices spread (Simmons et al. 2006). For example, learning often appears to play a critical role in understanding potentials and limitations of certain policy models. However, decisions about which model to choose or which changes to make may well turn into a competitive game involving stakeholders and media as well as policy-makers. Combining these two statements suggests a crude but differentiated expectation: while learning appears particularly important in developing the general principles of emissions trading and in further refining complex technical arrangements, the design of a system's main policy components will often be shaped more by (interest-driven) competition in international as well as domestic markets.[5]

Fourth, regarding the agents driving diffusion processes, we expect that when learning is the main mechanism of diffusion, *expert networks* found in research institutions, governments, ENGOs, industry/business and broader 'epistemic communities' (Haas 1990) will be important, particularly during the initial policy-making phases. Extending this line of reasoning, and drawing on our discussion of domestic politics as a mediating variable, we expect that when the process reaches the stage of competitive bargaining over the main policy components of an ETS, *policy-makers* and *industry/business stakeholders* will play more prominent roles – some as drivers, others as blockers (see also Steinberg and VanDeveer 2012; Bang et al. 2015). As noted, affected industries and utilities are likely to oppose costly policy components and use the political opportunity structure to lobby for modification or rejection of such policy components.

Fifth, regarding the relationship between diffusion mechanisms and outcomes, we expect that *emulation* will lead to upwards convergence, as a more advanced system is being copied; that *learning* will lead to more effective and efficient design but not necessarily to convergence; and that *competition* may generate a race to the bottom or to the top, depending on the circumstances. The expectation with regard to emulation is fairly straightforward: when policy-makers copy the design of a more advanced system, the outcome of the diffusion process will presumably be convergence upwards. However, with its simplistic approach, emulation involves the real risk of failure to adapt the imported model appropriately to the new setting. We expect learning – especially *sophisticated learning* – to lead to more effective and/or efficient designs, but not necessarily to convergence. Our main reason for emphasizing sophistication here is to point out that constructive learning need not refer only to 'successes' achieved by friendly neighbours: 'mistakes' made elsewhere may provide equally valuable information (see e.g. Gilardi 2010).

Finally, we expect that *competition* may generate upwards change as well as downwards change. One important determinant seems to be the kind of 'goods' or 'bads' generated by competition. When major foreign competitors cut prices (and/or taxes) on a given product, this will strengthen incentives for other companies (and governments) to respond with similar cuts, thereby fuelling a race to the bottom. As noted, competition in other settings could generate a race to the top, as in the 'California effect' (Vogel 1997) and in certification markets (Gulbrandsen 2010).

Parallel play and policy interplay

Our interest in international diffusion of policies and practices does not imply an assumption that diffusion will generally be the major factor in shaping ETS design. At least one alternative route of explanation calls for attention. This alternative sees policies, including the choice of policy instruments, as determined by the preferences and beliefs that domestic decision-makers have acquired, based – at least primarily – on their own assessments of the challenges encountered and the response options available.

According to this understanding, convergence cannot be taken as proof of international learning or adaption. Convergence may arise because different jurisdictions are likely to adopt similar policies when faced with similar challenges. Much economic and political science theory assumes that rational actors facing similar tasks will tend to come up with similar solutions – also in the absence of coordination. As noted earlier, the intellectual process leading actors to such convergence may be labelled 'parallel play'.

Similarly, the most intuitively compelling explanation of *divergence* in ETS design or use will point to differences in the challenges that countries encounter and/or in decision-makers' preferences and beliefs. Belief in the effectiveness of ETS in solving a country's problems seems particularly important – but climate-change mitigation policies often intersect not only with other mitigation *measures* but also with other *policy domains* such as electricity production and transport of people and goods. Thus, the introduction and design of ETS cannot be fully understood *solely* in terms of its effectiveness and efficiency in reducing greenhouse gas emissions (Steinberg and VanDeveer 2012; Bang et al. 2015).

One potential extension of this line of reasoning is to consider the interplay between ETS and other policy instruments serving a similar purpose. There are few examples anywhere in the world of a 'pure' ETS – an ETS implemented as the sole instrument for cutting emissions. In most cases where emissions trading has been introduced it was intended to complement, support or replace one or more other policy instrument(s). Its role in this broader policy context is important for understanding how emissions trading systems are designed and how they function once in place.

We may distinguish between the formal role of an ETS in the mix – whether emissions trading is a declared climate policy 'cornerstone' or merely one of several mitigation policies – and the actual role, which can be quite different. For example, ambitious policies for promoting renewables and enhancing energy efficiency have reduced emissions in the EU – and that, in turn, has been one contributing factor to the low demand (and prices) for EU ETS credits (Commission 2012; Wettestad and Jevnaker 2016).

Some scholars have even suggested that policy-makers will link emissions trading schemes to other policies precisely in order to make the full cost of trading schemes less transparent (see Victor 2009). Direct regulation in the form of general rules or fossil-fuel taxes can serve that purpose, but often to the disadvantage of groups that are poorly organized politically. Trading schemes layered on top of that basic logic are a kind of 'Potemkin' trading – a scheme that may look like real emissions trading when, in fact, most of the real 'work' in cutting emissions is being done through non-trading instruments (Victor 2009).

A central finding in the latest mitigation report from the Intergovernmental Panel on Climate Change (IPCC) is that policy interactions with price instruments (e.g. taxes) tend to add to the environmental effectiveness of *all* policy instruments, whereas interactions with quantity systems (e.g. emissions trading) are not always additive (IPCC Working Group III 2014: Chapter 15). That insight may lead policy-makers to look for alternatives to emissions trading or price-like mechanisms within ETS schemes. In that case, learning from the experience of others may be what triggers the exploration of alternative policy instruments, but the outcome of that exploration will probably be determined primarily by considerations of the country's own challenges and capabilities. Hence, at least in systems which have functioned for some years, 'internal learning' about design and functioning is likely to become increasingly important – one reason being that experience from the domestic setting may appear more solid and more directly relevant than observations from less familiar systems and more remote settings.

Finally, for more than two decades now, GHG mitigation policies have been subject to global negotiations under the auspices of the UN Framework Convention on Climate Change (UNFCCC). For most of this period, the substantive achievements have been meagre (Victor 2011), and no universal guidelines for emissions trading systems have been developed. However, the Intended Nationally Determined Contributions (INDCs) prepared for the Paris 2015 Summit indicate that IPCC reports and discussions in working groups have at least generated somewhat broader interest in ETS as a potential ingredient in emissions reduction policies. Although this hardly represents a breakthrough for emissions trading as a prominent tool for mitigation policies, we may expect the number of countries introducing some form of market-based systems to increase as they turn to implementation of their Nationally Determined Contributions (NDCs). And if more countries introduce such systems at the national level, the more likely it seems that some of these systems will (eventually) be linked.

Method, case selection and empirical coverage

Our research design is inspired by George (1979), who coined the expression 'structured, focused comparison' to refer to a general method of theory development in qualitative, small-N research. This design is what contemporary small-N methodologists often refer to as 'systematic and contextualized comparisons'. Our approach is 'systematic' in the sense that our case-study authors were asked to address the same ETS design features (to determine variation on the dependent variable) and to examine the same explanatory variables, across all cases. Our approach is 'contextualized' as it considers ETS diffusion in light of the unique historical, political, economic and institutional characteristics of the jurisdictions in question. Guided by the analytical framework, our case studies employ a similar structure, facilitating comparison. This makes for tightly integrated chapters that follow the same methodology and research design.

This volume is unique in its empirical coverage, examining almost the entire *universe* of systems that are in operation, or have been operational, worldwide: the EU ETS, RGGI, California, Tokyo, New Zealand, Australia, China, South Korea and Kazakhstan.[6] While various *proposed* trading schemes could have been examined,[7] we focus on key systems that have been operational for some time, since actual operation often reveals important diffusion dynamics and political influences not evident in hypothetical systems.

While we chose early on to employ a comparative case-study approach to exploring diffusion processes across jurisdictions, the contributing authors rely on within-case *process tracing* to identify causal chains of events and path dependencies that resulted in particular ETS design outcomes (George and Bennett 2004). The case studies are based on primary research on the role of diffusion in ETS design, employing a range of data sources. Process tracing was made possible by investigating policy processes and reconstructing the chain of events in the jurisdictions under scrutiny. All case studies draw on position papers and reports produced by stakeholders, impact assessments, policy reviews and the like; hearings and public discussions in legislatures and other decision-making institutions were also examined where relevant.

All case-study authors have conducted in-depth interviews with decision-makers, stakeholders and various experts to supplement the written sources, and some case studies have also benefited from participant observation by the authors through their work for international organizations or consultancy firms involved in establishing the ETS. As the interviews were conducted on the basis of differing 'ground rules' in the various case studies (some interviewees demanded anonymity; some did not), they are referenced in different ways.

The written material, interview data and other data sources have provided evidence of the forms of reasoning underpinning the design of carbon trading systems. Explicit and more implicit reference to diffusion mechanisms – emulation, lessons learned, competitive concerns and coercion – has provided evidence of diffusion. The evidence has been scrutinized to provide a comprehensive picture of the main societal actors and arguments shaping ETS designs, as well as to specify to what extent and how different diffusion mechanisms have operated. This triangulation of data sources has helped the case-study authors generate reliable and valid findings on the influence of policy diffusion on ETS design.

The empirical chapters of this volume have followed the same methodology and research design, all leading up to systematic comparisons across the cases and solid conclusions. We feel confident that the comparison of design features and diffusion influences across cases has provided a full and rich account of the role of diffusion in shaping ETS design.

Notes

1 As a guide for the case-study authors we initially developed a more fine-tuned set of potential scores on these eight dimensions (see Underdal et al. 2015). As expected, some of these distinctions proved more important and useful than others in describing and comparing ETS systems.

2 http://medical-dictionary.thefreedictionary.com/parallell+play. Accessed 5 May 2017.

3 Maggetti and Gilardi (2016) found that emulation is somewhat more frequently studied in diffusion research than (sophisticated) learning, the only exception being studies of policy success, where learning leads by a wide margin.

4 Gresham's law is a statement saying, in essence, that whenever the two co-exist and the latter is generally recognized as being the more valuable, 'bad' money drives out 'good' money.

5 We base this 'expectation' on propositions and observations from various other studies, including Simmons et al. 2006; Gilardi 2010; Ovodenko and Keohane 2012.

6 Main systems in operation not covered here are those in Saitama, Switzerland and Ontario and Quebec in Canada. See ICAP 2016.

7 This includes Brazil, Mexico, Ukraine, Thailand and Vietnam. See ICAP 2016.

References

Bang, G., A. Underdal and S. Andresen (eds.). 2015. *The Domestic Politics of Global Climate Change: Key Actors in International Climate Cooperation*. Cheltenham: Edward Elgar.

Baumgartner, F. and B. Jones. 1993. *Agendas and Instability in American Politics*. Chicago, IL: University of Chicago Press.

Biesenbender, S. and J. Tosun. 2014. Domestic politics and the diffusion of international policy innovations. *Global Environmental Change* 29, 424–433.

Börzel, T. A. and T. Risse. 2012. From Europeanisation to diffusion: Introduction. *West European Politics* 35 (1), 1–19.

Commission. 2012. *The State of the European Carbon Market in 2012*. Report from the Commission to the European Parliament and the Council. Brussels, 14 November, COM (2012) 652 Final.

Deutsch, K. W. 1966. *The Nerves of Government: Models of Political Communication and Control*. New York: Free Press.

Downs, G. W. and D. M. Rocke. 1990. *Tacit Bargaining, Arms Races, and Arms Control*. Ann Arbor: University of Michigan Press.

Elkins, Z., A. Guzman and B. Simmons. 2006. Competing for capital: The diffusion of bilateral investment treaties, 1960–2000. *International Organization* 60 (4), 811–846.

Elkins, Z. and B. Simmons. 2005. On waves, clusters and diffusion: A conceptual framework. *Annals of the American Academy of Political and Social Science* 598, 33–51.

Falkner, R. and A. Gupta. 2009. The limits of regulatory convergence: Globalization and GMO politics in the South. *International Environmental Agreements* 9 (2), 113–133.

Finnemore, M. and K. Sikkink. 1998. International norm dynamics and political change. *International Organization* 52 (4), 887–917.

George, A. L. 1979. Case studies and theory development: The method of structured, focused comparison. In *Diplomacy: New Approaches in History, Theory, and Policy*, edited by P. G. Lauren, 43–68. New York: Free Press.

George, A. L. and A. Bennett. 2004. *Case Studies and Theory Development in the Social Sciences*. Cambridge, MA: MIT Press.

Gilardi, F. 2010. Who learn from what in policy diffusion processes? *American Journal of Political Science* 54 (3), 650–666.

Gilardi, F. 2013. Transnational diffusion: Norms, ideas, and policies. In *Handbook of International Relations*, edited by W. Carlsnaes, T. Risse and B. A. Simmons, 453–477. London: Sage.

Gulbrandsen, L. H. 2010. *Transnational Environmental Governance: The Emergence and Effects of the Certification of Forests and Fisheries*. Cheltenham: Edward Elgar.

Haas, E. B. 1964. *Beyond the Nation State*. Stanford, CA: Stanford University Press.

Haas, P. M. 1990. *Saving the Mediterranean*. New York: Columbia University Press.

Harrison, K. and L. M. Sundstrom (eds.). 2010. *Global Commons, Domestic Decisions: The Comparative Politics of Climate Change*. Cambridge, MA: MIT Press.

Holzinger, K., C. Knill and T. Sommerer. 2008. Environmental policy convergence? The impact of international harmonization, transnational communication, and regulatory competition. *International Organization* 62 (4), 553–587.

Holzinger, K., C. Knill and T. Sommerer. 2011. Is there convergence of national environmental policies? An analysis of policy outputs in 24 OECD countries. *Environmental Politics* 20 (1), 20–41.

Hovi, J. and T. Skodvin. 2008. Which way to U.S. climate cooperation? Issue linkage versus a U.S.-based agreement. *Review of Policy Research* 25 (2), 129–148.

ICAP. 2016. *Emissions Trading Worldwide: International Carbon Action Partnership Status Report 2016*. Berlin: International Carbon Action Partnership (ICAP).

IPCC. 2014. *Climate Change 2014: Mitigation of Climate Change*. http://mitigation2014.org accessed 29 May 2017.

Kingdon, J. 1984. *Agendas, Alternatives, and Public Policies*. Boston, MA: Little, Brown & Co.

Kinne, B. J. 2013. Network dynamics and the evolution of international cooperation. *American Political Science Review* 107 (4), 766–785.

Klingler-Vidra, R. and P. Schleifer. 2014. Convergence more or less: Why do practices vary as they diffuse? *International Studies Review* 16 (2), 264–274.

Knill, C., K. Schulze and J. Tosun. 2012. Regulatory policy outputs and impacts: Exploring a complex relationship. *Regulation and Governance* 6, 427–444.

Maggetti, M. and F. Gilardi. 2016. Problems (and solutions) in the measurement of policy diffusion mechanisms. *Journal of Public Policy* 36 (1), 87–107.

Olson, M. 1965. *The Logic of Collective Action*. Cambridge, MA: Harvard University Press.

Overdevest, C. 2010. Comparing forest certification schemes: The case of ratcheting standards in the forest sector. *Socio-Economic Review* 8, 47–76.

Ovodenko, A. and R. O. Keohane. 2012. Institutional diffusion in international environmental affairs. *International Affairs* 88, 523–541.

Paterson, M., M. Hoffman, M. Betsill and S. Bernstein. 2014. The micro foundations of policy diffusion toward complex global governance: An analysis of the transnational carbon emission trading network. *Comparative Political Studies* 47 (3), 420–449.

Pierson, P. 1993. When effect becomes cause: Policy feedback and political change. *World Politics* 45 (4), 595–628.

Pierson, P. 2000. Path dependence, increasing returns, and the study of politics. *American Political Science Review* 94 (2), 251–267.

PMR/ICAP. 2016. *Emissions Trading in Practice: A Handbook on Design and Implementation*. Washington, DC: The World Bank.

Sabatier, P. A. 1988. An advocacy coalition framework of policy change and the role of policy-oriented learning therein. *Policy Sciences* 21 (2), 129–168.

Sebenius, J. K. 1983. Negotiation arithmetic: Adding and subtracting issues and parties. *International Organization* 37 (2), 281–317.

Shipan, C. R. and C. Volden. 2008. The mechanisms of policy diffusion. *American Journal of Political Science* 52 (4), 840–857.

Shipan, C. R. and C. Volden. 2012. Policy diffusion: Seven lessons for scholars and practitioners. *Public Administration Review* 72 (6), 788–796.

Simmons, B. A., F. Dobbin and G. Garrett. 2006. Introduction: The international diffusion of liberalism. *International Organization* 60 (4), 781–810.

Simmons, B. A. and Z. Elkins. 2004. The globalization of liberalization: Policy diffusion in the international political economy. *American Political Science Review* 98 (1), 171–189.

Skjærseth, J. B. and J. Wettestad. 2008. *EU Emissions Trading: Initiation, Decision-making and Implementation*. Aldershot: Ashgate.

Slaughter, A. M. 2005. *A New World Order*. Princeton, NJ: Princeton University Press.

Solingen, E. and T. A. Börzel. 2014. Introduction to presidential issue: The politics of international diffusion – a symposium. *International Studies Review* 16 (2), 173–178.

Steinberg, P. F. and S. D. VanDeveer (eds.). 2012. *Comparative Environmental Politics: Theory, Practice and Prospects*. Cambridge, MA: MIT Press.

Swank, D. 2006. Tax policy in the era of internationalization: Explaining the spread of neoliberalism. *International Organization* 60 (4), 847–882.

Tsebelis, G. 2002. *Veto Players: How Political Institutions Work*. Princeton, NJ: Princeton University Press.

Underdal, A. 1998. Explaining compliance and defection: Three models. *European Journal of International Relations* 4 (1), 5–30.

Underdal, A., D. G. Victor and J. Wettestad. 2015. *Studying the Global Diffusion of Emissions Trading: Key Building Blocks in the ETS DIFFUSION Project Research Design*. Lysaker: FNI Report 2/2015.

van Asselt, H. 2016. The design and implementation of greenhouse gas emissions trading. In *The Oxford Handbook of International Climate Change Law*, edited by C. P. Carlarne, K. R. Gray and R. G. Tarasofsky, 332–356. Oxford: Oxford University Press.

Victor, D. G. 2009. Potemkin trading. *Technology Review* (July/August), 12.

Victor, D. G. 2011. *Global Warming Gridlock: Creating More Effective Strategies for Protecting the Planet*. Cambridge: Cambridge University Press.

Victor, D. G. 2014. *A Political Theory of Water Governance*. San Diego: University of California, ILAR Working Paper 19. http://ilar.ucsd.edu/_files/publications/working-papers/working-paper-19.pdf accessed 29 May 2017.

Vogel, D. 1995. *Trading up: Consumer and Environmental Regulation in a Global Economy*. Cambridge, MA: Harvard University Press.

Vogel, D. 1997. Trading up and governing across: Transnational governance and environmental protection. *Journal of European Public Policy* 4 (4), 556–571.

Weishaar, S. E. 2014. *Emissions Trading Design: A Critical Overview*. Cheltenham: Edward Elgar.

Wettestad, J. and T. Jevnaker. 2016. *Rescuing EU Emissions Trading: The Climate Policy Flagship*. Basingstoke: Palgrave.

Wilson, J. 1973. *Political Organizations*. New York: Basic Books.

3 EU emissions trading

Frontrunner – and 'black sheep'?

Jørgen Wettestad and Torbjørg Jevnaker

Introduction

In the preparatory process of the 1990s, prior to the Kyoto Protocol, the European Union was sceptical of the idea of using flexible instruments such as emissions trading in the context of climate-change policy. At that time, emissions trading was used mainly for reducing the emissions of air pollutants in the US (see Chapter 5 of this book). Then, in 1998, the EU made a policy turn-about and started to develop an emissions trading system – the EU ETS.

The first EU ETS Directive, adopted in 2003, determined the key elements of the design of the system in a first trading phase (2005–7, the pilot phase) and the second phase (2008–12, the Kyoto Protocol commitment phase). The system was launched in 2005, making the EU a frontrunner in emissions trading. Initially, the system covered around two billion tons of CO_2 (and hence tradeable emissions allowances), corresponding to roughly 40 per cent of the EU's CO_2 emissions. The design was decentralized, with no common central cap, and decisions about allowance allocations were up to the individual member-states. Allowances were mainly handed out for free. Hence, the carbon price proved to be volatile and generally low, as member-states had handed out allowances generously and implemented the system differently (Skjærseth and Wettestad 2008, 2010).

Therefore, in 2008, a significantly changed design was adopted for the third phase of the system (2013–20). But at the same time the financial crisis hit Europe and lowered production and emissions. Responding to an increasing surplus of allowances and a rather low carbon price, a further reform process was initiated in 2012, resulting in the adoption of a Market Stability Reserve to start operating in 2019 (Wettestad and Jevnaker 2016; Jevnaker and Wettestad 2017). Thus, the design of the EU ETS has undergone multiple revisions.

The EU ETS is a pivotal system, the largest of its kind so far. Moreover, as an international carbon trading frontrunner, it is the system with the longest history. The EU ETS has gradually been complemented by other systems around the globe, as further discussed in other chapters of this book. As noted by Knox-Hayes (2016: 190), 'All of the emissions markets have been influenced to one degree or another by the EU ETS'. Hence, as the EU ETS is a major *sender* of policy impulses and lessons, it is certainly important to understand how its design has come about and developed over time. This chapter clarifies this gradual evolution. But the system has also been a *receiver* of policy impulses. Most importantly, it was preceded by a trading mechanism in the US for regulating air pollution. This point is discussed as well.

The long history of the EU ETS allows exploration of whether external policy diffusion may vary over time and across different phases. On the one hand, one might expect openness to the experiences of others to have been highest in the initial stage where uncertainty was relatively high and positions less fixed – and lower in later stages when positions became more settled, when internal path dependencies and internal lesson learning became more prominent. On the other hand, in the early years there were few other carbon trading systems the EU could learn from: it is only more recently that such systems have mushroomed. Paradoxically, then, as lessons from other ETS are becoming available, the EU may have become less open to drawing such lessons. We return to this later in the chapter.

How, then, does an ETS work in practice? The EU ETS provides ample evidence of the relationship between design and the actual functioning of the system, as expressed not least through the carbon price. As noted, there has been a volatile and generally rather low carbon price, plummeting to rock bottom in 2007 and on a serious downward trend since 2009. As this is a market-based system, policy-makers have restricted opportunities for controlling the price directly. Getting a 'reasonably high' price becomes an issue of framework conditions, some of which are subject to political control (not least the number of allowances in circulation), whereas others remain outside the control of policy-makers (e.g. economic growth). Add a complex EU decision-making process involving multiple and antagonistic players to the mix, and the result is an ETS that some today view as a 'black sheep', representing what *not* to do: a flawed design resulting in a carbon market haunted by problems. Did the EU bear the burden of frontrunning – and is it still paying the costs of this?

This chapter is based on examination of official documents from EU bodies and central governmental and non-governmental stakeholders, articles and books on the EU ETS, articles from news agencies such as *ENDS Daily* and *Carbon Pulse*, and interviews with stakeholders (see list of interviews in Annex).

Overview of the ETS and its emergence

A brief overview of the EU and how it adopts policy can be found in Box 3.1.

Box 3.1 Overview of the EU and how it adopts policy

The EU is not a standard international organization driven by intergovernmental negotiations among its 28 European member countries, but it is also not a supranational federal state. Although the decision-making competence of the EU varies by policy area, the EU is a political system in its own right, with three branches of government: it has an executive branch (the European Commission) that prepares legislative proposals that are adopted as EU law if approved (usually with amendments) by the legislative branch. The latter consists of two distinct entities: a EU-level parliament (the European Parliament) and an EU-level assembly of 28 national ministers (Council of the EU) that gather in sector configurations (e.g. each member state will be represented by its environmental ministers if environmental policy is on the agenda). Further, the judicial branch is represented by the European Court of Justice. Finally, there is the European Council, an assembly of 28 heads of state or government, which defines the EU's overall political direction and priorities. Although the European Council does not pass laws, it sometimes adopts positions on specific issues that are seen as de facto binding the Commission's policy preparation. In the Parliament and Council, majority voting rules are now the default option for most policy areas (an important exception being tax issues), whereas unanimity is required in the European Council.

(For further details, see e.g. Wallace et al. 2014.)

From 1998 onward, the EU ETS was developed as a new, cornerstone measure within climate policy (Christiansen and Wettestad 2003; Wettestad 2005; Skjærseth and Wettestad 2008; Convery 2009). As noted, this marked a break with the earlier scepticism towards flexible mechanisms. The ETS Directive was adopted in 2003, covering the pilot phase (2005–7) and the Kyoto Protocol commitment phase (2008–12).

The power sector was a central target group and implementer, together with several energy-intensive industries like steel and cement. The ETS was adopted as an EU-level cap-and-trade system, albeit with a significant degree of decentralization. Initially, there was no common central cap for the entire EU, and specific decisions about allowance allocations were up to the individual member-states. The outcome was that allowances were handed out for free, and rather liberally. To ensure additional flexibility, the ETS was also linked to the Kyoto flexibility mechanisms: the Clean Development Mechanism (CDM) from 2005 and Joint Implementation (JI) from 2008. No specific price-management mechanism was adopted.

Unsurprisingly for a 'grand experiment' (Kruger and Pizer 2004), the first years proved problematic: member-states implemented the system differently, and a surplus of allowances arose. With no possibility of saving allowances from the pilot phase to the next phase ('banking'), the carbon price plummeted to near zero in 2007. As noted, the two first phases were covered by the 2003 Directive: a first major reform was adopted in 2008. This reform was a central part of the EU's overall climate and energy package for 2020 and significantly changed the rules for the third phase of the ETS (2013–20). The reform introduced a single EU-wide cap with a common Linear Reduction Factor (LRF) and was intended to make the ETS a much more centralized and auctioning-based system from 2013 (Skjærseth and Wettestad 2010; Boasson and Wettestad 2013).

However, economic activity in Europe plummeted as the financial crisis unfolded from autumn 2008 onwards. The crisis meant lower production and thus also lower emissions, and a formidable surplus of allowances began accumulating (see e.g. Skovgaard 2013; Grubb et al. 2014; Wettestad 2014). The use of CDM credits was to be tightened from 2013, triggering a rush to use such credits before the tightening deadline. And growth in the production and use of renewables further reduced the demand for allowances.

The result was a volatile and generally low carbon price (down to EUR 5 in 2013). This was a far cry from the EUR 30–40 level deemed necessary for sparking a low-carbon transition (Dupont and Oberthür 2015). With insufficient economic signals from the EU ETS, the EU member-states had started considering national compensating measures. The UK was a frontrunner in adopting measures explicitly aimed at complementing the ETS: in 2011, it decided to introduce a carbon price floor, placing a fossil-fuels levy on the electricity bill. This came in addition to the EU carbon price already included there (see Sandbag 2012; Fankhauser 2013; House of Commons 2014).

The worsening ETS crisis from 2011 onwards also called for responses at the EU level. In 2012, the Commission initiated a reform process with two main elements: 'backloading' (postponing the auctioning of some allowances to 2019–20) and six options for structural reform, including a discretionary price-management mechanism (Commission 2012). Then, in spring 2013, the European Parliament (hereafter: Parliament) voted against backloading. However, the Parliament soon changed its mind, and a governmental shift in Germany – making it a more vigorous supporter of ETS reform – altered the dynamics among the member-states (Wettestad and Jevnaker 2016; Jevnaker and Wettestad 2017).

In early 2014, the Commission launched a proposal for introducing a Market Stability Reserve (MSR) from 2021. This mechanism would automatically withdraw or release allowances, depending upon the number of allowances in circulation, hence gradually reducing the accumulated surplus. After tough negotiations where both the UK and Germany pushed for an MSR start already in 2017, the MSR was adopted in spring 2015, with a compromise start in 2019. Proposals for a revised ETS Directive for the next trading period (2021–30) were tabled soon after.

In 2016 the carbon price fell again, moving between EUR 4 and 6.5. National frustrations over the ETS have increased – with, for instance, France launching proposals for further EU-level regulation of the carbon price and the introduction of a national price and Sweden announcing a unilateral, yearly cancellation of a limited number of allowances in the summer of 2016. The 2030 Directive proposal is currently going through the EU institutions, with a final decision expected in the course of 2017.

Table 3.1 Overview of ETS design

	Pilot phase (2005–7) and Kyoto phase (2008–12)	*Key changes for phase 3 (2013–20)*
Type of system	– Cap and trade – Banking from second phase on – Decentralized design	– More centralization and harmonization
Ambition level	– No common cap – Loose link to EU Kyoto target	– Common cap – 21% reduction by 2020 (1990) – Linear Reduction Factor (1.74% reduction annually)
Allocation mechanisms	– Mainly free allocation	– From 2013 40% auctioning; to increase
Coverage	– Power producers and several energy-intensive industries – Upstream focus ('direct' emissions) – CO_2 – Around 11,000 installations	– Airlines from 2012 – Also nitrous oxide and perfluorocarbons
Offsetting and linking	– CDMs from 2005; also JI from 2008 – From 2008, 10% offset limit – Linking with Kyoto ratifiers – Linking with Norway in 2009	– Certain credits/projects banned from 2013 – Vision of linked carbon markets in the Organisation for Economic Co-operation and Development (OECD) area by 2015
MRV (monitoring, reporting, and verification)	– Annual reports from installations, verified by third party – Initially EUR 40 penalty for non-compliance; then EUR 100	
Price and quantity management	– Initially nothing	– Loose rule about intervention if two years of high price – Market Stability Reserve adopted in 2015, to operate from 2019
Revenue earmarking		– Recommendation to use 50% of revenues for climate purposes

Explaining the turn to ETS in the EU

Why did the EU decide to turn to emissions trading as a key climate policy instrument back in 1998? A combination of internal and external factors was involved. On the whole, the adoption of the Kyoto Protocol in 1997 and the commitment for the EU to reduce emissions by 8 per cent created a clear need for the EU to come up with common policies with significant clout, which it had not managed to do earlier in that decade. Those years had seen a strenuous, politically highly controversial, and ultimately failed effort to establish a common carbon tax (Wettestad 2001). In addition to being controversial, legislating on tax issues at EU level would require unanimity among member-states, involving a rather high threshold for adoption.

The tax experience was an important formative influence on a small group of Commission officials and entrepreneurs, most of them economists. Some of these economists had their formal education from and had maintained good contacts in the US, making them open to drawing inspiration from US practice. This group managed to convince then environment commissioner Hedegaard of the virtues of carbon trading in 1998 – and the development of an EU ETS started (Christiansen and Wettestad 2003; Skjærseth and Wettestad 2008). Moreover, unlike a carbon tax, a carbon market measure could be adopted through the relatively easier procedure of qualified majority vote.

Thus we can note a certain policy diffusion influence from the US as to convincing the EU about the idea of emissions trading. Damro and Luaces Méndez (2003) see the 1997 negotiations that led up to the Kyoto Protocol as a venue for transferring lessons from the US to EU policy-makers. Basically, the EU needed a policy instrument that could reduce emissions in accordance with the EU's Kyoto Protocol commitment of an 8 per cent reduction and also be politically feasible, and contact with the US facilitated inspiration regarding a viable solution.

Explaining the evolving design of ETS

Deciding the rules for the two first phases

Type of system: diminishing US influence; EU stakeholder concerns take over

As noted prior, inspiration from the US clearly contributed to turning the EU towards a cap-and-trade ETS. The US link continued in the initial, more specific discussions on fleshing out a design appropriate for the EU. According to Zapfel and Vainio (2002: 7), in the immediate post-Kyoto phase, US actors such as Environmental Protection Agency (EPA) staff, environmental non-governmental organization (ENGO) Environmental Defense, and the think-tank Center for Clean Air Policy (CCAP) 'invested a lot of time and pressure in participating in the European [ETS] debate'.

However, given the different institutional, cultural, legal, and administrative nature of the EU, 'the value of the contributions by US experts declined steadily' (Zapfel and Vainio 2002: 9) – also due to the non-development of a national US ETS. Paterson et al. (2014) further support this view of very limited US influence on the more specific evolving design of the ETS, noting the important underlying division between US and European 'trading communities', with limited cross-community personal contacts.

Regarding inter-temporal safety valves, banking was to be allowed from phase 2 on, but not between phases 1 and 2. This was primarily because phase 1 was a pilot phase and the EU wanted to avoid transferring start-up errors into the second phase when it had formal Kyoto Protocol commitments. The governance level of the ETS was supranational, with the main rules decided at EU level. But considerable authority was given to member-states in the initial two phases, primarily as a response to member-state uncertainty about a policy instrument that was new to almost all of them (Paterson et al. 2014).

Ambition level: unclear and only loosely linked to Kyoto

The 2003 Directive did not establish a common cap for ETS phases 1 and 2. Instead a bottom-up approach was chosen, with the common cap emanating from the national caps put together. There was only a loosely worded link to the need for the ETS to contribute achieving the EU's Kyoto Protocol commitment of an 8 per cent reduction (points 2 and 5 in the Preamble). Here we should keep in mind that the ETS would cover less than 50 per cent of EU greenhouse gas (GHG) emissions and the lack of a specific common cap.

What were the major factors that shaped the initial ETS design of the ambition level? Peter Zapfel (of what was then the Commission's Environment Directorate) was among the chief initial ETS architects and 'present at the creation'. In his 2002 account of the ETS discussions in the EU thus far (written together with Matti Vainio) he places considerable emphasis on the several rounds of stakeholder consultations, with a majority of member-states and industries stating their clear preference for a decentralized design (Zapfel and Vainio 2002; Watanabe and Robinson 2005). As emissions trading was new to most member-states, they felt cautious about the introduction of this instrument and allowing the Commission 'too much' power in the initial implementation phase. There was also relevant activity on the part of industry – like the establishment of company-internal systems in BP and Shell and emissions trading simulations conducted by the power industry (GETS I and II) (Victor and House 2006).

The preferences of key industries and member-states undoubtedly shaped central design features in the directive proposal that was put forward by the Commission in October 2001. As discussed in greater depth in Skjærseth and Wettestad (2008), much of this design survived the subsequent EU decision-making process. Concerning the low degree of centralized steering of the system, the Commission chose to heed key sentiments among industries and member-states, rather than pushing its own preferences for centralization. There was very limited willingness among stakeholders to set up the Commission as a strong watchdog for the system.

Policy diffusion in the sense of learning did not play a significant role in this specific design attribute. But what about the competition mechanism? Here we should note that when the EU made a U-turn and started to develop emissions trading (from 1998 onwards), the EU saw itself as a frontrunner in global climate politics, as it indeed was at that stage (see Grubb et al. 1999; Christiansen and

Wettestad 2003). The initial ambitiousness of the ETS did not emanate from any fundamental need to adapt to the actions of others, in the sense of 'ratcheting up'.

Allocation method: much shaped by competitive concerns, but not policy diffusion

The 2003 Directive established a system where allowances were to be handed out basically for free to companies, based on previous emissions from each installation ('grandfathering'). In the pilot phase, there was to be at least 95 per cent allocation by member-state governments, each of which was to set up a National Allocation Plan (NAP); in phase 2, at least 90 per cent free allowances. This also meant that one of the eight design properties in focus in this book – rules for earmarking of auctioning revenues – was not particularly relevant in these initial phases, simply because little auctioning took place.

As to shaping factors, stakeholder consultations showed a clear preference for allowances to be handed out for free (Zapfel and Vainio 2002; Watanabe and Robinson 2005). The pioneering position of the EU ETS – 'the grand new experiment' – led to worries in important EU industries, primarily the energy-intensive industries competing in the global marketplace, about an uneven global economic and regulatory playing field (Skjærseth and Wettestad 2008; Wettestad 2009a). These concerns were voiced in the stakeholder consultations, as well as channelled through member-state inputs to the Commission.

This element clearly contributed significantly to the decision to establish an ETS where almost all allowances would initially be handed out for free. Thus we see that the choice of allocation method was shaped by the interaction of internal and external factors: internal uncertainty about the functioning of a new regulatory instrument and externally motivated concerns about competitive effects vis-à- vis countries and industries not subject to comparable climate policy constraints. Although the EU adjusted to the absence of comparable climate regulation imposed on companies competing with European industries, this significant external influence cannot be seen as 'policy diffusion' as defined in this book.

Coverage: practical reasoning and internal reference points

The main target group covered by the EU ETS was the energy-producing sector, referred to in the 2003 Directive as 'energy activities', but selected energy-consuming industries were also included: 'production and processing of ferrous metals' (like iron, steel); 'mineral industry' (cement, glass, ceramics); and 'other activities' (pulp and paper). Formal rules were not differentiated across sectors. Only CO_2 emissions were covered – approximately 40 per cent of EU CO_2 emissions.

As to shaping factors, coverage was discussed in the seminal Green Paper issued in 2000 (Commission 2000). Although in principle a broad and comprehensive system that would cover all six main GHGs and carbon sinks and all emission sources was seen as best, the Commission held that there were 'sound scientific and practical reasons', related to monitoring not least, for not necessarily pursuing that option further but for confining the scope to large fixed-point sources of CO_2 (Commission 2000: 10). Two earlier EU policies – the Large Combustion Plant (LCP) and the Integrated Pollution Prevention and Control (IPPC) Directives – were used to underpin the argument for why the ETS should focus only on such point sources. With no one to learn from, international policy diffusion did not play a significant role in the design here. Instead, the EU built on existing practice established in previous EU environmental legislation.

External offsetting and linking: covering new ground

The 2003 Directive opened up for the use of Kyoto Protocol offsets/credits (CDM/JI), although Article 30 stated that this use should be supplemental to domestic action. More specific rules were set out in a subsequent 'linking directive' (2004/101), which stipulated that only CDM credits could be used for compliance in phase 1, with JI credits also becoming useable in phase 2. No particular countries or sectors were given priority. But credits from nuclear power projects were banned; the use of credits from carbon sinks/forestry was limited to the pilot phase; and credits from hydropower plants were allowed as long as they took account of 'environmental and social impacts'. Regarding linkage with other emissions trading systems, Article 25 stated the general goal of entering into agreements with countries that had ratified the Kyoto Protocol, for 'mutual recognition' of allowances from their ETS.

As to shaping factors, the frontrunner position must again be emphasized. The EU was covering new regulatory ground, and there were no models to learn from as regards linking an emissions trading system to external offsets. A central worry for industry (particularly those that are energy intensive) and policy-makers was an overly high, 'runaway' carbon price within an isolated system (Sandbag 2012: 10). This was seen as calling for safety valves like access to offsets. Furthermore, the decision to link up to the CDM/JI system also had to do with the EU's overall strong support to the UN Framework Convention on Climate Change (UNFCCC) and the Kyoto Protocol, so there were also diplomatic motivations at work (Sandbag 2012: 9).

MRV (Monitoring, reporting, and verification) and enforcement: significant learning from the US

EU member-states were to ensure that emissions from the installations included were monitored in accordance with overall guidelines. Installations were required to report emissions annually, through reports prepared by accredited verifiers in line with specified criteria. Subsequently, the installations would have to hand in permits in accordance with the allowed maximum (i.e. the 'cap'). For oversight of the holding and transfer of allowances, member-states were also required to establish and maintain registries 'accessible to the public'. Member-states were also to submit yearly reports to the Commission about their application of the ETS

Directive. In the pilot phase, penalties were set at EUR 40 for each ton of emitted CO_2 beyond the number of permits held, increasing to EUR 100 per ton in phase 2 (2008–12).

This design element was much shaped by learning. Damro and Luaces Mendez (2003: 89) point out that key aspects of the design of the monitoring and verification system – the registry part but also the penalties regime – drew heavily on the example of the US SO_2 system. Interviews with central policy-makers at the time confirm scrutiny of the US system but also indicate some divergent choices, for instance with the monitoring approach (different from the continuous US emissions monitoring) and the EU's requirement for independent, third-party verification of companies' emission figures (interviews March 2015, January 2017).

Price or quantity-focused management mechanisms: not initially addressed

No price or quantity-focused management mechanisms were established in the 2003 Directive. Indeed, the regulatory history shows that this issue was virtually absent from the discussions. Although various design issues were discussed in the preamble to the 2001 proposal from the Commission, the issues of possible price development and the relationship to design were not commented upon.

In part, this probably had to do with a point noted prior: the central worry was about excessively *high* prices, not too low ones. And initially, the various safety valves – free allowances, some access to CDM/JI credits, member-states in control and the Commission as a weak watchdog – were probably seen as sufficient to avoid price spikes. Moreover, the other main ETS in operation at that time – the US SO_2 trading system – had no price-management mechanism.

Summing up: what role did policy diffusion play for the turn-about and initial design of the EU ETS?

It is important to distinguish between the turn-about and the initial design, because policy diffusion played differing roles for these processes. As to the turn-about, EU-external impulses were fairly important, since the EU would not have opted for this instrument without the Kyoto Protocol, both the negotiation process leading up to the Protocol and the EU target adopted. Also relevant, however, was a prior EU-internal policy failure: the failure to adopt a EU carbon tax. As there was an element of inspiration from the US, we hold that at least some of the external influence can be classified as policy diffusion. And how were the diffusion impulses mediated into the EU system? Primarily by a small group of economist entrepreneurs within the Commission who were fed up with the carbon tax debacle, some of whom had trained in the US.

The subsequent process of shaping the initial design was then less markedly shaped by policy diffusion, and to varying degrees. The learning mechanism did not play a very significant role, as it had become clear at an early stage that the US context was very different from that facing policy-makers in the EU. There were also issue area differences, as the US experience had concerned regulating air pollution, not climate change. The most notable US influence was on the MRV regime, mediated by Commission officials.

International competitive concerns were clearly important for the dominance of free allocation. This influence was mediated primarily through lobbying from energy-intensive industries but also through pressure from several member-states uncertain about ETS introduction. However, the specific policy for shielding exposed industries from environmental regulation had not emanated from outside the EU: it was developed internally, with a generous distribution of free allowances combined with access to international credits.

Improving the ETS design for 2013–20: major changes adopted in 2008

The pilot phase of the ETS did not function well, with a sharp price drop in 2006 and a carbon price close to zero in 2007 (Wettestad 2009b, 2011). Hence, when the design rules for the third phase (2013–20) were to be decided in 2008, significant changes were adopted (Skjærseth and Wettestad 2010; Boasson and Wettestad 2013; Wettestad 2015). What were the main changes made, and to what extent and how were they shaped by diffusion?

Fundamental system changes: harmonization and centralization

With regard to inter-temporal safety valves, banking was now to be allowed between phases. The governance level would become more clearly supranational, with greater harmonization and far less leeway and authority given to member-states. A longer phase was introduced (eight years: 2013–20). Furthermore, a novel feature was added, in reality entailing a much longer time horizon than eight years: from 2013 onwards, the number of allowances would be reduced by 1.74 per cent. This was termed the Linear Reduction Factor, and it was set to continue beyond 2020, with no end-date specified. We come back to the LRF in the following. In addition, a single, EU-wide cap would be introduced, with allowances allocated on the basis of fully harmonized rules for the period 2013–20. Thus, individual NAPs per member-state would be simply no longer needed.

As described prior, much of the background for these fundamental changes were the problems experienced in the pilot phase, with member-states interpreting ETS rules in sharply differing ways and a quite fragmented system emerging. Who were the main leaders/pushers? In essence, a coalition of key actors managed to put in place a significantly tighter system: among the member-states the UK was a national ETS frontrunner, with the long-serving ETS entrepreneurs in DG Environment, and power producers.

As noted in Chapter 2 of this book, the policy innovation literature points to the importance of 'failures of existing policies' and related 'shock events'. Such a political shock occurred within the ETS in the spring of 2006, when the verified emissions figures for the first year of the ETS were presented, confirming suspicions of an over-allocated market. This led to an immediate halving of the carbon price and a subsequent price decline in 2007 to near zero (Skjærseth and Wettestad 2008; Wettestad 2009b). These events contributed considerably to the growing realization that the initial ETS design was fundamentally flawed and that significant changes would have to be adopted.

The design changes can also be interpreted as the Commission entrepreneurs finally having it their way, as it is clear that a more centralized system had been their preference all along (Skjærseth and Wettestad 2008; Boasson and Wettestad 2013). With the ETS already up and running, the overall need for entrepreneurship had become less pressing. Still, the Commission played a central role as well this time; indeed, many of the same key persons in the climate unit (DG Clima) who had helped bring about an EU ETS in the first place were central in developing the markedly changed ETS design for phase 3 – among them Jos Delbeke and Peter Zapfel. The Commission's capacity for innovation was bolstered by expertise provided by external consultants: five such reports were listed in the annex to the Commission's Impact Assessment (Commission 2008).

However, there were also forces seeking to counter the role of the Commission and the development towards a far more centralized system. To understand the adoption of a model with a cap, but without supply flexibility, it is important to bear in mind member-state interests in retaining as much power as possible and hence seeking to restrict the Commission's areas of competence. Furthermore, as discussed in greater detail elsewhere (e.g. Boasson and Wettestad 2013), 2008 was a busy year for climate policy discussions in the EU. As to the ETS revision, the cap-setting issue seemed to drown amidst a myriad of other issues – likewise, the centralization of the system, the level of the cap, and the linear reduction factor. Discussions revolved predominantly around the *method of* allocation and the turn to auctioning in particular.

Concerning the length of trading periods, the Impact Assessment (IA) concluded that the option of a 'long' trading period, from 2013 to 2030, was 'too long . . . lacking flexibility to adapt to new information' (Commission 2008: 102). A period lasting to 2020 was deemed preferable, and the inclusion of a trend-line factor (i.e. the LRF) would provide additional long-term predictability. Such an approach would strike 'the best balance between predictability and flexibility' and also be 'most effective'. Thus, the move towards a more centralized design was fuelled by events like the price drop, but it was also affected by EU-level actors interested in European centralization and harmonization.

Ambition level: set prior to financial crisis and derived from overall 20 per cent target

As noted, a common EU-level cap was established for the ETS. This cap would be calculated on the basis of the overall EU target of achieving 20 per cent emissions reductions by 2020 at 1990 levels, as agreed by EU leaders in March 2007. The linear reduction consistent with this target amounted to 1.74 per cent per year, to result in a reduction of specific ETS sector emissions of 21 per cent below 2005 emissions. But as noted earlier, the 1.74 per cent reduction (LRF) did not stop in 2020. As a more long-term vision EU leaders adopted in 2009 an ambition of 80–95 per cent emissions reductions by 2050 compared to 1990 levels, 'in the context of necessary reductions according to the IPCC by developed countries as a group' (Commission 2009: 3). This long-term vision was later specified in the 2050 Roadmap launched in 2011 (Commission 2011).

Several factors shaped the overall ambition level of the EU, thereby indirectly determining the ETS cap. In addition to the overall GHG reduction target for 2020, explicit attention was paid to the cap-setting issue in the Commission's Impact Assessment (Commission 2008). What factors can help explain why the modelling process used estimates for economic growth that would later be proven overly optimistic? It is essential to recall that the years in focus here (primarily 2006–8) were pre–financial crisis years with rather stable growth and similar expectations for the future. The main GDP growth assumptions for the period 2005–30 in the IAs amounted to an increase of some 43 per cent by 2020 and 71 per cent by 2030 (Hermann and Matthes 2012: 27).

Interviewed Brussels insiders also point out that it was not seen as politically advisable for the Commission to indicate, in any way, to the member-states that economic growth might collapse. As one official explained, 'it is a system bias to be optimistic'. Furthermore, the later recession proved to be unexpectedly deep, and a significant future allowance surplus had simply not been conceivable back in 2007/8 (interviews, 2014).

Turning then to EU-external factors and policy diffusion, EU climate policy in the years 2006–8 was generally conducted with a view to the global context: EU policy and climate targets were meant to inspire and help bring about a positive outcome at the 2009 Copenhagen summit. But the EU's 20/20/20 targets were not shaped by global estimates or modelling linked to the global two-degree target which the EU had embraced already back in 1996.

As regards learning from others, as noted, initial ETS design discussions around the year 2000 had shown that the Commission favoured a quite centralized cap-setting model, inspired by the US SO_2/NOx model. Both Delbeke and Zapfel had studied this US emissions trading system. In the process leading up to the model for a revised EU ETS adopted in 2008, Commission ETS entrepreneurs took note of the developing Waxman-Markey climate bill in the US. They liked the long-term vision of the Waxman-Markey proposal and its linear trajectory, which inspired the 1.74 per cent linear reduction factor in the EU ETS (interviews, 2014).

Allocation: significantly more auctioning

Auctioning was to become the main principle from 2013. It was initially to be introduced in the power sector, with significant exceptions and special arrangements for the Central and Eastern European countries (CEECs). It was to be gradually phased in in the energy-intensive industries. Free allocations were to be based on benchmarking rules (i.e. with reference to the best performers in the different sectors), to be specified subsequently.

Similar to several other key changes of the system, the turn to auctioning was a preference initially held by the Commission. Furthermore, the turn was coloured by experiences from the pilot phase. Importantly, free allocations had led to a heated debate about power producers reaping windfall profits – receiving allowances for free and profiting from higher electricity prices (see Sijm et al. 2006). This debate had weakened the capacity of power producers to resist the turn to auctioning, and thus they largely accepted this change, which was also welcomed by many member-states. This became clear during a new round of stakeholder meetings held in 2007.

The opposing coalition consisted of CEECs led by Poland, with coal-based power production to protect, and energy-intensive industries, still fearing an uneven global playing field and industrial relocation ('carbon leakage'). The outcome must be characterized as a typical EU compromise, where auctioning proponents and opponents alike were accommodated. Thus, we see that prior events *and* the European opportunity structure influenced the changes in design.

International competitive concerns remained relevant, underpinning the argumentation of energy-intensive industries. But again, this cannot be termed policy diffusion, as the EU's specific policy response was internally driven.

Coverage changes: moderate broadening – but note airlines

Emissions from some additional sector (aluminium, some chemicals) and gases (nitrous oxides and perfluorocarbons) were to be added. Airlines were also now to be included (from 2012), the aim being to cover all aircraft operations flying into or out of the EU. However, this development had already been codified in Directive 2008/101. Around 50 per cent of EU CO_2 emissions were to be covered.

Apart from the inclusion of airlines, the changes in coverage were not really striking. The non-airline sectors now to be included had been part of the discussions in the early 2000s, indicating a clear internal pathway at work: previous steps affected prospective developments. As to the inclusion of airlines, the EU was again a frontrunner, as no other systems covered the sector then.

External offsetting and linking: both tightening and opening up

There was a certain tightening of the room for external offsetting, with an offset cap introduced. Rules were to be further specified, and in 2011 a ban on the use of industrial gas credits (from CDM projects seeking to destroy HFC-23 and N_20 gases) was adopted, to enter into effect in May 2013. Regarding possible linking with other emissions trading systems, a goal of a linked OECD market by 2015 was adopted in 2009 (Wettestad and Jevnaker 2014).

As to shaping factors, in 2008 very few CDM credits had actually been used as offsets in the ETS, so this was not based on negative experiences and internal learning (although ENGOs had warned against using external credits). The offset tightening must be seen as a precautionary measure, as part of the effort for better steering of the amount of allowances circulating in the system. The dominant causal drivers were hence EU-internal. Again, there were few pertinent lessons to be learned from others at this stage, so policy diffusion had little relevance here.

MRV and enforcement: harmonization and centralization

Instead of national registries, a single Community registry was to be introduced (Article 19, 1) in 2012. The penalty for non-compliance would continue to be EUR 100, but set to increase in accordance with the European index of consumer prices. Again, the main background here came from bad experiences with the decentralized approach in the initial years of the ETS. As to policy diffusion and possible learning, the other systems in operation or planned at this stage were national and subnational ones; a single registry was a natural choice – but not necessarily offering any lessons to the multi-state and complex EU.

Price management: a weak mechanism put in place

As a mechanism for countering extreme price fluctuations, a clause was introduced in the 2009 Directive: in the case of six consecutive months with a carbon price more than three times the average during the two preceding years, the Commission was to convene a committee meeting (Art. 29a).

It is likely that some of the background for the introduction of this weak mechanism was the significant price volatility experienced in the pilot phase, with prices first climbing to EUR 30, then dropping markedly in 2006 (after an 'over-allocated' pilot phase was confirmed), before reaching rock bottom in 2007. However, prices had certainly not skyrocketed. So some of the background for the clause was EU policy-makers' old fear that industries (particularly energy-intensives) would threaten to relocate outside of the EU.

As to policy diffusion, similar to the several other design features discussed here, at this stage there were still few models to learn from. True, the evolving Regional Greenhouse Gas Initiative (RGGI) and California systems in the US had complex price floors and ceilings. But the EU discussions had not been oriented towards external models. So policy diffusion does not appear influential here.

Earmarking for climate purposes

A recommendation to use half of auctioning revenues for climate-change mitigation and adaptation measures was introduced in the revised ETS Directive. The EU was among the design frontrunners in this regard.

As to shaping forces, this change must be viewed mainly against the backdrop of the general surge in the attention and weight given to fighting climate change in the EU in the years prior to the financial crisis. True, the emerging Californian system had a somewhat similar 'redistribution for climate purposes' design element. But there is no evidence of EU policy-makers looking to California in shaping this element of their ETS revision process.

In contrast, such attempts at earmarking can be understood in light of 'domestic politics': the EU's overall climate ambitions, where income from auctioning could be used to further stimulate emission reduction. Also the timing mattered, as the ETS Directive was negotiated together with the overall climate and energy package for 2020, making such connections more likely (Boasson and Wettestad 2013; Skjærseth et al. 2016). Still, the clause remained a recommendation and not a mandatory requirement, due to member-state opposition to EU intervention in how their money was to be spent.

Further tightening of the ETS 2012–15: mainly internal determinants?

The main design for the 2013–20 phase had been adopted in 2008, but due to a crisis – the build-up of a structural surplus that caused prices to tumble – further design changes were adopted during the years 2012 to 2015. These changes focused on the more limited but definitely important issue of the system's incentive effect, related to mainly the design issue of price-management mechanisms. As noted, a weak mechanism for limiting price surges had been included in the 2009 Directive. But things developed very differently: first, with the financial crisis lowering emissions and the demand for allowances; and then this effect being amplified by rapidly expanding renewables and massive use of CDM credits (before the adopted tightening, to take effect from 2013). Finally, companies had been allowed to save up allowances from the second trading period ('banking'), in which allocations had proved too generous.

Thus, the carbon price became volatile, falling to rather low levels. In June 2008 prices had peaked at EUR 28. But already by January 2009 the price had fallen to EUR 12, and by January 2012 further down to around 8. This led the Commission to initiate a tightening process in summer 2012, even before the third phase had started (Wettestad and Jevnaker 2016).

However, it should be borne in mind that there were highly differing problem perceptions within the EU at this point: some saw the low price as a symptom of a flagship in deep trouble, providing little impetus to the low-carbon transition in the long term. This view was held by the UK and several other Western member-states, as well as by DG Clima, green forces in the European Parliament, and the power industry. Others saw the low price as natural in a situation of low demand and argued against intervening in the market. Moreover, they regarded a low price as unproblematic as long as emissions stayed below the cap; those holding this view included Poland and the CEECs, DG Enterprise, most of the majority EPP group (the Conservatives) in the Parliament, and energy-intensive industries.

A first and temporary element of this reform was the postponement of auctioning of 900 million allowances to 2019–20 ('backloading'). This proposal was first voted down in the European Parliament in April 2013 (indicative of the strength of the 'ETS critics' within the Parliament), but was later adopted. The second and more important structural step was a proposal to establish a Market Stability Reserve, to start operating in 2021. The MSR can be seen as a 'market thermostat', whereby allowances are automatically released to the market if the number in circulation drops below 400 million allowances and withdrawn if the surplus exceeds 833 million. The MSR was adopted in May 2015. Following heavy political pressure from the most impatient/ambitious member-states and the European Parliament, the operational start date was moved forward to 2019.

As analysed in Wettestad and Jevnaker (2016), the main forces for shaping the changes in ETS design were internal to the EU. In the following, we focus on the MSR. Whereas backloading was a temporary emergency response for the third phase, the MSR represents a structural change to the design of the system, potentially affecting third-phase dynamics, but with main implications for the post-2020 years.

First, and more generally, there was internal learning from the failures of design and policy adopted thus far, indicated by the build-up of a large surplus of allowances and a carbon price that failed to function as a significant decarbonization incentive. As some factors affecting the demand for ETS allowances were beyond political control (e.g. economic growth rates), it was important to insert flexibility into the *supply* of allowances, to prevent carbon prices from becoming too low to incentivize long-term decarbonization.

In 2012 the Commission had issued a Carbon Market Report where it launched six proposals for reforming the ETS and bolstering the carbon price, including raising the 2020 target, deleting a significant number of allowances (a 'set-aside'), and the establishment of some sort of central bank for the carbon market. Most of these proposals would entail political feasibility problems, due to the differing problem perceptions and related positions, as outlined prior. The idea of a central bank was deemed not feasible, as it would involve transfer of discretionary power to an EU entity, which many member-states opposed. But an automatic 'market thermostat' with predefined triggers for regulating the amount of allowances in circulation stood out as far more acceptable.

Second, as to more specific shaping forces, changes in the domestic politics of the biggest EU member-state – Germany – were very important. Its elections in autumn 2013 ousted the ETS-sceptical FDP party from government; and ministry re-organization lessened receptiveness to energy-intensive industry in the powerful Ministry of Economy, where two new units were filled with staff from the Ministry of the Environment. This led to the subsequent adoption of a far more active and 'progressive' position on the part of pivotal Germany.

Third, the elections in the European Parliament in spring 2014 led to the entry of about 100 new radical and extremist parliamentarians. In order to retain control over legislative dossiers, the main party groupings sought closer cooperation, in particular the Conservatives (EPP) and the Social Democrats (S&D).

Fourth, the launch of negotiations on a new EU 2030 climate package opened up new possibilities for integrative bargaining which allowed the inclusion of several policy 'carrots' to the overall deal in order to get the support from coal-dependent East European member-states sceptical to further ETS tightening.

Furthermore, as in earlier phases, international competitive concerns played a significant role, particularly via the lobbying for exemptions and compensation by the energy-intensive industries and a group of reluctant countries led by Poland. This has to do with the general change in the context for climate policy development in the EU; first a 'green wave' in the years leading up to the climate and energy package in 2008, later increasingly replaced by 'crisis management' and concerns for economic competitiveness (see Boasson and Wettestad 2013; Skovgaard 2013).

What role did policy diffusion play in the MSR process? Learning from abroad did not play any significant role, although the Commission was aware of a MSR mechanism that was included in discussions on the US Waxman-Markey bill in 2009/2010 (but not in the bill itself) (interviews in Brussels 2015). At this point, other emissions trading systems had emerged globally, and several included some sort of price regulation. However, the idea of introducing a mechanism directly targeting the carbon price did not resonate well in an EU setting, as it came too close to resembling the contentious and therefore rejected carbon tax – part of the reason why the EU had turned to emissions trading in the first place. A discretionary price-management mechanism was not deemed appropriate in the EU, with even the Commission noting that it would change the very 'nature' of the EU ETS (Commission 2012). In other words, such design features did not diffuse to the EU.

Although price regulation was off the table, there were within the EU actors strongly calling for a solution to the rapidly growing allowance surplus. A volume-based mechanism for regulating supply (like the MSR) offered a practical compromise for introducing flexibility to supply – thereby making the EU ETS more similar to the ideal of a market. Moreover, this was a way of dealing with prices indirectly. While diffusion can be seen mainly as solution-driven, with model solutions spreading and being used for tackling various problems, the process of reforming the EU ETS could instead be characterized as problem-driven. Furthermore, the solution was tailored to the problems experienced within the EU ETS, showing that interests and ideas can interact to produce political feasibility of design elements.

Summing up, we find that the changes to the design of the EU ETS during the years 2012–15 were crisis-driven and that the solutions to these problems were found through introspection rather than searching for appropriate solutions among emissions trading systems elsewhere. Despite the availability of potential design lessons from other systems, often in the form of price floors, the EU developed a policy response in line with the established legacy of its own ETS: dealing with the quantity of allowances rather than 'interfering' directly to regulate the carbon price. Thus a certain path dependency can be observed here.

The political system of the EU is an important contextual factor. Regulating the supply of allowances has emerged as an EU competence, gradually centralized from the national to the EU level. Moreover, emissions trading did not exist prior at the national level in most EU member-states, with a few notable exceptions. In contrast, taxation is a policy area that has remained largely within the national domain even today. Direct regulation of the allowance price comes close to resembling a carbon tax, and an *EU* carbon tax is highly controversial indeed, as seen earlier in this chapter.

Given the unique political structure of the EU, solutions that challenge the national-supranational distribution of power and competence will not easily diffuse from other ETSs into the EU ETS. Such design elements will be seen as 'inappropriate' due to the historical trajectory whereby tax matters have remained a national prerogative even as the EU as a collective has gained increasing decision-making powers on climate policy. Thus, diffusion of solutions for price management from ETS elsewhere did not play a significant role when the EU was redesigning its EU ETS during these years.

Conclusions

The EU ETS is a frontrunner system that remains the biggest in the world – at least, until China's national ETS starts up in 2017 – and can serve a model for others to imitate – or avoid. That makes it especially important to get the lessons from that system right. This chapter has shown how policy diffusion has generally played a fairly insignificant role, as to be expected of a pioneering system. As to the impact of diffusion over time, the system appeared most open to external impulses in the form of learning in the early stages. That may appear paradoxical, as this was at a time where there were no other carbon trading systems to learn from. With regard to the EU's turn to emissions trading, we find external impulses emerging as the chief forces.

Furthermore, learning, primarily from the US, played a certain (but diminishing) role in the initial design of the system, primarily with initial MRV procedures learning from the US SO_2/NOx model. Even then, however, the design was adapted to the EU and climate-change context. In later rounds of revision, US experiences proved only moderately relevant, contributing ideas to the introduction of a Linear Reduction Factor in 2008 and the launching of the MSR option in 2013/14.

The role of international competitive concerns has been quite stable, perhaps increasing somewhat in importance over time. As indicated, the energy-intensive industries and the CEECs led by Poland have been the most vocal actors on the dangers of the EU adopting much more ambitious policies than global competitors.

Who have been the key 'mediating actors/agents' of external diffusion impulses? The main transmitter of lessons from abroad has been the small group of policy entrepreneurs in the Commission, establishing links to US consultants at an early stage. Having worked with a pioneering system, and becoming increasingly active as consultants to others, China not least (see Chapters 9 and 11 of this book), these entrepreneurs and the wider EU climate policy community may have adopted a rather EU-centric view on carbon market design. For instance, while promoting emissions trading over carbon taxes makes sense in the EU setting, the legal hurdle for taxes is significantly lower within unitary states (which, admittedly, still face the political battle). Moreover, champions of the EU ETS have shown little interest in lessons from other systems when revising their own ETS.

Symptomatically, the (re)design of the EU ETS has been chiefly internally driven, with EU politics at centre stage. The initial establishment put the EU ETS on the pathway of balancing between national and supranational interests and actors. Allowance allocation was subject to a gradual EU integration, becoming more centralized over time. In contrast, price regulation remained too contentious to handle at the EU level, although automatized regulation of the amount of allowances was acceptable, perhaps as this had already been tackled indirectly through climate target- and ETS cap-setting at the EU level. Moreover, initial sector coverage was also affected by prior EU developments, where the same sectors were included that were covered by pre-existing EU environmental legislation.

The EU ETS has been operational for more than a decade now. This has certainly been a bumpy ride, with volatile and generally low carbon prices and controversies involving powerful actors. This is probably one cost of frontrunning – but the EU has also had some bad luck, as when the financial crisis rendered the tightening of the ETS design in 2008 futile (Wettestad 2015). That in turn reminds us that design changes should be seen mainly as necessary conditions for effective systems, and not as sufficient conditions, because certainly not all factors are subject to political control.

The EU ETS has ended up partly as a 'black sheep' internationally, but with its design adjusted and improved several times, most recently with the adoption of the MSR in 2015, has the EU now got the design right? As recently concluded elsewhere (Wettestad and Jevnaker 2016; Jevnaker and Wettestad 2017), the adoption of the Market Stability Reserve appears to be as a significant improvement. Furthermore, the Linear Reduction Factor (which is to be upped to 2.2 per cent from 2021 following a decision made at the EU summit in October 2014) means that the EU ETS has a rather unique long-term horizon. We come back to this in Chapter 13 of this book.

However, after the MSR was adopted in May 2015, carbon prices have fallen again, triggering new efforts that were in progress at the time of this writing, efforts that seek to tighten the system further. Hence, we conclude that, although the EU ETS has indeed some institutional strengths (not least the LRF) and has been improved, further reforms and design adjustments will be needed in order to realize the system's full potential as a forceful driver of decarbonization.

References

Boasson, E. and J. Wettestad. 2013. *EU Climate Policy: Industry, Policy Interaction and External Environment*. Farnham: Ashgate.

Christiansen, A. and J. Wettestad. 2003. The EU as a frontrunner on greenhouse gas emissions trading: How did it happen and will the EU succeed? *Climate Policy* 3 (1), 3–18.

Commission. 2000. *Green Paper on Greenhouse Gas Emissions Trading Within the European Union*. COM (2000) 87 final. Brussels: European Commission.

Commission. 2008. *Impact Assessment, Accompanying Document to the Proposal for a Directive of the European Parliament and the Council Amending Directive 2003/87/EC so as to Improve and Extend the EU Greenhouse Gas Emission Allowance Trading System*, Commission Staff Document. Brussels, 28 January, COM (2008) 16 final.

Commission. 2009. *Brussels European Council 29/30 October 2009 – Presidency Conclusions*, Council of the European Union. Brussels, 1 December 2009.

Commission. 2011. *A Roadmap for Moving to a Competitive Low Carbon Economy in 2050*. Communication from the Commission to the European Parliament, the Council, the European Economic and Social Committee and the Committee of the Regions, Brussels, 8 March 2011, COM (2011) 112 final.

Commission. 2012. *The State of the European Carbon Market in 2012*, COM (2012) 652 final. Brussels: European Commission.

Convery, F. 2009. Reflections: The emerging literature on emissions trading in Europe. *Review of Environmental Economics and Policy* 3 (1), 121–137.

Damro, C. and P. Luaces Méndez. 2003. Emissions trading at Kyoto: From EU-resistance to Union innovation. *Environmental Politics* 12 (2), 253–275.

Dupont, C. and S. Oberthür. 2015. Conclusions: Lessons learned. In *Decarbonization in the European Union: Internal Policies and External Strategies*, edited by C. Dupont and S. Oberthür, 244–265. Basingstoke: Palgrave Macmillan.

Fankhauser, S. 2013. A practitioner's guide to a low-carbon economy: Lessons from the UK. *Climate Policy* 13 (3), 345–362.

Grubb, M., C. Vrolijk and D. Brack. 1999. *The Kyoto Protocol: A Guide and Assessment*. London: Energy and Environmental Programme, Royal Institute of International Affairs.

Grubb, M., J. C. Hourcade and K. Neuhoff. 2014. *Planetary Economics*. Abingdon: Routledge.

Hermann, H. and F. Matthes. 2012. *Strengthening the European Union Emissions Trading Scheme and Raising Climate Ambition*. Report by Öko-Institut for WWF and Greenpeace, Berlin.

House of Commons. 2014. *Carbon Price Floor*. Note SN/SC/5927. 14 May.

Jevnaker, T. and J. Wettestad. 2017. Ratcheting up carbon trade: The politics of reforming EU emissions trading. *Global Environmental Politics* 2, 105–124 (doi: 10.1162/GLEP_a_00403).

Knox-Hayes, J. 2016. *The Cultures of Markets*. Oxford: Oxford University Press.

Kruger, J. and W. A. Pizer. 2004. *The EU Emissions Trading Directive: Opportunities and Potential Pitfalls*. Discussion Paper RFF DP 04–24. www.rff.org/files/sharepoint/WorkImages/Download/RFF-DP-04-24.pdf accessed 15 May 2017.

Paterson, M., M. Hoffman, M. Betsill and S. Bernstein. 2014. The micro foundations of policy diffusion toward complex global governance: An analysis of the transnational carbon emission trading network. *Comparative Political Studies* 47 (3), 420–449.

Sandbag. 2012. *Help or hindrance? Offsetting in the EU ETS*. Sandbag Report, November, London.

Sijm, J., K. Neuhoff and Y. Chen. 2006. CO2 cost pass-through and windfall profits in the power sector. *Climate Policy* 6, 49–72.

Skjærseth, J. B. and J. Wettestad. 2008. *EU Emissions Trading: Initiation, Decision-making and Implementation*. Aldershot: Ashgate.

Skjærseth, J. B. and J. Wettestad. 2010. Fixing the EU emissions trading system? Understanding the post-2012 changes. *Global Environmental Politics* 10 (4), 101–123.

Skjærseth, J. B., P. O. Eikeland, L. H. Gulbrandsen and T. Jevnaker. 2016. *Linking EU Climate and Energy Policies: Policymaking, Implementation and Reform*. Cheltenham: Edward Elgar.

Skovgaard, J. 2013. EU climate policy after the crisis. *Environmental Politics* 23 (1), 1–17.
Victor, D. G. and J. C. House. 2006. BP's emissions trading system. *Energy Policy* 34 (15), 2100–2112.
Wallace, H., M. A. Pollack and A. R. Young. 2014. *Policy-Making in the European Union*. Oxford: Oxford University Press.
Watanabe, R. and G. Robinson. 2005. The European Union emissions trading scheme. *Climate Policy*, Special issue.
Wettestad, J. 2001. The ambiguous prospects for EU climate policy – a summary of options. *Energy and Environment* 12 (2 and 3), 139–167.
Wettestad, J. 2005. The making of the 2003 EU Emissions Trading Directive: Ultra-quick process due to entrepreneurial proficiency? *Global Environmental Politics* 5 (1), 1–24.
Wettestad, J. 2009a. EU energy-intensive industries and emission trading: Losers becoming winners? *Environmental Policy and Governance* 19 (5), 309–320.
Wettestad, J. 2009b. European climate policy: Towards centralised governance? *Review of Policy Research* 26 (3), 311–329.
Wettestad, J. 2011. EU emissions trading: Achievements and challenges. In *Towards a Common European Union Energy Policy: Problems, Progress and Prospects*, edited by J. S. Duffield and V. L. Birchfield, 87–113. New York: Palgrave.
Wettestad, J. 2014. Rescuing EU emissions trading: Mission impossible? *Global Environmental Politics* 14 (2), 64–81.
Wettestad, J. 2015. EU emissions trading. In *Research Handbook on Climate Governance*, edited by K. Bäckstrand and E. Lövbrand, 345–356. Cheltenham: Edward Elgar.
Wettestad, J. and T. Jevnaker. 2014. The EU's quest for linked carbon markets: Turbulence and headwind. In *Toward a New Climate Agreement: Conflict, Resolution and Governance*, edited by T. L. Cherry, J. Hovi and D. M. McEvoy, 266–279. London: Routledge.
Wettestad, J. and T. Jevnaker. 2016. *Rescuing EU Emissions Trading: The Climate Policy Flagship*. Basingstoke: Palgrave.
Zapfel, P. and M. Vainio. 2002. *Pathways to European Greenhouse Gas Emissions Trading History and Misconceptions*. FEEM Note 85, October.

Annex: Interviews

Deblock, Sarah, IETA (by telephone), 17 September 2015
De Clara, Stefano, IETA (by telephone), 13 January 2017
Egenhofer, Christian, CEPS, Brussels, 19 November 2012
Eggert, Axel, EUROFER, Brussels, 4 June 2014
Eickhout, Bas, European Parliament (by telephone), 29 November 2012; 17 March 2015
Ghonda, Jean-Paul, EUROFER, Brussels, 19 March 2015
Hein, Joachim, BDI, Berlin, 4 June 2015
Kumar, Sanjeev, Change Partnership/Friends of ETS, Brussels, 18 March 2015
Liese, Peter, European Parliament, Brussels, 18 March 2015
Lind, Øystein, Statoil Brussels office, 19 November 2012
Matthes, Felix, Öko-Institut e.V., Berlin, 2 June 2015
Oberthür, Sebastian, IES, Brussels, 17 March 2015
Ruhrberg, Martin, BDEW, Berlin, 29 May 2015
Schafhausen, Franzjosef, BMU, Berlin, 8 June 2015
Scott, Jesse, IEA (formerly at EURELECTRIC), 21 November 2012; 25 August 2015 (by telephone)

Tuma, Jan, Department of Energy and Climate Protection, Prague, 4 June 2015
van Ierland, Tom, DG Clima (by telephone), 1 July 2014
Vis, Peter, DG Clima, 26 January 2011; 4 June 2014
Wyns, Tomas, IES (formerly CCAP), Brussels, 19 November 2012; 17 March 2015
Zapfel, Peter, DG Clima, 20 November 2012; 5 June 2014; 18 March 2015; 11 January 2017 (by telephone)

4 The Regional Greenhouse Gas Initiative

US pioneer seeking to avoid EU mistakes?

Solveig Lygre and Jørgen Wettestad

Introduction

In 2005, the governors of seven Northeastern and mid-Atlantic US states[1] signed a memorandum of understanding (MoU) in which they agreed to establish a regional cap-and-trade scheme for CO_2 in the electricity sector. The Model Rule – which provides the framework for the participating states to establish individual CO_2 budget trading programmes through statutes or regulations (RGGI 2005) – was signed in 2008; the Regional Greenhouse Gas Initiative (RGGI, pronounced 'Reggie') became the first mandatory, market-based programme for reducing CO_2 emissions in the US, effective from January 2009 (RGGI 2016a). Maryland, Massachusetts and Rhode Island signed the MoU in 2007, whereas New Jersey withdrew in 2011 (RGGI 2016b). At present there are nine US states participating in this regional emission trading system (ETS).

RGGI regulates CO_2 emissions from the electricity sector only: the entities regulated are fossil fuel–fired power plants with capacity of 25 megawatts (MW) or more, 164 in total (RGGI 2016c). These units are responsible for approximately 20 per cent of CO_2 emissions in the region. The initial RGGI target aimed at stabilizing CO_2 emissions until 2015 and then reducing emissions by 10 per cent from the 2009 cap level until 2019 (RGGI 2005).

In its current form, RGGI is made up of nine individual state-level cap-and-trade programmes that allow the states to maintain their legal sovereignty while being coordinated at the regional level through the organization 'RGGI Inc.' (RGGI 2016a). Regional auctions have been held every three months since 25 September 2008. RGGI is the only ETS in the world that allocates most of its allowances through auctioning. In addition, the RGGI design is of interest because of its narrow sectoral coverage and the introduction of a price floor.

RGGI was established partly as a response to the lack of a federal climate policy in the US. The RGGI states wanted to take the lead and show that it was possible to do something about the climate-change problem, despite the inaction of the Bush administration. These states have a long history of environmental cooperation, and the experience of trading other gases through the Acid Rain Program and the Ozone Transport Commission (OTC) NOx Budget Program made a CO_2 ETS a readily recognizable solution to a similar policy problem. The fact that the EU was then in the process of putting in place an ETS might also have influenced the RGGI policy makers. This chapter discusses the role of diffusion relative to local and federal domestic factors and the relation between international and domestic causal drivers in the establishment of RGGI and in the subsequent design process of the programme, as well as how these factors have influenced the later revision of the design properties.

Data for this case study come from the RGGI archives and other public documents, as well as relevant books and articles. In addition, five semi-structured interviews were conducted with actors who were central in the RGGI establishing and design process: the three officials of the steering committee of the Staff Working Group (SWG),[2] the facilitator of the stakeholder process and a representative from the Environmental Defense Fund (EDF). (See Annex.)

Overview of the ETS and its emergence

In March 2001, President George W. Bush withdrew the US from the Kyoto Protocol. In response, a bottom-up climate policy began to emerge in many US states (Schreurs 2008). Governor George Pataki set up the New York Greenhouse Gas Task Force (the Task Force) that same year, to 'develop policy recommendations for reducing the state's GHG emissions' (CCAP 2003: ES2). One recommendation of the report published in connection with the Task Force was that New York should emplace a mandatory cap on emissions from electricity generation that would reduce the state's emissions to at least 25 per cent below 1990 levels by 2010; this was accompanied by a request to other states in the region to follow a similar strategy that would eventually permit interstate emissions trading (CCAP 2003).

The year 2001 also saw the creation of the New England states[3] and eastern Canada climate plan, with regional CO_2 reduction goals (NEG/ECP 2001). Individual state and provincial plans were worked out with local circumstances in mind. Short-, mid- and long-term goals were set for reducing regional greenhouse gas (GHG) emissions to 1990 levels by 2010, by at least 10 per cent below 1990 emissions by 2020 and ultimately by 75–85 per cent below 2001 levels, respectively (NEG/ECP 2001).

In 2003, Governor Pataki approached the governors of the six New England states and four other states in the region to propose the establishment of a system to cap emissions from the region's largest utility plants. Although most of the governors were Republicans, they agreed to establish a regional ETS for CO_2, and in 2005 the MoU was signed by seven of these states. From the time the MoU was signed until the Model Rule was adopted, it took three years. During those years, a comprehensive stakeholder process was organized by the SWG to make the design phase as open and inclusive as possible. Numerous topical workshops were held, where outside experts were brought in to speak to stakeholders and state staff, and various policy options were discussed amongst the participants.

The first allowance auction was held in September 2008, a few months before the first compliance period started. At the first auction, allowances had a clearing price (the price paid by all successful bidders) of USD 3.07 (Ramseur 2016). The first three-year RGGI compliance period started on 1 January 2009 with an annual emission budget of 188 million short tons[4] of CO_2. This cap, based on emissions from 2000–4, proved far too high, as total CO_2 emissions in the region in the period were only 153 million short tons (RGGI 2016d). The price dropped to the reserve price of USD 1.86 at the end of 2009 due to lower economic activity and the availability of more natural gas in the market.

When the second compliance period begun in 2012, the emissions budget was adjusted down to 165 million short tons a year, further lowered to 91 million in January 2014 (RGGI 2016d). As set out in the MoU, there was a comprehensive review of all components of the programme in 2012 (RGGI 2005: 6D), which resulted in the updated Model Rule of 2013. Major changes in the updated Model Rule were the lowering of the cap and the establishment of a cost containment reserve to replace the offset price triggers (RGGI 2013). Due to the lowered emissions cap, the auction price increased in March 2013, peaking at the end of 2015 at USD 7.50. Since the beginning of the third compliance period – January 2015 – the cap has declined by 2.5 per cent each year.

In 2016 came another RGGI programme review, with additional emissions reductions after the last compliance period among the issues for reflection (RGGI 2016e). At the 33rd auction in September 2016, the allowance price was USD 4.54.

Explaining the turn to ETS

To explain why RGGI was established, we must examine the internal and external political factors that may have influenced the decision to set up such a regional ETS. This was a time where the US had withdrawn from the Kyoto Protocol, and the European Union was designing the EU ETS. Were the initiators of RGGI influenced by international policy diffusion? What was the role of domestic US politics? And what about factors intrinsic to the nine key jurisdictions? Could a combination of these have driven the process?

In his campaign prior to the 2000 elections, George W. Bush had promised that he would seek a four-pollutant bill, controlling NOx, SO_2, mercury and CO_2 from power plants (Revkin 2001). Some six months into his term, President Bush retracted that pledge and withdrew the US from the Kyoto Protocol. The Republican governors of the Northeastern states had supported Bush when he was running for the presidency, but when he backed off this promise they publicly criticized their fellow-Republican president – a very unusual thing to do (Interview 1). To find out why RGGI was established, a good place to start looking is the non-existent federal climate policy: it was after George W. Bush took office in 2001 that things started to happen.

The Republicans of the Northeast have tended to be more pro-environmental than in the rest of the country. Faced with the Bush administration's lack of climate policy and the withdrawal of the US from the Kyoto Protocol, they were motivated to do something on their own (Tvinnereim 2013; Interview 3). In

2001, the Conference of New England Governors and Eastern Canadian Premiers (NEG/ECP)[5] formulated a regional action plan on climate change (NEG/ECP 2001). This action plan set short-, mid- and long-term goals for reducing regional GHG emissions to 1990 levels by 2010, then by at least 10 per cent below 1990 emissions by 2020 and ultimately by 75–85 per cent below 2001 levels, respectively (NEG/ECP 2001). New Jersey had also been working on a GHG reduction plan and would have taken the initiative on a regional ETS if New York had not done so first (Interview 3).

Also in 2001, Governor Pataki announced the formation of the New York State Greenhouse Gas Task Force, set up to find alternative ways of abating the state's GHG emissions (CCAP 2003). Establishing a CO_2 cap-and-trade programme for fossil fuel–fired power plants was a central recommendation in the report that was released in connection with the Task Force. The report also pointed out that by doing this New York would be likely to enjoy a 'first mover' advantage as regards carbon trading, given the expectations of a Canadian and a European trading programme (CCAP 2003: 51). Thus, we see that some attention was drawn to the issue of competition in this preliminary phase of the RGGI.

Even though the governors of seven of the RGGI states were Republicans, they decided to develop the first ETS for GHGs in the US. Given the traditionally weak environmental policy of the Republican Party, why did they take this leadership role? (See also Dunlap et al. 2001.) One explanation could be that Governor Pataki wanted to gain some 'environmental credentials' (Interview 4) before deciding to run for the presidency. Another explanation highlights the history of friendly competition amongst the Northeastern states in proving environmental leadership and influencing the national debate (Interview 3). Economic profit also enters into the picture as a major driver for Governor Pataki to establish an ETS for GHGs. New York had many low-cost reductions to make and thereby a good trajectory for selling its allowances to other states (Interview 2; see also CCAP 2003: ES9). Moreover, as the only state in the region without a climate plan, New York was exposed to considerable pressure from environmental non-governmental organizations (ENGOs) (Interview 2).

According to our interviewees, the EU ETS was not a notable driver for the establishment of the RGGI at all; in fact, being associated with Europe could even make it harder to sell the programme in the US (Interview 1). Nevertheless, the officials who led the RGGI establishment process did have contact with some of the actors that developed the EU ETS (Interviews 1, 2), and the EU reached out to the RGGI staff and gave them confidence that it was possible to create an ETS for CO_2 (Interview 2).

The most important background factor for establishing this regional ETS seems to have been the lack of federal climate-policy action. Realizing that nothing was going to be done about the climate-change problem at the national level, the governors in the Northeast wanted to show political leadership and put pressure on Washington (Interviews 4, 5), as they had often done on environmental issues.

Thus, the establishment of RGGI was driven largely not by policy diffusion, but by internal federal and local/regional factors in the US – in particular, the lack of federal climate policy, the historical tradition of the Northeastern states of taking the lead in environmental politics and previous experience with emissions trading in the region.

Explaining the RGGI design

Type of system: both path dependencies and anticipatory moves

The Regional Greenhouse Gas Initiative is a regional cap-and-trade system made up of nine individual state cap-and-trade schemes, covering fossil-fuel power plants with capacity of 25 MW or more. Unlimited banking of allowances is allowed between compliance periods.

The initiators of the RGGI plan never considered a tax or any other CO_2 regulation instead of a cap-and-trade scheme; from the beginning, the intention was to create a cap-and-trade programme similar to the Acid Rain Program. When the SWG started the design process they were instructed to create a cap-and-trade programme to emulate the sulphur programme. The fact that these states already had good experience with cap-and-trade – with the Acid Rain Program nationally and with the NOx programmes nationally and regionally – meant that cap-and-trade was familiar as a policy tool for emissions reductions. Our interviewees indicated that such previous experience was the decisive factor for choosing a cap-and-trade system as the policy solution to GHG reductions. Learning from the successful history of reducing SO_2 and NOx, they emulated these programmes.

Table 4.1 RGGI design overview

Type of system	Cap and trade Phase 1: 2009–11 Phase 2: 2012–14 Phase 3: 2015–20 Banking, but not borrowing
Ambition level	Caps through emissions budgets for each phase
Allocation mechanisms	Almost 100% auctioning
Coverage	Electricity generators larger than 25 MW in nine states Only CO_2
Offsetting and linking	Maximum 3.3% domestic offsets for each installation Goal: expand the geographic reach of the programme
MRV and compliance	Yearly reports through EPA system Penalty provisions, in two stages
Price and quantity management	Price floor and ceiling
Revenue earmarking	Revenues to support energy efficiency, renewable energy and direct bill assistance

By participating in these programmes administered from the federal level, the RGGI states learned how this policy tool could be used for reducing emissions from power plants.

Internal learning – in this case, learning from something involving the RGGI states within a greater jurisdiction, that of the US federal government – was the main factor in deciding the type of system. Path dependency is also relevant here as these states opted for emissions trading because they had done so together before.

The political feasibility of a cap-and-trade programme compared to emplacing a tax on CO_2 emissions also simplified the choice for policy makers. Americans in general oppose new or higher taxes, making tax-based policies to control GHGs difficult to enact in the US (Lachapelle et al. 2012). A tax would also have been more complicated to implement, whereas a cap-and-trade programme is easily enacted under the Clean Air Act CAA – as was done with the Acid Rain and the NOx programmes.

At the time when RGGI was planned, there were also expectations of a national ETS for GHG emissions. Those who designed RGGI felt it would be an advantage to be prepared for something that would ultimately be federal policy: leading the way for the federal government would help give them a competitive advantage (RGGI 2005). Interviewees also pointed out that the RGGI states wanted to put more pressure on the federal government to come up with a national cap-and-trade system (Interviews 4, 5).

Ambition level: worries about competitiveness

The initial target was to stabilize emissions in the first period (2009–14) and then cut by 2.5 per cent each year until 2018, resulting in a 10 per cent reduction of CO_2 emissions by 2019 from 2009 levels (RGGI 2005). The reduction target was set on the basis of estimated 2009 emission levels in 2005, but these proved to be much lower than the estimates, resulting in a surplus of allowances and low allowance prices.

Several factors influenced the rather weak ambition level of the RGGI designers. Policy diffusion was of minor importance. Still, one interviewee said that he found the EU ETS's early prices frighteningly high and wished to avoid such high prices with RGGI by setting a less stringent target (Interview 1).

The major reasons for not setting a more stringent reduction target were economic. Leakage was a chief concern. As the RGGI governors were the first to establish an ETS for CO_2 in North America, they had to take care not to set the target at a level that might scare off states from joining the programme (Interviews 2, 3, 4). It was deemed more important to establish a system that was well designed and would be robust, rather than having a stringent target. The idea was to get the programme up and running to create a model for a national programme. Thus, the programme was designed to make it possible to adjust the cap if it proved desirable to make it more stringent later on (as was indeed the case). One of the leaders of the design process stressed this as the main reason for the rather weak initial target, while also emphasizing that the intention had never been to try to match the EU (Interview 1).

Also important were the already high electricity prices in the region compared to the rest of the country and concerns that they would become even higher with a more stringent cap. This could hurt local economies by making it unattractive for companies to establish new industry in those states, rather than where electricity would be much cheaper. Thus, there were worries about leakage due to high electricity prices. As there is a market-based electricity system with an open grid in the Northeast, the designers were highly aware that higher electricity prices could lead to electricity from dirtier power plants outside the RGGI states getting in to the region (Interview 2).

Allocation mechanism: avoiding EU anomalies and benefitting from local structural changes

RGGI distributes the vast majority of emissions allowances through quarterly auctions, starting in September 2008. As of the end of 2016, 34 auctions had been held. These auctions follow a single-round, uniform-price, sealed-bid auction format: participants submit confidential bids for the amount of CO_2 allowances they want to acquire, subsequently receiving the quantity of allowances corresponding to their winning bids at a uniform clearing price (RGGI 2016f).

As yet, RGGI is the only ETS where almost all allowances are auctioned. When the design process started, nobody had thought it would be possible to auction all the allowances – programme designers imagined that at most one-third could be auctioned (Interview 2), whereas in reality some 90 per cent of the allowances have been auctioned (RGGI 2016f). Several factors influenced the shaping of this design property. Learning was central here: those who designed RGGI learned from what went wrong in the EU ETS. Most interviewees emphasized that the European experience was very important for the choice of auctioning instead of distributing allowances free, as in the sulphur and NOx programmes. They did not want to make the same mistake as the Europeans, who distributed allowances for free, resulting in windfall profits for the polluters (see Chapter 3 of this book). Also the ETS literature indicates that RGGI learned from the experience of the EU what not to do when designing the allocation mechanism (Carbon Market Watch 2015).

Moreover, the stakeholder process – in which environmental organizations in particular argued for auctioning – played an important role in the choice of allocation mechanism (Interviews 2, 4). Raymond (2016) points out how environmentalists successfully reframed the auctioning issue by highlighting broad distribution of any public benefits from polluters' use of resources. Also important were the reorganization of the electricity market in the region to wholesale markets and the breakup of utilities, as well as the revenues the auctions would provide to the states (Huber 2013; Interview 2). Thus, we find that a combination of international policy diffusion and local factors shaped this design property.

Sectors, gases and emissions covered: path dependency and feasibility

The RGGI covers CO_2 emissions from the power sector only, more specifically from power plants with capacity of 25 megawatts or more – 164 in total (RGGI 2016c). These sources cover approximately 20 per cent of the emissions in the region, a total of 135,731,651 short tons of CO_2 in 2014 (RGGI 2014).

There are several reasons why the power sector, and thereby only CO_2, was the sole sector and GHG included in the RGGI. Domestic path dependency is an important factor. The governors who initiated RGGI wanted to emulate the sulphur programme and keep it simple (Interview 2); limiting it to the electricity sector was the easiest way to do this. The initial plan was to get the programme up and running and then consider expanding to other sectors (Interviews 1, 2, 3). The electricity sector is the second-largest source of GHG emissions in the region (after transport). Since all the RGGI states adopted GHG standards for automobiles at the same time – finding that a better approach to reductions in the transport sector – the electricity sector was the place to start (Interview 1). Previous cooperation among the RGGI states on reducing other gases from the power sector made it logical to stick to this sector when establishing a new ETS.

As noted, before RGGI was planned, the New England states and some Canadian provinces had been working together on reducing GHGs in the region through the New England Governors and Eastern Canadian Premiers (NEG/ECP) Climate Change Action Plan 2001. Because the electricity system is highly interconnected among and between states, controlling power plants effectively on a state-by-state basis is not easy – making an ETS a better policy instrument for this task (Interview 2).

The decision to cover only the electricity sector made CO_2 the sole crucial gas to address: it is responsible for 95 per cent of emissions from power plants (EPA 2016a). Also, most of the power plants in question had already installed CO_2 monitoring systems under the CAA (EPA 2015), making it easy to implement. Including other gases would require new monitoring protocols for gases that accounted for only some 5 per cent of emissions from power plants. That was a major factor for choosing only CO_2 (all interviews).

External offsets: local concerns

An ‘offset’ is a project-based GHG emissions reduction or carbon sequestration achieved outside the capped electricity sector (RGGI 2016g). Initially, RGGI allowed regulated power plants to use offsets to meet up to 3.3 per cent of their CO_2 compliance obligation (RGGI 2016g). Offset projects permitted from the beginning were landfill methane capture and destruction; reduction in emissions of sulphur hexafluoride; sequestration of carbon due to afforestation; reduction or avoidance of CO_2 emissions from natural gas, oil or propane end-use combustion due to end-use energy efficiency; and avoidance of methane emissions from operations for managing agricultural manure (RGGI 2008: 10.3).

Policy diffusion was not an important driver in shaping this design property – internal economic factors were more decisive. The initial Model Rule from December 2008 allowed external offsets in the RGGI states and in 'any state or United States jurisdiction in which a cooperating regulatory agency has entered into a memorandum of understanding with the appropriate regulatory agencies of all participating states to carry out certain obligations relative to CO_2 emissions offset projects in that state or US jurisdiction' (RGGI 2008). Under certain circumstances, offsets were allowed anywhere in North America; 5 per cent of the CO_2 compliance obligation could be covered by offsets (RGGI 2008).

Economic factors were the main drivers for not allowing external offsets outside the region. In an environmental perspective, it does not matter where GHG reductions are made – the overall effect on the climate will be the same. However, the RGGI states wanted to keep the offset project in the region so that the economic benefits generated from offset projects could stay in the region (Interviews 1, 3).

A less significant driver was the fact that it was easier to track and monitor projects located within the region (Interview 4). The designers wanted to avoid any ethical/moral issues with the offsets: keeping them within the region made that easier to control (Interview 3).

Monitoring, reporting and verification (MRV) and enforcement: domestic path dependency

As noted, the RGGI's monitoring and reporting system is based on existing federal requirements established under earlier air-quality programmes. Part 75 of Volume 40 of the Code of Federal Regulations (CFR) requires continuous monitoring and reporting of SO_2, CO_2 and NOx emissions (EPA 2016b). The Acid Rain Program made it mandatory for coal-fired electricity-generating units (EGUs) – most of the RGGI sources – to install Continuous Emission Monitoring Systems (CEMS). The Environmental Protection Agency (EPA) keeps emissions data for emitters in the Clean Air Markets Division database in accordance with state CO_2 Budget Trading Program regulations and EPA regulations (ICAP 2012). Data are automatically transferred to the publicly available electronic platform, the RGGI CO_2 Allowance Tracking System (RGGI COATS). All units must surrender CO_2 allowances equal to their emissions in a compliance period, and each participating state sets the penalties for noncompliance.

Thus, according to all interviewees, with monitoring and reporting systems already in place, the shaping of the MRV mechanism involved simply following up already existing systems.

Price management: both policy diffusion and domestic drivers

In the initial MOU, RGGI established two mechanisms for price management, both in practice forming a price ceiling. First, the Compliance Period and Safety Valve mechanism would make it possible to extend the compliance period by up to three one-year periods if the safety valve was triggered. That would happen if the average regional spot price for the allowances equalled or exceeded the Safety Valve Threshold (USD 10, in 2005 terms), as adjusted by the Consumer Price Index plus 2 per cent per year from 2006, for a period of 12 months on a rolling average after the Market Settling Period (the first 14 months of each compliance period) (RGGI 2005: 2E).

Second, there was an 'offset price trigger', later removed from the Model Rule in the 2012 programme review and replaced with the Cost Containment Reserve Mechanism (CCRM). The CCRM releases allowances when the price is triggered, i.e. exceeds developing thresholds (RGGI 2013). When the turn to auctioning became clear, also a price *floor* was introduced. A reserve price was established as part of the auction design, in the first auction set at USD 1.86. In 2016 it was USD 2.10.

Some design elements in connection with the price management mechanism were shaped by policy diffusion. The reason for setting a price floor was a combination of recommendations from academic researchers and lessons learned from the EU experience (Interview 3). The price floor was adopted because those who designed RGGI did not want a repeat of what had happened in the first period of the EU ETS, when allowance prices plummeted from EUR 30 to zero (Interview 1). However, diffusion took place more by learning from what had gone wrong in the EU than through direct consultancy with EU staff. The RGGI designers had regular contact with the EU throughout the design phase, but in this case watching what happened in Europe was the most important factor (Interview 3).

Other important drivers for establishing a reserve price included local factors like economic benefits from auctions and reinvestment in energy efficiency (Interview 2), as well as utility-owner concerns that if the price dropped too low it would not justify their investments, especially since the cap was so weak (Interview 5). The Offset Price Trigger Mechanisms was a compromise made with Governor Romney of Massachusetts, who insisted on a price cap on the allowances, which the others strongly opposed (Interview 1). As noted, this was removed in the 2012 programme review.

Revenue earmarking: protecting consumers

The RGGI states reinvest almost all auction proceeds in strategic energy and consumer programmes. As all the RGGI states have their own individual regulations based on the Model Rule, all investment programmes are independently administered and operated by the states (RGGI 2016g).

The signatory states had agreed in the MoU to devote 25 per cent of auction proceeds to consumer benefit or strategic energy programmes (RGGI 2005: 2G). However, the states came to independent decisions on reinvesting the majority of the proceeds in strategic energy and consumer benefit programmes: auction proceeds of more than USD 1.3 billion have been invested in energy efficiency, clean and renewable energy, direct bill assistance and GHG abatement – with the first two categories receiving the greatest share (RGGI 2005). A return of USD

4.67 billion in lifetime energy-bill savings for 4.6 million participating households and 21,400 businesses is estimated (RGGI 2005).

The main drivers behind the decision to devote most of the proceeds to strategic energy and consumer benefit programmes were internal political factors. The RGGI designers wanted to protect ratepayers and lower electricity demand (Interview 3).

Discussion: the RGGI programme review

The 2005 MoU stipulated that there was to be a 'comprehensive review of all components of the program' (RGGI 2005: 6D) commencing in 2012. The updated Model Rule issued in February 2013 included a tighter cap, the introduction of interim adjustment for banked allowances and the replacement of the offset trigger mechanism with a cost containment reserve (RGGI 2013). The changes in the Model Rule were founded on a rigorous and wide-ranging evaluation based upon analyses and supported by an extensive stakeholder process underway since 2010 (RGGI 2016i). Lowering the cap by 45 per cent – to 91 million short tons in 2014 – and introducing the Cost Containment Reserve was a solution to the large surplus of allowances relative to actual emissions in the region. We find no external factors influencing the choice of the changes to these design elements. Political decisions taken after thorough analyses and a broad stakeholder process seem to have been decisive.

Conclusions

The initial idea of establishing an ETS for GHGs was driven predominantly by inaction at the federal level and previous experiences of cap-and-trade in the region and nationally in the US – a combination of domestic politics and local/regional path dependencies. Nevertheless, international policy diffusion arguably played a moderate role in the establishment and design phases of the Regional Greenhouse Gas Initiative, RGGI.

Main factors behind the establishment of RGGI involved a combination of the lack of a climate policy at the US federal level, the experience of previous cooperation amongst the Northeastern states, a tradition in the region of taking the lead in environmental politics and pressure from ENGOs, as well as economic profits. But even if our interviewees did not mention competition as a central factor, Governor Pataki might well have considered the possibility of gaining a 'first mover' advantage. Until then, the emergent carbon trading market had been dominated by European competition in London and Paris (CCAP 2003: ES9). As the Center for Clean Air Policy (CCAP) report – under the section 'impacts on and benefits for New York' – pointed out: 'the opportunity for Wall Street brokerages to get involved in linking the New York carbon trading program with neighboring states and international programs will be substantial' (CCAP 2003: 51). Also, the technological innovations expected from the expanded energy-efficiency and renewable energy sources programme would 'put New York on the cutting edge of technology research and development, while saving participating consumers money and improving commercial and industrial competitiveness' (CCAP 2003: ES9).

As to policy diffusion, the EU did not have much impact on the decision to establish RGGI. However, EU staff reached out in the early phase, sharing their experiences in establishing the EU ETS and convincing the RGGI initiators that their project was feasible. Even if the EU ETS was not a main driver for Governor Pataki, the officials were clearly inspired by it, and the Multi State Working Group had considerable contact with the EU staff – especially with Peter Zapfel, a central designer of the EU ETS – and this made the whole process easier for them. Influence from the EU may not have been the main driver for initiating RGGI, but the US withdrawal from the Kyoto Protocol, halting the prospects for an international ETS, spurred the beginning of a worldwide process – which included RGGI – of establishing local, national and regional carbon markets as the new policy tool for addressing climate change.

It is in the RGGI design process that we find more evidence of international policy diffusion. Our presentation of the various design properties has shown that some properties became as they did partly because of international policy diffusion. Especially in shaping the allocation mechanism and the price management mechanism, RGGI designers looked to the EU ETS, learning from what they perceived had gone wrong there. The decision to auction emissions allowances was in addition influenced by stakeholders, ENGOs and researcher recommendations in particular. Learning from the mistakes of the EU helped the RGGI staff shape these features so as to prevent large windfall profits from going to the polluters, instead providing the participating states with proceeds they could reinvest in green technology and consumer benefit programmes.

As regards the other design properties, internal factors were decisive for how they were shaped. The various stakeholder groups were deeply involved in the process, and it was important to establish a programme acceptable to all. Internal economic factors were an important driver in setting the level of ambition. With electricity prices already high, it was important to set the cap at a level that would not induce industry to relocate to states with lower electricity prices. Internal economic factors were also the main driver for choosing the limited offset rules. The economic benefits from the offset projects were meant to stay in the region. Also revenue earmarking was designed to benefit the RGGI states and their consumers. Investments in strategic energy and consumer benefit programmes have arguably served to lower the demand for electricity and create jobs. The region has experienced an 8 per cent growth in its economy, and CO_2 emissions have been reduced by 45 per cent since 2005 (RGGI 2016h).

For other design features, path dependency was an important factor, especially for the sectors and gases covered and for the MRV components. As the equipment for monitoring CO_2 was already installed in the power sector, it would have been far more expensive and complicated to involve other gases or sectors. Finally, it was easier to get stakeholders on board for something they were already familiar with, through positive experiences.

Notes

1 Connecticut, Delaware, Maine, New Hampshire, New Jersey, New York and Vermont.
2 The SWG was composed of two state-level representatives from each state: one from the environmental agency and one from the public utility agency. The SWG was tasked with the design of the RGGI and produced the MoU.
3 Connecticut, Maine, Massachusetts, New Hampshire, Rhode Island and Vermont. Note that New York is not a 'New England' state.
4 One US short ton is equivalent to 0.91 metric ton.
5 The NEG/ECP is an annual conference, held since 1973, involving the six US New England states and five Eastern Canadian provinces, aimed at advancing the interests of these states and provinces (Council of Atlantic Premiers 2015).

References

Carbon Market Watch. 2015. Towards a global carbon market: Prospects for linking the EU ETS to other carbon markets. http://carbonmarketwatch.org/wp-content/uploads/2015/05/NC-Towards-a-global-carbon-market-report_web.pdf accessed 9 November 2015.

CCAP/Center for Clean Air Policy. 2003. *Recommendations for Governor Pataki for Reducing*. New York: State Greenhouse Gas Emissions.

Council of Atlantic Premiers. 2015. www.cap-cpma.ca/about/new-england-governors-and-eastern-canadian-premiers-annual-conference-negecp/ accessed 30 November 2016.

Dunlap, R. E., C. Xiao and A. M. McCright. 2001. Politics and environment in America: Partisan and ideological cleavages in public support for environmentalism. *Environmental Politics* 10 (4), 23–48. (doi: 10.1080/714000580).

EPA. 2015. *Summary of the Clean Air Act*. www.epa.gov/laws-regulations/summary-clean-air-act accessed 18 February 2016.

EPA. 2016a. *Sources of Greenhouse Gas Emissions*. www.epa.gov/ghgemissions/sources-greenhouse-gas-emissions#t1fn2 accessed 31 September 2016.

EPA. 2016b. *Clean Air Markets – Emissions Monitoring*. www.epa.gov/airmarkets/clean-air-markets-emissions-monitoring#tab-2 accssed12 June 2016.

Huber, B. R. 2013. How did RGGI do it? Political economy and emissions auctions. *Ecology Law Quarterly* 40 (1), 59–106.

ICAP. 2012. *Fact Sheet: USA – Regional Greenhouse Gas Initiative*. https://icapcarbonaction.com/en/ets-map?etsid=50 accessed 2 September 2016.

Lachapelle, E., C. P. Borick and B. Rabe. 2012. Public attitudes toward climate science and climate policy in federal systems: Canada and the United States compared. *Review of Policy Research* 29 (3), 334–357.

NEG/ECP. 2001. *Climate Change Action Plan 2001*. www.novascotia.ca/nse/climate.change/docs/NEG-ECP.pdf accessed 29 November 2016.

Ramseur, J. L. 2016. *The regional greenhouse gas initiative: Lessons learnt and issues for Congress*. Congressional Research Service. www.fas.org/sgp/crs/misc/R41836.pdf accessed 21 November 2016.

Raymond, L. 2016. *Reclaiming the Atmospheric Commons – The Regional Greenhouse Gas Initiative and a New Model of Emissions Trading*. Cambridge, MA: MIT Press.

Revkin, A. C. 2001. Despite opposition in party, Bush to seek emissions cuts. *New York Times*. 10 March. www.nytimes.com/2001/03/10/us/despite-opposition-in-party-bush-to-seek-emissions-cuts.html accessed 29 November 2016.

RGGI. 2005. *Memorandum of Understanding*. www.rggi.org/docs/mou_final_12_20_05.pdf accessed 14 November 2016.

RGGI. 2008. *Regional Greenhouse Gas Initiative*. www.rggi.org/docs/Model%20Rule%20Revised%2012.31.08.pdf accessed 14 November 2016.

RGGI. 2013. *Summary of RGGI Model Rule Changes: February 2013*. www.rggi.org/docs/ProgramReview/_FinalProgramReviewMaterials/Model_Rule_Summary.pdf accessed 29 November 2016.

RGGI. 2014. *CO2 Emissions from Electricity Generation and Imports in the Regional Greenhouse Gas Initiative: 2014 Monitoring Report*. www.rggi.org/docs/Documents/Elec_Monitoring_Report_2014.pdf accessed 5 December 2016.

RGGI. 2016a. *Program Design*. www.rggi.org/design accessed 14 November 2016.

RGGI. 2016b. *Memorandum of Understanding*. www.rggi.org/design/history/mou accessed 14 November 2016.

RGGI. 2016c. *Regulated Sources*. www.rggi.org/design/overview/regulated_sources accessed 30 November 2016.

RGGI. 2016d. *The RGGI CO2 Cap*. www.rggi.org/design/overview/cap accessed 14 November 2016.

RGGI. 2016e. *2012 Program Review*. www.rggi.org/design/program-review accessed 17 November 2016.

RGGI. 2016f. *Fact Sheet: RGGI CO2 Allowance Auctions*. www.rggi.org/docs/Documents/RGGI_Auctions_FactSheet.pdf accessed 1 December 2016.

RGGI. 2016g. *CO2 Offsets*. www.rggi.org/market/offsets accessed 17 November 2016.

RGGI. 2016h. *Proceeds Report 2014*. www.rggi.org/docs/ProceedsReport/RGGI_Proceeds_Report_2014.pdf accessed 6 December 2016.

RGGI. 2016i. *Final Program Review*. www.rggi.org/docs/ProgramReview/_FinalProgramReviewMaterials/Recommendations_Summary.pdf accessed 5 December 2016.

Schreurs, M. 2008. From the bottom up: Local and subnational climate change politics. *Journal of Environment & Development* 17 (4), 343–355.

Tvinnereim, E. 2013. Paths towards large, unilateral climate policies. *Journal of Energy and Natural Resources Law* 31 (4), 379–405.

Annex: list of interviewees

Interview 1: Franz Litz, New York State Government, leader of the steering committee of the RGGI Multistate Working Group. Interview conducted 31 May 2016.

Interview 2: Sonia Hamel, Massachusetts State Government, member of the steering committee of the RGGI Multistate Working Group. Interview conducted 3 June 2016.

Interview 3: Christopher Sherry, New Jersey State Government, member of the steering committee of the RGGI Multi Sstate Working Group. Interview conducted 17 June 2016.

Interview 4: Jonathan Raab, helped design and facilitate the regional stakeholder process and was also involved in some of the internal meetings. Interview conducted 24 June 2016.

Interview 5: Eric Haxthausen, the Environmental Defense Fund. Interview conducted 14 July 16.

5 California's cap-and-trade programme

The role of diffusion

Guri Bang, David G. Victor and Steinar Andresen

Introduction

California adopted and designed its cap-and-trade system at a time when many countries and regions, notably the European Union, were experimenting with emissions trading.[1] By 2006, the US federal government under the leadership of George W. Bush had failed to adopt a nationwide strategy to cut emissions, and California moved ahead on its own. Those efforts took various forms, but the centrepiece was California Assembly Bill 32 (AB 32) – the Global Warming Solutions Act – that the California State Legislature adopted in 2006. While AB 32 did many things, its most visible accomplishment was to set in motion a process that led to a statewide cap-and-trade system that came into effect in 2012. This chapter investigates the role of policy diffusion, policy learning, copying and local political economy in shaping the design of that system.

On the surface, the AB 32 system is very similar to other cap-and-trade systems, but in practice there are many detailed differences that reflect efforts by California policy-makers to avoid the flaws they saw in other systems. The California system was designed to create the impression that efficient markets were being used to control emissions in the state – when, in fact, most of the real effort in cutting emissions came from more expensive regulatory and procurement mandates. California policy-makers also understood that the state was responsible for only a fraction of global emissions, so they designed their cap-and-trade system with the potential for other states and countries to link to California's carbon market. As implementation of AB 32 proceeded, California took on the role of a leader, seeking to encourage other states and the federal government to follow.

We examine the origins and operation of California's cap-and-trade system from two broad sets of theoretical frames. First, we focus on the roles of policy diffusion. Drawing on previous research, we examine the broad process of diffusion and active learning that unfolded as policy agents and organized interest groups sought to identify and apply lessons from other trading systems when designing and adjusting California's emissions trading programme. Previous literature shows that the implementation process, where the design of the cap-and-trade system is decided, is crucial for continued growth and support of climate policy (Klinsky 2013; Paterson et al. 2014; Houle et al. 2015). Such processes are intrinsically complex and responsive to many different actors, interests, administrative arrangements, institutions and ideas.

Second, we examine how organized political concerns within California have affected the design of the system. There is a huge literature on 'clean' or 'optimal' cap-and-trade systems, but relatively little on *how* political economy affects the design and operation of cap-and-trade schemes (but see Klinsky 2013 and Houle et al. 2015 for a comparison of emissions trading systems across several US and Canadian sub-federal jurisdictions). Indeed, as we expected, local political concerns – and not purely policy diffusion – proved instrumental for explaining the specific design elements and scope of the cap-and-trade system. Those local concerns have affected the coverage of the system – overcoming the opposition of California's politically well-organized oil industry was crucial to expansion of coverage to include the transport sector in the second compliance period (2015–17).

Strategies to overcome and redirect organized environmental and community interests were crucial to creating a cap-and-trade system in the first place. Many of these groups – such as those anchored in the environmental justice movement – were concerned that trading would lead to loopholes, local pollution 'hotspots' and other undesirable outcomes. In 2016, those concerns were instrumental in pushing forward the bill AB 197 to adoption in the California State Legislature. AB 197 specifically instructs the government to prioritize direct regulation of large emission sources and hence poses a potential challenge to continuation of the cap-and-trade system after 2020. Finally, an active strategy by policy entrepreneurs regarding how revenues from cap-and-trade auctions would be spent was also crucial to building political support. The cap and trade auctions have generated some USD 4 billion to date, which is then collected and deposited in the Greenhouse Gas Reduction Fund, where it is subject to appropriation by the state legislature.

Auction proceeds are channelled to infrastructure investments, projects for disadvantaged communities and other activities favoured by pivotal interest groups. The practice of using auctions to generate money for the state has been challenged in the courts on the grounds that it may conflict with the California constitution's requirement that all new taxes require a two-thirds majority in order to be adopted. AB 32 was not adopted by a two-thirds majority. After the 2016 election, however, the Democratic Party has a two-thirds majority in the state legislature, which they can potentially use to adopt appropriate legislation to allow the use of auctions. In the conclusion, we draw some inferences about how California is trying to move its ideas and market signals *outward* to influence other jurisdictions, in the US and abroad.

While the history of California's climate change policy is rich, the central purpose of this chapter is to explore why California adopted cap-and-trade and how California policy-makers designed and adjusted that system over time. We limit our case study to the pre-2020 period, where AB 32 gave specific authority to introduce a cap-and-trade system. In August 2016, the State Senate adopted SB 32, which extends California's climate policy to 2030 and requires a 40 per cent cut in greenhouse gasses (GHGs) below 1990 levels. With the adoption of

SB 32, it is clear that the California Air Resources Board (CARB) is required to continue regulating to meet the 40 per cent target – but whether cap-and-trade will be part of the regulatory package is an open question, due to the requirements in AB 197, as mentioned earlier. It is beyond the scope of this chapter to explore the consequences of SB 32 and AB 197, but these new laws will keep the debate about the design and implementation of the cap-and-trade system alive for years to come.

We employ data from position papers and reports produced by major actor groups, more formal stakeholder processes, impact assessments and policy reviews, as well as from hearings and public discussions in the state legislature and other decision-making institutions (notably CARB). These processes provide evidence of the forms of reasoning underpinning the design of the cap-and-trade system and explicit and more implicit references to external factors – lessons, competitive concerns and tactical concerns. The data have been scrutinized in order to provide a comprehensive picture of the main societal actors and arguments shaping the design and scope of the cap-and-trade system and specify to what extent and how different diffusion mechanisms were operating.

Complementing this with semi-structured interviews with key stakeholders enables firm process tracing to identify the causal chains of events and path dependencies that resulted in the design of the California cap-and-trade system. We conducted 13 semi-structured expert interviews in October 2015 (see Annex). Interviews started with a presentation of our research questions and were followed by approximately six open-ended questions related to the role of the organization/expert in shaping the design of the cap-and-trade programme, to identify who the key actors in the design process were and to assess where the idea of cap-and-trade originated. Interviews lasted between 45 and 90 minutes. We interviewed state politicians or their expert staff, experts at environmental non-governmental organizations (ENGOs), staff at relevant state agencies, and academics. We were not able to get interviews with utilities or oil industry representatives, which would have been desirable, for maximal representativeness of primary data material. Secondary data like *E&E News* and published literature have been employed to fill this gap in our interview data.

Overview and emergence of California's cap-and-trade programme

California is the most populous state in the United States, with 39 million residents. It relies heavily on natural gas for heating and electricity production (44 per cent of the total in 2015), but renewable energy is growing fast and reached 26 per cent in 2015 (California Energy Commission 2016). California is a leading industrial state, with an economy larger than that of many countries. Agriculture, technology, petroleum, tourism and the motion picture industry provide a wide range of jobs statewide. Political power is divided among the governor, the state legislature and the state supreme court. The Democratic Party has been in majority control of the state legislature continuously since 1970,[2] whereas the governorship has switched between Democrats and Republicans.

The California cap-and-trade experiment originated at a time when political attention to climate change was increasing rapidly but federal climate policy was in a gridlock. In the early 2000s, US policy in this domain became increasingly polarized, with Democrats in general more supportive of climate policy action than Republicans. At the federal level, the Republican-led US Congress essentially had no majority in favour of a federal climate policy act or support from President George W. Bush. Bipartisan efforts in the US Senate in 2003 and 2005 to pass cap-and-trade legislation – in parallel with the EU's introduction of an emissions trading system (ETS) – were not supported by the Republican leadership and quickly stalled.

In California, however, the Democratic Party had greater political strength, and there was a larger group of moderate Republicans interested in market-friendly environmental policies. With a strong history of environmental policy pioneering, California Democrats advocated the need for climate action.[3] In an alliance with Republican Governor Schwarzenegger, these legislators put climate policy on the agenda in the early 2000s and looked to the EU and the Kyoto Protocol experience for inspiration when they proposed the Global Warming Solutions Act (AB 32) (Interview 1). The California Legislature adopted AB 32 in 2006, and Governor Schwarzenegger signed it into law. AB 32 constitutes the basic building-block legislation that made possible the development of California's climate policy package. AB 32 requires California to reduce its GHG emissions to 1990 levels by 2020 – a reduction of approximately 15 per cent below emissions expected under a 'business as usual' scenario.

With AB 32 adopted, the California Air Resources Board was authorized to develop regulations to achieve 'the maximum technologically feasible and cost-effective GHG emission reductions'. AB 32 did not explicitly require emissions trading – instead, the political debate and implementing legislation made it clear that CARB 'may' use emissions trading as an option for implementing the objectives of the legislation.[4] This ambiguity reflected a political debate still alive in California in which political forces concerned about minimizing economic impacts (including Governor Schwarzenegger, who had threatened to veto any legislation that did not use emissions trading) were opposed to environmental justice groups that were suspicious of unfettered markets and concerned that trading would create pollution hotspots within disadvantaged communities (e.g. EDF/IETA 2015).

CARB developed an initial Scoping Plan in 2008, which outlined California's emissions reduction target and included a wide range of recommended strategies, direct regulations, market-based approaches, voluntary measures and other programmes – most of which CARB itself did not directly control. The most important policy programmes that affected emissions were the state's renewable portfolio standard (RPS), the low-carbon fuel standard (LCFS) and energy-efficiency measures. The cap-and-trade system, in CARB's logic, was to offer a 'backstop' and an insurance policy.[5] The backstop would help ensure that total emissions would not rise above prescribed levels. The insurance function, in tandem, would create a mechanism that could make up for emissions reduction efforts that were lost if any of the major complementary policies were to fail. This logic was extremely important to CARB's design because the agency knew that many of the policies that were expected to have large emission reduction impacts – like the state's low-carbon fuel standard and its rules setting fuel economy limits in terms of CO_2 emissions per mile – would face severe and possibly successful legal challenges (Wara 2014).

CARB turned the 'may' in the authorizing statute into an actual emissions trading programme by engaging an expert group of California's top economists to evaluate policy options – that group, almost by design, strongly recommended cap-and-trade as the most cost-efficient policy instrument (Economic and Allocation Advisory Committee 2010). CARB leaned heavily on the expert group's advice in choosing cap-and-trade as a central element in the state's climate policy package. Over the next three years, CARB's own experts developed the detailed rules of the cap-and-trade programme, consulting a range of external experts and stakeholders in the process. In 2011, CARB submitted final rules for the state's cap-and-trade programme, and the programme was implemented in January 2012 (CARB 2016). An update of the Scoping Plan, approved by CARB in 2014, includes new strategies and recommendations.

The California programme emerged in the vacuum created by the absence of a serious federal policy. Californian politicians and regulators described their efforts in terms of leadership, but they also knew that California's strategy would have to be designed to expand and influence a larger fraction of the nation's (and the world's) emissions. To that end, California helped initiate the Western Climate Initiative (WCI) from 2007 onwards. This was a regional collaborative initiative to develop a regional cap-and-trade programme, with seven US states (Arizona, California, Montana, New Mexico, Oregon, Utah and Washington) and four Canadian provinces (British Columbia, Manitoba, Ontario and Québec) as members. WCI emerged at the same time as a regional GHG reduction programme was established on the East Coast – the Regional Greenhouse Gas Initiative (RGGI; see Chapter 4 of this book for a detailed account of the emergence of RGGI).

Over a four-year period, several partner workshops and meetings planned the design elements of the WCI, making it close to implementation-ready by 2011. Those efforts may have been somewhat eclipsed by the arrival in 2009 of a new president in Washington – Barack Obama, whose Democratic Party also controlled both houses of Congress at the time. During a brief window of opportunity that year, several major legislative efforts were pushed forward – notably on health care and on climate change. When momentum was building for the Waxman-Markey bill in the 111th US Congress (also known as the American Climate and Energy Security Act of 2009), copies of the California climate regulator's implementation plan, the 2008 Scoping Plan, were distributed widely in Washington, DC, to show that climate mitigation policy was feasible and that California was showing the way. Eventually, the Waxman-Markey bill passed the US House of Representatives but failed to attract sufficient support in the US Senate, where the bill died without a formal vote. Rising political polarization on climate change was one important reason for the lack of traction for climate legislation in the

US Congress; some analysts have also pointed to lack of leadership by President Obama in efforts to persuade and negotiate with legislators (Lizza 2010).

After US midterm elections in 2010, a wave of new state governors took office, and the Democrats lost unified control of the federal legislative branch. That political pivot killed hopes for further climate legislation in Washington. It also undermined the WCI: almost all collaborating states had bowed out of the WCI by the end of 2011 (Rabe 2016). Only California and Québec remained committed to implementing cap-and-trade. In 2014, those two programmes were formally linked, now constituting one carbon market. Other WCI members have either abandoned cap-and-trade entirely or are still considering possible future implementation.

At the time, state-level climate action was buzzing as a result of low federal-level attention to the issue under President George W. Bush. In this context, California made strides to develop a climate policy model that other parts of the country could follow, actively seeking to shape the national debate.

Explaining the turn to emissions trading in California

Previous research points to a number of potential sources of learning as California designed its cap-and-trade programme. Emissions trading as a climate policy instrument originated in discussions related to the Kyoto Protocol in the late 1990s, inspired by the successful US experiences with the SO_2 trading market established under the Clean Air Act (Schmalensee and Stavins 2013). After initial scepticism, the European Union embraced the idea of a carbon market and started planning and implementing its pioneering ETS from 2001 onwards (Skjærseth and Wettestad 2008).

In a parallel process, the US Congress debated several proposals for adopting a federal cap-and-trade programme, but bills failed in the Senate in 2003, 2005 and 2008 (Bang 2010). Moreover, nine states on the East Coast formed RGGI in 2005 with the aim of establishing a regional cap-and-trade to cut GHG emissions from the electricity sector. The WCI was initiated on the heels of RGGI in 2007, with a broader scope (all sectors of the economy) and membership (11 states and provinces) (Rabe 2016).

In the early phase, politicians and regulators were interested in drawing lessons from the experiences made when the EU developed and implemented its emissions trading system. European politicians visited California and helped convince Governor Schwarzenegger that emissions trading would be a cost-effective and useful policy approach for California (Interview 13). Schwarzenegger eventually became an important driving force for a California cap-and-trade system. EU officials and technical experts visited California several times to share their knowledge and experience (Interview 2). Representatives from CARB also went on study trips to the EU to learn about emissions trading (Interview 6).

Other domestic emissions trading programmes gradually became increasingly important sources of influence in the design phase of California's cap-and-trade. Specifically, collaboration within the WCI inspired some important choices. For several years pursuant to and parallel to CARB's work with the Scoping Plan, WCI engaged in developing a multi-sector, market-based programme to reduce GHG emissions. Some of our interviewees pointed to an interactive process, where common WCI design elements were developed for offset and compliance, with the specific aim of future linkage between systems, and all participating states undertook lawmaking preparations (Interview 5). More critical voices hold that the WCI process was dominated by Californian ideas and expert knowledge, with California as the main provider of premises for other WCI members (Rabe 2016; Interview 11).

Between 2007 and 2012, CARB conducted a thorough preparatory process to develop the California cap-and-trade programme and the broader climate policy package. Drawing on the experiences with over-allocation and windfall profits in the EU ETS, CARB put considerable weight on ensuring that the data and rules were correct before implementation of the carbon market (Interviews 6, 11). Stakeholder involvement was important in this process: CARB organized 24 workshops with a broad range of stakeholders to facilitate learning and discussion about the design of the cap-and-trade system. More than 20 designated experts in CARB worked on developing the Scoping Plan. All new proposed design elements were subject to public hearing processes with long commenting periods, and thousands of comments were submitted and answered (Interview 5).

To summarize, the design of California cap-and-trade programme developed with an eye to the experiences from other emissions trading systems, in particular the EU ETS, RGGI and the regional WCI collaboration. The focus was on avoiding the mistakes of others, especially related to allocation of permits, compliance rules, offset practices and price-setting. In other words, diffusion took place by learning from errors rather than copying (Underdal 2013). Throughout the design process, domestic internal learning and diffusion were more important than the EU; learning from the EU by avoidance was most important initially and did not make much difference once the system was up and running.

Local political concerns: path dependency and political economy

In developing its climate policy programme, California's Democratic political majority and the regulatory authorities did not merely draw lessons from other emissions trading systems. Designing a system that took local concerns into account was crucial for garnering support from stakeholders and the general public, so local political concerns mediated how lessons were learned. California has a long history of serious air pollution problems and is vulnerable to serious impacts of climate change, like droughts, wildfires and water shortages. Californians express high concern for environmental degradation and climate change, and relatively strong support for climate policy, compared to other states (Yale Program on Climate Change Communication 2013; Howe et al. 2015).

When the Federal Clean Air Act was passed in 1970, California already had a long history of efforts to address local air pollution. CARB, for example, was established in 1967 and was already deeply engaged with understanding and responding to the state's unique geography (high-density urban centres located in arid basins where pollution concentrates – notably in Los Angeles). As a result, an exceptional number of people with high competence within the field have been working in key agencies like CARB, the California Energy Commission and the California Public Utility Commission. Previous literature and almost all our interviewees underlined this highly developed competence as crucial for California's ability to design its current climate policy programme (Houle et al. 2015).

A strong coalition of actors – including legislators, the governor's office and emissions trading experts in key state agencies and ENGOs – has been deeply involved in designing the climate policy package, with an intended interaction between direct regulation and cap-and-trade that leaned most heavily on the effect of direct regulation. First, Democratic legislators formed a strong majority in the state legislature that actively pushed through legislation that could support a strong climate policy, including cap-and-trade. Part of their mission was to organize regular hearings and debates in the state legislature in order to educate state politicians on the climate-change issue, so as to build a stable majority coalition that would support climate policy initiatives in both the assembly and senate (Interview 1). The 2014 midterm elections brought in a diverse group of Democrats who represented traditionally strong environmentalist strongholds like Los Angeles and San Francisco, but also more representatives of low-income voters and districts with industries and business sectors generally less enthusiastic about climate policy. These new legislators looked for amendments to the climate policy package that could take better account of their constituents' concerns. The adoption of AB 197 in 2016 – authorizing an extension of CARB's regulatory responsibility for cutting GHGs, but under new expectations towards the cap-and-trade system – was an example of the effect of these new concerns entering the state assembly.

Second, the governor's office has persistently supported cap-and-trade as a central piece of California's climate policy. Governors Schwarzenegger, Davis and Brown were instrumental in initiating and supporting ambitious climate policy initiatives (Houle et al. 2015). In close alliance with the Democratic majority in the state legislature they issued executive orders at crucial moments to initiate and implement climate policy instruments like the cap-and-trade that had initially failed to get direct support in the legislature. CARB has benefited from the support from legislation and from the governor: when the former is unsupportive, then the latter can assist CARB on new missions. In the case of climate policy, experts hired at CARB were selected and promoted for their support of the pro–climate policy approach. Continued support from the governor's office for cap-and-trade is expected by the Democratic majority in the state legislature, since it is unlikely that a governor unsupportive of a strong climate policy would be elected in California (Interviews 1, 2, 3, 4).

Third, the coalition includes experts from CARB, the Energy Commission and Natural Resources Defence Council (NRDC) that were instrumental in designing the climate policy package, based on strong expertise and decades of experience as described prior. Some of the top people involved have worked on environmental regulations since the 1970s. They represent a network of experts who have worked together over many years and largely agree on what the best policy solutions are. Drawing on lessons from previous regulatory processes, these experts were instrumental in designing a climate policy package for California, with direct regulation like the RPS, the LCFS and energy-efficiency regulations as the basic building blocks. Cap-and-trade, being a new and untested policy instrument, was designed to have less effect on emissions, at least in the early phases. For instance, in 2015 the cap-and-trade system represented only 20 per cent of total emissions cuts.

Explaining the design of California's cap-and-trade programme

Type of system: encompassing system tailored to local interests

California has a mandatory cap-and-trade system, with an absolute cap. Banking and limited borrowing are allowed, but under a general holding limit. Borrowing of future vintage allowances is not allowed, as allowances are allocated and auctioned within each calendar year. Some future-year allowances are offered for sale at each auction and may be traded but cannot be used for compliance until the compliance date for the vintage year (ICAP 2017).

When California adopted AB 32 and started to develop its cap-and-trade programme, regulators and politicians looked to other jurisdictions to learn from their experiences. Exchanges of knowledge with the EU ETS, WCI members and RGGI shaped key design mechanisms, with the effect that California decided on a different design for allocation of permits and offset rules to avoid mistakes like over-allocation, double counting and windfall profits to permit holders. Put differently, California 'learned' from early actors, but then proceeded into largely uncharted territory by designing and rapidly implementing a system that was much more complex and bespoke to California conditions than the other relevant emission trading systems that offered partial learning models. The easiest and most conspicuous lessons from other trading systems were the easiest to identify and learn from, although many of those lessons – such as risks of over-allocation – were also easy to spot from basic market theory. However, for most of what mattered – complex instrument design and administration – California was largely on its own.

Local political concerns were important as mediating factors in the diffusion process that helped shape the design of the cap-and-trade programme. First, California's established regulatory competence and experience in air-pollution policies played an important role in causing path dependency. Democratic legislators, the governor's office and regulators from CARB, the Energy Commission and California Public Utility Commission (CPUC) had developed competencies crucial for designing a climate policy package that gave traditional command-and-control measures like the RPS and the LCFS the main task of cutting emissions, while the cap-and-trade programme was designed to sweep up remaining emissions. Second, key stakeholders like investor-owned utilities (IOUs) and the oil

Table 5.1 Design features of the California cap-and-trade programme

	Initial design	*Key changes*
Type of system	Cap-and-trade system with a hard price floor and soft price cap.	No significant changes.
Ambition level	Stabilization of state emissions at 1990 levels by 2020.	As of 2016, emission reductions tightened to 40% below 1990 by 2030.
Allocation mechanism(s)	90% free allocation and 10% auction.	Gradual increase of auctioning, with 75% free allocation and 25% auctioning by 2019–20.
Coverage	All GHGs, initially 35% (mainly power sector and large industrial sources).	Expansion to include transport in 2015, for a total of 85% of state emissions.
Offsetting and linking	Maximum 8% offset permits for each covered entity; rigid assessment of eligible offset projects.	Linkage with Québec's cap-and-trade system from 2014, although the two systems operate in parallel and are not fully linked.
MRV and compliance	All covered entities to report on a yearly basis.	No significant changes.
Price/quantity management	Flexible price-containment mechanism, where the Allowance Price Containment Reserve builds up a pool of additional allowances that can be introduced into the market if permit prices exceeded specified levels. In effect, this creates a soft price ceiling. The programme also has a price floor that started at USD 10 per ton for 2012–13, then began increasing at a rate of 5% per year until 2020. The rate is 5% in real (not nominal) terms, defined as 5% plus the CPI index.	No significant changes.
Revenue earmarking	Revenue from auctions go into the Greenhouse Gas Reduction Fund, and proceeds are earmarked for low-carbon development projects in California. Those projects are determined through a separate mechanism and are not strictly scored according to their cost-effectiveness in cutting carbon.	No significant changes.

industry influenced the design elements in the cap-and-trade programme and the larger climate policy package, like the allocation mechanism, auctioning rules and how to include and regulate refined oil products through cap-and-trade and the LCFS. Adapting the cap-and-trade programme to make it politically acceptable for stakeholders and the public entailed, among other things, creating a price floor that gives predictability for stakeholders' investment horizons and starting with a low allowance price only gradually increasing to a level where it can have a real effect on emissions and green technology investments.

Academic advice also made a significant impact on the design of the cap-and-trade system. Notably, the independent Economic and Allocation Advisory Committee, with economists from California's top universities, gave important input to CARB. The committee's advice was quite influential for CARB's argumentation to establish a cap-and-trade system in California as a central part of the climate policy package. Several interest groups were initially opposed to trading – notably the environmental justice grassroots movement. Having obtained clear academic advice from the expert group, CARB had important support for moving ahead to design a climate policy package that included both emissions trading and more traditional command-and-control regulations (Borenstein et al. 2016).

Several analysts and independent academics have been quite critical to the design of the current climate policy package, pointing out that the *de facto* central role of the RPS and the LCFS is an indication that the cap-and-trade system is not working optimally (Interviews 9, 10, 11). Too many compromises have been made with stakeholders, opening up for leakage problems. For instance, resource shuffling involving creative ways of using coal-fired power from neighbouring states constituted a leakage problem caused by compromises between CARB and the utility sector in the first two compliance periods, but this has now been fixed (Interview 11). Even so, some critics claim that there is little reason for California to celebrate the cap-and-trade system as a cornerstone policy instrument as long as most emissions cuts are addressed through traditional command-and-control regulations. In essence, these critics say, the climate policy package has been carefully constructed to hide the marginal costs of climate action (Interviews 9, 10, 11). With a relatively low and stable carbon price in the cap-and-trade system attracting most attention, the much higher costs incurred by the less talked-about RPS and LCSF are not so visible for the public.

Ambition level: climate policy leadership

The Global Warming Solutions Act (AB 32) was adopted by the California State Legislature in 2006, and Governor Schwarzenegger signed it into law. AB 32 constitutes the basic building-block legislation that made possible the development of California's climate policy package. AB 32 requires California to reduce its GHG emissions to 1990 levels by 2020 – a reduction of approximately 15 per cent below emissions expected under a 'business as usual' scenario. Despite the signature status of the trading system, in fact California relies mostly on far less transparent and more costly direct regulation – notably the RPS, energy efficiency measures, and the LCFS – to cut GHG emissions. Our findings indicate that the climate policy package was purposely designed for interaction between cap-and-trade and complementary direct regulation to avoid high permit prices in the cap-and-trade programme, which would have caused political controversy. If allowance prices had been too high, mounting protests against cap-and-trade could potentially have jeopardized its continuance. Instead, the RPS and the LCFS now take the brunt of the carbon emissions cuts and represent the more costly policies without having a directly visible price for consumers.

In August 2016, the state senate adopted SB 32, which extends California's climate policy to 2030 and requires a 40 per cent cut in GHGs below 1990 levels, with the long-term target of cutting emissions by 85 per cent from 1990 levels by 2050. Democrats in the state legislature, in collaboration with ENGOs and a strong public-opinion push, have pressed for increasingly ambitious climate policy in California. Even in the face of the Trump administration's slashing of federal climate-change regulations, California's policy-makers seem set on continuing this policy.

Allocation mechanism and auctioning rules: avoiding mistakes, adapting to political economy

The allocation of permits was based on 90 per cent free allocation and 10 per cent auction in the first phase (2013–14), which covered only electricity and industrial sources. Utilities receive allowances on behalf of their ratepayers, while natural gas suppliers must consign an increasing percentage of allowances to auction each year. All natural gas and electrical utilities must use the allowance value for ratepayer benefit and for emissions reductions (ICAP 2017). Transport fuels became subject to the cap-and-trade programme in the second phase (2015–17), with a requirement for this sector to buy allowances at auctions (or to buy offsets from third parties).

In the case of auctioning rules, California seems to have converged towards the RGGI model with establishing a fund for surplus auction revenue that is used for investment in additional low-carbon projects. The effects of policy diffusion and learning were probably stronger in the early phase of developing the cap-and-trade than in later phases. Moreover, policy learning was more directed at avoiding some of the mistakes that the EU had made – leading to divergence in terms of specific design elements – while lessons from domestic cap-and-trade experiments, WCI and RGGI, resulted in some degree of convergence in design. Certain flexibility provisions in the California cap-and-trade programme were designed on the basis of lessons from the EU ETS and RGGI (Rabe 2016). Specifically, the number of covered entities will expand over time, thereby increasing the size of the market. The percentage of emission allowances to be auctioned rather than allocated without charge will also increase gradually, from 10 per cent in 2012 and reaching 25 per cent by 2020. The auctioning method is designed to generate government revenue for specific purposes, with some parallels to a carbon tax (Rabe 2016).

Local stakeholders were closely involved in shaping the design of allocation and auctioning mechanisms. California's IOUs – Pacific Gas & Electric, Southern California Edison and San Diego Gas & Electric – played an important role in the Scoping Plan process and were actively involved in workshops organized by CARB and in hearings and commenting regulatory proposals. As key stakeholders, these IOUs weighed in with their market expertise to shape the design. Of particular interest to utilities were the allocation mechanism and auctioning rules. In the cap-and-trade programme, most permits are distributed for free – including to utilities. The utility permits are consigned back to CARB for auction, which generates revenues that are then recycled to ratepayers – creating the impression that the net cost of these emissions control efforts is low. Moreover, the IOUs were highly aware that some of them had a historical legacy of importing large amounts of power through contracts with out-of-state coal-fired power plants. Emissions from those plants were high, creating the risk (or opportunity) for 'resource shuffling' if higher emitting power gets redirected to states not covered by a cap (Cullenward 2014; EDF/IETA 2015) – which could affect the carbon price, as well as undermining the efficacy of the cap-and-trade programme and California's ability to meet its emissions reduction targets (Cullenward 2014).[6] This risk has diminished, as nearly all those coal-fired contracts have now been unwound, and California's IOUs fully embrace emissions reduction as a central goal.

Californian IOUs are generally considered the most progressive in the US as regards climate-change issues; with the current design for allocation, auctions, reporting and compliance, they are not opposed to regulation. In fact, all three IOUs have been shifting from companies that generate power to 'wires' companies that specialize in transmission and distribution – areas with high capital investments and supervised, assured rates of return.

California's Independent System Operator (CAISO) is becoming more involved in a dialogue with CARB and CPUC as plans to expand the state's electricity market into a regional market are evolving. CAISO underlines the need to design an efficient day-ahead market to include more renewables, while also maintaining a well-functioning energy imbalance market. Interaction with the cap-and-trade system is especially important for price-setting in the electricity market (Interview 7).

Coverage: responding to local concerns

California's cap-and-trade system covers about 85 per cent of the state's total emissions and targets emitters of more than 25,000 tons of CO_2 equivalents annually. It covers all major sectors, including electricity producers and first deliverers, process industry and manufacturing, oil and gas producers and transport fuels. In total, some 450 entities are required to participate in the carbon market. The programme covers all major greenhouse gases.

The 'complementary policies' – the RPS, the LCFS and energy-efficiency measures – are in fact the most important components in California's climate policy package in terms of emissions reductions. The complementary policies were designed to take the bulk of emissions cuts (as much as 80 per cent in 2015), with the cap-and-trade system designed to be a backstop that would sweep up remaining cuts (not more than 20 per cent in 2015) not addressed through the RPS, energy-efficiency measures or the LCFS (Interviews 5, 6, 2, 3, 1).

The policy mix was purposely designed this way to avoid soaring permit prices and political controversy, according to regulators and legislators we interviewed (Interviews 5, 6, 2, 3, 1). CARB considered and planned the interaction between the complementary policies (RPS, LCFS) and the cap-and-trade programme to sweep up remaining GHG emissions not covered by complementary policies and designed the system with a price-control mechanism that allowed the carbon price to stay at a politically acceptable level (Interview 5). If allowance prices had been too high, protests could have mounted against cap-and-trade and potentially jeopardized its continuance. The climate policy package is built to gradually increase allowance prices, as well as gradually increase acceptance of cap-and-trade among stakeholder groups (Interviews 5, 6, 2, 3, 1). Hence, the design of the cap-and-trade system was aligned with intentions to increase legitimacy and acceptability with this innovative policy measure.

One sector in particular – fuel suppliers and the oil industry – has opposed the coverage of the climate policy package, especially the inclusion of the transport sector. The oil industry has given conflicting signals, indicating a preference for a cap-and-trade system over direct regulation, and has expressed deep disagreement with the LCFS on the grounds that the programme will be inadequate for producing enough low-carbon fuels to meet demand, resulting in insufficient supply and more costly fuels for the Californian transport sector (WSPA 2016). Oil and gas suppliers argue that the cap-and-trade programme best addresses climate-change concerns without placing undue burdens on the economy, the consumers and the transport sector. Since California's cap-and-trade programme now includes transport fuels, oil industry representatives see the LCFS not as a complementary policy but as a contradictory one (WSPA 2016). Even so, just prior to the inclusion of transport fuels under the cap-and-trade programme in 2015, the oil industry expressed support for a proposal from then state senate president Darrell Steinberg to exempt transport fuels from the cap, instead making them subject to a stand-alone carbon tax (Climatewire 2014).

Moreover, in 2014, an oil industry campaign was criticized for employing a strategy to thwart AB 32 by projecting an erroneous image of consumer protest against new climate policy initiatives – notably, by placing ads that appeared to voice grassroots citizen-activist views while in reality promoting oil industry priorities and working against the implementation of AB 32 (Bloomberg News 2014). In 2015, the industry launched a massive campaign to prevent new legislation that would have mandated a statewide reduction in oil consumption of 50 per cent by 2050. As the bill (SB 350) did not receive sufficient support in the state legislature in a decisive vote in October 2015, the lobby campaign appears to have had effect. Several interviewees described it as a very successful campaign (Interviews 2, 3, 12, 13). Still, it should be noted that this applied to only one element of the bill – the requirement to reduce the consumption of petroleum fuels in the transport sector. Two of the other primary measures were retained, and the bill was signed into law in 2015.

Offsetting: lessons from other carbon markets

The rules for offset purchasing are firm: they allow maximum 8 per cent offset permits for each covered entity, with quite rigid assessments of eligible projects. Only projects in the US are allowed (EDF/IETA 2015). CARB and the state government regard the current regulations as a rigorous approach to ensure the environmental integrity of offsets eligible to enter California's programme. CARB is responsible for adopting protocols that set guidelines that individual projects must meet and that make accounting and other practices consistent across like projects. CARB has approved six protocols so far: ozone depleting substances (ODS), livestock digesters, urban forests, US forest projects, mine-methane capture and rice cultivation (EDF/IETA 2015; CARB 2016).

In designing the cap-and-trade system, Californian policy-makers set out to avoid some of the key mistakes made by the EU regarding rules for offsets. In the EU ETS, offset rules had compromised the system's environmental stringency, and Californian politicians and regulators were set on not making the same mistakes. Hence, learning from the EU ETS focused on designing better offset rules for California. Experience from collaboration and learning in the WCI also played a key role in designing offset rules that would make linkage easier to accomplish (Interview 5). For California, linkage to other markets is subject to several requirements. Notably, the prospective linked cap-and-trade market must be substantially equivalent to that of California, across several dimensions. That both California and Québec used the standard WCI market design made such linkage much easier (Benoit and Côté 2015; Cullenward 2015).

ENGOs, in particular the NRDC and the Environmental Defense Fund (EDF), worked in close partnership with regulators in developing a design of offset rules important in ensuring environmental integrity (Interviews 12, 13, 9, 10, 11). Indeed, the NRDC was one of the key architects of the system, providing specific design proposals. As one example of close relations and transitioning of experience and knowledge in the decision-maker network we may mention Mary Nichols, the current CARB chair, who first worked as NRDC staff and later came to CARB as a key person during the Scoping Plan years. She has been the powerful board chair during implementation of state climate policy under AB 32. Some critics question ENGOs for having too close relations to regulators and for their lack of critical input to the policy-making process (Interview 11).

MRV and compliance: lessons from other carbon markets

To ensure reliable monitoring, reporting and verification of activities in the market and cuts in emissions, CARB requires all covered entities to report on a yearly basis. Independent third-party verification is required for emissions-data reports and their underlying data. Covered entities must implement internal audits, quality assurance and control systems for the reporting programme and the data reported (ICAP 2017). There are substantial penalties for failing to report under the Mandatory GHG Reporting Regulation. If an entity fails to surrender a sufficient number of compliance instruments to meet its compliance obligation, a separate violation is registered for each required compliance instrument that has not been surrendered. Further, the authorities make an automatic adjustment to the compliance obligation due that is equal to the number of allowances lacking, multiplied by four. A quarter of that amount is retired, and the remaining amount is auctioned by the state (ICAP 2017).

As with other design elements, Californian policy-makers set out to avoid some of the key mistakes made by the EU, also regarding rules for compliance. Hence, learning from the EU ETS focused on designing better compliance rules for California. Experience from collaboration and learning in the WCI also played a key role in designing compliance rules.

Price management mechanisms: attuned to local expert advice

During the preparation of the first Scoping Plan, the Economic and Allocation Advisory Committee gave important advice on the price-control mechanism (Interviews 9, 10, 11). California established a minimum price floor in the auction of allowances, which generally functions as a minimum price in the market (although secondary market prices briefly fell below this level during a crisis in mid-2016). California does not have a price ceiling, but there is a quantity-limited pool of allowances held in the Allowance Price Containment Reserve (APCR), available in three tiers at USD 40, 45 and 50 per tCO_2e. If that supply is depleted, however, there is no upper limit on prices. Concern that market prices could blow through the APCR has been a critical issue in ongoing market design questions, and the Emissions Market Assessment Committee (EMAC) – CARB's top academic advisors established to be a watchdog over the implementation of the market – voiced concern over this in 2013.[7]

Recent developments in California, with over-supply and a fall in the allowance price below the price floor, indicate that such undesired effects have not been avoided entirely, even though these specific design elements were chosen.

Revenue earmarking: strategic use of revenue to bolster climate policy support

Since the implementation of the cap-and-trade system, and increasingly in the second phase (2015–17), revenues generated from cap-and-trade auctioning have filled up the Greenhouse Gas Reduction Fund substantially. The funds are earmarked for reducing GHG emissions, but AB 32 mentions other important policy priorities that must be considered – like ensuring benefits to disadvantaged communities, cutting emissions cost-effectively and maximizing societal benefits to the environment, economy and public health (EDF/IETA 2015). The fund allows policy-makers to invest auction proceeds in programmes that cut GHG emissions and accelerate pollution reductions, while also delivering on some other key policy objectives. Hence, the fund has allowed the state government to support infrastructure investments, projects for disadvantaged communities and other low-carbon policies with fresh funding. The governor and state legislative majority have specific plans for using the proceeds to support green projects and build new infrastructure (CARB 2016). Our interviewees noted that politicians in Sacramento seem to find it especially pertinent to use the proceeds to support low-income constituents in electoral districts where the representative or senator is in a swing-vote position: using the proceeds strategically to build future support for even more ambitious climate policies (Interviews 2, 3, 6, 1, 4).

Critical voices question the way proceeds have been used so far and whether the activities supported really are 'green' projects – or if funds are used to pay off potential critics of the cap-and-trade programme, indicating that the process is shady (Interview 10). Moreover, since California's constitution requires a two-thirds majority to change taxes, the auctioning element face challenges. The question of whether the cap-and-trade programme's auctioning of government-owned allowances constitutes an impermissible tax is currently before state courts. At the time of AB 32 (in 2006), the state provision was called Proposition 13, which generally requires a two-thirds legislative supermajority to enact new taxes. Because Proposition 13 never defined the word 'tax', however, courts have created exemptions including 'regulatory fees' that may be passed by a simple majority (Coghlan and Cullenward 2016). Because AB 32 passed by a simple majority, whether the cap-and-trade auction constitutes a 'tax' or a 'fee' (or some other permissible category) will determine the legality of the current auctioning of state-owned allowances that raise government revenue.

It is important to distinguish this concern from a new and related concern. After AB 32 was adopted in 2006, anti-tax activists succeeded in passing a new ballot initiative in 2010, called Proposition 26. It closed the ambiguities in Proposition 13 by broadly defining the term 'tax' (Coghlan and Cullenward 2016). After 2010, new legislation that raises taxes on any taxpayer must pass by a two-thirds legislative vote, so a two-thirds vote will probably be needed to extend cap-and-trade. There is also a dispute over whether CARB needs new authority to extend cap-and-trade after 2020 (CARB claims it does not); and if new authority is needed, a two-thirds legislative vote will be required if the state is to retain any revenue collection, which is critical to the political economy of California's entire climate policy system. After the 2016 elections the Democratic Party has two-thirds majority control of both houses in the state legislature. The issues of Proposition 13 and 26 are, despite their unfortunate complexity, of increasing importance to the political economy of state climate policy (Coghlan and Cullenward 2016).

Overall, the climate policy package is designed to increase allowance prices gradually, while gradually increasing acceptance of cap-and-trade among stakeholder groups. Key stakeholders have played crucial roles in developing the specific design elements of the cap-and-trade system to make it work in the local context. Particularly important here are the rules to channel auction proceeds into the Greenhous Gas Reduction Fund and to earmark funds for investments in green infrastructure and projects that support disadvantaged communities.

Conclusions

Californian policy-makers see their cap-and-trade system as 'leading' other jurisdictions to adopt more stringent climate policies. Efforts to create such a lead programme have to some extent affected the design of the scheme – notably, as to how the California market might link to others. The linking of the California and Québec cap-and-trade programmes has expanded the scope of the two systems. Now the goal for California's legislators and regulators is to expand the system further and include more states and provinces currently considering cap-and-trade, like Ontario.

California legislators, regulators and ENGOs see potentials for linkage, emphasizing that other states or provinces can easily copy the design that California has developed. Other states might introduce similar systems, and then link to the California cap-and-trade, to achieve maximum cost-effectiveness in carbon emissions cuts. Not all elements in linked cap-and-trade systems need to be identical, but it would be important to keep the integrity of California's offset rules intact. For instance, linkage through common offset practices would be a good option.

On the other hand, some carbon-market experts are highly sceptical of the potential for linking California's cap-and-trade system to other US states. Because California is a unique case in several respects, it is unlikely that other states in the US will be able to adopt similar systems. First, the Democratic majority in California's state legislature is very strong and stable, with a long history of championing environmental policy. This political landscape is not very common in other states, or indeed at the US federal level. Second, California has very little coal left in its energy mix, after policy reforms related to air-pollution control caused a switch from coal to natural gas (and increasingly, renewables) as the major source of electricity generation. Most other US states rely on coal for a much larger share of their power production. Third, in California, public support for ambitious climate and environmental policy is very strong and stable, which is not the case in many other states. Fourth, and perhaps most significant, California has very strong competencies in its regulatory agencies, available for developing and implementing complex and comprehensive environmental policies. No other state has such a deep administrative base, which means that no other state is likely to find it easy to copy California's approach of blending a complex cap-and-trade system with an even more complex suite of administrative policies. Indeed, California's cap-and-trade system alone has required extraordinary technical and legal expertise.

This does not mean that other states will not be able to adopt such policies, but they will need to build administrative capacity, tolerate erratic implementation or outsource the needed administrative functions to other bodies. Washington State, for example, has recently adopted a market-based approach to emission reduction that relies extensively on private standards bodies to develop implementing rules. One implication of this is that the implementing rules for future cap-and-trade systems might vary substantially (and perhaps unpredictably) on a state-by-state basis, making it very difficult to achieve deep linkages between various cap-and-trade systems. This in turn might lead to a more 'balkanized' global trading system that could erase many of the economic and environmental advantages of flexible market-based approaches to pollution control. Furthermore, according to some interviewees, the linkages to Québec (and possibly Ontario in the future) were created basically to show off politically, while the environmental effects are very modest (Interviews 9, 10, 11).

On the surface, California appears to be integrating with other systems, notably that of Québec, but our study has shown that the California cap-and-trade system has developed mostly in its own special political context in later phases of system design. Adaption of the cap-and-trade programme to local conditions and needs makes it more difficult to link with other carbon markets, since they too will have local contexts to take into account. This gives rise to questions about how emissions trading systems will achieve greater effectiveness and more cross-border trading, as many analysts have claimed and hoped. Linking carbon markets effectively and without carbon leakage can be a very challenging exercise.

While this chapter has focused on diffusion and lessons – emphasizing how the California design has diverged from other markets – it is important to recognize that, from the political perspective, the forces that have arrayed in favour of California's cap-and-trade system have viewed themselves through the lens of learning, but more in evangelical mode. They have been seeking to control emissions in California and to get others to follow, since climate change is a truly global problem and California's emissions represent less than 1 per cent of the global total. As such, this study suggests that the literature on policy learning and diffusion has focused too much on the learning process from the perspective of receivers and not enough from the perspective of senders. What is the most effective course of action for policy entrepreneurs seeking to change policies at home while also generating followers in other jurisdictions? Our study indicates that Californian policy-makers have not paid adequate attention to that question because they have designed a system that relies heavily on the unique capabilities of California and therefore is not readily replicated elsewhere.

Notes

1 This chapter represents a significantly revised version of Bang et al. (2017).
2 Except for a brief period in 1995–96 when the Republican Party had majority control of the state assembly.
3 At this writing, a similar pattern is playing out again in the United States – with likely gridlock or even reversals in environmental policy under the Trump administration and aggressive efforts in California to push ahead with even stricter rules.
4 California Health & Safety Code § 38562(c). www.leginfo.ca.gov/cgi-bin/calawquery?codesection=hsc
5 Special thanks to Danny Cullenward, who helped us understand the interplay of the backstop and insurance functions.
6 The cap-and-trade regulation specifies 13 'safe harbours' that are not considered as resource shuffling. First deliverers must report electricity deliveries to CARB with emissions calculated under the specific compliance obligations (EDF/IETA 2015).
7 See EMAC's letter to CARB on this matter in November 2013: www.arb.ca.gov/cc/capandtrade/emissionsmarketassessment/priceceiling.pdf

References

Bang, G. 2010. Energy security and climate change concerns: Triggers for energy policy change in the United States? *Energy Policy* 38 (4), 1645–1653.

Bang, G., D. G. Victor and S. Andresen. 2017. California's cap-and-trade system: Diffusion and lessons. *Global Environmental Politics* 17 (3), 12–30.

Benoit, J.-Y. and C. Côté. 2015. Essay by the Québec government on its cap-and-trade system and the western climate initiative: Origins, strengths, and advantages. *UCLA Journal of Environmental Law & Policy* 34, 42–60.

Bloomberg News. 2014. Leaked: The oil lobby's conspiracy to kill off California's climate law. www.bloomberg.com/news/articles/2014-11-25/leaked-the-oil-lobbys-conspiracy-to-kill-off-californias-climate-law accessed 19 June 2016.

Borenstein, S., J. Bushnell, F. A. Wolak and M. Zaragoza-Watkins. 2016. *Expecting the Unexpected: Emissions, Uncertainty and Environmental Market Design*. Energy Institute at Haas, Working Paper #274.

California Air Resources Board. 2016. *Assembly Bill 32 Overview*. www.arb.ca.gov/cc/ab32/ab32.htm accessed 9 March 2016.

Climatewire. 2014. Democratic leader's pitch to make carbon tax part of broader reform meets some scepticism. 21 February.

Coghlan, A. and D. Cullenward. 2016. Structural oversupply and credibility in California's carbon market. *Electricity Journal* 29, 7–14.

Cullenward, D. 2014. How California's carbon market actually works. *Bulletin of the Atomic Scientists* 70 (5), 35–44.

Cullenward, D. 2015. The limits of administrative law as regulatory oversight in linked carbon markets. *UCLA Journal of Environmental Law & Policy* 34, 1–41.

EDF/IETA. 2015. *The World's Carbon Markets: A Case Study Guide to Emissions Trading*. EDF/IETA, May.

Economic and Allocation Advisory Committee. 2010. Allocating Emissions Allowances Under a California Cap-and-Trade Program: Recommendations to the California Air Resources Board and California Environmental Protection Agency from the Economic and Allocation Advisory Committee. Report. Available at http://www.climatechange.ca.gov/eaac/documents/eaac_reports/, accessed 7 June 2017.

Houle, D., E. Lachapelle and M. Purdon. 2015. The comparative politics of sub-federal cap-and-trade: Implementing the Western Climate Initiative. *Global Environmental Politics* 15 (3), 49–73.

Howe, P. D., M. Mildenberger, J. Marlon and A. Leiserowitz. 2015. Geographic variation in opinions on climate change at state and local scales in the USA. *Nature Climate Change* 5, 596–603.

ICAP. 2017. Emissions Trading Worldwide: Status Report 2017. International Carbon Action Partnership, Available at https://icapcarbonaction.com/en/?option=com_attach&task=download&id=447, accessed 2 October 2017.

Klinsky, S. 2013. Bottom – up policy lessons emerging from the Western Climate Initiative's development challenges. *Climate Policy* 13 (2), 143–169.

Lizza, R. 2010. As the world burns: How the Senate and the White House missed their best chance to deal with climate change. *The New Yorker*. 11 October.

Paterson, M., M. Hoffmann, M. Betsill and S. Bernstein. 2014. The micro-foundations of policy diffusion toward complex global governance: An analysis of the transnational carbon emission trading network. *Comparative Political Studies* 47 (3), 420–449.

Rabe, B. 2016. The durability of carbon cap-and-trade policy. *Governance* 29 (1), 103–119.

Schmalensee, R. and R. Stavins. 2013. The SO2 allowance trading system: The ironic history of a grand policy experiment. *Journal of Economic Perspectives* 27 (1), 103–122.

Skjærseth, J. B. and J. Wettestad. 2008. *EU Emissions Trading: Initiation, Decision-making and Implementation*. Aldershot: Ashgate.

Underdal, A. 2013. Meeting common environmental challenges: The co-evolution of policies and practices. *International Environmental Agreements* 13 (1), 15–30.

Wara, M. 2014. California's energy and climate policy: A full plate but perhaps not a model. *Bulletin of the Atomic Scientists* 70 (5), 26–34.

Western States Petroleum Association. 2016. *Climate Change*. www.wspa.org/issues/climate-change accessed 19 June 2016.

Yale Program on Climate Change Communication. 2013. *Climate Change in the American Mind: Focus on California, Colorado, Ohio and Texas Report*. 2 October.

Annex: list of interviews, Sacramento and San Francisco, October 2015

Interview 1: California Democratic state senator, 13 October.

Interview 2: Legislative assistant for the California State Senate Energy, Utilities and Communications Committee, 13 October.

Interview 3: Legislative assistant for democratic state senator, 13 October.

Interview 4: Legislative assistant for democratic state senator, 13 October.

Interview 5: California Air Resources Board, 12 October.

Interview 6: California Energy Commission, 12 October.

Interview 7: California Independent System Operator, 12 October.

Interview 8: Statkraft San Francisco office representative, 14 October.

Interview 9: Legal scholar, Stanford University, 14 October.

Interview 10: Two researchers, Hoover Institute, 14 October.

Interview 11: Legal scholar, University of Berkeley, 11 October.

Interview 12: NextGen, 15 October.

Interview 13: NRDC, 15 October.

6 Tokyo's emissions trading system

Japan's first mandatory cap-and-trade scheme

Masahiko Iguchi

Introduction

This chapter examines the establishment of the Tokyo greenhouse gas emissions trading system (the Tokyo ETS) and the main internal and external shaping forces involved. Launched in 2005 and operative from 2010, this is the first city-level ETS that covers CO_2 emissions from large office buildings. It also holds significant implications for Japan's future climate policy, as the Tokyo ETS is the only mandatory cap-and-trade scheme to succeed in reducing CO_2 emissions by 23 per cent in the absence of a nationwide ETS.

There is a rich literature on the outcomes and effectiveness of the Tokyo ETS (for example, Nishida and Hua 2011; Rudolph and Kawakatsu 2012; Satou and Yamamoto 2012), but less attention has been paid to the possible causal role of international policy diffusion in shaping its properties. This chapter asks: Did Tokyo learn from the experience of other ETSs? And if so, how? How have local factors and actors influenced the policy diffusion process in the Tokyo context? The chapter also discusses the possibility of spillover effects from the Tokyo ETS to other local governments, spurred by the adoption of the Paris Agreement in December 2015, which might contribute to the creation of a nationwide ETS.

This chapter argues that while policy diffusion played a role in shaping the design properties of the Tokyo ETS, most of the process has been driven by domestic factors aimed at adapting to the internal context. First, although the EU emissions trading system (EU ETS) influenced the design of allowance allocation method under the Tokyo ETS, Tokyo avoided the problem of over-allocation by drawing on comprehensive data collected through the mandatory reporting system. Second, the Tokyo ETS is designed to be the main driver for improving energy efficiency and sets a longer compliance period. Under this system, trading can start only after the actual reductions have been made and verified by the Tokyo Metropolitan Government (TMG). Hence, the Tokyo ETS can be considered as a complementary measure, rather than as a major instrument for reducing CO_2 emissions.

Japan's ETS and its emergence

National-level climate policy

Many attempts have been made to create a general, non-legally binding framework for climate-change policy in Japan, including an Action Plan to Arrest Global

Warming (1990), the Basic Policy on Measures to Tackle Global Warming (1999) and the Outline for Promotion of Efforts to Prevent Global Warming (1998, 2002). However, these frameworks did not contain specific policy instruments to reduce greenhouse gas (GHG) emissions, and they did not create an institutional basis for an ETS. This is because Japanese climate policy has been dominated by voluntary actions by industry and business, which have generally been able to avoid direct regulation (Iguchi et al. 2015). In particular, industry and business created the Voluntary Action Plan (VAP) through the central business network 'Keidanren' in 1997, prior to Kyoto Protocol negotiations, aimed at keeping CO_2 emissions in the period from 2008–12 from industrial and energy-conservation sectors below 1990 levels.[1] Keidanren has firmly opposed a mandatory nationwide ETS on the grounds that it would harm the competitiveness of Japanese industry and that the VAP was adequate.[2]

The first nationwide cap-and-trade ETS, the Japan Voluntary Emissions Trading Scheme (JVETS), was introduced by the Ministry of the Environment (MOE) in 2005. This was a voluntary approach that aimed to support the GHG reduction activities of Japanese companies not included under the Keidanren VAP. Therefore, the JVETS was limited in scale, attracting only 288 participants by 2008 (Mochizuki 2011). In January 2008, the ministry continued to explore other design schemes for a nationwide ETS by establishing an advisory committee, which, in its interim report published in May 2008, proposed four options[3] for cap-and-trade (MOE 2008). In addition, the Japanese government started the experimental introduction of an integrated domestic market for emissions trading in October 2008 for achieving the Kyoto target, without any intentions of introducing a mandatory system.

A window of opportunity opened when the Hatoyama administration (Democratic Party of Japan, September 2009–June 2010) pledged 25 per cent reductions against 1990 levels by 2020 to the 2009 Copenhagen Accord. To deliver on this international commitment, the bill of the Basic Law on Global Warming Countermeasures was approved by the Hatoyama Cabinet on 12 March 2010. The bill proposed the establishment of a domestic emissions trading scheme and carbon tax, along with the introduction of a feed-in tariff applicable to all renewable energies, to raise the share of renewable energy in total energy supply to 10 per cent by 2020. It also led to the establishment of the Domestic Emissions Subcommittee under the Central Environment Council at the MOE in April 2010 to study various scheme designs of the domestic ETS. However, the bill was not passed in the Diet due to the resignation of the Hatoyama Cabinet following political pressures in connection with the re-location of the US Marine Corps Air Station. Since then, there has been no momentum for establishing a national ETS in Japan.

Overview and history of the Tokyo ETS

Despite the stagnant process of establishing a mandatory nationwide ETS, the TMG successfully established a cap-and-trade system in 2010. The TMG is the largest sub-national government in Japan, covering a population of more than 13 million. Tokyo emitted 63.8 million tons of carbon dioxide equivalent (tCO_2e)

in 2013 – more than Scandinavian counties such as Denmark (39 tCO_2e) or Norway (35 tCO_2e) and accounting for about 5 per cent of Japan's total emissions (TMG 2016a).

Tokyo's top two GHG emitters are the commercial and residential sectors, which have been increasing (Figure 6.1). The structure of Tokyo's GHG emissions can be characterized as a low rate in the industrial sector (accounting for less than 10 per cent), but with high rates in the commercial, residential and transport sectors.

The shaping of the Tokyo ETS took place in three stages (Ohno 2013). In the first stage (FY 2000–4), the TMG required large-scale buildings and business and commercial sectors to report their detailed emissions and reduction plans under the Tokyo CO_2 Emissions Reduction Program (CERP), introduced as part of the Tokyo Metropolitan Environmental Ordinance in 2000. Furthermore, by launching the Tokyo Green Building Program in 2002, it aimed to increase the market for energy efficiency in buildings in Tokyo. To this end, the TMG implemented a rating and reporting system for measuring the environmental performance of buildings. In 2010, it became mandatory to consider the introduction of renewable energy for buildings.

In the second stage (FY 2005), the TMG aimed to strengthen the reporting system. By revising the CERP in March 2005, it introduced a mechanism for large-scale buildings and business and commercial sectors to inform on emissions reduction plans, and it also evaluated the plans submitted. Under this system, the facilities covered were rated on a five-point scale made publicly available to encourage facilities to reduce emissions.

In the third stage (FY 2006–10), in December 2006, the TMG launched an ambitious GHG reductions target of 25 per cent below 2000 level by 2020. The

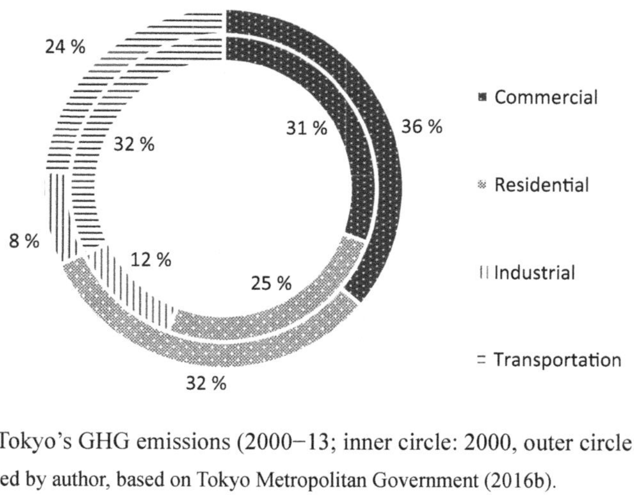

Figure 6.1 Tokyo's GHG emissions (2000–13; inner circle: 2000, outer circle: 2013)

Source: Created by author, based on Tokyo Metropolitan Government (2016b).

Table 6.1 Milestones of Tokyo's climate policy and the ETS

Stages	*Year*	*Milestones*
First stage	2000	Launch of the Tokyo CO_2 Emissions Reduction Program (CERP)
Second stage	2005	Revised CERP
Third stage	2006	Announcement of GHG reduction target of 25% below 2000 level by 2020
	2008	Creation of the Tokyo Greenhouse Gas Emissions Trading System
	2010	Launch of the Tokyo Greenhouse Gas Emissions Trading System

Source: Created by the author.

main intention here was to take leadership in climate-change policy before the national government. Although the CERP in 2000 required the targeted sectors to report and submit their emissions and reduction plans, it did not set a mandatory reduction target. As a result, the average reduction rate was only 2 per cent by 2003, which motivated Tokyo to set an ambitious reduction target. It adopted two plans (the Tokyo Climate Change Strategy and the Tokyo Metropolitan Environmental Master Plan) for setting its climate-change strategy for the next decade, which then led to the creation of the Tokyo ETS. Table 6.1 summarizes the development of the Tokyo ETS.

Explaining the turn to ETS in Tokyo

The TMG turned to emissions trading because of domestic causal factors. As noted prior, Tokyo had introduced various policies for reducing GHGs emissions to fulfil the target set under the Kyoto Protocol from 2000–6. In particular, Tokyo's GHGs reduction target of 25 per cent below 2000 level by 2020 pushed the TMG to introduce a cap-and-trade programme.

Two domestic factors were critical in enabling the TMG to introduce the ETS (see following section 'Domestic factors and actors' for details). First, Tokyo had been taking the lead in environmental policy prior to the national level, and the absence of a nationwide ETS motivated Tokyo to launch its ETS. In particular, the then-governor of the TMG, Shintaro Ishihara, strongly supported the creation of the nation's first cap-and-trade programme.

Second, the TMG possessed detailed data on GHG emissions, amounts of energy consumption and sector-wise energy-conservation performance, collected under the CERP since 2000. Drawing on this information, the TMG succeeded in convincing opposing voices and could introduce the cap-and-trade programme.

Explaining the design of the ETS

This section examines six design features of the Tokyo ETS, as outlined in Table 6.2. Design features regarding revenue earmarking will not be covered, as this is not applicable to the Tokyo case.

Type of system: nation's first mandatory cap-and-trade programme

The Tokyo ETS is the first mandatory cap-and-trade programme in Japan. It involves two compliance periods: Phase 1, from fiscal year 2010 to fiscal year 2014 that set 6–8 per cent reduction below base-year emissions; and Phase 2, from fiscal year 2015 to fiscal year 2019 that set 15–17 per cent reduction below base-year emissions. The base year is set by a covered entity which selects the average CO_2 emissions from any three consecutive years from 2002–7. As for intra-temporal safety valves, banking is allowed between two compliance periods, but borrowing is not permitted to ensure reduction ahead of schedule.

The TMG adopted this mandatory cap-and-trade programme mainly to fulfil the GHG reduction target of 25 per cent below 2000 level by 2020. As

Table 6.2 Design elements of Tokyo's ETS

Design Element	*Tokyo's ETS*
Type of system	Cap-and-trade scheme
Ambition level	25% reduction by 2020 relative to 2000 level
Allocation mechanism(s)	Grandfathering based on historical emissions
Sectors, gases and emissions covered	1. Office, commercial and public buildings 2. District heating and compliance In total about 1,300 facilities (approximately 1,000 commercial and institutional buildings and approximately 200 industrial facilities) Covers around 40% of commercial and industrial sectors' emissions
External offsets/credits/ linkages	Four types of credits: 1. Small- and Medium-sized Facility Credits 2. Outside-Tokyo Credits 3. Renewable Energy Credits 4. Saitama Credits
Monitoring, reporting and verification (MRV) and enforcement	Facilities are required to submit annual reports and emissions reduction plans verified by third party
Price management	No price controls by the TMG; in case of excessive price evolution, the TMG may increase the supply of credits available for emissions trading
Revenue earmarking	Not applicable

mentioned, the JVET, introduced by the MOE in 2005 as a *voluntary* cap-and-trade programme, aimed to support further GHGs emissions reduction activities of Japanese companies. In contrast to this stagnant climate policy at the national level, the TMG sought a stronger programme for achieving its targets. Here we can say that domestic politics influenced this design property independently.

Ambition level: formulated based on GHG reduction potentials

In 2000, Tokyo launched its independent target of 25 per cent reduction by 2020 relative to 2000 levels. The Tokyo ETS covers 20 per cent of all of Tokyo's CO_2 emissions, with base emissions set as 13.627 million tCO_2e. Since its launch in 2010, the Tokyo ETS has successfully encouraged emissions reductions. Already in March 2011, emissions had been reduced to 11.824 million tCO_2e (equivalent to a 13 per cent reduction from base-year emissions), thanks to active reduction measures taken by the facilities covered under the system (Tokyo Metropolitan Government 2012a). The crisis of the Great East Japan Earthquake in March 2011 further spurred facilities to achieve significant electricity savings. As a result, the ETS achieved a reduction to 10.636 million tCO_2e (22 per cent reduction from base-year emissions) by March 2012 and 10.267 million tCO_2e (25 per cent reduction from base-year emissions) by March 2015 (Tokyo Metropolitan Government 2013a, 2014a, 2015a, 2016c).

The reduction targets set under the Tokyo ETS were formulated with regard to the GHG reduction potentials of targeted sectors based on information gathered through the CERP.[4] Hence, the reduction targets were not influenced by policy diffusion from other ETS, but reflected a bottom-up approach.

Allocation mechanism: grandfathering, with longer compliance period

Tokyo's ETS does not employ allocation by the market (e.g. auctioning). Allocations are made by the TMG, which distributes free allowances at the beginning of each compliance period, based on grandfathering drawing on historical emissions, like the EU. Thus, Tokyo has developed its ETS here by learning from the design property of the EU ETS (see section 'Discussion' for further discussion).

However, while the EU ETS set the length of compliance period to one year, the Tokyo ETS operates with five-year periods in order to encourage long-term investment in energy conservation of the sectors targeted. Unlike the EU ETS, only the amount of allowances that exceed the reduction target is saleable, which in turn means that trading can start only after the actual reductions have been made and verified by the TMG. The amount of trade was very limited in the beginning of the first compliance period but has gradually increased (Figure 6.2).

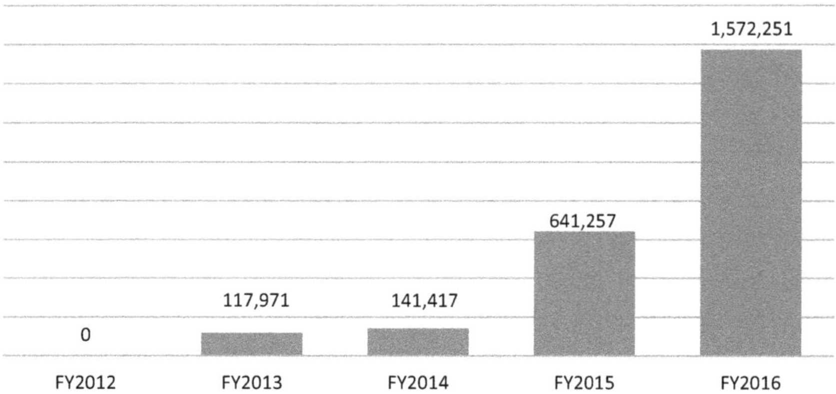

Figure 6.2 Amount of emissions trading under Tokyo's ETS (2012–16)

Source: Created by author based on Tokyo Metropolitan Government (2012b, 2013b, 2014b, 2015b, 2016d).

Sectors, gases and emissions: unique coverage of large-scale office buildings and factories

The Tokyo ETS is the world's first city-level cap-and-trade system to focus on commercial activity and end-use of energy. It covers CO_2 emissions from offices, commercial and public buildings, district heating and industrial facilities.

Sectors and gases to be targeted under the Tokyo ETS were determined on the basis of domestic factors: international policy diffusion did not influence this design property. In total, about 1,300 facilities are targeted by the Tokyo ETS, covering around 40 per cent of commercial and industrial sector emissions. Only CO_2 is targeted, reflecting the composition of most of Tokyo's GHG emissions.

Targets and rules are differentiated across sectors according to categories and differing compliance factors. Higher compliance requirements (8 per cent by 2014; 17 per cent by 2019) apply to office buildings and district and cooling plant facilities. Lower compliance requirements (6 per cent by 2014; 15 per cent by 2019) apply, *inter alia*, to office buildings, facilities with heavy use of district and cooling plants and factories.

External offsets/credits/linkages: four main domestic offsets

There are two types of credits under the Tokyo ETS. The first is excess credit, which is issued when actual annual reduction exceeds annual reduction obligation. The other involves four types of offset credits, all of which must be verified by verification agencies. The first type of offset credit is the 'Small- and Medium-Sized Facility Credits' generated from the total amount of emissions reductions from non-covered small- and mid-sized facilities in Tokyo as a result of emissions reduction measures and can be used without limit.

Second, there are the 'Outside-Tokyo Credits', generated from the total amount of emissions reductions from large facilities outside the Tokyo area as a result of emissions reduction measures. These credits can be used for compliance for up to one-third of reductions obligations.

Thirdly, 'Renewable Energy Credits' come from electricity production generated from solar, wind, geothermal, hydro or biomass under 1,000 kilowatts and can be used without limit.

Finally, the Tokyo ETS is linked with province-level ETS in Saitama. This ETS is modelled on the Tokyo ETS: the two local governments have established the 'Saitama Credits', where credits from excess emissions reductions and small- and medium-sized facility credits can be traded between the two jurisdictions.

Monitoring, reporting and verification (MRV) and enforcement: the CERP matters

Regarding the procedures used to monitor compliance, facilities are required to submit annual reports and emissions reduction plans verified by a third party. Seven GHGs are to be monitored and reported: CO_2, CH_4, N_2O, PCFs, HFCs, SF_6 and NF_3. With the mechanisms used to facilitate or enforce compliance, including penalty levels, the name of facilities will be made public and penalized by fines up to JPY 500,000 (USD 4,692), and surcharges will be imposed. In case of non-compliance with the fines, facilities are required to reduce their emissions by the amount of the shortfall multiplied by a factor of 1.3.

The MRV and enforcement arrangements under the Tokyo ETS were shaped by domestic factors. The reporting mechanism has been implemented since 2000 under the CERP. As for penalties in case of non-compliance, the JPY 500,000 fine penalty reflects the maximum amount that local governments are entitled to impose under their authority. Also, 'the amount of the shortfall multiplied by 1.3' is in line with similar arrangements under the Kyoto Protocol.

Price management

Generally, the TMG does not control carbon prices, which are determined by the market. However, the TMG attempts to prevent excessive price rises by increasing the supply of credits available for emissions trading, through measures such as increasing the small and medium-sized facility credit supply, and increasing the supply of excess credits by promoting CO_2 reduction measures. If supply remains scarce and excessive price increases are foreseen despite these measures, the eligible credits available for compliance will be expanded (Tokyo Metropolitan Government 2012c).

In December 2011, the average price of excess credit marked JYP 10,000 per tCO_2e (USD 89, when USD 1 = JPY 110) – a high level, compared to US or EU

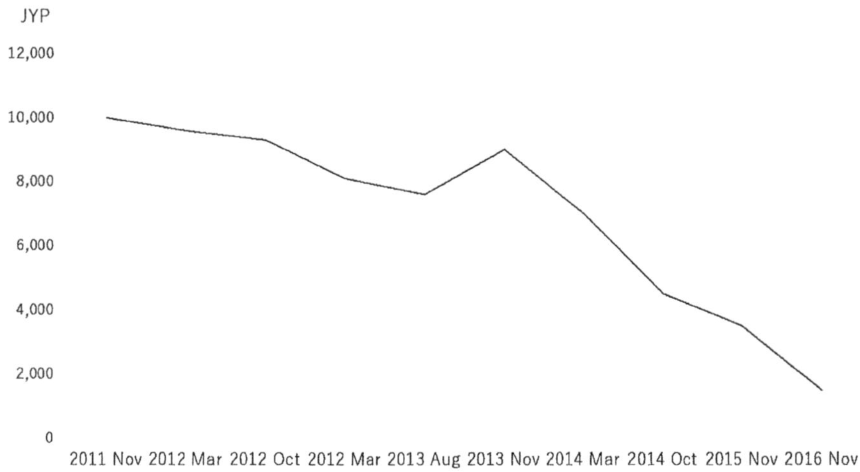

Figure 6.3 Trends of excess credit price (December 2011 to November 2016)

Source: Created by author, based on Tokyo Metropolitan Government (2014c, 2015c, 2016e).

prices. Since then, the price has been falling, as shown in Figure 6.3. The average price of excess credit in November 2016 was JPY 1,500 per tCO_2e (USD 13).

As to policy diffusion, it seems unlikely that design features of other models influenced the price management of the Tokyo ETS: the Regional Greenhouse Gas Initiative (RGGI) system in the US had a price floor, and the EU ETS had a ceiling, whereas the Tokyo ETS involves neither of these.

Discussion

The role of policy diffusion

Among the many ETSs existing today, two ETSs established prior to the Tokyo ETS influenced its design properties. They are the EU ETS, which started in 2005, and RGGI, established in 2009. According to an interview with a former TMG official who headed the formation of the Tokyo ETS, its design was developed by considering the merits and shortcomings of the EU ETS and RGGI in order to fit to the circumstances applicable to Tokyo.[5] Therefore, the aim of policy learning – rather than material factors like coercive pressures (Dolowits and Marsh 1996) or the 'California effect'[6] (Vogel 1997) – stands out as a factor more influential in shaping the design properties of the Tokyo ETS. However, the role of policy diffusion was rather limited, despite the intention to learn lessons from the EU ETS and RGGI. Most of the process was driven by domestic actors and factors, as noted earlier.

Table 6.3 compares and contrasts the basic designs of the three ETSs. Comparing the Tokyo ETS with the EU ETS, for example, we see that both employ grandfathering for the distribution of allowances. However, in contrast to the one-year compliance period of the EU ETS, Tokyo operates with a five-year period.

One reason why Tokyo opted for grandfathering and not auctioning was that Japan has never experienced emissions trading systems, and policy-makers were concerned that introducing auctioning could create heavy opposition from targeted sectors by imposing significant costs on them.[7] This contrasts with the US, where an emissions trading system was introduced as a popular policy tool for controlling air pollution and the RGGI employs auctioning as an allowance distribution method.

Another concern was the problem of over-allocation. In the case of the EU ETS, this was caused by an oversupply of emissions allowance as a result of grandfathering. This led to a low allowance price and weakened industry investments in low-carbon technology. Therefore, many were concerned about its effectiveness (Ellerman and Buchner 2008). Japanese industry was no exception. Keidanren issued a position paper opposed to the introduction of cap-and-trade, on the grounds that it would not only harm industrial competitiveness and inhibit technological innovation but also because 'the reduction effect of the EU ETS is not proved' (Keidanren 2007a, 2007b).

To these criticisms, Tokyo argued that its ETS could avoid the problem of over-allocation as the TMG had comprehensive data about GHG emissions from large-scale buildings and business and commercial sectors as a result of the mandatory reporting system under the CERP. Here the TMG emphasized the differences between the Tokyo ETS and EU ETS and held that the Tokyo system would effectively reduce GHG emissions from the targeted sectors (Tokyo Metropolitan Government 2007b, 2007c).

As mentioned, Tokyo set the compliance period of five years, much longer than the EU ETS and RGGI. According to an interview with a former policy official at TMG, this longer period was intended to encourage companies to invest in energy

Table 6.3 Tokyo ETS compared with the EU ETS and RGGI

	Tokyo ETS	*EU ETS*	*RGGI*
Length of compliance period	5 years	1 year	3 years
Allowance distribution	Grandfathering	Grandfathering (about 40% to be auctioned from 2013)	Auction
Targeted sectors	Industry and commercial sectors	Industry (e.g. power sector) Aviation included from 2012	Fossil-fuel power plants 25MW and larger

Source: Created by author.

conservation in order to meet their cap.[8] Hence, one of the distinctive characteristics of the Tokyo ETS is that it gives weight to emissions reductions through energy conservation, and the ETS is designed to be the main driver to improve energy efficiency. Its longer compliance period is intended to encourage gradual emissions reductions through energy conservation, with emissions trading seen as a complementary measure rather than as the main mechanism for reducing GHG emissions.[9] Further, while the EU ETS allows the sale of allowances before the actual reductions have been made, the Tokyo ETS allows emitters to sell allowances only after this has been achieved.

Domestic factors and actors

The role of leadership

The political leadership of Shintaro Ishihara, former governor of the Tokyo Metropolitan Government (Independent, in office from 1999 to 2012), was indispensable for the introduction of a cap-and-trade emissions trading system. Ishihara criticized the stagnation of national-level climate policy and emphasized that Tokyo could be the first model city to introduce a mandatory ETS prior to a national-level regulation. For example, in a speech in 2008, one year before Tokyo's decision to join the International Carbon Action Partnership (ICAP), he stated: 'Tokyo should participate in ICAP regardless of the intentions of the national government, so that Tokyo's participation could pressure the national government to join' (Asahi Shimbun 2008). This political leadership on the part of the TMG can be explained by its history of leading environmental policies in advance of the national government. This point will be further explored as regards path dependency in the following.

Decision-making process

In the absence of a mandatory nationwide ETS, the main decision-making process for designing the Tokyo ETS involved three 'stakeholder meetings' arranged between July 2007 and January 2008. These meetings were intended to discuss the introduction of a cap-and-trade system from the viewpoint of various stakeholders, including academia, energy companies and business organizations, consumer organizations and environmental non-governmental organizations (NGOs) (Tokyo Metropolitan Government 2007a).

What was notable about this process was that it was open to all stakeholders, in contrast to the 'iron triangles' often noted in connection with Japan's decision-making process where the dominant Liberal Democratic Party, industry and the bureaucracy form a powerful 'government-industrial complex' (Pempel and Tsunekawa 1979; Samuels 1987; Pempel 1998). By contrast, the TMG has a well-organized network with environmental NGOs and academia, with high expertise, knowledge and practical know-how to support the introduction of the Tokyo ETS

(Ohno 2013). An expert from an environmental NGO who participated in the stakeholder meetings noted that the TMG consulted with various stakeholders prior to the meetings and prepared detailed institutional arrangements in order to build consensus.[10]

Debates at the stakeholder meetings were between industry, which emphasized GHG emissions reduction through industry self-regulation, and the TMG and environmental NGOs, which argued for a mandatory cap-and-trade system (Aoki 2010). Industry strongly opposed the introduction of such a system, holding that it would harm economic activities and lead to a decline in the international competitiveness of Japanese industry (Keidanren 2007a, 2007b). Further, it maintained that grandfathering would be highly unfair to companies that had already achieved good energy efficiency, as grandfathering tends to reward historically high emitters.

Against heavy opposition from industry, the TMG insisted that the allocation of allowances would not be unfair to emitters, referring to rich data on GHG emissions collected through reporting system under the CERP. Further, environmental NGOs argued for the need for a mandatory cap-and-trade system, stressing the potential advantages for large offices and buildings. A major climate-related NGO, the Kiko Network, stated: 'We welcome Tokyo's effort to introduce a mandatory cap-and-trade system for large offices and buildings as an economic instrument to reduce GHGs, as it is not only an adequate but also a necessary measure' (Kiko network 2007).

Thus, two major factors led to the successful establishment of the Tokyo ETS. First, the TMG had strong information power to convince opposing industry that much had been gained through the reporting system under the CERP since 2000. By requiring large-scale buildings and business and commercial sectors to inform on their emissions reduction plans and by evaluating the plans submitted (and then making them publicly available), the TMG possessed detailed information on actual GHG emissions, energy consumption and the actual energy-conservation performance of each sector.

The second factor concerned the structure of Tokyo's GHG emissions by sector. As noted, some 40 per cent of Tokyo's overall emissions are from commercial sectors, with the industrial sector accounting for less than 10 per cent. Hence, the main target of the Tokyo ETS is commercial and institutional buildings, not energy-intensive industrial sectors such as power generation or steel production. In contrast to the industrial sector, which often opposes ETS introduction due to concerns about carbon leakage, commercial sectors do not have the incentives to relocate their offices outside Tokyo, as the city is home to one of the world's major international financial centres. Therefore, even though industry was deeply opposed to the introduction of cap and trade, it did not function as a 'veto player' (Tsebelis 2002). In this sense, industry did not possess strong influence over Tokyo's decision-making, unlike the case of national-level climate policy (Fisher 2004).

Path dependence, lock-in effects and shocks: history matters

Tokyo has been a leader in environment policy, especially as regards air pollution, and has introduced several regulations in advance of the national government. For example, Tokyo regulated the use of a fuel that became a source of sulphur dioxide pollution during the 1960s; it required the installation of exhaust-gas reduction devices for motor vehicles during the 1970s; and it introduced a regulation on particulate matter emissions from diesel cars in 2000.

The latest regulation successfully promoted a market for diesel particulate filter technology, thereby proving that the TMG could introduce a stringent environmental regulation before the national government did so. This city-level regulation gradually helped bring about a national-level regulation, thereby causing a spillover effect.

These successful experiences encouraged TMG policy officials to create a *mandatory* ETS in advance of the central government (Aoki 2010). In this sense, the first *voluntary* nationwide ETS established in 2005 did not influence the design of the Tokyo ETS. Tokyo launched the CERP in 2000 as the next step of its leadership in environmental policy; in 2006, it announced the target of 25 per cent CO_2 reduction below 2000 level by 2020, and it launched the Tokyo ETS from 2010.

Conclusions

This chapter has examined the effect of policy diffusion on the design of the Tokyo ETS. First, the Tokyo ETS idea caught the interest of decision-makers, as there had been no mandatory cap-and-trade system at the national level. There is a voluntary nationwide ETS established in 2005, but this is limited in scope, as it was intended to complement the GHG reduction activities of Japanese companies. TMG policy-makers were motivated to create a mandatory cap-and-trade system to limit rising CO_2 emissions based on their leadership success in environment policy.

Second, as the Tokyo ETS is a city-level cap-and-trade system, its design properties have been modified to apply to the situation in Tokyo. Notably, the Tokyo ETS is designed to be the main driver for improving energy efficiency: its long compliance period of five years has been set to encourage companies to invest in energy conservation in order to meet their cap. Emissions trading is seen more as a complementary measure, especially as allowances are accorded only after the actual reductions have been made.

Third, learning was instrumental in establishing the Tokyo ETS. However, the precise role of policy diffusion is hard to ascertain, although there was certainly the intention to learn lessons from the EU ETS and RGGI. In practice, domestic factors came to shape much of the design of the Tokyo ETS. For example, while employing the same allocation method as the EU ETS, Tokyo sought to avoid the problem of over-allocation by utilizing comprehensive data on GHG emissions from large buildings and business and commercial sectors, collected through the mandatory reporting system under the CERP.

Finally, in the domestic decision-making process, open stakeholder meetings provided the main venue for formulating the Tokyo ETS, with participation from academia, energy companies and business organizations, consumer organizations and environmental NGOs. There was a split between industry, which held that GHG reduction should be based on self-regulation, and the TMG and environmental NGOs, arguing for the introduction of mandatory cap-and-trade. This can be contrasted to the traditional Japanese climate policy-making process, where the voice of industry has been fairly strong and NGOs have had only modest influence. That the TMG has a well-organized network with environmental NGOs supporting the introduction of the emissions trading system created an environment that weakened the role of industry as a potential veto player.

Tokyo successfully established Japan's first mandatory ETS in 2010. However, the major challenge remains: to establish a national-level ETS. Several studies have examined whether the Tokyo ETS could have spillover effects to other local governments, perhaps leading the creation of a nationwide ETS (see e.g. Suzuki 2009; Aoki 2010). In fact, the Tokyo ETS did spill over to the creation of the Saitama ETS,[11] but no other local governments have created similar systems. One reason is that introducing an ETS requires considerable funding and human resources, and not all local governments can simply copy and paste the Tokyo ETS. That being said, however, mandatory reporting systems for collecting detailed data on actual GHG emissions, energy consumption and energy conservation performance are a widespread feature of local governments in Japan.

While this could be a stepping-stone for introducing a national-level ETS, there seems no critical momentum to create such a policy. In May 2016, the Japanese government launched new emissions reduction targets of 3.8 per cent by 2020 and 25.4 per cent by 2030 (both in reference to the 2005 level) and 80 per cent reduction by 2050 (no reference level). As the government had once proposed a 25 per cent reduction by 2020 in reference to 1990 levels, this indicates a significant retreat in climate policy. Furthermore, although Japan has proposed a new energy mix plan for doubling its renewable energy use between 22 and 24 per cent by 2030 (from around 10 per cent at present), fossil fuels still remain the major source of electricity generation (liquefied natural gas 27 per cent, coal 21 per cent, oil 3 per cent) (METI 2015).

According to the most recent plan for dealing with global warming, approved in May 2016 by the Abe administration (Liberal Democratic Party, December 2012–), 'the creation of a domestic emissions trading scheme will carefully be considered by taking into account of various factors, including effects on employment, trends of foreign ETS, and progress of industry's voluntary action schemes' (Cabinet of Japan 2016). This indicates that, while the introduction of a mandatory nationwide cap-and-trade system is still on the negotiating table, priority is to be given to economic conditions over the creation of a nationwide ETS.

Notes

1 The VAP reduced 12.1 per cent CO_2 emissions from the 1990 level by 2012 (Keidanren 2013). This plan was upgraded as 'Keidanren's Commitment to a Low Carbon Society' for the year 2020.
2 A survey conducted by Keidanren in September 2010 showed that 61 companies (out of 64) opposed the introduction of ETS and none favoured its introduction (Keidanren 2010).
3 All four options consider a mandatory cap-and-trade system. One option considers upstream allocation, and the other three consider downstream allocations. The details are as follows: 1) upstream allocation, which allocates allowances to produces, importers and distributors of fossil fuels; 2) downstream allocation (end-users), which allocates allowances to large users of fossil fuels and electricity; 3) downstream allocation (power companies), which allocates allowances to power companies and to other large users of fossil fuels; 4) downstream allocation (responsibility sharing), basically the same as option 2, with enterprises responsible for their emissions intensity, but with activity level treated separately.
4 Based on interview with Teruyuki Ohno, executive director, Renewable Energy Institute, Tokyo, 1 July 2016.
5 Based on interview with Teruyuki Ohno.
6 According to Vogel (1997: 561−562), the 'California effect' refers to:

> Political jurisdiction which have developed stricter product standards often force foreign procedures in nations with weaker domestic standards either to design products that meet those standards, since otherwise they will be denied access to markets. This, in turn, encouraged those producers to make the investments required to produce these new products as efficiently as possible. Moreover, having made these initial investments, they now have a stake in encouraging their home markets to strengthen their standards as well, in part because their exports already meeting those standards.

7 Ibid.
8 Based on interview with Teruyuki Ohno.
9 Based on interview with Naoyuki Yamagishi, leader of climate and energy group, WWF Japan, 29 July 2016, at WWF Tokyo Office.
10 Based on interview with Kimiko Hirata, international director, Kiko Network, 28 July 2016, at Kiko Network Tokyo Office.
11 Saitama Prefecture, which is a part of the Greater Tokyo Area, created the Saitama ETS in April 2011. The design of the ETS is identical to the Tokyo ETS, and these two ETSs are linked with each other. In 2013, Saitama ETS achieved 22 per cent emissions reductions from base year.

References

Aoki, K. 2010. On the (im)possibilities of policy diffusion of the Tokyo Metropolitan Government's cap-and-trade. *Kankyokagakushi* 23 (4), 321–331.

Asahi Shimbun. 2008. Tokyo Metoropolitan Governer Ishihara announces coordination with Europe and the US over emission trading. www.asahi.com/special/070110/TKY200803170004.html accessed 7 October 2016.

Cabinet of Japan. 2016. *Global Warming Plan (Chikyuondanka taisaku keikaku)*. Document approved by the Cabinet of Japan. May 2016.

Dolowits, D. and D. Marsh. 1996. Who learns what from whom: A review of the policy transfer literature. *Political Studies* 44, 343–357.

Ellerman, A. D. and B. Buchner. 2008. Over-allocation or abatement? A preliminary analysis of the EU ETS based on the 2005–06 emissions data. *Environmental and Resource Economics* 41, 267–287.

Fisher, D. 2004. *National Governance and the Global Climate Change Regime*. Lanham, MD: Rowman & Littlefield.

Iguchi, M., L. Alexandru and S. Andresen. 2015. Japan's climate policy: Post-Fukushima and beyond. In *The Domestic Politics of Global Climate Change: Key Actors in International Climate Cooperation*, edited by G. Bang, A. Underdal and S. Andresen, 119–140. Cheltenham: Edward Elgar.

Keidanren. 2007a. *Towards Construction of International Framework on Climate Change After the Kyoto Protocol*. Tokyo: Keidanren.

Keidanren. 2007b. *Requests on an Introduction of Tokyo's Emission Trading System*. Tokyo: Keidanren.

Keidanren. 2010. 'A Result of a Survey Conducted with Japanese Companies on an Introduction of a Nationwide Emission Trading Scheme' (in Japanese). www.keidanren.or.jp/policy/2010/081.pdf accessed 1 October 2017.

Keidanren. 2013. *Results of Fiscal 2013 Follow-up to the Voluntary Action Plan on the Environment (Summary)*. Tokyo: Keidanren.

Kiko network. 2007. *An Additional Opinion to the First Stakeholder Meeting for Tokyo's ETS*. Tokyo: Kiko network (in Japanese).

Ministry of the Economy, Trade and Industry of Japan (METI). 2015. *Japan's Electricity Market Reform*. Tokyo: METI.

Ministry of the Environment of Japan (MOE). 2008. *Approach to Japanese Emissions Trading Scheme Interim Report (Executive Summary)*. Tokyo: Ministry of the Environment, Japan.

Mochizuki, J. 2011. Assessing the designs and effectiveness of Japan's emissions trading scheme. *Climate Policy* 11 (6), 1337–1349.

Nishida, Y. and Y. Hua. 2011. Motivating stakeholders to deliver change: Tokyo's cap-and-trade program. *Building Research and Information* 39 (5), 518–533.

Ohno, T. 2013. *Energy Strategy of Local Governments: The USA and Tokyo (Jichitai no enerugi senryaku: amerika to tokyo)*. Tokyo: Iwanami.

Pempel, T. J. 1998. *Regime Shift: Comparative Dynamics of the Japanese Economy*. Ithaca, NY: Cornell University Press.

Pempel, T. and K. Tsunekawa. 1979. Corporatism without labor? The Japanese anomaly. In *Trends Toward Corporatist Intermediation*, edited by G. Lehmbruch and P. C. Schmitter, 231–270. Beverly Hills, CA: Sage.

Rudolph, S. and T. Kawakatsu. 2012. Tokyo's Greenhouse Gas Emissions Trading Scheme: A model for sustainable megacity carbon markets? *Joint Discussion Paper Series in Economics*, 77–93.

Samuels, R. 1987. *The Business of the Japanese State: Energy Markets in Comparative and Historical Perspective*. Ithaca, NY: Cornell University Press.

Satou, H. and K. Yamamoto. 2012. An evaluation of carbon dioxide emissions trading among enterprises: The Tokyo Cap and Trade Program. *Journal of Communication and Computer* 9, 1008–1020.

Suzuki, M. 2009. Outlook on climate change policy of local government: Viewing introduction process of Tokyo Emission Trading System. *Kwansei Gakuin Policy Studies Review* 11, 15–34.

Tokyo Metropolitan Government. 2007a. *List of Members to the Stakeholder Meeting Regarding to an Introduction of Tokyo ETS (in Japanese)*. Tokyo: TMG.

Tokyo Metropolitan Government. 2007b. *The Response of TMG to Questions Regarding Tokyo ETS at the Second Stakeholder Meeting (in Japanese)*. Tokyo: TMG.

Tokyo Metropolitan Government. 2007c. *Comparison Between Tokyo ETS with the EU-ETS (in Japanese)*. Tokyo: TMG.

Tokyo Metropolitan Government. 2012a. *The Tokyo Cap-and-Trade Program: Results of the First Year of Operation*. Tokyo: TMG.

Tokyo Metropolitan Government. 2012b. *Information Regarding Emissions Trading, FY 2012 (in Japanese)*. Tokyo: TMG.

Tokyo Metropolitan Government. 2012c. *Tokyo Cap-and-Trade Program for Large Facilities*. Tokyo: TMG.

Tokyo Metropolitan Government. 2013a. *The Tokyo Cap-and-Trade Program Achieved 23% Reduction in the 2nd Year*. Tokyo: TMG.

Tokyo Metropolitan Government. 2013b. *Information Regarding Emissions Trading, FY 2013 (in Japanese)*. Tokyo: TMG.

Tokyo Metropolitan Government. 2014a. *The Tokyo Cap-and-Trade Program Achieved 23% Reduction in the 3th Year*. Tokyo: TMG.

Tokyo Metropolitan Government. 2014b. *Information Regarding Emissions Trading, FY 2014 (in Japanese)*. Tokyo: TMG.

Tokyo Metropolitan Government. 2014c. *Assessment Result of Transaction Price (in Japanese)*. Tokyo: TMG.

Tokyo Metropolitan Government. 2015a. *The Tokyo Cap-and-Trade Program Achieved 23% Reduction in the 4th Year*. Tokyo: TMG.

Tokyo Metropolitan Government. 2015b. *Information Regarding Emissions Trading, FY 2015 (in Japanese)*. Tokyo: TMG.

Tokyo Metropolitan Government. 2015c. *Assessment Result of Transaction Price (in Japanese)*. Tokyo: TMG.

Tokyo Metropolitan Government. 2016a. *Final Energy Consumption and Greenhouse Gas Emissions in Tokyo (FY2013)*. Tokyo: TMG. www.kankyo.metro.tokyo.jp/en/climate/files/e2a1ae8695c1f0f9709a4249d5fbbfb3.pdf accessed 21 April 2017.

Tokyo Metropolitan Government. 2016b. *The Result of CO2 Emissions Reduction Program in FY2015 (in Japanese)*. Tokyo: TMG.

Tokyo Metropolitan Government. 2016c. *The Tokyo Cap-and-Trade Program Achieved 23% Reduction in the 5th Year*. Tokyo: TMG.

Tokyo Metropolitan Government. 2016d. *Information Regarding Emissions Trading, FY 2016 (in Japanese)*. Tokyo: TMG.

Tokyo Metropolitan Government. 2016e. *Assessment Result of Transaction Price (in Japanese)*. Tokyo: TMG.

Tsebelis, G. 2002. *Veto Players: How Political Institutions Work*. Princeton, NJ: Princeton University Press.

Vogel, D. 1997. Trading up and governing across: Transnational governance and environmental protection. *Journal of European Public Policy* 4 (4), 556–571.

7 Adopting and designing New Zealand's emissions trading scheme

Tor Håkon Jackson Inderberg, Ian Bailey and Nichola Harmer

Introduction to NZ ETS

In 2008, New Zealand introduced the New Zealand Emissions Trading Scheme (NZ ETS) as its primary instrument for reducing greenhouse gas (GHG) emissions, following a failed attempt three years earlier to introduce a carbon tax.[1] The scheme has been heralded by some as innovative and comprehensive because of the sectors covered and its inclusion of all six Kyoto gases (Bullock 2012) – but it has also been heavily criticized for failing to produce emissions reductions or to set a meaningful price on carbon emissions and for lacking a concrete national cap on emissions (Bertram and Terry 2010).

The performance of any such scheme will be strongly related to its design features. The adoption and design of the NZ ETS has been influenced, albeit modestly, by international models, on the one hand, and national domestic needs and opportunistic interests on the other. Other ETS 'models' – in particular the EU ETS and the failed Australian Carbon Pollution Reduction Scheme (CPRS) – were scrutinized during the process of formulating the NZ ETS design elements. However, the model that emerged showed appreciable differences from these 'templates' in the sectors and gases included, its approach to emissions caps and subsequent revisions to the scheme (Bertram and Terry 2010; Emissions Trading Scheme Review Panel 2011; Bullock 2012; Calel 2013; Bailey and Inderberg 2016). These features align with important characteristics of New Zealand's economy. In particular, the importance of forestry and agriculture and an unusually high share of renewables in the energy mix called for a different design from the main international model of the EU ETS. New Zealand's emissions portfolio is particularly characterized by the fact that agricultural emissions are significantly higher than those of most other developed economies and that around 80 per cent of electricity is already generated from renewable sources (New Zealand Government 2015: 42). With a population of around 4.5 million, New Zealand contributes 0.15–0.2 per cent of global emissions; however, per capita emissions place the country 12th globally, as a result of its emissions-intensive primary export industries and heavy reliance on private transport (New Zealand Government 2007a: 2). Industry groups also provided strong input into the NZ ETS's design through formal consultations. In addition, there was a change in government shortly after the scheme was adopted, making it pertinent to investigate to what degree and in which ways changes in government influenced the design of the NZ ETS.

This chapter accordingly explores the main factors that have shaped the adoption and design choices of the NZ ETS, to enable broader inferences to be drawn about the relationship between diffusion and domestic factors in the design and evolution of ETS. More specifically, the chapter addresses three questions: *why was an ETS adopted in New Zealand; what factors explain its design and evolution; and what wider lessons can be gained about interactions between diffusion and domestic influences during processes of climate policy development?*

The processes that created the shape of the NZ ETS require deeper investigation to enable more general inferences about the role of diffusion and other factors in the design of ETS and other climate policy models. The analysis is based on scrutiny of official reports, party and cabinet papers, industry reports and research documents, combined with 22 expert interviews. The interviews were conducted with five New Zealand politicians, four government officials, seven independent analysts and six industry-related experts or representatives who were involved in designing, advising or commenting on the scheme. The industry representatives represented a variety of sectors, mainly from within agriculture and forestry. Further details are provided in the Annex. While secondary documents were important for establishing data about the shape and change of the NZ ETS, the interviews provided significant information about the more informal processes that accompanied the development of the NZ ETS, the influence of different actors and the extent and nature of different international and national influences. The interviews were conducted in July and August 2015 and were semi-structured so that interviewees were asked similar questions unless there were specific aspects of the NZ ETS with which they were unfamiliar. This approach also enabled interviewees to reflect freely and to raise issues they regarded as particularly important.

We begin with overviews of diffusion and domestic influences on climate policy and events surrounding the adoption of the NZ ETS. Next, we analyse factors that shaped its adoption and main design features, paying particular attention to interactions between international and domestic influences on the initial design and evolution of the scheme. We conclude by suggesting agendas for future research on diffusion and climate policy design.

New Zealand politics and the emergence of the NZ ETS

The NZ ETS was established as New Zealand's cornerstone climate mitigation policy under the Climate Change Response (Emissions Trading) Amendment Act in September 2008 (New Zealand Government 2008). The scheme has since been amended several times, most importantly in 2009, 2011–12 and 2015–16 (with parts of the last review being postponed to 2017). From the outset the ETS stipulated single-year allowance trading and compliance periods using mostly freely allocated emissions units and surrender obligations based on historic absolute emissions. Initially, participants in the NZ ETS were required to surrender one

NZ unit for each ton of CO_2e emitted, but although the number of NZ units issued is limited, unrestricted access to international units was also permitted. This led to an ETS without a fixed national cap (Moyes 2008) and meant that the scheme did not incorporate set emissions reductions for the national jurisdiction, but instead related to New Zealand's Kyoto commitment to return emissions to 1990 levels by 2008–12 (New Zealand Government 2007a). This approach was intended to add a cost to emissions so as to promote emissions reductions via trading, rather than genuine cap-and-trade (Bertram and Terry 2010).

The 2008 legislation envisaged a gradual phasing in of sectors: forestry (2008), liquid fossil fuels (mainly transport, 2009), stationary energy and industrial processes (2010), agriculture (originally 2013, now deferred indefinitely) and waste (2013) (New Zealand Government 2007a). Phasing was based principally on the perceived feasibility of each sector entering the ETS rather than any clear prioritization in reducing emissions: the main contributors to New Zealand's emissions profile at the time were agriculture (49 per cent), energy (43 per cent) and transport (19 per cent of total emissions and 45 per cent of energy emissions) (New Zealand Government 2007a). With the change from a two-party electoral system to a proportional representative multi-party system through various reforms since 1996, a tradition of more frequent coalition governments with three-year terms had begun to emerge (Miller 2015). In November 2008, following the passage of the ETS Act the previous September with support from the Green Party, the Labour government led by Helen Clark lost the general election and was replaced by a minority coalition led by PM John Key and the National Party, with the ACT Party, Maori Party and United Future. The NZ ETS quickly became a target for revision by the National Party.

The first two revisions of the NZ ETS took place in 2009 and 2012, and a review and revision was made in 2016–17. The first revision included several transitional arrangements that reflected the new government's agenda and attempts to align the NZ ETS with the CPRS model being developed in Australia (Bullock 2012). These included: delays to the inclusion of some sectors, most notably agriculture to 2015; the creation of a 'one-for-two' measure permitting certain sectors to surrender one New Zealand Unit (NZU) for every two tons of emissions; and a NZD 25 per ton cap on NZU prices (Bullock 2012: 662f). Another significant change was to alter the basis of allowance allocations from absolute allocations based on 1990 emissions to intensity-based allocations on output measured against estimated industry averages. The 2012 revision was more notable for the government's refusal to enact changes recommended by the Emissions Trading Scheme Review Panel (2011) – a body established to provide independent advice on changes needed to meet the scheme's objectives – that transition measures should be phased out and agriculture phased in, although a recommendation to remove pre-scheduled reviews of the ETS was adopted. The most recent revision in 2016–17 ended the 'one-for-two' measure and further postponed inclusion of agriculture by defining it out of the revision in the first place.

Finally, the prices for NZUs have fluctuated somewhat. From 2010 to mid-2011, the NZU price remained close to NZD 20, but then gradually declined to under NZD 2 in 2013. Prices remained around NZD 5 in 2014 but gradually rose again to just over NZD 17 between mid-2015 to the end of 2016 (Carbon Forest Services 2017).

Explaining the adoption of the NZ ETS

As the responsibility for the future of the scheme passed from Labour to the National Party coalition just after the adoption of the act, we analyse the adoption of the scheme separately from the revisions that followed. For an overview of the major design features at the time of adoption in 2008, see Table 7.1.

Some international diffusion mechanisms had important influences on the adoption of the NZ ETS in the period leading up to adoption in 2008. In particular, *the ideational and material impacts of the Kyoto protocol* had a direct influence on adoption. This was the only material-consequences coercive mechanism found for New Zealand because failing to provide a policy response to Kyoto would not have been seen as acceptable by the international community,[2] and several interviewees involved in developing the scheme argued that Kyoto was a significant driver for adopting the ETS. Internal policy notes and official references further indicate that the international trend towards ETS added to the momentum for this solution, while other documents note reputational factors, not least the NZ ETS as being the '[f]irst domestic scheme in the world to include obligations for agriculture' (New Zealand Government 2007b: 7).

However, these international impacts extended beyond the Kyoto obligations to incorporate political and ideational influences from other ETS arrangements. As one technical expert interviewed put it: 'The EU ETS was very important because

Table 7.1 General design features of the NZ ETS in 2008

General design features	*NZ ETS at time of adoption*
Type of system	National carbon trading scheme, with a market-based price open to international allowances. No national cap.
Ambition level	Generally recognized as weak: no stated goals for quantified emissions reductions.
Allocation mechanism	Governmental allocation (grandfathering) with mostly free allocations of national emission units. International units accessible through the market.
Scope (sectors and gases)	Gradual phasing-in of the economy intended by the design (later to be delayed). All six Kyoto gases included.
Linking and external offsetting	In 2008 almost completely open to the use of international credits.
Monitoring, reporting and verification (MRV) and enforcement	Self-reporting from individual companies, with some audits.
Price management	Market based.
Revenue earmarking	None.

it proved to the world that emissions trading could work'. Additionally, although assessments of other schemes such as the EU ETS arrived at mixed conclusions about their suitability for New Zealand, the evidence suggests that participation in international networks, and in particular interaction with EU officials, helped persuade the Clark government of the overall merits of an ETS.

Although these international diffusion mechanisms played an important role, national factors and interests were also significant drivers for the adoption of an ETS. The first came from the challenges created by New Zealand's atypical emissions portfolio compared with other OECD countries, with low electricity-based emissions and high agricultural emissions. This distribution has created domestic political challenges for the NZ ETS, not least the limited scope for further decarbonization of the electricity sector, technological and economic obstacles to reducing agricultural emissions and the limited impact on global emissions of reducing New Zealand's emissions, combined with high potential economic impacts of stringent climate policies (Jiang et al. 2009).

The adoption of the NZ ETS was also significantly conditioned by other developments in domestic politics. By the time the ETS was negotiated in 2008, the Labour Party had held power for three consecutive terms under Helen Clark, and it was widely expected that Labour would lose the 2008 election. Additionally, the government had proposed a carbon tax in 2005 as its response to New Zealand's Kyoto obligation, but this had been abandoned following fierce resistance from the National Party aligned with major interest groups, who dubbed it and a previous government proposal for a research levy on agriculture emissions 'the fart tax' for including methane emissions from ruminant animals. These two factors significantly narrowed the Clark government's policy options for meeting New Zealand's Kyoto obligations (New Zealand Government 2007b) and contributed to the ETS emerging as the main candidate policy for achieving this. This pressure was intensified by the government's previous reliance 'on voluntary and informational instruments' a policy approach that allowed New Zealand's emissions to increase to 24.7 per cent above 1990 levels by 2005 (Bührs 2008: 65).

A national characteristic mentioned by several interviewees was that New Zealand's highly neoliberalized approach to economic management corresponded well with the use of market-based instruments to expedite economic and environmental reforms. This was arguably a further obstacle to the carbon tax and increased the political feasibility of an ETS. Interviewees referred to the 'Rogernomics'[3] economic reforms that began in 1984 as a starting point for far-reaching market-led restructuring and deregulation, which has since solidified into a strong preference for market-based approaches. These perspectives were particularly championed by the Treasury, a strong institutional actor supporting an ETS over a tax.

Although forestry is an international consideration under the Kyoto Protocol, we include it as a domestic characteristic because of the large potential impact of land-use activities on New Zealand's national emissions and the emissions impacts of converting land from forestry to agriculture, especially high-emissions activities such as dairying. Also connected to the adoption of the NZ ETS was keen awareness of the need for any climate policy instrument to manage other forestry issues. Discussions focused particularly on potential emissions liabilities arising from deforestation, and the climate and financial benefits from creating forestry-related credits within the ETS, with the latter becoming an important driver for the adoption of a market-based mechanism (New Zealand Government 2007a).

Other important drivers can be traced to interplays between material consequences and national characteristics. A dominant argument among interviewees was that the Kyoto target was portrayed as a significant future financial liability for New Zealand which, if unaddressed, could compromise the competitiveness of the country's specialized and trade-exposed economy. Kyoto was further presented as a burden on taxpayers if the government was forced to buy large quantities of international units. The accompanying logic was that an ETS could devolve the financial risk and incentivize abatement by pricing carbon in an open market, a view reinforced by the early inclusion of mandatory obligations for pre-1990 forests to reduce deforestation liabilities. In theory, this liability could also have been managed using a carbon tax. However, weight was added to the argument for an ETS because of another forestry-related material consequence: that New Zealand could gain financially from an ETS through the sale of afforestation credits from post-1989 forests on international markets. Allied to this was New Zealand's efficiency in key sectors, especially agriculture, and that international trading with an ETS could offer greater protection of these efficiencies. This latter argument mixes elements of protectionism with country-specific comparative advantages, although forest credits have become a potential liability for New Zealand more recently because low NZU prices have not incentivized new plantation or deterred harvesting and the conversion of forest to dairying (Luth Richter and Chambers 2014).

Summing up, the analysis indicates that international learning mechanisms created significant drivers for the establishment of an ETS. Additionally, international economic liabilities in the form of competition concerns were very evident and contributed to the adoption of a relatively weak ETS, although these are more accurately regarded as general influences rather than discrete diffusion mechanisms. However, these competitive concerns also led to the creation of an ETS with highly distinctive national characteristics, principally in response to domestic political pressures.

Explaining the specific design features of the NZ ETS

Moving from the process of adoption to pressures shaping the ETS, many of the same structural drivers are still evident, but with some changes in the level and form of influence of domestic political drivers. To help understand interactions between these factors and the political ethos affecting the NZ ETS's design features, we first identify the main actors involved in the design process. Arguably the most influential was the Treasury, through its role in the Emissions Trading Group (ETG) – the cross-government team tasked with developing proposals for the scheme's design – and other ministerial fora. The ETG was led by the Ministry for the Environment and made up of technical experts from Environment, Treasury, Economic Development, Transport and Agriculture and Forestry, but it was housed at the Treasury.

Alongside the ETG, other expert groups advising on the ETS design at a strategic or operational level included the Climate Change Leadership Forum, with high-level representation from relevant ministries and the private sector (agriculture, energy, forestry and industry), and more sector-specific groups such as the Electricity Allocation Factor Contact Group and Business Opportunities Working Group. The composition of these groups guaranteed industry strong representation and direct links to government officials and also ensured a prominent role for the Treasury in defining the goals and financial boundaries of the ETS. Divisions of opinion were also evident between the governmental departments involved in the ETS design. As might be expected, the Ministry for the Environment favoured stronger ETS design features, while Treasury and Business, Innovation and Employment advocated a more business-friendly design. The Ministry for Primary Industries manoeuvred between these camps, aiming to maximize the benefits of forest credits while protecting its sectors. The government, technical and lobby groups were nevertheless instrumental in filtering international diffusion influences through perceptions of national interest during the detailed design of the NZ ETS.

The design of the 'cap': no cap, but trade

One of the most striking examples of the filtering of international influences was the decision to construct the carbon cap differently than those of most other ETS by treating the cap and the Kyoto target as effectively one and the same, with no scheme-specific cap and only a weak link between the number of units available to emitters and national emissions targets (Bertram and Terry 2010). This and other design choices primarily reflect the adaptation of diffusion influences to improve their fit with identified national characteristics and the protection of strategic primary industries. In this case, the absence of defined caps drew strongly on the logic of the Kyoto trading design, rather than other cap-and-trade schemes like the EU ETS. Several interviewees, and in particular public officials involved in the early design process, referred to the cap design being based on 'deciding on economic first principles' (making basic strategic design choices first) and then designing features that were seen as effective and suited to New Zealand's open trading economy. Prior to 2008, a design working group had undertaken a detailed review of the EU ETS but decided that problems with the EU scheme, such as absolute cap and allocation issues, as well as major differences from the New Zealand context, meant that the EU scheme mainly 'provided examples for how not to do it'. After the limitations on the use of international allowances in the NZ ETS were imposed in 2015, it has been argued that the scheme has moved closer to a real cap, as the issuing of national NZUs will resemble a real cap (ICAP 2017). However, this issue was not discussed extensively with interviewees.

Scheme ambition: low and unspecified but aligned with Kyoto targets

Similar reasoning informed the emissions reduction ambition of the NZ ETS, which is generally regarded as low but aligned with New Zealand's Kyoto target. However, it has been accompanied by the almost complete absence of complementary measures, such as renewable energy targets, direct expenditure or other policies – reflecting the strong neoliberal ethos in the New Zealand political economy and the influence of the Treasury over ETS design. Interviewees who expressed support for the ETS tended to show a greater-than-average belief, although not outright consensus, that pricing carbon using a well-designed ETS would flow dynamically through all sectors of the economy to incentivize abatement and that there was no case for creating regulatory 'double jeopardies' through the use of complementary measures. Apart from the loose alignment with the Kyoto structure little evidence was found of diffusion influences shaping the ambition of the NZ ETS.

Allocation method: output-intensity for trade-exposed industry

Many allowances are allocated free of charge to participants based on varying rationales. Fisheries (although not mandatory participants) receive allowances based on historical emissions; owners of pre-1990 forests receive fixed free allocations; energy-intensive, trade-exposed industrial sectors receive 90 per cent free allowances based on output-intensity modelling; and moderately exposed sectors receive 60 per cent free allocation (ICAP 2016). This change occurred after the 2009 revisions, when the scheme moved from an absolute historic emissions allocation mechanism to production-based allocations. The latter allocations were based on design work completed for the Australian CPRS and were criticized by some interviewees as inappropriate for New Zealand because even comparable industries have divergent fuel sources and emissions profiles. This was the closest example of simple copying from another country, but it still caused controversy when dairying failed to qualify for free allowances based on these metrics. This was cited by several independent experts and public officials as a key factor delaying the inclusion of agricultural emissions (except energy) from the scheme.

Coverage and scope (sectors and gases): broad ambitions, modest realities

In theory, the NZ ETS has broader sector and gases coverage than any other national ETS, although its 'all-gases, all-sectors' approach has been eroded by transitional periods introduced in the 2009 revisions (Diaz-Rainey and Tulloch 2016). The initial decision to include all gases and sectors was prompted by the heavy representation of agriculture and forestry in New Zealand's emissions profile (New Zealand Government 2007b). Interviewees representing politicians, public officials and independent experts indicated that this inclusion was seen as essential to target achievement because stationary electricity is predominantly derived from renewables (New Zealand Government 2015: 42). By mid-2015 2,295 entities had surrender obligations under the scheme (ICAP 2017). While the 'all gases' approach copied the Kyoto structure, the successive delays to the inclusion of agriculture again reflect domestic sectoral lobbying about competitive material consequences created by a lack of affordable options for reducing biological emissions and the dangers of increasing production costs for low value-added, export-oriented sectors like dairying and meat.

In terms of responsibilities for reporting emissions reductions, the government's strong preference has been to place points of obligation as far 'upstream' as possible within sectors to reduce the number of entities monitored and administrative complexity/costs. Again, this reflects domestic preferences: in this case, New Zealand's first principles of ETS design and neoliberal economic discourses that have construed the Kyoto target as a financial burden and the main purpose of the ETS as providing a low-cost policy for discharging the burden. Officials confirmed that they examined the EU's target installations approach and instead opted for upstream obligations to reflect institutional preferences for administrative efficiency and because sectors like aluminium and steel consist of just one or two players. The main conflict on obligations has concerned agriculture, where the ministries again preferred upstream obligations, whereas the sector has pressed for on-farm obligations to create incentives where emissions reductions can be best achieved and rewards best recognized. This has again impeded the full inclusion of agriculture within the NZ ETS.

Offsets and linking: open then closed to international credits

Several interviewees noted that, until June 2015, the NZ ETS was almost entirely open to international credits to offset domestic emissions (although some restrictions were implemented in 2011 and 2012 to reduce 'hot air' problems and uphold the integrity of the scheme). The NZ ETS is not officially linked to other schemes, but discussions did take place with the EU and Australia to investigate linking possibilities. Additionally, prior to deciding not to ratify the Kyoto Protocol second commitment period (CP2) for 2012 to 2020, New Zealand had a stronger-than-average reliance on external offsets to discharge its international commitments, justified by the perceived lack of technically feasible and/or affordable abatement options in agriculture. Coupled with this was the opportunity for New Zealand to benefit financially from selling forestry credits overseas: again both represent domestic pressures and material consequences linked to maintaining competitiveness. The decision to close the ETS to international credits was taken in May 2015, and is attributed to New Zealand's decision not to join Kyoto CP2 (Diaz-Rainey and Tulloch 2016). Some restrictions were placed on the sale of units overseas during the transition period (legislated to end on 31 December 2012) to add robustness to the theoretical cap and informed by EU ETS design features. However, this connection is fairly notional as it excludes forest-removal credits, an issue that led to significant differences of opinion between New Zealand and the EU during discussions on linking the two schemes. In general, there are few traces of international diffusion beyond remaining open to the potential benefits of selling forestry credits abroad.

Monitoring and enforcement: drawing on experience from domestic tax reporting

Monitoring in the NZ ETS differs from that in many other schemes in that it principally involves self-reporting by target entities, with only selective third-party auditing to ensure integrity or when participants apply to use non-standard emission factors. The main justification for this mentioned by interviewees was that self-reporting works well in the New Zealand tax system and proved robust during preparatory work on emissions reporting for the carbon tax. As with point-of-obligation requirements, officials scrutinized approaches used elsewhere but preferred self-reporting, whereas interviewees maintained that the system has operated efficiently. Overall, there is little evidence of international diffusion on monitoring, reporting and verification.

Price management and revenue earmarking: price ceiling and two for the price of one

A price ceiling of NZD 25 per ton was introduced under the 2009 ETS reforms, but, to date, no price floor has been established. No other government had set a price ceiling at the time (Australia's fixed price was not adopted until 2011), so this is again attributable mainly to domestic lobbying to protect trade-exposed primary industries against upwards price risk prior to the collapse of Clean Development Mechanism (CDM) prices from 2011. A further unique price-management measure was the decision in 2009 to require stationary-energy, fossil-fuel and industrial entities to surrender only one NZU for two tons of carbon dioxide equivalent emitted. Although officially a temporary measure, this has been extended on the grounds that competitors, particularly the US and Australia, have not introduced emissions trading, even though this is a priority issue under the 2015–16 ETS review (Ministry for the Environment 2015). Additionally, while the government has maintained faith in the allocative efficiencies of a market-based instrument, the NZ ETS contains only peripheral commitments to earmarking revenues and remains the dominant policy for curbing emissions. See Table 7.2 for an overview of the most important changes in the NZ ETS design features between 2008 and 2016.

Although interviewees maintained that the main features and parameters of the ETS design were informed primarily by *sophisticated learning in response to domestic pressures* and *the material consequences of New Zealand's Kyoto target*, evidence also exists of active scrutiny and the adapted incorporation of technical features from other ETSs. Major examples of this include the emissions-conversion factors used for different sectors, which were largely borrowed from the Australian CPRS, and the design of rules for forestry to ensure their compatibility with Kyoto accounting standards.

Most design characteristics were finalized by the ministries-led ETG, but, as noted, technical discussions also involved a range of cross-sectoral groups such as: the Technical Advisory Group; Electricity Allocation Factor Contact Group;

Table 7.2 Changes in NZ ETS design features 2008–16

Design features	*NZ ETS 2008*	*NZ ETS 2016*
Type of system	National carbon trading scheme, with a market- based price open to international allowances. No national cap.	Same as for 2008, but more closed to international allowances, leading to something closer to a national cap in practice
Ambition level	Generally recognized as weak: no stated goals for quantified emissions reductions.	Generally recognized as weak: no stated goals for quantified emissions reductions.
Allocation mechanism	Governmental allocation (grandfathering) with mostly free allocations of national emission units. International units were accessible through the market.	Intensity-based allocation for trade-exposed industry (from 2009).
Scope (sectors and gases)	Gradual phasing-in of the economy intended by the design (later to be delayed). All six Kyoto gases included.	Several sectors, such as Transport and Agriculture, delayed indefinitely. All six Kyoto gases officially included.
Linking and external offsetting	Almost completely open for the use of international credits.	As of 1 June 2015 international units are not eligible for surrender in the NZ ETS due to NZ discontinuing involvement in Kyoto CP2.
MRV and enforcement	Self-reporting from individual companies, with some audits.	Same as 2008.
Price management	Market based.	Market based, but with a price ceiling of NZD 25 from 2009.
Revenue earmarking	None.	None.

Agriculture; Forestry Measurement; Stationary Energy and Industrial Processes; Transport Fuels; and Waste, representing industry sectors, ministries, local government and independent analysts. This presented affected industries with multiple opportunities to raise issues and influence technical design issues. These groups were further aided by more dynamic domestic factors, not least the election of the National Party government, who supported an ETS in principle and worked in government via the 2009, 2012 and 2016 revisions to tailor its provisions while preserving the overarching architecture of the scheme.

Discussion

So far, the analysis has indicated causes behind the adoption of an ETS and its most important design features. This section summarizes the findings and utilizes these to explore a more integrated perspective on the design of climate policy development.

The general picture is that international diffusion played a fairly modest role in the design of the NZ ETS. Diffusion influences which existed were closely scrutinized in terms of their compatibility with 'agreed first principles' of emissions trading developed by the New Zealand government. According to interviewees, designing the market proved reasonably straightforward once these principles were established and suitable cross-ministerial expertise was enlisted. The process was also facilitated by the technical competence gained from New Zealand's earlier failed carbon-tax proposal, which aided the analysis of design elements from schemes from other countries with New Zealand's circumstances and perceived national interests. Because internal expertise was appreciably controlled by the Treasury, both the first principles and the ETS were steered towards a design that emphasized cost reduction in meeting New Zealand's Kyoto target.

For these reasons, *competition* emerged as the overarching diffusion influence on the initial design and revisions of the NZ ETS, although *ideational influences* were more evident in the decision to adopt an ETS. The absence of an overall emissions cap, the ceiling price, measures allowing some sectors to surrender one NZU for every two tons of emissions and the exclusion of agricultural biological emissions all indicate divergence from other national schemes, underpinned by a defensive approach to mitigating international material consequences.

The prominence of international *material* consequences suggests that national interests and domestic politics exerted powerful conditioning effects on the design of the NZ ETS. Decisions on the adoption and timing of a market-based instrument also showed domestic political influences, not least Labour's commitment to introduce the NZ ETS before the 2008 election following the failed carbon tax and subsequent moves by the National Party government to revise the scheme in response to key constituencies in the agricultural and business sectors.

However, domestic influences appear to have extended beyond pure interest-group lobbying (Benwell 2008) to the wider processes used to determine New Zealand's national interests on climate mitigation. Interviewees frequently cited general equilibrium models of the impact of different emissions and carbon-price scenarios produced by New Zealand–based organizations such as Motu, NZIER[4] and Infometrics. This indicates sophisticated learning by officials and politicians, whereby modelling was matched with higher-level first principles, rather than design features being shaped foremost by the adaptation of design features from other schemes. Much of the shape of the NZ ETS can thus be understood in terms of 'goodness of fit' between key officials and politicians' interpretations of national interests and design features found in other ETSs (Börzel and Risse 2003). In general, *diverging goodness of fit* between domestic priorities and ETS design models prompted active sophisticated learning, leading to diverging ETS outcomes.

Party politics are also evident in the adoption and revision of the scheme, and the change in government from Labour Party to National Party corresponds well with the revisions of the scheme. Labour had invested a great deal in the original design of the 2008 version of the scheme, while the National Party had a stronger support base within agriculture and the business sector. This enabled and drove revisions, in particular in the face of the global financial crisis, to protect New Zealand's export economy by 'reducing the bite' of the NZ ETS.

Other national entities outside party politics were also important, however. The Treasury's standing was strong, especially as a result of hosting the ETG described earlier. Although the ETG was led by the Ministry for the Environment and included representation from several ministries, the Treasury had considerable influence on the scheme's design, according to many interviewees. It was also the ministry most heavily involved in direct meetings with the minister for the environment, David Parker, during the design phase, and it became something close to a veto actor in setting the premises for much of the process and the design choices that were made.

The legacy of previous political efforts on carbon pricing emerged as another important factor shaping the government's room to manoeuvre when adopting the NZ ETS. The failure to adopt the carbon tax in 2005 left the country in a situation of having ratified Kyoto, but without significant policies to reduce carbon emissions. The ETS was one of few remaining options for filling this policy vacuum. This is likely to have influenced also the National Party's decision to revise the scheme but not to abandon it altogether, despite the party's opposition to the ETS act in 2008.

The discussion thus far has examined diffusion and domestic influences on the design of the NZ ETS separately when, in reality, those designing the scheme were required to evaluate multiple factors simultaneously under changing political circumstances. Drawing the strands of the investigation together, a number of observations can be made on the extent and ways in which international diffusion and domestic factors may interact to influence the design of ETSs.

First, evidence from New Zealand suggests that international diffusion mechanisms – both learning and material consequences – are often most pronounced during initial decision-making on the adoption of emissions trading. The Kyoto Protocol targets provided a key propellant for politicians to initiate a broad-based debate on New Zealand's climate mitigation response, while the EU ETS helped engineer political space for the NZ ETS by demonstrating that GHG trading was politically and technically feasible. Such interactions also drew politicians and officials into international networks that exposed them to further dialogue on the advantages and methodologies of emissions trading. However, international diffusion still only provides a partial explanation for the adoption of the NZ ETS. Two domestic considerations appear particularly salient: the failure of the carbon-tax proposal, which narrowed the options available for the government to respond to the normative agenda of the Kyoto Protocol, and the development of economic first principles establishing strategic goals for the ETS. Whilst the first consideration is traceable to international influences insofar as developing a national climate response was critical to maintaining New Zealand's reputation as a Kyoto signatory (and, more generally, its clean, green image), the latter is indicative of efforts by the government to broaden support for an ETS by assessing its economic and social implications and offering reassurances that the scheme would not endanger key national and sectoral interests. Both were underpinned by a cultural preference for market-based approaches to economic reform whose roots can be traced to the neoliberalism of 1980s Rogernomics.

Second, the evidence supports arguments that domestic factors exerted a growing – and arguably dominant – influence on strategic decision-making about ETS design features. Although analysis of other schemes is a common feature of ETS design, the main motivation in this case was to scrutinize their fit with New Zealand's economic and emissions circumstances. This draws attention to an important analytical distinction between diffusion influences motivated by learning and those where international interactions and assessment of other ETS is motivated primarily by a desire to ensure preferred design features and calibrations do not create competitive or other disadvantages, such as problems with linking. Although both diffusion influences involve elements of learning and have the potential to lead to novel design features that might later themselves diffuse (Jordan and Huitema 2014), they involve distinctive cognitive processes. Outright learning is more strongly associated with the diffusion of knowledge and ideas and may lead to radical policy developments in the recipient country (Jordan et al. 2013). The second diffusion process can be labelled 'competitive impact assessment' and is more analogous to a corporation conducting research on competitors to safeguard markets. As such, scrutiny is oriented less towards learning about ETS design and more towards confirming or recalibrating previously made design choices and avoiding a policy miscalculation. Such diffusion forces are consequently likely to produce more cautious and bounded changes in scheme design, unless a major design disparity with implications for competitiveness or linking is identified, as a result of established preferences about the goals the policy should achieve (Jordan et al. 2003; Klingler-Vidra and Schleifer 2014). Active lesson-drawing, involving mimicking or sophisticated learning from practices that are deemed to be effective and appropriate to national circumstances, might become more prominent during the technical stages of policy development once key design parameters have been established, and less politically risky incremental changes become possible.

Alongside international and domestic political influences, a series of events provided leverage or otherwise contributed to revisions to the NZ ETS. The global financial crisis that began soon after the ETS was legislated hit New Zealand hard, giving interest groups increased leverage over revisions to the scheme's design. Equally, the weak outcome of the 2009 UN climate conference in Copenhagen sent additional signals that New Zealand should retain a cautious approach to carbon pricing. This situation was compounded in 2010 by the collapse of the proposed Australian CPRS, which closed off an important prospective link and fuelled competitiveness concerns. New Zealand and Australia have strong trade links, and many companies operate across the two countries, adding to fears that some might decide to relocate activities to Australia to avoid carbon pricing. Third, the 2010 and 2011 Christchurch earthquakes placed additional pressures on the economy, related particularly to funding reconstruction and increased insurance premiums, and further weakened arguments for repealing the transitional measures introduced during the 2009 ETS reform.

Finally, the open nature of the NZ ETS left NZU prices highly exposed to the collapse of CDM prices in 2011 (Diaz-Rainey and Tulloch 2016). Interviewees referred to this as 'unfortunate', and no obvious links were traced to modifications to the scheme. It could equally have been used as a pretext for tightening the scheme to boost NZU prices but did not appear to induce this, perhaps indicating the influence of different interest groups and path dependency in government attitudes towards climate policy vis-à-vis economic competitiveness. The effects of events are difficult to predict, but in the case of New Zealand they appear to have focused attention further towards domestic issues and suggest the need for more detailed analysis of the effects of events that run with or against the grain of mainstream political and business preferences.

These findings underscore the value of analysing the temporal dimensions of climate policy design. New Zealand's experiences lend weight to the view that greater change (and openness to diffusion) may exist during the early stages of policy experimentation when politicians and officials are more inclined to investigate promising design features from overseas and from other relevant areas of domestic policy,[5] whereas the political latitude for change diminishes as policy design and adaptation 'mature'. Although the establishment of strategic goals for the NZ ETS prior to detailed work being undertaken on its design would seem to run counter to this proposition, at that stage those developing the ETS had limited information on its possible impacts on the New Zealand economy. As work on the ETS design progressed, accumulated knowledge about impacts and increased attention to the ETS added to existing barriers to radical innovations that were regarded as contravening accepted first principles.

Finally, further understanding of how domestic and international factors interact during policy design may emerge from targeted examination of the effects of longer-term strategic and shorter-term political factors and events on diffusion processes. Broadly speaking, strategic factors such as New Zealand's emissions profile, dependent economic relationships and neoliberal traditions exerted relatively stable influences on the ETS's design, creating predictable and narrow channels of change based on 'goodness of fit' with established national characteristics. Conversely, short-term political factors and events – such as changes in government and recessionary periods – might facilitate more noticeable shifts in policy design (Bailey and Wilson 2009), although the evidence found for this study is ambivalent. Interestingly, in New Zealand these factors have usually contributed to greater introspection rather than more openness to external ideas, driven by an increased sense of vulnerability and the need to ensure design features contributed towards achieving key 'national' preferences.

Conclusions

The integrated analysis of international, domestic and temporal factors affecting the design of emissions trading explored in this chapter offers a rich understanding of the processes and patterns shaping climate policy by better reflecting the complex, disjointed and dynamic contexts faced by decision-makers and officials. We have considered domestic influences together with international diffusion, drawing attention to the importance of distinguishing between international interactions driven by learning or coercion and those motivated by 'competitive impact assessment' aimed chiefly at avoiding negative material consequences. In so doing, this chapter makes important contributions to explaining the existence of both convergent and divergent policy outcomes resulting from international interactions.

In New Zealand, coercive pressures and experiences from other countries were instrumental in creating the political latitude to adopt a market-based instrument by creating pressure to act and demonstrating the viability of the approach. However, the dominant influence over the detailed design of the NZ ETS was undoubtedly management of the potential material consequences of climate action through the establishment of New Zealand 'first principles' of emissions trading; alignment of the scheme with that of its major trading partner, Australia; and the inclusion of various transitional and other measures (including unrestricted access to international credits) aimed at lessening the economic impact of the scheme. Further, the change in government opened a way for party politics to exert a direct influence on the scheme through post-adoption revisions. At the same time, stable institutional actors, and in particular Treasury, have played a very strong role in shaping the design of the NZ ETS.

These findings indicate several potentially fruitful avenues for future research on climate policy development. First, highlighting the need to look beyond diffusion influences draws attention to the possibilities of greater mutual engagement between diffusion studies and 'goodness-of-fit' and related theories (Bailey 2002; Börzel and Risse 2003) to help explain divergences in the design of policies like emissions trading. Second, it highlights the value of temporal analysis for developing deeper understandings of how diffusion and learning interact across the strategic and technical phases of climate policy development. Third, the New Zealand case raises questions about whether ETS are in fact as complex and unfamiliar a form of policy intervention as is sometimes assumed and, thus, about the prominence of – and need for – 'learning' from other jurisdictions in its purer sense compared with learning in the sense of information gathering to avoid making excessive commitments. Many of the actors involved in developing the New Zealand ETS already had wide-ranging experience in designing regulated markets and, at a technical level at least, saw carbon markets as another not particularly major variant of this process.

Deeper investigation of the factors contributing to convergence and divergence in the processes and outcomes of climate policy design represents an important frontier in climate politics research. In this chapter, national characteristics, policy legacies, party politics, institutional actors and economic interests have all been shown to be crucial mediators of international diffusion influences. Understanding diffusion outcomes and how they differentiate between the adoption and implementation phases of policy development thus necessitates venturing beyond (or 'below') the international level and directing equal attention to tracing the longitudinal dimension of innovation journeys within domestic political arenas.

Notes

1 This chapter represents a significantly revised version of Inderberg, Harmer and Bailey (2017).
2 However, one respondent spoke of the government's 'cavalier' adoption of the Kyoto target and saw it as opening up a Pandora's box for New Zealand businesses.
3 A portmanteau term drawing parallels between economic reforms initiated in the 1980s under Minister of Finance Roger Douglas and US 'Reaganomics'.
4 New Zealand Institute of Economic Research at http://nzier.org.nz/
5 Analogies may exist here with the concept of 'innovation niches' in the multi-level transitions literature (Smith 2007).

References

Bailey, I. 2002. National adaptation to European integration: Institutional vetoes and goodness-of-fit. *European Public Policy* 9 (5), 791–811.
Bailey, I. and G. Wilson. 2009. Theorising transitional pathways in response to climate change: Technocentrism, ecocentrism, and the carbon economy. *Environment and Planning A* 41 (10), 2324–2334 (doi: 10.1068/a40342).
Bailey, I. and T. H. J. Inderberg 2016. New Zealand and climate change: What are the stakes and what can New Zealand do? *Policy Quarterly* 12 (2), 3–12.
Benwell, R. 2008. Linking as leverage: Emissions trading and the politics of climate change. *Cambridge Review of International Affairs* 21 (4), 545–556 (doi: 10.1080/09557570802452870).
Bertram, G. and S. Terry. 2010. *The Carbon Challenge: New Zealand's Emissions Trading Scheme*. Wellington: Bridget Williams Books.
Börzel, T. A. and T. Risse. 2003. Conceptualizing the domestic impact of Europe. In *The Politics of Europeanization*, edited by K. Featherstone and C. Radaelli, 57–80. Oxford: Oxford University Press.
Bührs, T. 2008. Climate change policy and New Zealand's 'national interest': The need for embedding climate change policy into a sustainable development agenda. *Political Science* 60 (1), 61–72.
Bullock, D. 2012. Emissions trading in New Zealand: Development, challenges and design. *Environmental Politics* 21 (4), 657–675.
Calel, R. 2013. Carbon markets: A historical overview. *WIREs Climate Change* 4, 107–119 (doi: 10.1002/wcc.208).
Carbon Forest Services. 2017. *New Zealand Unit (NZU) & Emission Reduction Unit (ERU) Chart*. www.carbonforestservices.co.nz/nzueru-chart.html accessed 15 May 2017.
Diaz-Rainey, I. and D. J. Tulloch. 2016. *Carbon Pricing in New Zealand's Emissions Trading Scheme*. USAEE Working Paper No. 16–255. https://papers.ssrn.com/sol3/papers.cfm?abstract_id=2759284 accessed 15 May 2017.
Emissions Trading Scheme Review Panel. 2011. *Doing New Zealand's Fair Share: Emissions Trading Scheme Review 2011: Final Report*. Wellington: Ministry for the Environment.
ICAP. 2016. *New Zealand Emissions Trading Scheme (NZ ETS), 2016*. Berlin: International Carbon Action Partnership.

ICAP. 2017. *New Zealand Emissions Trading Scheme (NZ ETS), 2017*. Berlin: International Carbon Action Partnership.

Inderberg, T. H. J., I. Bailey and N. Harmer. 2017. Designing New Zealand's emissions trading scheme. *Global Environmental Politics* 17 (3), 31–50. (doi:10.1162/GLEP_a_00414).

Jiang, N., B. Sharp and M. Sheng. 2009. New Zealand's emissions trading scheme. *New Zealand Economic Papers* 43 (1), 69–79.

Jordan, A. and D. Huitema. 2014. Innovations in climate policy: The politics of invention, diffusion, and evaluation. *Environmental Politics* 23 (5), 715–734 (doi: 10.1080/09644016.2014.923614).

Jordan, A., M. Bauer and C. Green-Pedersen. 2013. Policy dismantling. *Journal of European Public Policy* 20 (5), 795–805 (doi: 10.1080/13501763.2013.771092).

Jordan, A., R. Wurzel and A. Zito. 2003. Comparative conclusions – 'new' environmental policy instruments: An evolution or a revolution in environmental policy? *Environmental Politics* 12 (1), 201–24 (doi: 10.1080/714000667).

Klingler-Vidra, R. and P. Schleifer. 2014. Convergence more or less: Why do practices vary as they diffuse? *International Studies Review* 16, 264–274.

Luth Richter, J. and L. Chambers. 2014. Reflections and outlook for the New Zealand ETS: Must uncertain times mean uncertain measures? *Policy Quarterly* 10 (2), 57–66.

Miller, R. 2015. *Democracy in New Zealand*. Auckland: Auckland University Press.

Ministry for the Environment. 2015. *New Zealand Emissions Trading Scheme Review 2015/16. Discussion Document and Call for Written Submissions*. Wellington: New Zealand Government.

Moyes, T. E. 2008. Greenhouse gas emissions trading in New Zealand: Trailblazing comprehensive cap and trade. *Ecology and Law Quarterly* 35 (4), 911–965.

New Zealand Government. 2007a. *The Framework for a New Zealand Emissions Trading Scheme*. Wellington: Ministry of Environment and the Treasury.

New Zealand Government. 2007b. *A New Zealand Emissions Trading Scheme: Key Messages and Strategic Issues*, edited by Cabinet Policy Committee. Wellington.

New Zealand Government. 2008. *Climate Change Response (Emissions Trading) Amendment Act*. 2008 No. 85.

New Zealand Government. 2015. *Energy in New Zealand*. Wellington: Ministry of Business, Innovation and Employment.

Smith, A. 2007. Translating sustainabilities between green niches and socio-technical regimes. *Technology Analysis Strategic Management* 19 (4), 427–450.

Annex: list of anonymized interviewees

Independent expert, 14 July 2015.
Industry consultant, 15 July 2015.
Academic, 15 July 2015.
Public official, 6 July 2015.
Politician, 16 July 2015.
Independent expert, 17 July 2015.
Industry representative, 21 July 2015.
Politician, 21 July 2015.
Politician, 21 July 2015.
Politician, 22 July 2015.

Industry representative, 22 July 2015.
Industry representative, 23 July 2015.
Public official, 23 July 2015.
Public official, 23 July 2015.
Politician, 24 July 2015.
Academic, 27 July 2015.
Industry representative, 29 July 2015.
Academic, 30 July 2015.
Industry representative, 7 August 2015.
Independent commentator, 7 August 2015.
Independent expert, 12 August 2015.
Public official, 12 September 2015.

8 Australia

Domestic politics, diffusion and emissions trading design as a technical and political project

Ian Bailey and Tor Håkon Jackson Inderberg

Introduction

Australia has a long history of designing emissions trading schemes (ETS) but a far patchier one in introducing and maintaining policies for pricing greenhouse gas (GHG) emissions. Early work on an ETS began shortly after the Kyoto Protocol negotiations and continued throughout the early 2000s, albeit somewhat disjointedly as different groups vied for leadership. It took until 2009, however, before the first proposal for a national ETS, the Carbon Pollution Reduction Scheme (CPRS), was debated by the Australian parliament, and it was not until 2011 that the Carbon Pricing Mechanism (CPM) was introduced by the Labour government as part of the Clean Energy Future Package. This policy proved to be short-lived, and the CPM was repealed in 2014 by the Liberal–National Coalition (hereafter Coalition) government.

Australia's interest in emissions trading stemmed mainly from concerns about achieving its international commitments on emissions reduction[1] in ways that accommodated the needs of the country's trade-exposed and emissions-intensive economy. An ETS with international linking enabling access to Kyoto and other sources of credits was widely seen as attractive for maintaining flexibility and avoiding excessive burdens in the absence of strong mitigation actions by Australia's major trading partners, principally the US and China (Crowley 2013a). However, features of the Australian economy have severely problematized carbon pricing, including: a strong reliance on coal-based electricity generation and high exports of coal, natural gas and other minerals; significant land-use and land-use change emissions; and high per capita emissions compared with other OECD countries.

These factors have contributed to the intense politicization of climate issues in Australia and greater public debate on ETS adoption than has occurred in the European Union and other jurisdictions. Key aspects of this have included: highly adversarial party politics, with support for carbon pricing by Labour governments but more conflicting stances within the Coalition; strong lobbying against carbon pricing or individual ETS design features by generators and energy-intensive, trade-exposed industries (EITEIs); and inflammatory discussion of carbon pricing in the Australian media and society.

Australia thus represents an important case study of how diffusion and domestic forces intertwine during ETS design in resource-intensive economies where climate policy affects core commercial concerns and becomes embroiled in electoral politics. Additionally, Australia's expertise in ETS design provides opportunities to analyse the operation of diffusion and domestic factors across the political and bureaucratic branches of government. Explanations of ETS design frequently stress that greater political space for diffusion exists in the earlier stages of policy development, when governments have less experience of ETS and are more influenced by external forces and ideas, but lessens as domestic pressures and institutional processes exert more influence on policy design (see Chapter 2 of this book). However, few accounts differentiate between the outlooks of government departments and their political leaders towards diffusion and domestic influences and how these actors interact during the design of national ETS.

The main argument in the chapter is that although the politics of designing and defending an Australian ETS have been dominated by domestic factors, at the bureaucratic level ETS design has involved sustained sophisticated learning about avoiding the shortcomings of other national ETS and/or their mismatches with the Australian economy and about meeting imperatives created by domestic debates on ETS while still promoting ETS as an effective and cost-efficient mechanism for reducing emissions. The analysis is based on reviews of secondary documents and academic literature combined with interviews with politicians, government officials, industry groups and independent analysts involved in, or commenting on, Australian ETS models. Documents examined include issues papers published by the Australian Greenhouse Office; the Shergold and Garnaut I and II reviews; legislative proposals for the CPRS and CPM; analyses by the Productivity Commission, Climate Change Authority, industry and NGOs; and parliamentary papers. Semi-structured interviews were conducted in two phases: 31 interviews were completed in 2010, focusing on the CPRS; and 20 further interviews were conducted in 2015 examining the design, introduction and repeal of the CPM. The interviews targeted experts from the major government departments and agencies involved in designing the CPM, including the ex-Department of Climate Change and Energy Efficiency, Garnaut reviews, Clean Energy Regulator and Climate Change Authority, to help understand how interactions between politicians, government departments, industry, the media and other groups influenced ETS design in Australia. A breakdown of respondents by sector is provided in Table 8.1. However, because all interviews were given on the basis of anonymity and confidentiality in accordance with ethical requirements related to the political sensitivities of Australian climate politics, the names and institutional affiliations of respondents cannot be disclosed.

From appeal to repeal: the emergence and demise of emissions trading in Australia

Shortly after the conclusion of the Kyoto Protocol in late 1997, the government began work on how to meet Australia's Kyoto target by instructing the Australian Greenhouse Office (AGO)[2] to produce a series of papers setting out the issues that

Table 8.1 Profile of interviewees by sector

	Politicians	*Officials/ government regulators*	*Industry*	*Consultancy*	*Non-governmental organization (NGO)*	*Academic*	*Total*
2010	4	4	9	2	6	6	31
2015	1	8	4	2	0	5	20
Total	5	12	13	4	6	11	51

needed to be addressed, an initial ETS design and approaches to land-use change (AGO 1999a, 1999b, 1999c, 1999d). At the time, there appeared to be broad support for an ETS with international linking as a way of shielding Australia's trade-exposed sectors from competitive disadvantages if other major countries failed to introduce emissions reduction programmes. Although government support for an ETS dissipated when Prime Minister John Howard announced in 2002 that he would not ratify Kyoto, design activity continued at the state level, leading in 2003 to the introduction of the New South Wales Greenhouse Gas Abatement Scheme (NSW GGAS), a baseline-and-credit trading scheme, as the world's first legislatively based ETS for regulating GHG emissions (Zahar et al. 2013).

Work on an Australian ETS gained further momentum in 2004, when the states and territories governments, frustrated by Howard's intransigence on climate policy, formed the National Emissions Trading Task Force (NETTF) to investigate a state-led, but nationally operating, ETS. NSW Premier Bob Carr enlisted personnel involved in GGAS to the NETTF, hoping GGAS would be replicated nationally. However, issues with GGAS's baseline-and-credit approach persuaded the task force to pursue a cap-and-trade design, and it submitted its 'possible design' for a national GHG ETS in August 2006 (National Emissions Trading Taskforce 2006).

By 2006, the government was coming under growing pressure on climate policy as the new Labour leader Kevin Rudd made climate change a key point of differentiation between the parties in the run-up to the 2007 election (Bailey et al. 2012; Crowley 2013b). Howard responded by commissioning his own Prime Ministerial Task Group on Emissions Trading, led by Peter Shergold, with Martin Parkinson as its secretary. The Shergold Review's ETS design was similar to the NETTF model, convincing Parkinson that an ETS suited to Australia's economic profile had emerged and that attention should be directed towards implementing this regardless of the 2007 election result.

In a further stream of work beginning in April 2007, Rudd commissioned Ross Garnaut from the Australian National University (ANU) to conduct the first Garnaut Climate Change Review. The review was published in September 2008 and drew in expertise from ANU and other research institutions (Garnaut 2008). Garnaut's approach was to make the case that, contrary to John Howard's view, action on climate change was in Australia's national interest. The review pursued this task by examining the impacts of climate change on Australia's economic and social well-being, using economic modelling to argue that an ETS was the least-cost method of achieving climate goals while protecting competitiveness, achieving equitable burden sharing and stimulating investment (Garnaut 2008).

The Garnaut Review and NETTF involved extensive state-federal and international interactions, especially with EU and GGAS officials, but also contributed to the development of considerable domestic expertise in designing an ETS tailored to the needs of the Australian economy. However, neither the Garnaut reviews nor the NETTF or Shergold reports were legislative proposals. Rather, they discussed issues affecting Australia and options for resolving these to lay the foundations for a formal ETS legislative proposal, the Carbon Pollution Reduction Scheme (Department of Climate Change 2008a, 2008b).

Despite the lessons and technical proficiency in ETS design amassed in the preceding years, the passage of the CPRS through the House of Representatives and Senate became polarized, as industry groups and the Coalition parties attacked it on the grounds of competitive impacts, insufficient protection of resource-dependent sectors and burdens on households, while the Greens and NGOs criticized it for lack of ambition and over-generous compensation for large polluters (Bailey et al. 2012).The process also coincided with the global financial crisis, the failure of the UN Copenhagen climate conference and perceptions that Australia was pursuing an ambitious ETS when other major powers were doing nothing (Christoff 2013). This embroiled the CPRS in national political and economic issues, and although Department of Climate Change officials were examining technical design issues, political factors overshadowed the parliamentary debate. Rudd came close to brokering Coalition support for the CPRS with the opposition leader, Malcolm Turnbull, but rather than securing this, Rudd sought to drive a wedge between the Liberals (the Coalition majority party, which was divided on climate change) and Nationals (many of whom opposed an ETS) to strengthen Labour's hold on government. This backfired when Turnbull was ousted by Tony Abbott, a staunch opponent of carbon pricing. Several interviewees commented that this ensured the CPRS's downfall (Behm 2015).

Despite two rejections of the CPRS by the Senate and the removal of Kevin Rudd as prime minister by Julia Gillard, the 2010 election created a further opportunity to introduce an ETS by giving the balance of power to three independents and the Greens in the House and Senate respectively (Rootes 2011). The new Carbon Pricing Mechanism was based on the CPRS but also contained important changes, discussed in the next section. Negotiating the CPM nonetheless required various trade-offs with the Greens and independents to allow its introduction under the Clean Energy Future Act in 2011.

Linking with other ETS was always seen as essential for maintaining flexibility and reducing the cost of meeting Australia's emissions target. In August 2012, the Australian government and the European Commission released a linking proposal involving an initial one-way link that would enable Australian firms to purchase EU allowances, to be superseded in 2018 by a two-way link. Full linking required the parties to agree on several design issues, including international offsets and land-sector credits. Although the Commission recommended opening formal negotiations (European Commission 2012), the CPM continued to come under attack, with Tony Abbott declaring a 'blood oath' to repeal the scheme if the Coalition gained power in the 2013 election (Gratton and Wroe 2011). Despite Gillard's replacement as prime minister by Kevin Rudd, the Coalition won a decisive election victory, and in July 2014 Abbott repealed the CPM after he secured majority Senate support for the move (Rootes 2014).

Key elements of ETS design

Emissions trading in Australia has involved multiple streams of investigation that culminated in two linked, but not entirely continuous, legislative proposals. Table 8.2 summarizes the main design features of the CPRS and the CPM to aid comparison of individual design elements. Because the CPM evolved out of the CPRS to counteract design issues that had impeded adoption of the CPRS, the following sections do not provide separate analyses of the factors that influenced the design of each scheme. One key distinction to note, though, is that the CPRS was intended to be Australia's main instrument for emissions reduction, whereas the CPM formed part of the wider Clean Energy Future (CEF) Plan that also included: the Renewable Energy Target; the Carbon Farming Initiative; the establishment of the Clean Energy Finance Corporation; and the creation of an independent Climate Change Authority to advise government on emissions targets and other areas of climate policy (Australian Government Department of the Environment 2011; Commonwealth of Australia 2011). As such, the CPM moved Australian climate policy away from reliance on an ETS and towards a policy portfolio involving an ETS alongside a range of complementary and support measures.

Diffusion and domestic influences on ETS design

Type of system: flexibility for an uncertain world

Interview and documentary evidence indicate that the adoption of a cap-and-trade system transitioning from fixed to floating prices under the CPM reflected both diffusion and domestic influences, underpinned by the ambition to ensure the ETS met the needs of Australia's resource-dependent and trade-exposed economy. The Garnaut and NETTF teams interacted extensively with EU officials, and were facilitated in their ability to utilize ideas by the fact that their remit was to explore the case for an ETS, rather than to develop a formal legislative proposal. These dialogues provided both positive and negative lessons, as one NETTF member recalled:

> In 2005–7, there was little to go on elsewhere; just the EU ETS really, and one key thing we learned was not to prevent connections between phases by prohibiting banking and borrowing, because this truncated market development by creating artificial boundaries. Nonetheless, we weren't going to do

Table 8.2 CPRS and CPM design features

	Carbon Pollution Reduction Scheme	*Carbon Pricing Mechanism*
Type of system	Cap-and-trade with price cap until 2015 (Jotzo and Betz 2009); unlimited banking between compliance years except fixed-price permits 2011–12; short-term borrowing to ease transition costs, up to 5% of participant's obligation (Jotzo and Betz 2009).	Hybrid scheme with fixed price of AUD 23 tonne^{-1} 2012 but no cap; full cap-and-trade over 3 years via transitional phases (Lo and Spash 2012; Peel 2014); annual compliance and no banking in fixed price period (Center for Energy and Climate Solutions 2011); banking from 2015; borrowing up to 5% of emissions limit (Patay and Sartor 2012).
Ambition level	Unconditional 5% reduction from 2000 by 2020; conditional 15%–25% dependent on commitments by other countries; 60% below 2000 by 2050 (Curran 2011; Firsova et al. 2012).	Unconditional 5% reduction from 2000 by 2020; conditional 15%–25% dependent on commitments by other countries; 80% below 2000 by 2050 (Australian Government Department of the Environment 2011; Pearse 2011; Talberg and Swoboda 2013).
Coverage	75% of national emissions and all six Kyoto gases; mining, steel, aluminium, cement, plastics and chemicals sectors with agriculture from 2015; around 1,000 entities (Bailey et al. 2012).	60% national emissions and only CO_2, methane, nitrous oxide and PFCs; heavy industry, energy, fugitive emissions, implied emissions domestic aviation, maritime and rail, landfill waste (Patay and Sartor 2012); only liable entities exceeding 25,000 tons $C0_2e$; around 377 entities.
Allocation mechanisms	Free allocation up to 95% for some energy-intensive trade-exposed industries (aluminium, iron and steel, cement); otherwise auctioning, with fixed price of AUD 10 tonne^{-1} of CO_2e in first year (2011–12) (Curran 2011)	Free allowances up to 94.5% of emissions for strongly trade-exposed sectors, 66% moderately exposed sectors (aluminium, steel, pulp and paper, glass, cement, petrol refining). Calculated on industry average baselines, declining 1.3% annually (Talberg and Swoboda 2013; Peel 2014).
Offsetting and linking	One-sided international linkages with unlimited purchases of Clean Development Mechanism (CDM) and Joint Implementation (JI) units. Export of Australian units prohibited (Jotzo and Betz 2009).	No international credits until flexible pricing; carbon offsets from farming up to 5% of obligation up to 2015, unlimited thereafter; 12.5% obligation from CDM and JI; negotiations on EU link and interest in other links (Commonwealth of Australia 2012; Redmond and Convery 2014).

(*Continued*)

Table 8.2 (Continued)

	Carbon Pollution Reduction Scheme	*Carbon Pricing Mechanism*
Reporting and verification		Climate Change Authority: strategic advice on targets and CPM design; Clean Energy Regulator: allocation, auctioning, monitoring, reporting, verification and disbursement of funds (Peel 2014); penalties 1.3x permit price, rising to 2x; Productivity Commission: review assistance and actions by other countries (CoA 2011).
Price management	Price cap 2010–15, starting at AUD 40 tonne^{-1} CO_2e, increasing 5% per year to AUD 51 by 2015. Sale of additional permits at fixed price to relax cap if necessary to reduce business costs (Jotzo and Betz 2009).	Fixed-price phase AUD 23 (indexed); market price from 1 July 2014; price ceiling AUD 20 above international price in fixed price, rising 5% annually; no price floor in flexible price period; ceiling removal in floating price phase.
Revenue earmarking	Direct financial assistance to coal-fired power sector; compensation for 5.3 million low- and middle-income households (Firsova et al. 2012).	50% of income earmarked for Household Assistance Package; 90% households; household payments for energy efficiency (CoA 2011); support for export exposed industries and investment in low carbon technologies (Center for Energy and Climate Solutions 2011) via Jobs and Competitiveness Program; energy-efficiency support for small firms; Energy Security Fund Coal-Fired Generators Assistance.

> baseline-and-credit. We'd learned its weaknesses from GGAS, but we did like the EU's cap-and-trade approach.

The type of system nevertheless also showed strong domestic influences. For example, Garnaut recommended a hybrid and flexible system to 'accommodate uncertainty over the shape of post-2012 international climate change arrangements' (Peel 2014: 437), while the fixed-price period was intended to 'allow firms to become familiar with the scheme and to establish and test the necessary institutional and administrative infrastructure' (Peel 2014: 439). However, while these arrangements partly aimed to familiarize industry with the CPM's technicalities, they also sought to diffuse industry and Coalition criticisms of industry's financial exposure by providing clarity about immediate liabilities while allowing price adjustment if the initial fixed price exceeded prices in other countries.

Ambition level: horizon scanning to remain respectably towards the back of the pack

The ambition levels of the CPM and the CPRS were unambiguously the product of domestic political processes, although indirect diffusion – or, more accurately, general consideration of developments in the international climate negotiations and other countries during target setting – can be identified where policy-makers drew on analyses of other national climate programmes and Australia's abatement opportunities. The 5–15 per cent target range showed consistency with modelling in the final Garnaut Review, which indicated that 'the expected economic costs of reductions within that range were likely to be modest' (Department of Climate Change 2008b: 4–16). The range was intended to signal Australia's willingness to work towards an ambitious global agreement as confidence increased that deep cuts in emissions were consistent with continuing economic growth. However, bipartisan support for a target from Labour and the Coalition was needed to provide a foundation for action, notwithstanding disagreements on methods for achieving the target (Climate Institute 2013). The main dissenting voice came from the Greens, who had opposed the CPRS for locking Australia into a 'weak' 5 per cent target. No progress was made between the government and the Greens on targets during the CPM negotiations; however, because the government wanted quick passage for the CEF Bill before the 2013 election, the issue was circumvented by adopting the AUD 23 initial fixed price. As several interviewees argued, 'the fixed price was relatively uncontroversial because it gave industry price certainty during a bedding-in period – until the EU ETS price dropped below the CPM price', although others argued that the 5–15 per cent target 'won few friends'.

Sectors and gases covered: everything with exceptions

The sector and GHG coverage of the CPRS and CPM can be attributed largely to domestic factors, not least Prime Minister Rudd's ambition to seal his political legacy by developing the world's 'best' emissions trading scheme (Behm 2015). This encouraged Rudd to differentiate himself from both the Howard government on climate change and the EU's approach of including only carbon dioxide and large emitters from fewer sectors in the first phase. However, the broad coverage of the CPRS and CPM also recognized that land-use change formed a major element of Australia's emissions and abatement portfolio: according to the 2006 GHG inventory, methane and nitrous oxide from livestock and cropping accounted for 16 per cent of national emissions (Department of Climate Change 2006). The government nevertheless recognized the complexities of reducing agricultural emissions and deferred its inclusion until 2015, with a final decision in 2013. The main external interaction here was with New Zealand, where agriculture again formed a prominent part of its ETS. Land use also featured during linking negotiations with the EU ETS and is discussed shortly.

The CPM's more modest GHG coverage reflects political constraints on gaining support for a revised ETS model, but there was little evidence of the same factors influencing sector coverage, except for modification of the approach to transport fuels (Utz 2011). Concessions instead mainly took the form of additional assistance to fugitive emissions from 'gassy' coal mines, liquid natural gas projects, steel manufacturers and stationary energy, particularly lignite generation. More generally, diffusion influences were characterized by politically directed learning from other ETSs, whereby officials scrutinized the provisions of other schemes but politicians made final decisions on issues like sector and gas coverage to meet domestic political goals. In the case of the CPRS, this was dominated by Rudd's aspiration to develop an ambitious ETS, and for the Gillard government a desire to fast-track the CPM legislation in the hope of embedding it prior to the 2013 election.

Allocation mechanisms: transparency and trade-offs

The CPM allocation mechanisms owe their existence chiefly to domestic negotiations to make the CEF acceptable to affected industries but their development was supported by analysis of the EU's allocation system. As one official recalled:

> We looked at the EU ETS to assess how fundamental design features worked in practice. The pilot phase provided good lessons on what could happen with over-allocation and disconnected phases. We did also look at RGGI; principally it made us conscious of the need to understand the effects of allocations on price.

The main focus of these analyses was nevertheless on informing the management of domestic stakeholder concerns. As Behm (2015: 176) notes, 'we appreciated fully that the carbon price would impose yet another cost on industries that were struggling with a high exchange rate, high labour costs, declining productivity, lack of scale and strong international competition'. Circumstances, however, differed between sectors: aluminium smelting faced a bleak future regardless of carbon pricing, but the same was not true for steel. Officials argued that the government worked hard to compensate the steel sector, and representatives reciprocated by being 'entirely professional in their dealings with the government' (Behm 2015). However, some minerals producers took a more combative stance, with some engagements being: 'snide, supercilious or aggressive . . . to the point of offence', with attempts 'to use bluster to extort subsidies and concessions' (Behm 2015: 178–179). Either way, the main communication channels for finalizing allocation mechanisms and other transitional measures were between industry executives, ministers and chiefs of staff, with departmental officials then liaising to flesh out more detailed mechanisms.

Departmental interviewees stressed: 'we were clear throughout about levels of assistance and how design arrangements interacted across the scheme'. Another key principle was transparency, because secrecy would have damaged government – industry relations and undermined the task of reducing emissions. This was acknowledged as risky if it gave groups advocating stronger policy opportunities to accuse the government of weakness – but it helped promote constructive discussions and persuade the Greens to support the design and then work for tighter measures rather than derailing the CPM. Officials claimed that industry was also comfortable with the way assistance measures were communicated because it gave clearer information than they had received for the EU ETS,

> which made statements like '100 per cent free allocation', but when one trawled through the detail, it was up to 100 per cent with a range of conditions, so the headline statement wasn't transparent. We were up-front about having two tiers of free allocations based on emissions intensity and trade exposure of 66 per cent and 94.5 per cent. Industry could relate to that because everything was up-front and transparent.
>
> (interview, government official)

Although the CPM's allocation mechanisms were heavily influenced by domestic political interactions, the Productivity Commission, Garnaut and officials also scanned mechanisms in other countries to estimate relative burdens and abatement achieved in addition to the scrutiny of the EU ETS mentioned earlier. However, the Productivity Commission only considered electricity generation and transport and did not analyse specific allocation or assistance mechanisms (Productivity Commission 2011). In contrast, there was limited scrutiny of the New Zealand Emissions Trading Scheme (NZ ETS) because Australia was ahead of New Zealand on many issues – New Zealand instead took its industry assistance model from Australia. Another internal quasi-diffusion influence stemmed from the involvement of officials who designed the NSW GGAS, although interviewees again noted that 'the GGAS provided mainly cautionary tales on allocation and industry assistance'.

External offsetting and linking: looking over the neighbour's fence

According to one senior government official interviewed, 'offsetting and international linking was always essential to Australia. There was an almost philosophical belief here that an international market was needed to make ETS fulfil their potential. Carbon was no different to any other commodity in this regard'. A second motivation for allowing international units was to create safety valves for industry, but interviewees maintained that 'the first driver always dominated because, over time, Australian carbon prices would align with international prices'. Accessing international units nevertheless exposed the CPM to the rules and procedures of the CDM and JI. This prompted Garnaut to follow the EU in recommending limits on international offsets to encourage simplicity and investor confidence (Garnaut 2008). Some of the reasons for this followed a similar logic to the EU ETS and, thus, indicate diffusion influences, notably the desire to protect the integrity of the market mechanism from doubtful international credits. At the same time, allowing credible offsets to shield industry and households from cost shocks was crucial to maintaining the CPM's political credibility following its turbulent inception, while another more blatantly domestic motivation for restricting offsets was to stimulate interest in Australia's large potential supply of domestic offsets generated by the Carbon Farming Initiative.

Another cost-mitigation factor underpinning the desire to link with other ETS, according to one interviewee, was the 'lumpiness' of Australia's carbon profile and the fact 'Australia needed to replace 30–40 per cent of its energy infrastructure over the next decade because most existing capacity was near the end of its working life' (interview, consultant). Linking and international offsets were both seen as smoothing this transition. The focus of linking activity between 2011 and 2012 was with the EU ETS, although discussions were also held with New Zealand. As mentioned earlier, the intention was to establish an initial one-way agreement that would allow Australian entities to purchase European Union Allowances (EUAs) and to buy Kyoto Certified Emissions Reductions (CERs) up to 12.5 per cent of each entity's obligation, supported by a CPM floor price calculated as a weighted average of CER prices (up to the 12.5 per cent limit) and prevailing EUA prices. The second phase of two-way linking required removal of the Australian floor price because this did not exist in the EU scheme. Some economists preferred to retain the floor price to maintain incentives, but it became a *quid pro quo* for the linking agreement. Linking, by definition, necessitates scrutiny of partner schemes to address inconsistencies that might hinder trades or scheme integrity. The respective sizes of the schemes meant Australia would, in effect, adopt the EU price. Australia is often a price-taker in international trading, but 'this still prompted a small sovereignty debate, though it soon faded away because all parties wanted the flexibility and cost-effectiveness that linking offered' (interview, official).

The Department of Climate Change completed extensive studies of the EU ETS to support the negotiations, but interviewees denied this was dominated by one-way learning or attempted harmonization. Rather, they emphasized mutual learning and checking for inconsistencies that might have impeded linking. For example, Commission officials visited Australia to examine the GGAS: this was a baseline-and-credit scheme rather than cap-and-trade, but it preceded the EU ETS, and EU officials were keen to learn from Australian experiences. Equally, during the talks, the two parties engaged in mutual exchanges of information. However, these were again described as 'looking over each other's fences to see how their ETS worked, so learning from each other'. The key aspects of the CPM were seen by Australian officials as 'pretty textbook', and the main challenges for linking were how to manage electricity prices and assistance for EITEIs. Officials described the CPM as being designed with linking in mind but not as the primary influence.

A major domestic motivation for linking was to reassure companies that they would not have to pay appreciably more than international permit prices. Among other things, this encouraged adoption of the initial CPM fixed price to create broad parity with EUA prices. However, when EUA prices plunged in 2012, the government was inundated with complaints that Australian companies were paying AUD 23 per ton, whereas EU firms were paying AUD 8 per ton (Koch et al. 2014). This strengthened the case for linking to align CPM prices with EUA prices, but 'it also fuelled controversy about the idea of emissions caps in other countries dictating Australian prices. This was a difficult idea to defend against opposition and media campaigning' (interview, official; see also Crowley 2013a, 2013b; Rootes 2014). Another discussion involved how linking would affect industry lobbying for compensation. Officials noted that "trans-national companies would compare schemes and petition their governments if they identified discrepancies in compensation levels or rules. Advance cooperation on the terms and levels of compensation was therefore essential'.

The linking discussions ran smoothly because the EU saw that the CPM was well managed and compatible with the EU ETS on caps, assistance and most other features. However, the EU was uneasy about linking with New Zealand, or about Australia linking with New Zealand (creating an indirect link between New Zealand and the EU), because of New Zealand's approach to land use and access to international credits. The EU also had reservations about links between the Carbon Farming Initiative (CFI) and the CPM because the EU ETS does not accept land-based credits. However, they were satisfied the CFI had strong governance and that it was only a small part of the CPM and did not compromise the EU ETS.

Summing up, the negotiations show clear diffusion influences motivated by the economic and risk-management advantages of linking the CPM with the world's largest carbon market. The chief aim of these interactions was to clarify how the CPM would need to be adjusted in areas like industry assistance and price management; as such, compatibility rather than out-and-out learning provided the major lens for analysing the EU ETS. Equally, rather than unidirectional influence, the linking talks represented the latest stage of longstanding dialogue between the EU and Australia in which learning from Australia was also an important feature. As interviewees also argued:

> Two schemes catering for different emissions profiles and levels of trade exposure would never adopt the same designs. Pressure for harmonization might increase if linking becomes more widespread globally, but the critical factors for both sides were that the schemes were sufficiently compatible to allow linking and both were well governed.

Monitoring, reporting and verification (MRV): home-grown expertise

Australia developed significant expertise and infrastructure for MRV prior to the adoption of the CPM; hence, its systems have been shaped largely by domestic technical considerations. Monitoring and reporting of emissions and abatement action became mandatory for participants in Australia's voluntary Greenhouse Challenge and Greenhouse Challenge Plus programmes from 1995 onward, and in 2007 the National Greenhouse & Energy Reporting (NGER) scheme was introduced as part of preparations for the CPRS. As one government regulator noted: 'we had excellent reporting systems already, so were well prepared, but the main lesson we gained from Europe was the problems of not having well-established MRV before the scheme started operating'. The NGER continues to be overseen by the Clean Energy Regulator despite the repeal of the CPM (International Energy Agency 2016). One industry regulator reported that some industries regard the NGER as having onerous data requirements but that it produces reliable figures and offers a robust approach to establishing baselines and targets. Although NGER uses a similar downstream obligation to the EU ETS (requiring each liable entity to report emissions annually; Clean Energy Regulator 2016), no evidence of diffusion was found. For instance, the Garnaut reviews made no reference to methods for reporting business emissions.

Price management: fixed risk, floating risk

The decision to establish an initial fixed price of AUD 23 per ton was chiefly the result of domestic political factors. The only other country to establish comparable price management measures at the time was New Zealand, which introduced a NZD 25 ceiling price in 2009 (Bailey and Jackson Inderberg 2016).[3] According to one commentator, the fixed price owes its existence to two factors:

> The government's desire to reassure industry about their financial exposure and defuse the Coalition's attacks on the CPM by setting a fixed price that mirrored EU ETS prices; and bridging disagreements with the Greens over targets by offering an initial fixed carbon price until the CPM matured.[4]

The first rationale backfired because Gillard had promised, prior to the 2010 election, that there would be 'no carbon tax under any government I lead', although she claimed she was always clear about introducing carbon pricing. However, she then appeared to concede that it was a tax, an 'admission' that enabled the Coalition and media to brand Gillard a liar even prior to the collapse of EUA prices. According to one consultant, 'this sealed the fate of both the CPM and the Gillard government'.

These experiences underscore the importance of party politics and institutional opportunity structures to ETS design in Australia. Turning first to institutional structures, Australia's bicameral parliamentary system meant the CPM required support from both parliamentary chambers and gave the Greens an important veto in the Senate. This was a credible threat because the Greens had already rejected the CPRS in 2009. The government therefore faced the choice between compromising on targets – further alienating industry and the Coalition – fixed pricing, or another defeat on carbon pricing. In contrast, the Coalition could not defeat the

CPM in the Senate, despite holding 34 out of 76 seats, because Labour and the Greens held 31 and 9 seats, respectively. These negotiations also illustrate the influence of party politics on price management because, without inter-party compromises, the chances of gaining approval for the CEF were greatly reduced. Whether the fixed-floating price transition reflected only domestic political factors is less clear, given the motivation for mitigating competitive risks; nevertheless, there is little to indicate anything other than internal political debates about indirect diffusion pressures.

Revenue earmarking: money can't buy you love

Revenue earmarking was an area where the CPM deviated markedly in scale and scope from the CPRS and other national ETSs. Although the CPRS and CPM both earmarked revenue for industry assistance, 50 per cent of the CPM's expected AUD 9 billion annual revenue was allocated to the Household Assistance Package in response to concerns about the material implications of carbon pricing for Australia's resource-dependent and trade-exposed sectors and discontent with the CPM among large portions of the Australian electorate (Meng, Siriwardana and McNeill 2013).

Criticisms by the Coalition increased pressure on the government to provide reassurances about the financial implications of the CPM, both to defend the legislation and to mitigate damage to the minority Labour government. As one interviewee stressed:

> Intensive stakeholder engagement had secured industry acceptance of the principles and levels of transitional assistance to be provided. However, industry was equally happy to support repeal given the opportunity and to use this as leverage to extract more concessions.
>
> (interview, consultant)

Any agreement, therefore, remained fragile amid public opposition to the CPM stoked by media attacks. One official nevertheless recalled how the government used revenue earmarking extensively to reduce the financial impact of the CPM for households: 'the department was instructed to track the implications of different carbon prices for each household category in Australia and then to scour every element of the tax system to identify all plausible assistance opportunities'. Although another expert described the Household Assistance Package as an 'outstanding exercise in equity', the same official conceded that it failed to improve public approval of the CPM because the government opted not to link the package to the CPM, given the latter's political toxicity, and instead presented it as a tax gift to boost the government's kudos with the electorate. In so doing, ministers missed a critical opportunity to refocus public debate on climate change and how an ETS reduced the costs of climate action. Either way, domestic factors linked to curbing the material and political fallout of carbon pricing formed the primary influence over revenue earmarking in the CPM.

Discussion

Drawing together the analysis, diffusion and domestic factors both influenced the design of emissions trading in Australia, but to differing degrees at different stages. Diffusion influences tended to be more prominent during the early stages of ETS development, with the Kyoto Protocol and its flexibility mechanisms providing the initial impetus for debates on an ETS as an adaptable and cost-effective way of meeting emissions targets. Further diffusion influences were evident throughout the preliminary design work on an Australian ETS 'model'. The NETTF and Garnaut reviews both incorporated scrutiny of the EU ETS and, to a lesser extent, RGGI, the NZ ETS and the NSW GGAS to inform internal discussions on ETS design technicalities and to build faith in the political feasibility of an Australian ETS.

Lesson-drawing during this period nevertheless centred to a significant degree on critical assessment of the suitability of ETS design features for Australia's energy-intensive sectors, particularly allocation mechanisms, industry and household assistance and international linking. As such, domestic political concerns about the economic consequences of an ETS featured strongly from the outset, prompting high levels of sophisticated learning and the modification or rejection of design features employed in other ETSs. Domestic influences continued to gain ascendancy during the development of the CPRS and CPM proposals, where party politics and political opportunity structures were critical in shaping government thinking and in enabling industry and media actors to lobby for the rejection or amendment of design features. The polarization of Australian climate politics, combined with constraints imposed by Australia's bicameral parliamentary system, left the government with little choice but to adapt targets, price management, allocation, assistance and offsetting to appease domestic political, business and public audiences. This often involved offering concessions to one group that antagonized others – leaving the schemes, in the words of one government interviewee, 'friendless in every quarter', but for contrasting reasons.

Although this tells a familiar story of diminishing openness to diffusion as policy development encounters political exigencies, a leading advisor on Australian climate policy suggested that international factors remained marginal throughout. He argued that economic modelling formed the mainstay of the Garnaut reviews, followed by domestic political-economy factors and lesson-drawing from previous experiences with carbon pricing in Australia. In contrast, domestic political-economy factors drove government decision-making, followed by past experiences with carbon pricing in Australia (again, indicating domestic political-economy stimuli) and economic modelling – but in both cases, international factors were least influential. The explanation for this was that the media and public profile of carbon pricing (Bailey et al. 2012; Christoff 2013; Crowley 2013a) meant the chief task for politicians was to make the scheme acceptable to key veto players and opinion shapers in Australian society. This in turn required advisory groups and government departments to ensure proposals responded first and foremost to domestic political pressures.

Müller and Slominski (2016) consequently argue that federal policy-makers used learning from other schemes strategically to facilitate the introduction of an Australian ETS, using lessons to enhance argumentative power vis-à-vis other stakeholders as much as to identify legislative designs that might expedite the policy process. Accordingly, learning was selective, as policy-makers acted on politically opportune lessons but avoided those involving high political costs. This was especially evident in the rejection of EU ETS design features, such as its approach to allocation and price management, and the CPM's innovative household assistance package, a feature not found in the EU ETS. As one official noted, this was essential because 'Australia isn't Europe and the European scheme isn't working'.

However, the evidence also suggests that diffusion operated somewhat differently between the political and bureaucratic branches of the Australian government. The challenge for politicians was to secure the CPM legislation without further damaging a vulnerable government by utilizing every political device available to improve the CPM's acceptability to industry and the electorate. Officials were answerable to their ministerial leads, and responded to their priorities, but, in keeping with conventions of political neutrality (Behm 2015), directed their attention towards finding technical solutions to political obstacles. This encouraged scrutiny of other schemes alongside economic modelling to assess the appropriateness of different design features and calibrations. This was especially pronounced during preparatory work for the CPRS and the CPM, but evidence exists of external scrutiny occurring throughout the history of ETS design in Australia. Concurrently, the expertise in ETS design accumulated since 1998 meant that review teams had less need to learn from other schemes in an absolute sense. For example, a senior official involved in the EU linking negotiations described the relationship with EU officials as one of 'co-equals working to detect and address design incompatibilities that might obstruct linking rather than one dominated by the transfer of ideas by one or other party'. Either way, the emphasis of officials and independent analysts remained on finding technical solutions to political obstacles to the CPM, acting as an ETS epistemic community advising government on design issues (Haas 1992).

In contrast, politicians evaluated and applied lessons from other ETSs more tactically. Despite Kevin Rudd's attempts to frame Australian climate change as a 'great social, economic and moral challenge' (Rudd 2008), it became apparent that addressing distributive issues was critical to countering political and stakeholder opposition, and learning was oriented towards this goal. Critical examples of this included the adoption of an initial fixed allowance price, targeted provisions for EITEIs and the decision not to squander political gains from the Household Assistance Package by publicizing its links to the CPM. As such, politicians' openness to, and interpretation of, ETS design possibilities from both internal and diffusion-related processes falls closer to Müller and Slominski's (2016) description of how learning from other ETSs informed the development of emissions trading in Australia.

However, Australian politicians were keenly aware of technical design lessons communicated by officials and advisory bodies and showed high comprehension of how individual features worked and might be used to address political challenges. Instead, the impression was of a symbiotic (although not always consensual) learning relationship between the political and bureaucratic branches of government, but with the two sets of actors applying lessons to suit their respective priorities. Experts and officials engaged in extensive technical learning from internal and external sources, to inform evaluations of their potential to address functionality or acceptability issues – whereas politicians' learning centred on using ETS design ideas to solve domestic political obstacles to the CPM and risks to the government from other political parties, industry, the media and the electorate. One critical lesson from the Australian case, therefore, is that what appears in policy may not always fully reflect the nature of learning processes accompanying ETS design and policy development.

Conclusions

Australia represents an important case study of factors shaping the design of emissions trading schemes in resource-intensive economies, where pricing carbon affects key economic interests and provokes strong lobbying and political and public debates. Alongside its standalone interest, therefore, Australia provides useful hints on how the politics of designing ETS may unfold in other carbon-profligate countries, such as the US and Canada, where national ETSs have yet to be introduced but where media coverage, public opinion and party politics are likely to have a bearing on whether, and in what form, emissions trading takes root.

The design – if not the operation – of ETS in Australia has a lengthy history, with early design work taking place concurrently with the negotiation of the EU ETS. The main triggers for this were undeniably international: Australia's participation in the Kyoto negotiations and a 'broad but shallow' consensus that pricing and trading carbon in flexible national and international markets offered the best prospects for meeting international commitments while protecting the country's resource-intensive, export-oriented sectors. Such factors contributed to keen interest by the NETTF and Garnaut teams in ETS design features in other jurisdictions, but, given the challenges facing Australia, a critical feature of such interactions was scrutiny of the appropriateness of design features for the Australian context.

These assessments produced sophisticated learning about ETS design, expressed in outright rejection of design features (annual compliance); adoption but in modified form (transitional assistance for energy-intensive, trade-exposed industries); and/or the introduction of features not found in other ETSs (household assistance and floor prices prior to the EU linking negotiations). Throughout much of this period, Australia also had few international comparisons – the EU ETS and, to an extent, RGGI and the New Zealand scheme – but it did have a domestic scheme, the GGAS, from which to gather lessons.

The preparatory investigations also contributed to the accumulation of significant expertise in ETS design within Australia, with experts moving between organizations as new initiatives emerged. Although this diminished the need for pure learning, the incentives for evaluating design features used in other jurisdictions to demonstrate the cost-effectiveness and equity of Australian ETS models intensified during the CPRS and CPM debates and EU linking negotiations. The Garnaut and 2011 Productivity Commission reviews had both an international and a domestic focus, but with a shared imperative of limiting the economic impacts on energy generators, EITEIs and households to assist the government in navigating political wrangling over climate policy.

In addition to producing distinctively Australian ETS innovations, the need to manage external and internal pressures arguably produced different learning orientations among department officials and independent analysts compared with government ministers. International (and domestic) interactions by officials were primarily concerned with technical evaluations and the refinement of design features to meet the government's objectives of linking and promoting equity. In contrast, ministers viewed design issues through more overtly domestic lenses, assessing lessons for their potential to enhance the government's reputation and limit the political damage arising from adopting an ETS. Although politicians ultimately determined the design features that were adopted, interactions with their overseas counterparts and their officials (acting as 'learning intermediaries') also contributed to significant technical learning by ministers about ETS design features that aided assessment of the implications of different design choices. In addition to providing glimpses of the complexity of identifying sources of influence on ETS design, the inevitability of political influence in how lessons are interpreted and applied provides grounds for arguing that divergence and co-evolution of ETS design are likely to be major features of international policy diffusion (Simmons et al. 2006; Underdal 2013).

If international linking becomes more widespread, this may provide impetus for greater idea-sharing and convergence between schemes. However, there is reason to believe this will occur mainly between more mature schemes where greater mutual trust in scheme integrity exists. Evidence from Australia indicates that path dependencies resulting from the need to accommodate domestic institutional and political demands will mean that international interactions will be characterized by reciprocal scrutiny to identify and address design inconsistencies but that significant diversity will persist in the goals and construction of carbon markets.

Notes

1 In the Kyoto Protocol, Australia committed to return its emissions to 108 per cent of 1990 levels by 2008–12. Although Australia did not ratify Kyoto until 2007, John Howard's Coalition government always maintained that it would achieve its Kyoto target. Australia's current target is to reduce emissions to 5 per cent below 2005 levels by 2020 (Australian Government 2012).

2 The government agency established in 1998 to manage national greenhouse gas abatement programs.

3 This price ceiling is largely notional because NZ ETS prices have rarely exceeded NZD 18.

4 Another part of the deal was independent scrutiny of emissions caps by the Climate Change Authority once the CPM was operating and its effects had become clearer.

References

AGO. 1999a. *National Emissions Trading: Establishing the Boundaries, Discussion Paper 1*. Canberra: AGO.

AGO. 1999b. *National Emissions Trading: Issuing the Permits, Discussion Paper 2*. Canberra: AGO.

AGO. 1999c. *National Emissions Trading: Crediting the Carbon, Discussion Paper 3*. Canberra: AGO.

AGO. 1999d. *National Emissions Trading: Designing the Market, Discussion Paper 4*. Canberra: AGO.

Australian Government. 2012. *Ministerial Statement: Securing a Clean Energy Future, Chapter 5: Supporting Energy Markets*. www.budget.gov.au/2012-13/content/ministerial_statements/climate/html/climate_change-06.htm accessed 15 May 2017.

Australian Government Department of the Environment. 2011. *The Clean Energy Future Plan and the CFI*. www.climatechange.gov.au/reducing-carbon/carbon-farming-initiative/carbon-farming-initiative-handbook/clean-energy-future accessed 15 May 2017.

Bailey, I., I. MacGill, R. Passey and H. Compston. 2012. The fall (and rise) of carbon pricing in Australia: A political strategy analysis of the Carbon Pollution Reduction Scheme. *Environmental Politics* 31 (5), 691–711 (doi: 10.1080/09644016.2012.705066).

Bailey, I. and T. H. Jackson Inderberg. 2016. New Zealand and climate change: What are the stakes and what can New Zealand do? *Political Quarterly* 12 (2), 3–12. http://apo.org.au/files/Resource/i_bailey_nz_and_climate_change_pq_may_2015.pdf accessed 15 May 2017.

Behm, A. 2015. *No Minister: So You Want to Be a Chief of Staff?* Melbourne: Melbourne University Press.

Center for Energy and Climate Solutions. 2011. *Australia's Carbon Pricing Mechanism*. www.c2es.org/docUploads/Australia_Pricing_Mechanism.pdf accessed 15 May 2017.

Christoff, P. 2013. Climate discourse complexes, national climate regimes and Australian climate policy. *Australian Journal of Politics and History* 59 (3), 349–367 (doi: 10.1111/ajph.12020).

Clean Energy Regulator. 2016. *About the National Greenhouse and Energy Reporting Scheme*. www.cleanenergyregulator.gov.au/NGER/About-the-National-Greenhouse-and-Energy-Reporting-scheme accessed 15 May 2017.

Climate Institute. 2013. *Coalition Commitments to 5–25 per cent Emissions Reduction Targets*. www.climateinstitute.org.au/verve/_resources/TCI_MediaBrief_Coalitiontargets_5September2013.pdf accessed 15 May 2017.

Commonwealth of Australia. 2011. *Securing a Clean Energy Future: The Australian Government's Climate Change Plan*. www.acci.asn.au/Files/Government-Carbon-Tax-Plan accessed 15 May 2017.

Crowley, K. 2013a. Pricing carbon: The politics of climate policy in Australia. *Wiley Interdisciplinary Reviews: Climate Change* 4 (6), 603–613 (doi: 10.1002/wcc.239).

Crowley, K. 2013b. Irresistible force? Achieving carbon pricing in Australia. *Australian Journal of Politics and History* 59 (3), 368–381 (doi: 10.1111/ajph.12021).

Curran, G. 2011. Modernising climate policy in Australia: Climate narratives and the undoing of a prime minister. *Environment and Planning C: Government & Policy* 29 (6), 1004–1017 (doi: 10.1068/c10217).

Department of Climate Change. 2006. *National Greenhouse Gas Inventory*. Canberra: Department of Climate Change.

Department of Climate Change. 2008a. *Public Consultations Carbon Pollution Reduction Scheme Green Paper*. Canberra: Department of Climate Change.

Department of Climate Change. 2008b. *Carbon Pollution Reduction Scheme: Australia's Low Pollution Future*. Canberra: Department of Climate Change.

European Commission. 2012. *Australia and European Commission Agree on Pathway Towards Fully Linking Emissions Trading Systems*. http://ec.europa.eu/clima/news/articles/news_2012082801_en.htm accessed 15 May 2017.

Firsova, A., V. Strezov and R. Taplin. 2012. After 20 years of creating Australian climate policy: Was the proposed Carbon Pollution Reduction Scheme a change in direction? *Australasian Journal of Environmental Management* 19 (1), 21–34 (doi: 10.1080/14486563.2011.646751).

Garnaut, R. 2008. *The Garnaut Climate Change Review*. Cambridge: Cambridge University Press.

Garnaut, R. 2011. *The Garnaut Review 2011: Australia in the Global Response to Climate Change*. Port Melbourne: Cambridge University Press.

Gratton, M. and D. Wroe. 2011. *Abbott's Blood Oath to Repeal Carbon Tax*. www.smh.com.au/national/abbotts-blood-oath-to-repeal-carbon-tax-20111012-1ll80.html accessed 15 May 2017.

Haas, P. 1992. Epistemic communities and international policy coordination. *International Organization* 46 (1), 1–35 (doi: 10.1017/S0020818300001442).

International Energy Agency. 2016. *National Greenhouse & Energy Reporting System (NGERS)*. www.iea.org/policiesandmeasures/pams/australia/name-24097-en.php accessed 15 May 2017.

Jotzo, F. and R. Betz. 2009. Australia's Emissions Trading Scheme: Opportunities and obstacles for linking. *Climate Policy* 9 (4), 402–414 (doi: 10.3763/cpol.2009.0624).

Koch, N., S. Fuss, G. Grosjean and O. Edenhofer. 2014. Causes of the EU ETS price drop: Recession, CDM, renewable policies or a bit of everything? – New evidence. *Energy Policy* 73, 676–685 (doi: 10.1016/j.enpol.2014.06.024).

Lo, A. Y. and C. Spash. 2012. How green is your scheme? Greenhouse gas control the Australian way. *Energy Policy* 50, 150–153 (doi: 10.1016/j.enpol.2012.07.052).

Meng, S., M. Siriwardana and J. McNeill. 2013. The environmental and economic impact of the carbon tax in Australia. *Environmental and Resource Economics* 54 (3), 313–332 (doi: 10.1007/s10640-012-9600-4).

Müller, P. and P. Slominski. 2016. *Strategic Experimentation with GHG Emission Trading in Australia*. COST/INOGOV workshop, 'The Global Turn to Greenhouse Gas Emissions Trading: Experiments, Innovation, Actors, Drivers and Consequences', 8–9 February, University of Leuven.

National Emissions Trading Taskforce. 2006. *Possible Design for a National Greenhouse Gas Emissions Trading Scheme*. Canberra: Government of Australia.

Patay, M. and O. Sartor. 2012. *Australia's Clean Energy Future Package: How Does It Compare with the EU's Approach?* Institute for Climate Economics. www.cdcclimat.com/IMG/pdf/12-05_climate_brief_15_-_ets_australia.pdf accessed 15 May 2017.

Pearse, G. 2011. The climate movement: Australia's patrons of climate change activism. *The Monthly Essay*. www.themonthly.com.au/issue/2011/september/1316399650/guy-pearse/climate-movement accessed 15 May 2017.

Peel, J. 2014. Australian Carbon Pricing Mechanism: Promise and pitfalls on the pathway to a clean energy future. *Minnesota Journal of Science and Technology*, 15 (1), 429–467. http://conservancy.umn.edu/handle/11299/162654 accessed 15 May 2016.

Productivity Commission. 2011. *Carbon Emission Policies in Key Economies: Productivity Commission Research Report*. Melbourne: Commonwealth of Australia.

Redmond, L. and F. Convery. 2014. The global carbon market-mechanism landscape: Pre and post 2020 perspectives. *Climate Policy*, 15 (5), 1–23 (doi: 10.1080/14693062.2014.965126).

Rootes, C. 2011. Denied, deferred, triumphant? Climate change, carbon trading and the Greens in the Australian federal election of 21 August 2010. *Environmental Politics* 20 (3), 410–417 (doi: 10.1080/09644016.2011.573363).

Rootes, C. 2014. A referendum on the carbon tax? The 2013 Australian election, the Greens, and the environment. *Environmental Politics* 23 (1), 166–173 (doi: 10.1080/09644016.2014.878088).

Rudd, K. 2008. *Building a Better World Together*. Speech at Kyoto University 9 June 2008. http://pmtranscripts.dpmc.gov.au/release/transcript-15955 accessed 15 May 2017.

Simmons, B., F. Dobbin and G. Garrett. 2006. Introduction: The international diffusion of liberalism. *International Organization* 60 (4), 781–810 (doi: 10.1017/S0020818306060267).

Talberg, A. and K. Swoboda. 2013. *Emissions Trading Schemes Around the World*. Parliament of Australia. www.aph.gov.au/About_Parliament/Parliamentary_Departments/Parliamentary_Library/pubs/BN/2012-2013/EmissionsTradingSchemes accessed 15 May 2017.

Underdal, A. 2013. Meeting common environmental challenges: The co-evolution of policies and practices. *International Environmental Agreements*, 13 (1), 15–30 (doi: 10.1007/s10784-012-9203-0).

Utz, C. 2011. *Carbon Price, Carbon Copy? What's the Difference Between the Carbon Price Mechanism and the CPRS?* www.lexology.com/library/detail.aspx?g=2e909ce2-dc36-4048-bc08-31cd67a8785c accessed 15 May 2017.

Zahar, A., J. Peel and L. Godden. 2013. *Australian Climate Law in Context*. Port Melbourne: Cambridge University Press.

9 South Korea

East Asian pioneer learning from the EU

Katja Biedenkopf and Jørgen Wettestad

Introduction

This chapter analyses the most prominent greenhouse gas (GHG) emissions trading system (ETS) in Asia besides China: that of South Korea. The EU ETS has been important as a benchmark and source of lessons, but domestic factors have played a dominant role in shaping several unique features of the South Korean ETS. Understanding the specific circumstances of South Korea's economy, industry structure and energy market can help explain a policy design and implementation that includes not only elements from other ETSs but also several unique features tailored to the local context and politics. Some specific design decisions resemble the Chinese GHG ETS pilot projects and China's plan for a national system. These similarities are grounded in similar domestic factors such as government-controlled electricity prices. Given these shared circumstances and South Korea's pioneering role in East Asia, the South Korean GHG ETS could develop into a model for an East Asian variant of greenhouse gas emissions trading, inspiring other countries in the region. Trilateral ETS collaboration amongst South Korea, China and Japan has been initiated but is still in its infancy.[1]

South Korea has undergone a tremendous and rapid economic transformation in recent decades, making it an important case for understanding the design and implementation of ETS and climate policy in general. South Korea is amongst the top 10 global GHG emitters from fossil-fuel use, with a 1.7 per cent share of global emissions in 2015 (Olivier et al. 2016: 33). It also is a crucial case for analysing the transfer and adoption of GHG ETS as a policy tool, since it was the first East Asian country to adopt a nationwide system. The South Korean carbon market is the second largest after the EU, at least until China launches its national GHG ETS. It has some unique features, not least its comprehensive scope that includes a wide range of sectors and GHGs. Further, it covers direct emissions as well as indirect emissions arising from the use of electricity and heat. The allowance price has been amongst the highest globally, but some volatility must be noted. Although the South Korean carbon price might suggest a relatively ambitious system, some observers deem the current cap insufficient to reach the country's established GHG emissions reduction target (Interview 11). Low levels of trading and delaying strategies instead of investment in low-carbon technology appear to hamper the carbon market's functioning.

Although domestic factors can arguably provide the main explanation for the adoption and design of the South Korean ETS, external factors should not be ignored. South Korea's rapid industrialization and growth in emissions, combined with the desire to be a respected member of the international community, led to pressures to make climate change–related commitments. The GHG ETS is the main policy tool for achieving South Korea's internationally proclaimed climate-change mitigation targets. Inspiration and learning from the EU's experience with GHG emissions trading, and to a lesser extent from other jurisdictions, have been important in the technical design and implementation of the South Korean system. This chapter examines this interaction amongst South Korean and external actors and ETS models.

We draw on various sources of information. Twenty expert interviews were conducted with South Korean and European experts involved in the design and implementation of the South Korean GHG ETS. A first set of interviews was conducted during a research stay in Seoul in October 2013, followed by a second one in January 2017. Policy documents, academic studies and news reports from sources such as *Carbon Pulse* provided additional insights for our qualitative investigation of external and domestic drivers of eight design elements of the South Korean ETS.

The South Korean ETS and its emergence

In the 1997 Kyoto Protocol, South Korea was defined as a non-Annex I country, which meant that ratification was not accompanied by any emissions reduction obligations. In the ensuing decades, South Korean GHG emissions grew rapidly conjointly with the country's economic growth. With the developed countries' GHG emissions increasing only slightly or declining during the same period, South Korea joined the group of major GHG-emitting countries. That resulted in growing international pressure to act on climate mitigation.

An important development in this regard was President Lee Myung-bak's launch of the Low Carbon, Green Growth Strategy in 2008. One year later, South Korea made its first (voluntary) international climate pledge, aiming at a 30 per cent reduction of GHG emissions below the business-as-usual (BaU) scenario by 2020. The 2010 Framework Act on Low Carbon, Green Growth enshrined this target in domestic law and also provided the foundations for adopting a GHG ETS. The framework law requires large emitters and energy consumers to report their GHG emissions and energy consumption every year. For this purpose, the GHG Inventory and Research Centre (GIR) was established in 2010.

The Low Carbon, Green Growth Act outlined three options for climate-change mitigation: a GHG-Energy Target Management System (TMS), a carbon tax and a GHG ETS. While a carbon tax was never seriously deliberated, a TMS was implemented and preceded the development of South Korea's ETS. In November 2012, the Enforcement Decree on Allocation and Trading for Greenhouse Gas Emissions Allowances Act (ETS Act) was adopted, and in January 2015 South Korea launched its ETS.

The Target Management System can be seen as a precursor and preparatory exercise for the GHG ETS. Implemented in 2012, it has similarities with an ETS, since it introduced an infrastructure for the measurement, reporting and verification (MRV) of GHG emissions and set emissions targets; however, it lacked the allowance-trading element of an ETS. Installations that emitted more than 20 $ktCO_2e$ per year or consumed more than 90 TJ per year were required to submit their annual GHG emissions and energy consumption data to GIR. Business entities were categorized into seven sectors. Each entity was assigned a reduction target for the subsequent year based on grandfathering. It was calculated on the basis of the entity's average emissions in the previous three years. At first, this method was retained for the GHG ETS, with a few exceptions. Covered entities were required to submit implementation reports, to be verified by third parties. The governance structure of the TMS initially built the basis for the GHG ETS (Bloomberg New Energy Finance 2013: 3; Kim and Lim 2014: 85; Park and Hong 2014: 74).

In 2012, the South Korean Parliament adopted the ETS Act with a large cross-party majority. President Lee Myung-bak strongly supported its adoption. However, the act was not uncontroversial: fierce resistance came from the Ministry of Knowledge Economy (in 2013, renamed the Ministry of Trade, Industry and Energy) and from business groups. The main criticisms concerned increased costs and loss of international competitiveness. The GHG ETS, it was argued, would raise the costs of production for South Korean manufacturers in an international context in which major competitors, in particular China and the US, have no comparable national regulation (Bloomberg New Energy Finance 2013: 6; Hermanns 2015: 119). Despite this opposition, the GHG ETS was adopted, but some concessions were made – most importantly, the start was postponed from 2013 to January 2015.

The system has an overarching cap, which is based on a BaU forecast. This overall cap is broken down into sectoral caps – a unique feature of the South Korean GHG ETS. Three phases have been determined so far, the first two running for three years and the third for five years: 2015–17, 2018–20 and 2021–25. The initial economy-wide ambition level was to reduce GHG emissions by 30 per cent below the BaU scenario by 2020. However, South Korea's Nationally Determined Contribution (NDC) to the international Paris Agreement on climate change sets a 37 per cent reduction target below the BaU scenario by 2030, which is now considered the guiding target also for the GHG ETS. During the first trading phase, allowances were allocated for free, with the phasing-in of auctioning of 3 per cent of the allowances planned for the second phase and 10 per cent in the third phase.

Initially, the Ministry of Environment was the lead administration guiding the implementation process and drafting the implementation rules of the South Korean ETS. The Ministry of Strategy and Finance hosted the Emissions Allowance Allocation Committee, but the Ministry of Environment was the competent authority in charge of managing the general ETS process (Park and Hong 2014: 75) (Interview 10). Coordination between the two ministries proved challenging

Table 9.1 ETS design elements of the South Korean ETS

	South Korean ETS
Type of system	Cap-and-trade Phase 1: 2015–17 Phase 2: 2018–20 Phase 3: 2021–25 Banking allowed; borrowing within (but not between) phases
Ambition level	By 2020: 30% below BaU (no longer actively pursued) By 2030: 37% below BaU (536 $MtCO_2e$). This represents a 22% reduction below 2012 GHG emissions
Allocation mechanisms	Initially 100% free allocation, based on grandfathering Gradually phase in benchmarking from 2018 Gradually a limited auctioning from 2018
Coverage	5 sectors, 23 industries: 1. Power combustion-energy (power combustion-energy) 2. Industrial processes (mining, food and beverages, textile, wood, paper, oil refining, petrochemical, glass ceramics, cement, steel, nonferrous metals, machinery, semiconductor, display, electricity, electronics, motor vehicle, shipbuilding) 3. Public waste materials (water service, waste materials) 4. Building sectors (building, communications) 5. Transportation (aviation) Approximately 525 large emitter companies in the power and several energy-intensive industry sectors Six GHGs: CO_2, CH_4, N_2O, PFCs, HFCs, SF_6 Includes both direct and indirect emissions; indirect emissions come mainly from the building sector
Offsetting	Max 10% offsets; only domestic: qualitative restrictions No international credits in phase 1 (max. 5% in later phases)
MRV (monitoring, reporting and verification)	Annual reports, verified by a third party Governmental registry If an entity fails to comply with the obligation to surrender emissions permits, it shall return emissions permits that are left over or pay penalty surcharges (three times the market price within the scope of 100,00 KRW per tCO_2e).
Price and quantity management	Allocation Committee (Ministry of Strategy and Finance): The Allocation Committee may decide to implement market stabilization measures in the following cases: 1. The market allowance price of six consecutive months is at least three times higher than the average price of the two previous years. 2. The market allowance price of the last month is at least twice the average price of two previous years and the average trading volume of the last month is at least twice the volume of the same month of the two previous years. 3. The average market allowance price of a given month is smaller than 40% of the average price of the two previous years. In 2015 and 2016, the price threshold is KRW 10,000 (EUR 7).
Revenue earmarking	Revenues to contribute to Low Carbon Green Fund (being established)

Source: Most of the information is based on ICAP (2017a).

(Interviews 2, 3). In June 2016, lead responsibility was shifted to the Ministry of Strategy and Finance, and overall coordination was downgraded from the president's office to the Office for Government Policy Coordination at the prime minister's office (Carbon Pulse 2016a).

In the course of 2016 and 2017, the South Korean allowance price rose to the highest of all global GHG ETS, apparently due to the very low degree of trading and market liquidity. In early 2015 when the ETS started, the allowance price was just above 7,800 Korean Won (KRW) (approx. EUR 6.30); it remained unchanged until June 2016, when it doubled. After a continued slow but steady increase in the second half of 2016, the allowance price peaked in February 2017 at 26,500 KRW (approx. EUR 21.25), gradually falling to approx. 20,000 KRW (or EUR 16.70) in April 2017. The trading volume for the entire year 2015 was zero; it remained low throughout 2016, picking up slightly in 2017.[2] The allocation plan that was adopted in January 2017 increased the allowance volume for the 2017 compliance period above the previous goal, in response to the price hike and the 2030 GHG reduction target.

Explaining the turn to ETS in South Korea

The interplay between international and domestic dynamics can explain South Korea's decision to use GHG ETS as the main tool to curb emissions. After the turn of the century, South Korea's rapid economic rise led to international pressure on the country to mitigate its GHG emissions. Although generally seen as a climate policy, South Korea's ETS fit well with President Lee Myung-bak's (2008–13) Low Carbon, Green Growth Strategy, which prioritized economic growth but attempted to achieve this through growth in low-carbon technology and innovation. The tension between serving as an industrial policy while at the same time addressing climate change can be observed throughout the history of the South Korean ETS, especially in the decisions of President Park Geun-hye's administration (2013–17), de facto lowering the level of ambition.

International dynamics: growing pressure to act; familiarization with carbon markets

South Korea's remarkable economic development has changed its role and responsibility in international climate governance. While it was considered a developing country in the early climate negotiations in the 1990s, by the turn of the century it had joined the club of major GHG emitters. International norms can play an important factor in eliciting domestic policy change (Hermanns 2015: 106), which arguably happened in the South Korean case. By the 2009 Copenhagen Conference of the Parties (COP), South Korea could no longer claim that it was a developing country of which no GHG emissions reduction commitments could be required, given its rapid economic and emissions growth. For this reason and as a result of international persuasion, President Lee Myung-bak (voluntarily) pledged in Copenhagen that his country would reduce GHG emissions by 30 per cent below the BaU scenario by 2020. This pledge was transposed into domestic law with the adoption of the Framework Act on Low Carbon, Green Growth in April 2010. The South Korean GHG ETS is a major part of the country's efforts to live up to its international promise.

Interaction with the international carbon market familiarized South Korea with emissions trading. The Clean Development Mechanism (CDM) devised as part of the Kyoto Protocol constituted South Korea's first encounter and acquaintance with carbon markets. In March 2005, the first CDM project hosted by South Korea was registered. Between 2005 and 2013, almost 100 CDM projects were registered with South Korea as their host country. Most of them were approved. Compared to countries such as China and India, however, the number of South Korean CDM projects is relatively low.[3]

Bilateral interaction with other countries, including dialogues on climate change, seems to have contributed to persuading South Korea to engage in climate mitigation policy. The EU and the US played a key role in this process. For example, the EU and South Korea concluded a Free Trade Agreement in 2010, with a binding chapter on sustainable development that stresses the importance of ratifying international environmental agreements like the Kyoto Protocol and their implementation in domestic policy. Similarly, the Korea–US Free Trade Agreement contains a chapter dedicated to the environment. Trade and dialogue with major economies that push for international and domestic climate action seem likely to have created a context that exerted some pressure on South Korea to act on its domestic climate policy. South Korea's growing interdependence and interaction with countries such as the EU and the US as well as its embeddedness in international governance architectures and processes have contributed to setting the political agenda and to starting the process towards adopting a GHG ETS.

Domestic dynamics: seeking a new growth engine in a challenging context

International pressure and developments are only one of the factors that have triggered the turn to ETS in South Korea: domestic dynamics have contributed another important set of factors. The origins of the South Korean GHG ETS can be traced back to President Lee Myung-bak's Low Carbon, Green Growth Strategy, announced in the beginning of his presidency in 2008. He made green growth a key priority and provided political impetus for the adoption of a GHG ETS in South Korea (Interviews 2, 4, 5). In South Korea, policy-making is generally driven top-down from the government, rather than bottom-up as a result of societal pressure (Hermanns 2015). This makes the priorities of the president and the government an important factor for explaining climate policy dynamics in South Korea.

President Lee Myung-bak's (2008–13) motivations for pursuing green growth were grounded primarily in economic developments. Economic growth had dropped from the high levels of the 1990s, and President Lee searched for a new growth engine for his country. Efficiency gains and growth from low-carbon innovations were considered a way to generate new economic growth. Considerations of energy security also seem to have played a role, with climate mitigation only a secondary goal (Kim 2016a: 457–459). Renewable energy did not figure prominently. The focus rather was on the expansion of nuclear electricity (Hermanns 2015: 117–118). President Lee Myung-bak pursued the vision of using green growth to make the Korean economy stronger. The ETS was seen as an economic strategy and a tool for decarbonizing the economy so as to seize economic opportunities arising from the global low-carbon transition (Interviews 2, 3, 4, 6, 10). The choice of adopting a GHG ETS can thus be explained largely by its good fit with the Green Growth Strategy of President Lee Myung-bak.

The rapid growth of the South Korean economy was accompanied by an equally rapid growth in GHG emissions. Increased demand for products from the manufacturing sector, largely export driven (Hermanns 2015: 116), led to growing GHG emissions per capita, as opposed to decreasing emissions per capita as seen in many other countries. Rising GHG emissions were not significantly curbed by technological progress. Investment in low-carbon innovation to mitigate South Korean GHG emissions seems limited (Kim et al. 2015: 147–150). A carbon price set by an ETS or a carbon tax could create incentives for low-carbon technology investments.

A second major contributor to South Korea's rise in GHG emissions is household electricity consumption, which has increased significantly since the turn of the millennium. The government-controlled low electricity price appears to have been one driver of this expansion, given the few incentives to invest in efficiency (Kim et al. 2015: 151–152). A carbon price could contribute to steering household electricity consumption behaviour, but South Korea's GHG ETS is not used to this end. Instead, the system design is constructed to accommodate the situation of government-controlled electricity prices, which explains the inclusion of indirect emissions in the scope of the ETS.

The high level of South Korean GHG emissions is rooted in the country's heavy reliance on coal. Coal consumption has steadily increased 3.5-fold since 1990 (BP 2016: 33). In 2015, South Korea accounted for 2.2 per cent of global coal consumption – more than, for example, Germany, whose global share was 2 per cent in 2015, a 0.6 per cent decrease from the previous year. Electricity from renewable sources constitutes only a minor share of South Korea's energy mix. Hydropower consumption accounted for 0.7 per cent of total electricity consumption. Other renewable sources, like wind, solar, biomass and geothermal, accounted for 1.6 per cent of 2015 electricity consumption, a 29 per cent increase over the previous year (BP 2016: 36, 38).

The South Korean industry structure is quite unique, with a few large conglomerations dominating the economy. Those large companies are influential players also in policy-making since their significant contribution to the country's GDP makes them crucial to its economic growth (Hermanns 2015: 116–117). This power became evident when industry voiced its firm resistance to the GHG ETS. To get the ETS adopted, the government had to invest considerable efforts in convincing industry and had to make several concessions, most notably ensuring free allocation in the first trading phase and postponing the system's start from 2013 to 2015 (Interviews 2, 3, 4, 9).

Explaining the design of the ETS

Type of system: inspiration from the EU and others, with domestic tweaks

Although the Low Carbon, Green Growth Act outlines three options for climate change mitigation policies, a carbon tax never featured substantively in the political deliberations. The Target Management System served as a transitional tool rather than a stand-alone policy instrument, intended to familiarize companies and other actors with the MRV procedures crucial for an ETS. Establishing a GHG ETS with an overall cap and flexibility for businesses and policy-makers was compatible with President Lee Myung-bak's Green Growth Strategy.

In addition to the good fit of GHG ETS with domestic political priorities, interaction with the EU in particular, as well as some other external actors, appears to have provided impetus for emissions trading as opposed to an alternative policy tool. EU–South Korea interaction in the issue area of climate change started in 2008, when the Korean Ministry of Environment organized a workshop together with DG Climate Action experts (Interview 6). As explained in the following, this collaboration has gradually developed and expanded since then.

The first two trading periods are for three years, the third is for five. The shorter duration of the first two can be explained by the gradual phase-in of some of the provisions, especially auctioning and offsetting. Constructing a carbon market is a challenging task for the authorities and covered entities alike, with the risk of various unintended and unanticipated events. Beginning with a pilot phase and improving the ETS step-by-step resembles the EU's approach, which would indicate a certain degree of inspiration.

The Korean ETS includes provisions on banking and borrowing. Covered entities may bank allowances without restrictions, whereas borrowing is limited to 20 per cent of an entity's overall obligations and can be conducted only within a given trading period. Initially, the maximum borrowing limit was 10 per cent, but, as part of the amendments enacted in May 2016, it was doubled in an attempt to ease the pressure on companies short on allowances. This could lead to delayed investments in low-carbon technologies, since companies can opt to wait and see how the policy develops, while borrowing from future allocations (Carbon Pulse 2016b). The 2016 adjustment indicates that the borrowing and banking provisions have been shaped by domestic dynamics, while the similarity to the EU and other systems suggests that the initial design decision could have been inspired by external experiences.

Ambition level: international pressure mitigated by domestic challenges

President Park Geun-hye, who took office in 2013 (–17), dropped green growth as the government's underpinning strategy, advocating instead the idea of creative growth – which is less related to environmental protection and climate change. Nonetheless, the ETS was further implemented under her presidency and became established as a core climate policy. President Park revised several earlier decisions, including the climate mitigation targets set under Lee Myung-bak's presidency and the ministerial responsibilities for the ETS. In June 2015, South Korea announced the target of reducing its GHG emissions by 37 per cent below the BaU scenario by 2030: 25.7 per cent from domestic reductions and 11.3 per cent from international offsets. The previous 2020 target was more ambitious. Under Lee Myung-bak, overall responsibility for the ETS was with the Presidential Committee on Green Growth in the president's office under Lee Myung-bak but was downgraded to the prime minister's office under Park Geun-hye (Interviews 9, 20).

Despite the lowering of ambitions, the ETS was further implemented during the Park Geun-hye presidency. The shifting of implementation responsibilities from the Ministry of Environment to the Ministry of Strategy and Finance can be considered as putting an environmentally less ambitious authority in charge, but it can also be seen as putting a politically more influential entity in the driver's seat. The Ministry of Strategy and Finance has the political clout to counterbalance opposition from the strong Ministry of Trade, Industry and Energy and from business groups. Moreover, the Ministry of Strategy and Finance seems more familiar with market-based policy instruments (Interviews 13, 19). On the other hand, it has little experience with climate change or ETS, which could give the Ministry of Trade, Industry and Energy the upper hand. The Ministry of Strategy and Finance has, however, employed an ETS expert from the Ministry of Environment to lead its ETS work (Interviews 13, 16, 17).

Unlike other GHG ETSs, the Korean system contains sector-specific caps. This means that the overall cap was broken down into the reductions expected from each of the sectors. The allocation of allowances is adjusted to these sectoral targets. This is a special feature of the Korean ETS, as is the BaU target. That necessitates some adjustments in the ETS design, since it is a figure that results from modelling and calculations (Interview 5). This makes the ETS vulnerable to criticism. The government's BaU forecast differed from the forecast that business actors had calculated. Although emissions grew faster from 2010 onwards than forecast in the 2009 calculation of the BaU scenario, the government has not implemented any significant changes (Kim 2016b). Outlining the future trajectory of the cap contributes to market predictability and enables companies to plan and devise a strategy, which is a challenging task (Jotzo and Löschel 2014). For this reason, an EU–Korea ETS capacity-building project, described in the following, includes workshops on carbon pricing modelling (Interview 15). Learning at the technical level has thus been institutionalized and reinforced between the EU and South Korea.

South Korea's GHG emissions reduction target was in part a response to international developments and pressure (Park and Hong 2014: 73). As noted, given the country's rapid economic development and steep rise in GHG emissions, it could no longer claim to be a developing country of which no climate mitigation action could be required. International persuasion and pressure contributed to President Lee Myung-bak (voluntarily) pledging to reduce GHG emissions by 30 per cent below the BaU scenario by 2020. This target was enacted in April 2010 in the Framework Act on Low Carbon, Green Growth, where the Korean GHG ETS is a major element.

However, the initial overall ambition level was weakened in South Korea's Intended Nationally Determined Contribution (INDC) by committing to a 37 per cent reduction below the BaU scenario by 2030. 'Business as usual' was calculated as 850.6 $MtCO_2e$ in 2030, which sets an overall cap for the entire country of 536 $MtCO_2e$ – 81 per cent above 1990 levels. Parts of the target are intended to be reached through carbon credits from international market mechanisms, which means that the domestic GHG emissions reduction is below the set percentage target. For the first trading phase, the emissions cap was set at 573 $MtCO_2e$ in 2015, 562 $MtCO_2e$ in 2016 and 551 $MtCO_2e$ in 2017. The difference between the 2017 cap and the anticipated 2030 cap, if the BaU calculation is not changed, is marginal when we consider the 13-year interval. Hence, some climate experts have evaluated South Korea's INDC as a low level of ambition (Climate Action Tracker 2016).

Initially, the Korean ETS was relatively ambitious in some regards, but certain provisions were weakened in the course of its implementation. The costs of reducing emissions seem comparatively high in South Korea, given its low share of renewable electricity, an industrial structure heavily reliant on energy-intensive production, its export focus and the (initially) limited use of offsets. A *Bloomberg New Energy Finance* study (2013: 11) based on early GHG ETS plans (and thus not reflecting the later changes) concluded that annual demand for abatement was significantly higher in South Korea than in the EU, the (failed) Australian or the Californian systems. While international dynamics appear to have been involved in triggering the Korean ETS, domestic factors seem dominant in the decisions concerning its level of ambition, as expressed in the cap and related provisions.

Allowance allocation: EU inspiration and technical learning, with fierce domestic contention

The Korean ETS started with full free allocation of allowances to all covered entities. Auctioning of a small share of allowances is gradually phased in, with 3 per cent in phase 2 (2018–20) and 10 per cent in phase 3 (2021–25). Energy-intensive and trade-exposed sectors will retain the prerogative of 100 per cent free allocation. The gradual phasing in of auctioning resembles and was inspired by the EU's approach, but it was also part of the concessions made to industry in the highly contested policy-making process, as described prior.

In the first phase, allocation was largely based on grandfathering, calculated as average historical emissions over the previous three years. The January 2017 decree on phase 2 includes the option to switch to benchmarking from 2018 onwards. The total of a sector's calculated emissions is adjusted to the cap for the sector in question. For the cement, oil refining and aviation sectors, allocation is based on benchmarking, which takes efficiency and production into account (Kim 2016b). Grandfathering and benchmarking of emissions were discussed in the design process, and EU experience was examined in this context (Interview 9).

South Korean regulators studied European experiences with regard to allocation, over-allocation, free allocation and auctioning in designing their own rules (Interviews 1, 2, 5, 8, 9). However, because of South Korea's regulation of electricity prices, sectoral targets were included in the ETS. This is a new dimension of allocation, necessary due to the specific South Korean context (Interview 5). The large extent of free allocation was also a result of political bargaining with industry, which had been fairly resistant to the adoption of an ETS and needed to be convinced by concessions as regards allocation. South Korean regulators were thus well aware of the problem of windfall profits that occurred in the EU (Interviews 1, 5, 9). They drew lessons from this experience – but, for political reasons, they adopted a 100 per cent free allocation approach in the first phase, knowing about the potential problems.

Allocation is a very contentious issue in South Korea. Almost 250 companies have filed complaints against allocation decisions, in more than 40 lawsuits. In some cases, the Ministry of Environment accepted the complaints and allocated additional allowances from the reserve (Carbon Pulse 2016b, 2016d; Kim 2016b) but other cases were rejected. For example, in February 2017, 34 companies lost a lawsuit they had filed, accusing the government of having allocated them too few allowances. Yet, in light of the 2030 climate mitigation target, which is less ambitious than the previous 2020 target, in January 2017 South Korea's Cabinet approved an allocation plan that adds a further three million allowances to the major increase announced in December 2016. The decrease in the level of ambition in the economy-wide climate mitigation target has thus been translated into the allocation of more allowances. This also responds to the comparatively high allowance prices, which triggered industry to call for the government to step in to make regulatory changes.

In 2016, the Korean allowance price rose to the highest globally, apparently due to the very low degree of trading and market liquidity (Carbon Pulse 2016b). The limited trading activities can be explained by the fact that most companies had sufficient allowances for the 2016 compliance period or, had borrowed from their 2017 allocation in anticipation of a relaxation of the cap (Carbon Pulse 2016c). Companies seem to have chosen to keep their allowances rather than trading them, given the lack of a long-term perspective (Carbon Pulse 2016b). The government auctioned some allowances from the market stability reserve below the market price in June 2016 (Carbon Pulse 2016b).

The Korean ETS does not seem to have triggered investments in low-carbon technologies and alternatives so far, as shown by the plan to build new coal-fired power plants. It might, however, be revised under newly elected President Moon Jae-in. Rather than searching for low-carbon solutions to lower demand for allowances and thereby the price, industry has called for the government to issue more allowances. While examination of external experiences informed Korean policy-makers, their ultimate decisions regarding allocation were shaped by domestic politics and interests.

Coverage: dominant domestic features with a link to Kyoto

The Korean ETS has a relatively broad scope, in terms of industrial sectors, greenhouse gases and types of emissions. Five sectors and 23 industries are covered, as shown in Table 9.2. Companies that emit more than 125 ktCO_2e at company level and 25 ktCO_2e at installation level fall within the scope of the system. This results in the inclusion of about 525 large emitters that account for approximately 68 per cent of South Korea's overall GHG emissions (ICAP 2017a). The GHGs CO_2, but also CH_4, N_2O, HFCs, PFCs and SF_6, are included.

The explanation for the broad sectoral coverage can be found in domestic structures, especially the dominant position of a few large conglomerations. South Korea hosts a few very large conglomerations such as Samsung, which generate a large share of domestic GDP. A narrow scope would have meant that only an extremely small number of companies would be covered, which in turn would have made trading inefficient, or companies would probably not have engaged in trading. The country's top 10 GHG emitters account for approximately 60 per cent of the total emissions covered by South Korea's ETS (Shim and Lee 2016: 2).

The covered GHGs match those covered by the Kyoto Protocol, which arguably influenced the South Korean choice. However, the decision to include a broad range of sectors also required the inclusion of gases other than CO_2. While the scope in terms of industries and GHGs covered is broader than that of many other ETSs, the scope of carbon market participants is narrower than, for example, in North America (see Chapters 4 and 5 of this book) or Europe (see Chapter 3). During the first two commitment periods, foreign companies or individuals are not allowed to participate in trading, which is restricted to the covered entities and four public banks (Carbon Pulse 2016b; Park and Hong 2014: 81). This appears to be one reason for the relatively low level of trading activities.

The Korean ETS covers direct *and* indirect emissions.[4] This means that it regulates indirect emissions from the consumption of electricity, in addition to the direct release of GHG emissions that stem from an installation's own production of electricity and other industrial processes. Indirect emissions typically originate from the purchase of electricity. This provision can be explained by South Korea's government-controlled electricity prices, which pre-empts the transfer

Table 9.2 Sectors and industries covered by the South Korean GHG ETS

Sectors	*Industries*
Power combustion-energy	Power combustion-energy
Industrial processes	Mining, food and beverages, textile, wood, paper, oil refining, petrochemical, glass ceramics, cement, steel, nonferrous metals, machinery, semiconductor, display, electricity, electronics, motor vehicle, shipbuilding
Public waste materials	Water service, waste materials
Building sectors	Building, communications
Transportation	Aviation

of the carbon price to consumers. Retail electricity prices are controlled by the government, and industry receives subsidies to compensate for electricity prices (Hermanns 2015: 116). In a complex system, the electricity price is determined so that some consumer groups are subsidized by paying less than the average cost of electricity generation, whereas other consumer groups pay more (Kim and Lim 2014: 85–86).

Including the indirect emissions of large-scale consumers can be a partial remedy, enabling the costs of carbon to be transferred from the production to the consumption side (Shim and Lee 2016: 2). It can also allow for the equal distribution of the burden of emissions abatement among a broad set of sectors. Since only large emitters are included in the ETS, the electricity price for households has remained unchanged. The downside of such an approach is that double counting can occur, i.e. allowances can be required twice for the same emissions: once at the production of electricity or heat, and a second time at the consumption stage (Oh et al. 2015: 14983–14984). Electricity generators could reap windfall profits if their allowances are allocated for free and exceed their actual emissions. If emissions reduction is achieved though reductions by other entities whose indirect emissions were covered, the system and its allowance allocation can be distorted (Shim and Lee 2016: 1).

The inclusion of indirect in addition to direct emissions is a characteristic feature of GHG ETSs in East Asia, given the challenge of government-controlled electricity prices, which does not allow allowance costs to be passed on to consumers (Kim and Lim 2014: 85). Both the Tokyo Metropolitan Area ETS (see Chapter 6) and the Chinese pilot projects (see Chapter 11) include indirect emissions, whereas the EU ETS (see Chapter 3) covers only direct emissions. This aspect of the EU system was studied by the South Korean authorities, but, in view of the South Korean context of regulated electricity prices, a different design was deemed necessary (Interview 6).

Offsets and linking: opposite direction to the EU

Originally, offset credits were permitted only from domestic projects, and then for a maximum of 10 per cent of an entity's compliance obligation. International carbon credits were allowed earlier than originally planned. Initially devised to apply from the third trading phase onwards, this option was moved forward to the second phase, but limited to offsets from projects in which South Korean companies are directly involved. In light of the NDC, which specifies that a share of South Korea's climate mitigation commitment will be covered using international market mechanisms and in response to demands from industry, up to 5 per cent of a company's overall allowance obligation may be fulfilled by international offsets. Setting a maximum limit on the number of credits that can be used to fulfil obligations under the ETS resembles the EU's approach pre-2020 and could have been inspired by it.

However, the overall approach runs counter to that of the EU, which allowed carbon offsets in the EU ETS until 2020 but adopted an economy-wide 2030 climate mitigation target that must be achieved by domestic efforts only. Through its involvement in the CDM, South Korea has gained some experience in designing offset projects, which seems to have influenced the practice of accepting converted domestic CDM credits. Given the low price for credits from CDM projects and the demand for additional allowances in the Korean carbon market, some domestic CDM project developers have converted their credits into Korean Offset Credits (KOC) that can subsequently be exchanged for Korean Credit Units (KCUs), which are traded at a higher prices than CDM credits (Carbon Pulse 2015). While some inspiration from external sources can be noted here, the evolution of the offsetting provisions seems influenced mainly by domestic considerations.

MRV and enforcement: using standard international approaches, building domestic capacity

Establishing a measurement, reporting and verification infrastructure is a challenge for most jurisdictions. For this reason, South Korea started with a preparatory stage to establish MRV processes and build the administrative capacity of industry, consultants and the administration. The TMS served this purpose, requiring MRV and target setting while not including an allowance-trading element. The Korean ETS includes annual emissions-reporting requirements. Emissions reports must be verified by third parties and submitted to the GHG Inventory and Research Centre, established in 2010. Failure to comply with the obligation to surrender emission allowances is penalized with fines of up to three times their market price but not exceeding 100,000 KRW per tCO_2e.

The MRV approach that South Korea has adopted as the basis for its ETS strongly resembles that of the EU and many other systems, indicating inspiration and learning from these external examples. Since a solid and well-functioning MRV system requires significant technical and skills-related capacity, support from the EU in particular has contributed to implementing the Korean system. The EU–Korea Emissions Trading System cooperation project has included workshops on MRV-related issues: for example, a workshop aimed at equipping verifiers with advanced skills and knowledge to strengthen the South Korean compliance cycle was held in January 2017. While the MRV system is a standard approach applied in similar ways in all ETSs, the EU has supported South Korea in enhancing its capacity. However, domestic preparation through the TMS played a more important role in establishing the basic MRV infrastructure, especially in the early phases. EU capacity-building support grew throughout the first ETS phase and with the implementation of the EU–Korea Emissions Trading System cooperation project.

Price and quantity management: options for avoiding problems elsewhere

The Korean ETS includes provisions that aim to stabilize the carbon price in cases of high volatility. The market stabilization mechanism can be triggered when one of four events occurs: 1) the allowance price throughout a period of six months is at least six times higher than the average of the previous two years; 2) the average allowance price for one month exceeds twofold the average price of the previous two years; 3) the allowance price is 60 per cent below the average price of the preceding two years; 4) market supply is insufficient to meet demand. The fourth trigger of the market stabilization mechanism was not contained in the original law but was added in March 2017 in response to growing pressure from industry to address the soaring allowance prices.

Various market stabilization options are available – including modifying the allowance reserve, limiting borrowing, regulating offset credits and setting a floor or ceiling price. The Emissions Allowance Allocation Committee decides which measure to enact. In June 2016, the government auctioned some allowances from the market stability reserve below the market price, in response to the doubling of the price from 8,000 KRW to 16,600 KRW (Carbon Pulse 2016b). South Korea has reacted to rising prices also in 2017, when it issued more allowances than initially anticipated – 17 million above the previous goal. This was the result of a recalculation of the cap in light of the 2030 emissions target that watered down the initial 2020 target (ICAP 2017b).

The observed price volatility in the EU ETS seems to have contributed to South Korea devising price control and market stabilization measures (Park and Hong 2014: 79). Korean regulators followed closely the EU debate about backloading and the Market Stability Reserve (MSR) (Interviews 1, 5, 6, 9; see also Chapter 3). Including a market stabilization mechanism in the form of ceiling and floor price provisions had been discussed prior to the EU's problems with the price drop of allowances, but this European experience confirmed the necessity for such a provision in the South Korean system (Interview 1).

Revenue earmarking: provisions not fully developed, potential for external inspiration

Since South Korea does not include auctioning in the first ETS phase, provisions concerning the use of revenues have not fully been developed and implemented, and it is still too early to identify clear patterns. However, it seems likely that the international debate in the EU and elsewhere has informed South Korean decisions and practices. In the next section, we turn to the role and contribution of international factors in South Korean ETS policy-making, to identify the specificities and relative importance of the various external GHG ETS experiences in domestic South Korean processes.

Discussion: international factors in South Korea ETS policy-making

The fact that the Korean ETS needed to be adjusted to the country's specific context does not exclude the possibility that external experiences and ETS designs may have informed and inspired Korean decisions. It is extremely difficult to gauge precisely and deterministically the relative importance of international versus domestic drivers of Korean decisions, but we can note some tendencies, drawing on the previous section, which found several instances of external influences. Detailed evaluation of each of the eight design elements shows that learning (from the EU in particular) has been greatest with respect to technical details like implementation of the MRV system. Intensified EU capacity-building initiatives have supported this process. Inspiration from external experiences seems to have affected less technical, higher-level decisions such as the system type, allocation methods and revenue earmarking.

However, the details of those and several other decisions appear to have been determined largely by domestic politics, interests and (economic) structures. Design elements with distributive consequences, such as the scope of sectors covered by the ETS and allocation modalities, as well as elements that could lead to deep economic restructuring, such as the level of ambition, have been determined mainly by domestic politics and considerations. Overall, the EU ETS has played an important role as benchmark and source of lessons, but domestic factors have played a dominant role in shaping several unique characteristics of the Korean ETS.

Our expert interviews indicate a central role for the EU ETS as source of experiences and information. It was described as a deliberate choice to appoint an official with good English-language skills to lead the ETS task force in the Ministry of Environment during the early drafting phase of the implementing regulation, intended to facilitate exchange with external actors (Interview 5). EU–South Korea relations in general were reinforced with the entry into force of the Free Trade Agreement (FTA) in 2011 and the conclusion of the Strategic Partnership in 2010. The Framework Agreement, negotiated alongside the FTA as an overarching agreement on political cooperation, entered into force in 2014. It includes strengthened cooperation in various policy areas, among them climate change and energy security.

Cooperation and exchange on GHG emissions trading is highly developed between the EU and South Korea. For 2013–16, a Korean official was seconded to the ETS unit of the European Commission's Directorate General (DG) for Climate Action. He established links between South Korean and EU ETS experts. Besides contributing to the work of DG Climate Action, his role was to act as a contact point for Korean actors with questions about GHG ETS design and implementation and to put them in touch with European experts (Interviews 1, 5, 8). Several South Korean expert delegations visited Europe to study EU experiences with implementing its ETS (Interviews 1, 5).

EU experts and high-level policy-makers, including former Climate Action commissioner Connie Hedegaard and DG Climate Action director-general Jos Delbeke, visited South Korea and included ETS in their meeting agendas (Interviews 6, 10). From the beginning, the EU delegation in Seoul was engaged in discussions leading to the adoption of the ETS Act and its implementation, and DG Climate Action funded a two-week training course for Korean actors on GHG ETS, implemented by the International Carbon Action Partnership (ICAP) (Interview 6).

In 2016, the EU started a three-year capacity-building project with South Korea (Interview 12). It has a budget of EUR 3.5 million and is funded under the EU's

Foreign Partnership Instrument. DG Climate Action and the Korean Ministry of Strategy and Finance jointly steer this project, which is seen as an important part of the EU–Korea Strategic Partnership and a 'new chapter in climate change cooperation' (DG Climate Action 2016). The purpose of the project is to share expertise and technical assistance from the EU with Korean regulators and ETS stakeholders. The emphasis is on benchmark-based allocation, auctioning and modelling (Interview 15). The project follows upon positive experiences with a similar project with China (Interviews 14, 18).

Not only the EU but also individual European countries, notably the UK, Germany and Norway, have engaged with South Korea on ETS design and implementation. In addition, US and Australian actors have been involved. The UK was the most active partner in the early design stages of the Korean ETS, engaging in bilateral dialogues and projects with policy-makers, think-tanks and academia. It hosted an annual ETS workshop in the early phases of developing the Korean ETS (Interviews 2, 4, 5, 6, 8, 10).

As our evaluation of the eight design elements shows, South Koreans seem to have learned lessons from various EU ETS design elements. Lessons were drawn from the EU's first and second ETS phases (Interview 1). Here we may note that the EU's first phase was also considered an experimentation phase by the EU itself for testing its own system. Actors central to the Korean ETS design process described the EU ETS as a benchmark for designing the Korean system. The EU system seems to be the system to which Korean regulators looked most because of the many similarities – for example, in term of the sectors covered (Interviews 5, 8, 10). Another motivation could be considerations about linking, which are included in the ETS Act. Linking with other systems will be possible from the third phase of the Korean ETS, starting in 2021.

One reason for studying the ETS experiences of other jurisdictions was the fact that South Korea had to start from scratch, without any prior experience with an emissions trading system (Interview 1). The US non-governmental organization (NGO) Environmental Defense Fund (EDF) organized a workshop presenting the North American systems (Interview 3), and Korean regulators have maintained contacts with ETS experts in California and the Regional Greenhouse Gas Initiative (RGGI); also, Australia has supported Korea in its ETS design process (Interviews 5, 8). In addition, Chinese ETS experts have engaged in dialogues with Korean counterparts; this sharing of information seems to occur at the level of individual experts and academics rather than at the governmental level (Interviews 2, 3).

However, domestic politics have also mattered. South Korea has some domestic structures that require a different design from the ETSs of the EU or other jurisdictions. One such factor is the structure of the Korean electricity market: it is not liberalized, and electricity prices are regulated. The drafting of the ETS implementation regulation coincided with difficult choices about South Korea's domestic energy mix and investments (Interview 6). The then- Korean government decided to invest in the construction of new coal-fired power plants, which does not seem very compatible with an ambitious climate policy. South Korea imports more than 90% of its energy, which influences its energy and climate policy decisions. Yet newly elected President Moon Jae-in ordered the temporary shutdown of eight old coal-fired power plants shortly after his election in May 2017, and a new approach to coal is expected for his presidency, but details remain to be seen (Carbon Pulse 2017).

The South Koran economy is heavily focused on external trade – to a greater degree than is the EU economy. This makes the international competitiveness angle an important consideration for the regulator. The structure of Korean companies, with their large conglomerates, means that only a relatively small number of companies are involved in the system; moreover, the number of installations covered is far lower than in the EU. This leads to the question of whether it is possible to run an ETS with such a small number of very large companies (Interview 3). Given the structural differences between the EU and South Korea, most ETS design elements have been adjusted to the Korean context (Interview 5).

Conclusions

The relatively extensive interaction with external experts supports the finding that South Korea's decision to adopt a GHG ETS was influenced and fostered in parts by experiences of other jurisdictions, most notably the EU. The interaction with external actors provides a strong indication that learning and emulation have contributed to South Korea's turn to GHG ETS. International pressure and persuasion served as additional mechanisms of influence at the agenda-setting stage. Learning has been strongest on technical details, supported by EU capacity-building initiatives. There has been some inspiration from external experiences as regards less technical, higher-level decisions, such as the type of system. Nonetheless, the domestic factors seem even stronger, ultimately explaining most of the specific design features – especially those with distributive consequences, such as the allocation modalities.

Commissioner for Climate Action Miguel Arias Cañete expressed his vision of the Korean ETS constituting a model and becoming a pioneer for similar policy developments in the East Asian region: 'I hope that China's and now Korea's experience can be a trigger to expand emissions trading systems across the region' (DG Climate Action 2016). The EU ambassador to South Korea voiced similar hopes at the launch of the EU–Korea ETS cooperation project: 'Through this technical cooperation and successful KETS, we will set a good example in the region' (EEAS 2016). For instance, China might be able to learn from South Korea as regards the functioning of a GHG ETS in a government-controlled electricity market (Jotzo and Löschel 2014: 4).

The current debate about the implementation and possible adjustment of the Korean ETS is an interesting process to follow. On the one hand, the present cap is not sufficient to achieve the GHG emissions reduction target (Interview 11). Coal is a key challenge here. While the government has announced its plans for closing 10 old coal-powered plants by 2025 and temporarily shut down 8 of them in spring 2017, it has also built new ones with greater power generation capacity than the obsolete facilities. The addition of 20 coal-powered plants generating 10.2 GW by 2022 was initially announced; later 3.7 GW capacity was deducted, to be replaced by nuclear sources.

Newly elected President Moon Jae-in is said to be rethinking South Korea's approach to coal, but details remain to be seen (Carbon Pulse 2017). In 2015, coal was responsible for about half of South Korea's emissions from fossil-fuel combustion in 2015, mainly from the electricity generation sector (Chung 2016; Olivier et al. 2016: 33). The share of coal in the South Korean energy mix is not projected to decrease significantly by 2030, which would appear to clash with an ambitious ETS that drives low-carbon technology deployment. The tension between the expansion of coal capacity and climate mitigation is reflected in some of the changes that have been implemented to reduce the level of ETS ambition.

Thereunto, the South Korean allowance price is currently relatively high, compared to that of the EU and other GHG ETSs. This has raised some concern amongst Korean (industry) actors. The current low EU allowance price and critical voices about the EU ETS could be used by Korean industry to delay or water down the Korean system (Interview 6). All in all, the system in South Korea is at a crossroads. With the election of President Moon Jae-in in May 2017, changes in South Korea's climate and energy policy are expected, but whether and the extent to which they will influence the level of ambition of Korea's ETS remains to be seen.

Notes

1 The authors would like to thank Min Ji Kim for her excellent research assistance, as well as all interviewees who agreed to share their expert insights. Parts of this research were funded by the KU Leuven Research Fund (Bijzonder Onderzoeksfonds KU Leuven) and the Research Foundation Flanders (FWO).
2 Korea Exchange: https://global.krx.co.kr/contents/GLB/05/0506/0506030102/GLB0506030102.jsp (accessed 26 April 2017).
3 A list of all CDM projects can be found in the UNFCCC CDM database: http://cdm.unfccc.int/Projects/projsearch.html (accessed 26 April 2017).
4 According to the Framework Act on Low Carbon, Green Growth (Article 2.10): 'both direct emission of greenhouse gases, which emits, discharges, or leaks greenhouse gases generated as a consequence of human activities, and indirect emission of greenhouse gases, which discharges greenhouse gases by using electricity or heat (limited to those from a heat source generated with a fuel or electricity) supplied by another person', are covered.

References

Bloomberg New Energy Finance. 2013. *South Korea's Emissions Trading Scheme*. White Paper, 10 May.

BP. 2016. *BP Statistical Review of World Energy*. London: British Petroleum.

Carbon Pulse. 2015. *Korean Carbon Traders to Switch Offsets from CDM to Korea ETS*. London, 6 March.

Carbon Pulse. 2016a. *South Korean Cabinet Approves Climate Power Shake-up, Loosens ETS Rule*. London, 17 May.

Carbon Pulse. 2016b. *What Now for South Korea's Emissions Trading Scheme?* London, 5 July.

Carbon Pulse. 2016c. *South Korea Carbon Trade Dries up as ETS Passes First Compliance Deadline*. London, 30 June.

Carbon Pulse. 2016d. *Korea to Release 900k Allowances from Reserve, Sends CO2 Price Tumbling*. London, 27 May.

Carbon Pulse. 2017. *South Korea's New President Moves to Curb Coal-fired Generation*. London, 15 May.

Chung, J. 2016. *South Korea to Shut 10 Ageing Coal-fired Power Plants by 2025*. Reuters, 5 July. www.reuters.com/article/us-southkorea-coal-idUSKCN0ZM06A accessed 26 April 2017.

Climate Action Tracker. 2016. *South Korea*. http://climateactiontracker.org/countries/southkorea.html accessed 2 February 2017.

DG Climate Action. 2016. *EU Launches €3.5 million Emissions Trading Cooperation Project with Korea*. Brussels. http://ec.europa.eu/clima/news/articles/news_2016070801_en accessed 26 May 2017.

EEAS. 2016. *EU and the Republic of Korea Launch € 3.5 million Emissions Trading System Cooperation Project*. Seoul. https://eeas.europa.eu/headquarters/headquarters-homepage_en/16712/EU and the Republic of Korea launch %E2%82%AC 3.5 million Emissions Trading System cooperation project accessed 26 May 2017.

Hermanns, H. 2015. Ecological modernization and the development of emissions trading schemes in Australia and South Korea. *Pacific Focus* 30 (1), 103–125.

ICAP. 2017a. *Korea Emissions Trading Scheme*. Berlin: International Carbon Action Partnership. ETS Detailed Information.

ICAP. 2017b. *Republic of Korea Releases 2017 Allocation Plan*. https://icapcarbonaction.com/en/news-archive/435-republic-of-korea-releases-2017-allocation-plan accessed 26 May 2017.

Jotzo, F. and A. Löschel. 2014. Emissions trading in China: Emerging experiences and international lessons. *Energy Policy* 75, 3–8.

Kim, E. 2016a. The politics of climate change policy design in Korea. *Environmental Politics* 25 (3), 454–474.

Kim, S. 2016b. Current status and issues of the Korean Emission Trading Scheme. *IEEJ Energy Journal* 11 (2).

Kim, Y. and J. Lim. 2014. An emissions trading scheme design for power industries facing price regulation. *Energy Policy* 75, 84–90.

Kim, Y., J. Yoo and W. Oh. 2015. Driving forces of rapid CO2 emissions growth: A case of Korea. *Energy Policy* 82, 144–155.

Oh, Inha, Y. Yeo and J. Lee. 2015. Efficiency versus equality: Comparing design options for indirect emissions accounting in the Korean Emissions Trading Scheme. *Sustainability* 7, 14982–15002.

Olivier, Jos G. J., G. Janssens-Maenhout, M. Muntean and J. A. H. W. Peters. 2016. *Trends in Global CO2 Emissions: 2016 Report*. The Hague: PBL Netherlands Environmental Assessment Agency.

Park, H. and W. K. Hong. 2014. Korea's Emission Trading Scheme and policy design issues to achieve market-efficiency and abatement targets. *Energy Policy* 75, 73–83.

Shim, S. and J. Lee. 2016. Covering indirect emissions mitigates market power in carbon markets: the case of South Korea. *Sustainability* 8 (583), 1–11.

Annex: list of interviews

1. Korean official, Brussels, 17 September 2013.
2. Korean think-tank researcher, Seoul, 1 October 2013.
3. Korean academic, Seoul, 1 October 2013.
4. Korean academic, Seoul, 7 October 2013.
5. Two Korean officials, Seoul, 8 October 2013.
6. Three European diplomats based in Seoul, Seoul, 10 October 2013.
7. Korean NGO representative, Seoul, 16 October 2013.
8. Official, President's Office, Seoul, 17 October 2013.
9. Korean NGO representative, Seoul, 17 October 2013.
10. Korean official, Brussels, 21 November 2013.
11. EU official, Brussels, 25 March 2015.
12. EU official, e-mail, 11 January 2016.
13. Korean think-tank researcher, Sejong City, 16 January 2017.
14. Two EU consultants/Korea ETS experts, Seoul, 17 January 2017.
15. Two Korean officials, Seoul, 18 January 2017.
16. European diplomat based in Seoul, Seoul, 19 January 2017.
17. European diplomat based in Seoul, Seoul, 19 January 2017.
18. Two European diplomats based in Seoul, Seoul, 20 January 2017.
19. Korean official, Seoul, 20 January 2017.
20. Chinese consultant, Beijing (phone), 8 February 2017.

10 Emissions trading in Kazakhstan

Complicated application of the 'EU model'

François Sammut, Lars H. Gulbrandsen and Jørgen Wettestad

Introduction

This chapter investigates the role of international policy diffusion and domestic politics in shaping the design of emissions trading in Kazakhstan.[1] The development of its emissions trading system (KzETS) has received little attention thus far, but deserves closer review, for several reasons. Kazakhstan was the first country in Asia to implement an economy-wide ETS (in 2013). It is also the first former Soviet republic to implement an ETS and as such could serve as a relevant case for other former Soviet states looking to implement emissions trading – for instance, Ukraine. After all, Kazakhstan does not have a long history of climate policy entrepreneurship or leadership, and its centralized and autocratic character does not make it a country one would naturally expect to turn to (decentralized) emissions trading.

It is fair to say that Kazakhstan has been a trailblazer in the region with respect to climate policy. The Kazakh government has championed the 'National Concept for Transition to a Green Economy', with legislation to promote energy saving, energy efficiency and renewable energy; numerous government programmes and strategies have been updated to reflect the country's commitment under the Paris Agreement. The centrepiece of Kazakhstan's Green Economy concept is the KzETS, covering all major emitting sectors in the country. The case of Kazakhstan and its ETS is noteworthy when we consider the size of the country, with a territory larger than Western Europe. Further, Kazakhstan has become a dominant Central Asian country in economic terms, due largely to its oil and gas industry but also its mineral resources. Its greenhouse gas (GHG) emissions are also considerable, with ETS-sector emissions around 147 Mt in 2013 (greater than France, for instance).

In this chapter, we ask: First, why did Kazakhstan, as a centralized and autocratic country, turn to emissions trading? Second, to what extent and how can the design of the KzETS be explained, specifically in the context of international policy diffusion? As various international consultants and experts have been involved in assisting the Kazakh authorities set up the system, it is relevant to explore to what extent and how the system has been initiated 'from the outside' and shaped by learning from or even copying other systems. Further, as the political system in

Kazakhstan must be characterized as centralized and autocratic, it is interesting to explore how this type of political system has influenced the design and functioning of a market-based policy instrument, fundamentally based on decentralized decisions and actions.

As further elaborated in the following, Kazakhstan's turn to emissions trading featured the adoption of three central laws in 2010, 2011 and 2012, as well as a one-year pilot phase that started in 2013. However, further operation of the system has now been put on hold, and we discuss the causes and possible consequences of this development. The data and analysis for this chapter draw on a review of publicly available information, combined with one author's long-standing professional experience in supporting the Kazakh authorities during development of the KzETS.[2]

Kazakhstan's ETS and its emergence

The Republic of Kazakhstan is located in the centre of the Eurasian continent. With an area of 2.7 million km2, it is the ninth largest country in the world, and also the world's largest landlocked country. Kazakhstan's current population is 17.7 million, with a growth rate of 1.5 per cent in 2014 (World Bank 2016). The population is predominantly urban (54.9 per cent), although the rural element remains significant. The country shares an extensive border with Russia in the north, as well as borders with China, Kyrgyzstan, Uzbekistan and Turkmenistan, in addition to a significant portion of the Caspian Sea coastline.

Kazakhstan became the last Soviet republic to declare its independence, on 16 December 1991. Its communist-era leader, Nursultan Nazarbayev, has remained the country's president. Kazakhstan has a parliamentary system, with the president as head of state. The president sets foreign policy, can initiate legislation, serves as commander-in-chief of the armed forces and, subject to parliamentary approval, appoints the prime minister. The supreme legislative body is the parliament, consisting of two chambers, the Senate (Upper House) and the Mazhilis (Lower House). Members of the Senate are indirectly elected representatives of regional assemblies and appointees of the president, whereas the Mazhilis is composed of elected deputies. Members of the parliament are elected for four-year terms.

As the largest economy in Central Asia, Kazakhstan generates 60 per cent of the region's GDP, due mainly to its significant natural resources such as oil, gas, minerals and metals. Exploitation of the natural resource potential has been the main source of economic growth. In 2015, Kazakhstan produced 77 million tons of oil and natural-gas condensate and 45.7 billion cubic meters of natural gas. According to World Bank statistics, the share of mineral products (including oil and gas) and metals in the total value of exports from Kazakhstan exceeded 80 per cent in the first half of 2016.[3] Kazakhstan also has considerable agricultural potential with its vast steppe lands suitable for both livestock and grain production.

Kazakhstan experienced consistent economic growth from 2000 to 2008, with an annual GDP growth rate of around 9 per cent as the norm. However, growth was severely hit during 2008 and 2009 as a result of the global economic crisis; although it picked up from 2010–13, growth in 2015 and 2016 was low, as a result of the slump in oil prices. The EU has become Kazakhstan's primary trade partner, with an almost 40 per cent share in its total external trade. The value of exports to the EU totalled EUR 12.8 billion in 2016, whereas imports from the EU amounted to EUR 5.2 billion in the same year (European Commission 2017).

The energy system of Kazakhstan is dominated by thermal generation; the electricity system includes about 70 power plants with total installed capacity of around 18 GW. Combined heat and power plants (CHP) represent installed capacity of 6.7 GW; they serve residential district heating networks and industrial end-users, covering about 40 per cent of heat and 46 per cent of electric power consumption in Kazakhstan. Thermal generation is primarily powered by locally available coal (75 per cent), followed by natural gas (10 per cent) and oil (5 per cent). Five large hydroelectric plants, mostly located on the Irtysh river, provide roughly 10 per cent of electricity generation. Other renewables are largely undeveloped, although Kazakhstan has further potential, especially in wind and solar power. Renewable energy sources could prove particularly attractive in isolated rural areas.

As explained in the following, Kazakhstan's status under the Kyoto Protocol is unique and is probably one of the original reasons for its decision to implement an ETS. Kazakhstan is a non-Annex I country with respect to the 1992 UN Framework Convention on Climate Change (UNFCCC), but an Annex I country under the Kyoto Protocol. As an Annex I Party without Annex B status, Kazakhstan has been barred from participating in any of the Kyoto flexibility mechanisms – Clean Development Mechanism (CDM), Joint Implementation (JI) or International Emissions Trading (IET).

The legislative foundations for a Kazakh ETS can be traced back to 2007, when the government adopted the Environmental Code of Kazakhstan, which attempted to consolidate and harmonize legislation related to the preservation and restoration of the environment and the use of natural resources. Specifically, the Environmental Code set a requirement for specific legal entities (e.g. industrial companies, power plants and oil and gas operators) to prepare an annual inventory of GHG emissions, and made provisions for annual reporting on the results of the inventory to the Committee for Environmental Regulation and Control of the then Ministry of Environment (MEP). As specified in Kazakhstan's III–VI National Communication to the UNFCCC, 'the organization of the system of accounting of greenhouse gas emissions at the level of individual industrial units was based on the intention to establish a national cap-and-trade market for greenhouse gas emissions in the country' (UNFCCC 2013).

Against this background, the decision to implement an ETS, with a specific focus on a market mechanism for reducing GHG emissions which should include 'international trade in allowances between the countries that have quotas and/or GHG emissions reductions and their legal entities', can be interpreted as a political decision, approved at the highest level, to take a more proactive and, it was hoped, more successful role in the international carbon market.

In August 2009, the MEP was appointed the authorized body for coordinating implementation of the Kyoto Protocol. In addition, the MEP was placed in charge

Table 10.1 Overview of the key design features of the KzETS

Type of system	Cap and trade; Phase 1: 2013; Phase 2: 2014–15: Phase 3 planned for 5 years (2016–20 but start postponed to 2018) Banking not allowed; borrowing only within phases
Ambition level	Phase 1 (pilot phase): allocation equal to 100% of the non-verified emissions reported by companies for the reference year (2010) Phase 2: 1.5% reduction in emissions by the end of 2015 compared to a company's average emission level 2011–12 Phase 3: Emissions to be kept at 2013–14 levels until 2020
Allocation mechanisms	Free allocation, based on grandfathering
Coverage	3 sectors: 1. Energy (electricity and heat production) 2. Industry (mainly non-ferrous metals (aluminium, zinc, copper), ferro-alloys, iron and steel, cement) 3. Coal mining, oil and gas extraction Around 166 enterprises covered by the National Allocation Plan (NAP) during Phase 2 Only CO_2 emissions included
Offsets and linking	Domestic offsets
Monitoring, reporting and verification (MRV) and enforcement	Annual, verified reports No penalties initially

of implementing an industry-wide programme, 'Zhasyl Damu' ('Green Growth'), which aims to achieve reductions in GHG emissions and mitigate the impact of climate change on the environment. The programme includes the development of proposals for the Government of the Republic of Kazakhstan to create a legal framework for the implementation of the Kyoto Protocol and post-Kyoto agreements, proposals for domestic policies and measures to reduce GHG emissions and, importantly, proposals for the development of market mechanisms for the reduction of GHG emissions.

At the national level, activities related to GHG reduction intensified after the publication of the Strategic Development Plan of the Republic of Kazakhstan to 2020, approved by Presidential Decree (No. 922) on 1 February 2010. This was followed by an amendment to the Environmental Code adopted, on 3 December 2011,[4] specifying that a market mechanism for reductions of GHG emissions should include:

- Trade in national GHG emissions allowances.
- Trade in certified emissions reductions (CERs), emissions removal units (ERUs) and units from domestic offset projects.
- International trade in allowances between the countries that have quotas and/or GHG emissions reductions and their legal entities.

Although the establishment of the KzETS predates the Paris Agreement and submission of the Kazakh INDC (Intended Nationally Determined Contributions), the system is now deemed an integral part of any commitment made with respect to the latter. Kazakhstan's INDC commits the country to achieving the unconditional target of 15 per cent reduction of all emissions from a 1990 baseline by 2030, as well as a 25 per cent reduction for the same period, conditional on international financial support.

Phase 1 of the KzETS, essentially a pilot phase, was launched on 1 January 2013. Phase 2 ran from 2014–15. In April 2016, the KzETS was suspended until January 2018 to allow time for amendments and clarifications to be made to the relevant legislation. The market had been over-allocated in the first three years, with prices ranging from USD 0.20 to USD 4 per ton of CO_2 (Carbon Pulse 2016). Table 10.1 provides an overview of the central design features of the KzETS.

Explaining the adoption of KzETS

After various delays, Kazakhstan ratified the Kyoto Protocol on 19 June 2009, focusing on participation in the regulated carbon market. At the time of ratification, Kazakhstan was a non-Annex I country with respect to the UN climate change convention, but an Annex I country for the purposes of the Kyoto Protocol.[5] Kazakhstan, however, did not declare that it wished to be bound by the commitments of Annex I Parties under the Convention when the Protocol was adopted and therefore had no emissions target listed for it in Annex B. Being considered an Annex I Party without Annex B status meant that Kazakhstan could not participate in any of the flexible mechanisms: the CDM, JI or IET (Climate Focus 2010).

Kazakhstan repeatedly requested an amendment to Annex B to the Kyoto Protocol to enable it to participate in the flexible mechanisms. A decision regarding this request at the meetings of the parties to the Kyoto Protocol was repeatedly postponed to the next meeting, mainly due to procedural issues and the country's proposal for a quantified GHG emissions limitation or reduction commitment of 100 per cent of the 1992 level. Because of these delays and postponements, Kazakhstan never gained any economic benefits from the flexible mechanisms, unlike its direct and close neighbours, in particular China and to a lesser extent Russia and Ukraine.

Against this background, the decision to implement an ETS, with a specific focus on a market mechanism for reductions of GHG emissions which should include 'international trade in allowances between the countries that have quotas and/or GHG emissions reductions and their legal entities', can be interpreted as a top-level political decision to take a more proactive and, one hoped, more successful role in the international carbon market.

Explaining the design of KzETS

Type of system: EU inspiration but also significantly 'home-brewed'

The KzETS is a conventional cap-and-trade system, divided into several phases. It started operating on 1 January 2013. The National Allocation Plan, approved in mid-December 2012, specified the allocation procedure and the duration of the pilot phase (one year, i.e. 2013). Once the pilot phase was completed, the KzETS entered a second trading period, 2014–15. A third trading period, originally planned for 2016–20, has been postponed, with a new start date planned for 1 January 2018.

The overall framework for Kazakhstan's ETS is inspired by the EU ETS, although divided into three much shorter phases. A main reason is that the relevant amendment to Kazakhstan's Environmental Code which set the start date of the pilot phase to 1 January 2013 was not adopted until December 2011. Just over a year before the pilot phase was due to start, all that was in place was the primary legislation which provided an outline; further legislative instruments (government decrees and ministerial orders) had to be developed during 2012. The second phase, 2014–15, therefore had an intermediary character which went beyond that of a pilot phase, but which still involved dealing with and developing fundamental aspects of a working ETS.

Due to the lack of time and resources, most issues and procedures related to matters like installation-level data, allocation approach, MRV, fundamental design of the system (e.g. on auctioning of allowances or whether GHGs other than CO_2 are to be covered), set-up of the allowance registry and design of the market oversight system were poorly defined (if at all) at the start of the pilot phase (Carbon Limits and Thomson Reuters Point Carbon 2013). Kazakhstan had no 'domestic tradition' of using economic instruments in environmental/climate policy upon which to build an operational ETS. The fact that policy-makers and legislators assumed that it could be possible to establish an operational ETS from scratch in just over 12 months shows an inadequate grasp of the complexities of such a market-based system and the need for mechanisms, regulations and institutional capacity to ensure transparency and confidence in the system. The resources – in terms of finance, manpower and know-how needed to fast-track implementation of the KzETS – were simply not available.

The objectives of the pilot phase were stated as being 1) to establish the trade infrastructure (national registry, methodological basis, monitoring system, verification and reporting for operators, accreditation of verifiers, infrastructure of secondary market, etc.) and 2) to clarify/amend legislation. With hindsight, we can see that more of these items should have been defined prior to the start of the pilot phase, which could then have been used for fine-tuning and amending the relevant procedures. Also, although Kazakhstan has received significant donor assistance in relation to developing its ETS, the first ETS-specific technical assistance programme was not launched until 2013 – again, due to the fast-tracked implementation process which did not allow sufficient time to notify the donor community.

Similarly, formal cooperation and exchange between Kazakhstan and the international community concerning the KzETS started late in relation to its actual implementation (that is, after the adoption of the relevant amendment to the Environmental Code in December 2011). For example, Kazakhstan became a technical partner of the World Bank's Partnership for Market Readiness (PMR) only in March 2014 – after the start of phase 2 of the KzETS. The upshot was that, by end of the pilot phase, significant technical issues remained unresolved, and many of the required procedures had not been defined. Phase 2, originally planned as the fully operational long-term phase, became in practice an intermediary phase, a hybrid between pilot and operational, since the official one-year pilot phase had proven insufficient for fully resolving all design issues.

Level of ambition: Doha pledge, but also appeasing industry

Both international and internal factors have shaped the ambition level of the KzETS. In the international context, Kazakhstan pledged to decrease its GHG emissions by 7 per cent through to 2020, as a percentage of the 1990 reference year, as part of its commitment made at the UN Climate Change Conference in Doha, December 2012. This pledge has influenced the level of ambition of the KzETS. Although allocation during the pilot phase was equal to 100 per cent of the emissions reported by companies for 2010, phase 2 foresaw a 1.5 per cent reduction in emissions by the end of 2015 compared to a company's average emission level in 2011/12. If this annual 1.5 per cent reduction were to continue until 2020, emissions from the 'ETS sector' would be projected to be reduced by at least 7 per cent (Carbon Limits and Thomson Reuters Point Carbon 2015).

Opposition to introduction of the KzETS from key target groups – operators in the power sector in particular – has characterized the roll-out of the system since its early days (Nabiyeva 2014). Attempts to appease this opposition have influenced the level of ambition, although this was not reflected in the original NAP. Rather, this influence led to an increase of nearly 9 million allowances compared to the government's allocation plan (Carbon Pulse 2015). This attempt to appease industry proved inadequate: Kazakhstan subsequently suspended its emissions trading scheme until 2018 as a result of opposition from industry, which claimed that the emissions reduction demands under the system were too strict and would lead to competitiveness concerns, and also that the legal foundations were too weak (Climate Policy Observer 2016).

The law On Amendments and Additions to Some Legislative Acts of Kazakhstan on Environmental Issues came into force on 22 April 2016. These amendments had the dual purpose of making changes to the Environmental Code which clarified various terms related to the KzETS and eliminated conflicts concerning distribution, issuance, change and redemption of quotas, as well as of suspending the scheme until 1 January 2018 (Ministry of Energy of the Republic of Kazakhstan 2016; ICAP 2016). When the KzETS restarts in 2018 it is expected to introduce new allocation methods based on benchmarking (as opposed to grandfathering), better-defined MRV processes and regulations and trading procedures for all market participants.

Allocation mechanisms: borrowing from the EU

The choice of free allocation, and the allocation methodology (grandfathering), have been copied from the early phases of the EU ETS. During the pilot phase of the Kazakh ETS, allocation was based on the grandfathering approach, being equal to 100 per cent of the non-verified emissions reported by companies for the reference year of 2010. This approach was retained for phase 2, with allocation based on an average of reported emissions for 2011–12. For phase 3, however, allocation is to be based on a benchmarking approach as adopted by the EU for allocating emission allowances under the EU ETS from 2013 onwards. Work is currently underway on developing appropriate benchmarks for the various sectors and products in Kazakhstan.

Any benchmarking approach adopted in Kazakhstan is expected to be based on the EU approach. However, it is unlikely to be a direct application of the EU or other relevant ETS approaches and benchmark figures, as it will need to reflect the specific conditions and economic burdens for the sectors in Kazakhstan. The various industrial sectors held slightly differing positions on the allocation mechanism (grandfathering vs benchmarking), which reflected their general view of the scheme and whether they considered their sector to be more, or less, advanced compared to international standards. The power sector has in general been opposed to a benchmarking approach, which mirrors its overall opposition to the KzETS. The oil and gas sector and the industry sector in particular have been more receptive to the idea of a benchmarking approach, providing the benchmarks chosen are specific to Kazakhstan and reflect operating conditions there.

Coverage: looking to the EU

Both CO_2 and methane are subject to monitoring and regulation in Kazakhstan,[6] but only CO_2 emissions are covered by the KzETS. Ever since the inception of the scheme, discussions have been ongoing as to whether methane emissions should be covered at a later date; however, this is not reflected in any current legislation or relevant documentation, and it is not expected to happen in the foreseeable future.

Coverage of the KzETS focuses on easy-to-monitor large fixed-point sources of emissions in the energy and power sector and in industries where combustion is part of the production cycle. In this respect, the KzETS would have been mostly compatible with the first two phases of the EU ETS. The operators and activities covered in phases 1 and 2 are grouped into three main sectors of the Kazakh economy: power; production of coal, oil and gas; and industry. According to the Environmental Code, the KzETS is also intended to cover agriculture and transport, but by the start of implementation of the pilot phase it had become clear that these are sectors with very specific challenges with respect to monitoring and ownership, especially in the agricultural sector, and where there is little if any international experience which can be emulated with respect to emissions trading.

Operators with annual CO_2 emissions exceeding 20,000 tons per year ('major emitters') and which belong to one of the three sectors mentioned prior are covered by the KzETS. It should be noted that the 20,000 tons per year threshold was applied at operator, or company, level and not for individual sites, and each company is therefore likely to operate several discrete sites which may be subject to a cap. An amendment to the legislation was originally proposed which would oblige companies to report data on an installation-level basis as opposed to an entity-level basis, which would be akin to the boundaries used by the EU ETS.

Offsets and linking: domestic drivers, international vision

The KzETS differs significantly from the EU ETS regarding the use of international and domestic crediting. The Environmental Code allows for implementation of offset projects in Kazakhstan under the existing international offset mechanisms (JI and CDM); a domestic crediting mechanism to reduce emissions; and a mechanism for environmental (green) investments. With respect to the domestic crediting mechanism (offset mechanism) a nine-point priority list of project types that can be implemented as offset projects in Kazakhstan has been specified by government decree, as follows: 1) mining and metallurgy (utilization of mine methane); 2) agriculture; 3) housing and communal services; 4) forestry; 5) prevention of land degradation; 6) renewables; 7) processing of municipal and industrial waste; 8) transport; and 9) energy-efficient construction. Unlike the KzETS, which at present covers CO_2 only, projects which reduce emissions of any GHG can be implemented as domestic offset projects.

To prevent double counting, the legislation specifies clearly: ‘project mechanisms cannot be carried out on installations or production objects that fall under greenhouse gas emission allocation requirements established by the National Allocation Plan’. This implies that domestic offset projects cannot be implemented at installations that are covered by the NAP. At present, there are no regulations that limit the amount of carbon units from domestic offset projects which can be used by an operator. In other words, as the regulation currently stands, theoretically a company could use 100 per cent of domestic offset units for compliance. With respect to CERs and ERUs, their use for compliance is not envisaged, so only units generated from domestic offset projects may be applied to this end.

The potential for linking with systems in other jurisdictions and for trading with these systems has been a point of interest to the architects of the KzETS from an early stage. This is demonstrated by the Environmental Code, which specifies that a market mechanism for reductions of GHG emissions should allow for ‘international trade in allowances between the countries that have quotas and/or GHG emissions reductions and their legal entities’.[7]

In addition, one stated aim of the pilot phase of the KzETS was ‘launching consultation in regard to linking with the EU ETS’. Based on this objective, the Preparedness for Emissions Trading in the EBRD Region (PETER)[8] project, supported by the European Bank for Reconstruction and Development (EBRD), was undertaken: among the chief aims was to assess the ‘market readiness’ of the KzETS for linking with other carbon markets. This analysis of the compatibility of the KzETS with the key features of the main operational trading schemes globally – the EU ETS, the Regional Greenhous Gas Initiative (RGGI) and the Western Climate Initiative (WCI) in North America – concluded that linking with EU ETS appeared the most promising, at least from the perspective of market design. Both RGGI and WCI have complex cost-containment procedures and elaborate market-support schemes that would not be compatible with the outline of the KzETS currently.

MRV and enforcement: copying the EU

With regard to MRV (monitoring, reporting and verification) and the rules for carrying out these tasks, the KzETS has copied many features of the EU model. Some components of the system are still under development, but it is eventually expected to be similar to its EU counterpart. For example, a monitoring plan must be prepared and submitted for third-party verification prior to approval by the Competent Authority (CA); there are monitoring and reporting regulations based on the EU Monitoring and Reporting Regulation; the annual emissions report is to be based on the monitoring plan and must be verified and confirmed by an independent third party. As in the EU ETS, uncertainty assessments are to be undertaken; moreover, the concept of tiers is included in the Kazakh MRV system.

Concerning enforcement, the Zhasyl Damu – the executive body of the Kazakh government responsible for drafting the secondary legislation, modelling the allocation procedure, including defining the NAP, and the collection and compilation of emissions data from operators – also originally performed many of the roles assigned to the ETS regulators under the EU system, including granting and maintaining permits, reviewing monitoring plans and reviewing verified annual emission reports. At the end of 2014, however, the functions of the Zhasyl Damu for overseeing company data and reporting were permanently transferred to the Committee on Environmental Regulation and Control (CERC), the institution that handles pollution control and environmental licenses. Such ETS functions are new to the CECR, and its approaches towards MRV compliance appear to be geared towards pollution control rather than handling reporting of the market, with a stronger focus on enforcement as opposed to providing follow-up instructions and secondary legislation. As of June 2014, any operator which fails to surrender sufficient allowances to meet its cap will be liable to a fine of 5 MCI (Monthly Calculation Index) for each ton of CO_2 in excess (currently equivalent to approximately USD 30).[9] In addition, administrative fines, for example for deficiencies or delays in reporting of emissions, were to be enforced during the 2014–15 period.

Discussion

This examination of the influence of policy diffusion on ETS design has shown that the overall framework for the ETS in Kazakhstan has been inspired by the EU ETS, with many of its design elements based on the EU system. In this respect, the key mechanism of policy diffusion could be seen as one of emulation, although learning has also played an important role, mainly through the support of donor agencies and international financial institutions. The EU ETS appears to have been the main model for the Kazakh system, but the latter has taken more general lessons from other systems as well, not least US-based systems like the WCI and

RGGI, through United States Agency for International Development (USAID)-supported programmes. Importantly, coercion as a policy diffusion mechanism has not been particularly evident. Thus far, the EU has showed limited interest and provided little if any support – which might seem surprising, since the design of the KzETS owes so much to the EU ETS. Perhaps because the EU has paid significant attention to China in the field of 'carbon trading assistance', it has had limited capacity to engage elsewhere.

As implementation of the KzETS initially enjoyed high-level backing in the government, and emphasis was placed on a 'fast-track' approach, it was politically important to ensure that the operational phase followed on directly from the one-year pilot phase – but the length of the pilot phase may not have been sufficient to iron out all possible problems in the system. The fast-tracked nature of the implementation process did not allow sufficient notification to the donor community to mobilize much-needed technical support until the pilot phase was completed. Donor agencies like the EBRD, the World Bank, the Norwegian Ministry of Foreign Affairs and USAID have provided significant and valuable assistance and support – but, had the Government of Kazakhstan requested this assistance prior to initiation of the pilot phase, many of the problems that led to the current postponement of the system could probably have been resolved.

The key domestic influences on the adoption and design of the KzETS have shifted in the course of the implementation period. The system was initiated, and strongly supported, by the highest levels within the government. Institutional changes in Kazakhstan – specifically, the status of the environmental portfolio within the government – and ministerial changes have influenced the government's stance, however. In parallel, opposition to the system on behalf of industry has become stronger. This opposition has resulted in design changes, such as the increase of 9 million allowances, and then postponement of the system until 2018.

Various factors have contributed to the growing opposition to the system on the part of the power, oil and gas and industrial sectors. First, although economic growth initially picked up during 2010–13 after the global economic crisis, growth in 2015 and 2016, when the KzETS was in its operational phase, was severely depressed as a result of plummeting oil prices. The slump in the country's economy is reflected in the value of the Kazakhstan currency unit, the tenge, which has more than halved compared to the US dollar, from around 150 tenge/USD at the start of 2014 to 330 tenge/USD by the end of 2016. Experiencing economic difficulties during this period, companies became averse to the perceived possibility of further financial burdens that could result from implementation of the KzETS.

Specific issues related to the tariff-setting mechanism for energy prices have also contributed to the vocal opposition from the power sector. Although the Kazakh power sector is largely deregulated and the state cannot impose tariffs, any changes to the latter must be proposed by operators and forwarded to the monopolies commission, based on an approved list of cost elements (e.g. cost of fuel). The cost of carbon is currently not included on this list, so any additional expenditures to a power company resulting from, for example, the need to purchase quotas cannot be passed on to the consumers.

Conclusions

The government of Kazakhstan can be seen as a trailblazer in Central Asia with respect to its vision on greening the economy and in developing policies and formulating targets that emphasize the need for low-carbon growth. The implementation of emissions trading has been a fundamental element of this vision. During the design of the KzETS, considerable emphasis was placed on learning and borrowing from the most established and largest operating system at the time: the EU ETS. This was a logical approach, as the EU is one of Kazakhstan's main trading partners; geographically, it was the closest operating system and could be taken as a template due to its relative longevity. Moreover, the architects of the KzETS aimed at eventually linking their system to other systems and saw the EU ETS as a potentially important market for Kazakh emissions reductions.

We have described how the ETS in Kazakhstan was launched, underwent a one-year pilot phase and then entered a hybrid pilot/operational phase which lasted two years, with implementation of a fully operational system slated to begin on 1 January 2016. Now the KzETS has been postponed until 2018, following complaints from industry that the emissions reduction demands under the system are too strict and the legal foundation too weak (Carbon Pulse 2016). To what extent are these complaints well-founded?

Starting with the legal foundation, there were indeed significant weaknesses in the original legislative design (the original amendments to the Environmental Code) of the KzETS. A main reason was the 'fast-track' nature of its implementation. As pointed out, legislation specifying the start date of the pilot phase was adopted less than 13 months prior to the start phase itself. It proved impossible to develop, fully and appropriately, all the necessary secondary legislation, procedures, tools, organizations and other elements by the start date. To the credit of the government officials who were given responsibility for managing and operating the system when it was launched, these deficiencies were indeed identified, and work was undertaken to make relevant changes to the legislation and to develop the required tools – but that was a difficult task to undertake once the system was already officially operating. Designing an ETS takes time and requires resources, and rushing the implementation through before the scheme is fully developed may prove counter-productive.

Are the emissions reduction demands under the system too strict? Our interpretation is that this relates more to enforcement than to the actual targets themselves. Responsibility for enforcing the KzETS was shifted from the Zhasyl Damu to the Committee on Environmental Regulations and Control, which traditionally handles pollution control and environmental licenses. CERC has seen the KzETS more as a permissions system than a trading system, and that view may undermine its nature as an effective market mechanism. The perceived risk entailed in this emphasis on permissions is a focus on identifying incidents of non-compliance and the application of penalties, instead of developing a workable trading mechanism to allow operators to meet their emissions targets in the most cost-effective manner. It is important to ensure that whoever enforces an ETS recognizes that the application of penalties is an option of last resort, especially if that ETS is not yet fully formed or operational. In such cases, a more flexible approach might be more appropriate.

The ETS of Kazakhstan is a fundamental element of the country's green growth initiative, and the adoption of a workable and effective trading system will be essential if Kazakhstan is to meet its international commitments cost-effectively. The overall framework for the KzETS has been inspired by the EU ETS, with many design elements based on the EU system. Policy diffusion mechanisms – particularly emulation and learning – can help explain some of the design similarities between the two systems, not least regarding allocation mechanisms, coverage and MRV. This observation is consistent with the traditional understanding of emulation as leading to *convergence*, as actors adopt a policy or practice initiated by more prestigious peers. Domestic political concerns have, however, also been important as mediating factors in the diffusion process that helped shape the design of the KzETS, resulting in design *divergence* rather than convergence. This applies particularly to ambition level, the offset rules and specific elaborations of design features. Thus, even with emulation as the key diffusion mechanism, the outcome of a diffusion process may be policy divergence. While this gives rise to questions about the feasibility of linking carbon markets more effectively, we conclude that having a clearer understanding of the role of policy diffusion can be of both theoretical and practical value for following up the ambitious climate policy goals adopted in Paris in 2015.

Notes

1 This chapter represents a significantly revised version of Gulbrandsen et al. (2017).

2 François Sammut, Carbon Limits, has been supporting the Kazakhstan government on ETS and climate change issues since 2010 through various donor-funded projects.

3 World Bank, Kazakhstan Trade Statistics, http://wits.worldbank.org/CountryProfile/en/KAZ (accessed 10 January 2017).

4 Law No. 505-IV, On Amendments and Additions to Certain Legislative Acts of the Republic of Kazakhstan concerning Environmental Issues (the law 'On Amendments').

5 By virtue of Protocol Article 1, para 7.

6 Government Decree #840, 'On Approval of the Rules for Monitoring/Control of the GHG inventory', 26 June 2012.

7 Article 94–7 of the Environmental Code.

8 See www.ebrdpeter.info/

9 The fines are equal to 10 multiplied by the monthly calculation index, which is subject to annual approval. One MCI in 2013 is equal to 1731 KZT, according to the Law No. 54-V dated 23 November 2012, On Republic Budget for 2013–2015.

References

Carbon Limits and Thomson Reuters Point Carbon. 2013. *The Domestic Emissions Trading Scheme in Kazakhstan*. Carbon Limits/Thomson Reuters. www.ebrdpeter.info/uploads/media/report/0001/01/d3cc004ab04df5be2d66179669998c2869992b15.pdf accessed 2 May 2017.

Carbon Limits and Thomson Reuters Point Carbon. 2015. *An Analysis of the Potential for Linking with External Emission Trading Schemes*. Carbon Limits/Thomson Reuters (report on file with authors).

Carbon Pulse. 2015. *Kazakhstan Proposes 4% Drop in Allowances for Third Phase of ETS*. http://carbon-pulse.com/12738/ accessed 10 January 2017.

Carbon Pulse. 2016. *Kazakhstan Suspends Its ETS Until 2018 – Minister*. https://carbon-pulse.com/16179/ accessed 20 April 2017.

Climate Focus. 2010. *Option Review for Kazakhstan to Participate in the International Carbon Market*. Climate Focus. www.ebrd.com/downloads/sector/eecc/kaz.pdf accessed 2 May 2017.

Climate Policy Observer. 2016. *Kazakhstan ETS to Be Suspended Until 2018*. http://climateobserver.org/9443-2/ accessed 6 January 2017.

European Commission. 2017. *Trade, Policy, Countries and Regions, Kazakhstan*. http://ec.europa.eu/trade/policy/countries-and-regions/countries/kazakhstan/ accessed 20 April 2017.

Gulbrandsen, L. H., F. Sammut and J. Wettestad. 2017. Emissions trading and policy diffusion: Complex EU ETS emulation in Kazakhstan. *Global Environmental Politics* 17 (3), 115–133.

ICAP. 2016. *Kazakhstan ETS Suspended Until 2018*. https://icapcarbonaction.com/ru/news-archive/387-kazakhstan-ets-suspended-until-2018 accessed 12 October 2016.

Ministry of Energy of the Republic of Kazakhstan. 2016. *Press Release*. http://energo.gov.kz/index.php?id=5355 (in Russian) accessed 12 October 2016.

Nabiyeva, K. 2014. *Businesses Urge Kazakhstan to Halt Asia's First Carbon Trading Scheme*. Thomson Reuters Foundation News, January 1. http://news.trust.org//item/20140101144716-ef4xl/ accessed 12 October 2016.

UNFCCC. 2013. *The III-VI National Communication of the Republic of Kazakhstan to the UN Framework Convention on Climate Change*. Ministry of Environment and Water Protection of the Republic of Kazakhstan. http://unfccc.int/files/national_reports/annex_i_natcom_/application/pdf/kaz_nc3,4,5,6_eng.pdf accessed 20 April 2017.

World Bank. 2016. *Population Data*. www.data.worldbank.org/indicator/SP.POP.TOTL accessed 12 October 2016.

11 China's carbon market

In it to learn it

Iselin Stensdal, Gørild Heggelund and Duan Maosheng

Introduction

In 2011, it was officially announced that China would 'gradually establish a carbon emissions trading market' (12th Five-Year Plan 2011: ch.6.21.1.). Rapid progress had been made in climate policies: not until 2007 did climate change become a national priority issue, with the release of the National Climate Change Programme (Stensdal 2014: 122; Heggelund and Nadin 2017). Just as China is the largest greenhouse gas (GHG)-emitting country in total terms, accounting for 29 per cent of global CO_2 emissions in 2015 (Le Quéré et al. 2016: 630), the national market is expected to become the world's largest in emissions covered (Zhang 2015: S118). However, it was not a given that China, with its long tradition of 'command and control' policies, would establish an emissions trading system (ETS).

This chapter explores the role of various causal drivers – international diffusion and, as a complementary explanation, domestic conditions – and how these affected both the decision to launch a carbon market and the design process. There is an extensive literature on the development of China's carbon market that focuses on the current status of the pilot projects and the national market (Cheng and Xu 2011; Duan et al. 2014; Hübler et al. 2014; Zhang et al. 2014; Liu et al. 2015; Jiang et al. 2016; Dong et al. 2016). Less attention has been paid to the reasons and drivers behind China's choice of a market mechanism and the factors that have shaped the specific design elements. These are research gaps that this chapter addresses.

The Chinese national market is set to commence in 2017. In order to prepare for emissions trading, China has been determined to learn from previous carbon-market experiences abroad and by creating learning opportunities domestically. Preparations for a national market started in 2011, with the approval of seven jurisdictions as carbon-market pilots. The pilots, which began operations in 2013–14, were intended to test out designs and provide lessons for designing the coming national market. There have also been various bilateral cooperation projects aimed at preparing for the pilots and the national market, as well as capacity-building training of stakeholders. The *ideational impact* from donor countries and multilateral organizations' lobbying would probably not in itself have 'tipped'

China to ETS unless the domestic conditions were present. An important feature here is what we call *internal learning*: the deliberate and focused process of establishing ETS trial areas, where the first few years of the national system are seen as a period for capacity-building and learning.

Data for this come from a range of written sources like official local and national documents and 25 interviews conducted in 2015 and 2016 with a range of stakeholders – policy-makers, consultancies, researchers, international donor partners, companies involved in the pilots and national market and third-party verifiers. It is also informed by participation in training seminars and workshops in China. We have drawn on written sources in Chinese and English and our interviews in order to determine to what extent diffusion mechanisms and domestic factors played a role in turning China onto ETS and in specific design decisions. Where applicable we have compared with pre-established carbon-market regulations, such as the EU ETS regulations, to identify any similarities between them and China's regulations.

In the following, we present some background, analyse the conditions for the adoption of a carbon market mechanism in the context of China's climate policies and then move on to the pilots and a discussion of possible diffusion regarding the design features and sectors. The national market and rationale for choices made in design and sector are then presented, followed by concluding remarks.

The emergence and evolution of emissions trading

China today is very different from the China which in the late 1970s embarked on reforms and opening up. The unparalleled annual growth in GDP, often double-digit percentages between 1978 and 2000 (World Bank 2016), which lifted millions from poverty, was driven largely by energy-intensive and heavy industry. It came at a price in the form of environmental degradation and high carbon emissions. As the economy expanded, so did energy consumption (Andrews-Speed 2012: 11–13). The main source of energy in China has been, and remains, coal. Coal stood for around 70 per cent of primary energy consumption between 1978 and 2012; only from 2012 has the share of coal been less than 70 per cent for consecutive years, reaching a record-low 64 per cent in 2015 (Andrews-Speed 2012: 11–13; NBS 2016: ch.9.2).

At the turn of the millennium, China saw itself as a developing country and would not accept a cap on its emissions. Instead, policies addressed energy concerns. Despite increases in energy consumption, energy intensity – the amount of energy needed to produce one unit of GDP – declined annually from 1980–2001. China was becoming more energy effective. From 2002–5 the energy intensity rose unexpectedly, caused by surges in industrial development and energy-intensive production, as well as an increase of coal in the energy mix. From 2003 there were energy shortages of commercial energy in China. Under the leadership of then-premier Wen Jiabao, the national government put efforts into regaining control of the energy sector (Andrews-Speed 2012: 16–20). China's main policy direction is driven in five-year cycles by the socioeconomic five-year plans (FYP). The

11th FYP (2006–10) addressed the energy-intensity issue with a target of reducing energy intensity by 20 per cent within those five years.

In 2006, a bilateral China–EU climate dialogue started. The following year, 2007, it became known that China had surpassed the US as the largest CO_2-emitting country in total terms (PBL 2007). During the 11th FYP period, energy-intensity reduction reached 19.1 per cent. In some areas it was very challenging to fulfil the local energy-intensity reduction targets, so temporary solutions like closing down factories and shutting off power were used in 2009 and 2010. This was an eye-opener to the leaders in Beijing, showing that old 'command and control' policy tools had their limitations as regards delivering effective yet maintainable policies (Qiu 2011).

The carbon market was not China's first encounter with market mechanisms for controlling gas emissions. The first emissions-scheme pilots in China came in the 1980s, concerning sulphur dioxide (SO_2) trading (Zhang et al. 2016: 876). More SO_2-emission trading studies and pilots followed from 1999, as a collaboration between the State Environmental Protection Administration (SEPA) (now Ministry of Environmental Protection, MEP) and the US Environmental Protection Agency. Between 2007 and 2016, the MEP, working together with the Ministry of Finance (MoF), initiated 11 pilots on trading of SO_2 and chemical oxygen demand (COD) emission permits (Zhang et al. 2016: 877). The experience with these SO_2 trading pilots was mixed (Hart and Ma 2014; Tung 2015) due to difficulties of implementation and regulations, combined with little previous familiarity with market mechanisms (Zhang et al. 2016: 876). However, this did not stop China from trying other market mechanisms, like the Clean Development Mechanism (CDM), part of the UN Framework Convention on Climate Change's (UNFCCC) Kyoto Protocol's flexible mechanisms. Initially sceptical to CDM, China came to embrace the mechanism as it fit well with the domestic priorities of economic development and energy, as well as brought in international project support (Heggelund et al. 2010: 246). By 2007 China alone accounted for about 60 per cent of all CDM projects in the pipeline, most of them renewable energy projects (Kinkead 2012: 2–5). Extensive support for CDM capacity-building was provided by donor countries and international organizations, as with the capacity-building projects under the UN Development Programme (UNDP) and the EU (Buhr et al. 2012: 81; UNDP 2012: 27–28).

The State Council is the highest executive body in the People's Republic of China. There is also the legislative National People's Congress (NPC) and a judiciary branch. Under the State Council, ministries and commissions are delegated responsibilities within their domains (Donald and Benewick 2005: 56–57; Saich 2015: 142). The National Development and Reform Commission (NDRC) is responsible for matters concerning climate change, energy and the carbon market. The National Climate Change Leading Group (NCCLG), chaired by the premier, was established in 2007; it serves as the national coordination institution on climate change. Other NCCLG members are representatives from ministries and commissions with relevant responsibilities for carrying out climate policies. The NCCLG signalled that climate issues were of importance at the highest levels of the Chinese government. Establishing leading groups to coordinate important issues among the relevant commissions and ministries is not an uncommon practice in China. The NDRC serves as secretariat for the NCCLG (Heggelund and Buan 2009: 306; Liu 2011: 85; Stensdal 2015: 56). Before major policy decisions are made, negotiations and bargaining are common – horizontally, as among various ministries, and vertically within the government (Saich 2015: 265). The 2007 launch of the National Climate Change Programme signalled that consensus on climate change among the Chinese top leaders had been reached (Liu 2011: 84).

The first political target directly aimed at curbing carbon emissions was declared prior to the 2009 climate summit in Copenhagen in 2009, when China announced its target of achieving, by 2020, a 40–45 per cent reduction from 2005 levels of tons of carbon emitted per produced amount of GDP (carbon intensity) (Reuters 2009). This would still allow emissions to rise with a growing economy, whereas an absolute cap would have set a carbon ceiling. The carbon-intensity target was, together with a continued energy-intensity target, incorporated into the next FYP, the 12th (2011–15), as a mandatory target. The goals were to reduce carbon intensity by 17 per cent and energy intensity by 16 per cent in the five years (12th Five-year plan 2011: ch.1.3).

On 29 October 2011, NDRC issued the Notice on Carrying out Carbon Emissions Trading Pilots (NDRC 2011), approving seven emissions-market pilots: in the two provinces of Guangdong and Hubei and the five cities of Beijing, Chongqing, Shanghai, Shenzhen and Tianjin. In China, it is common to test policies and new mechanisms in smaller areas before deciding on nationwide adoption. Following this, the State Council on 1 December 2011 released the Work Program for Controlling Greenhouse Gas Emissions in the 12th Five-Year Plan Period (Government of China 2011), calling for the development of a general plan on establishing a national market for trading in carbon emissions in China.

Launched in 2013 and 2014, the seven ETS pilots have provided substantial learning experience for the national system. These pilots were stand-alone markets with differing designs and allowance prices varying from less than USD 1 to more than USD 10. Also the fluidities varied – with trading volume in the Hubei pilot accounting more than half of total transactions. To further prepare the ground for the ETS, the NDRC issued the Interim Management Rules on Emissions Trading in December 2014 (NDRC 2014). Moreover, to strengthen the implementation basis, in December 2015 the NDRC submitted a draft national ETS regulation to the State Council, according to which the NDRC would be responsible for designing the market, with province-level development and reform commissions responsible for implementation and enforcement. The State Council included work on the ETS regulation in its work plan for 2016 (State Council Office 2016), indicating that a regulation might be in place by 2017. Further, a key document was issued in 2016, setting out key work to be conducted before the launch of the national carbon market in 2017 (NDRC 2016; Roldao 2016).

The 13th FYP (2016–20) was approved at the National People's Congress in March 2016. It sets the binding objectives of a 15 per cent reduction in energy intensity, and an 18 per cent decline in carbon intensity by 2020, as well as the establishment of a carbon market (13th Five-Year Plan 2016: ch.3 and 46.1). China also released its 13th Five-Year Plan on Greenhouse Gas (GHG) Emissions Control, in which the carbon market is set to play an important role in dealing with emissions (State Council 2016). In 2016, the State Council also approved approaches for setting a CO_2 cap for the national carbon market (Carbon Pulse 2016).

Explaining the adoption of ETS in China

China's decision to commence with ETS was shaped by a combination of domestic considerations and international influences. The diffusion mechanism of ideational impact came from the CDM experience and from ETS lobbying from the EU and other governments and international organizations (China Carbon Forum 2016: 4). Several interviewees agreed that the EU had been of special importance. The China–EU dialogue was probably helped by the good relationship between Connie Hedegaard of Denmark[1] and Xie Zhenhua, NDRC vice-chairman at the ministerial level from 2007 and one of China's key negotiators in the UNFCCC negotiations until he retired in 2015. EU strongly advocated the idea of ETS to China before 2010, and in bilateral cooperation it has been the strategy of the EU to empower the Chinese side to choose design options which are technologically and politically feasible, as shown later in this chapter. The experiences learned from CDM can help to explain why China was able to commence with the pilots so quickly. CDM also demonstrated emissions-market mechanisms in practice to companies and contributed to public awareness of carbon trading. The concept of emissions trading as a feasible mechanism for controlling emissions in China gradually gained the support of the central government.

The adoption of an ETS was also influenced by domestic factors. The concurrent economic development and energy situation, coupled with heightened awareness of the negative impacts of climate change on China, are central dimensions for explaining China's decision to establish an ETS. Managing GHGs with market mechanisms also fit well with China's larger path to development. The 12th FYP prescribed, in addition to a gradual carbon market establishment, to 'let the market play a fundamental role in resources allocation' (12th Five-Year Plan 2011: ch.1.1). The attitude that China would not accept emission cuts at home changed over the decade; combined with experiencing cost-effectiveness through CDM, the carbon market began to be perceived as a feasible policy option for China.

An important change occurred when the EU announced in 2009 that it would only accept offsets from least developed countries in EU ETS Phase 3, from 2013.[2] It is plausible that the approaching end to the CDM mechanism, with many actors and stakeholders facing an uncertain future, influenced the decision to start emissions trading (Tung 2015: 87). In order to address, *inter alia*, the coming reduction in foreign demand for certified emission reductions (CERs), Chinese certified emission reductions (CCERs) were created.[3]

China's previous SO_2 trading probably had limited impact on the NDRC's perceptions, as these pilots were managed by the MEP and not the NDRC. However, the learning experience may have been important for individuals. Xie Zhenhua, who was instrumental in promoting ETS in China, was head of SEPA and responsible for the SO_2 trading-pilot before becoming vice-chairman of the NDRC. As such, the CDM might have been more directly important for NDRC, as the commission was in charge of the CDM and is also in charge of the ETS (Buhr et al. 2012: 83; China Carbon Forum 2016: 4).

According to our interviews, the NDRC started considering a carbon market for China as a policy option in 2009 and 2010 and lobbied higher levels of government for this option. There were those who held that China should implement a carbon tax rather than a carbon market, among them researchers, counsellors, the Ministry of Finance and Ministry of Environmental Protection. However, developing the ETS gained important support from several top leaders, with the opinion that China should not follow the same emissions path as developed countries. In addition, President Xi Jinping, who rose to power the year after the decision was made, has emphasized building an ecological civilization which includes dealing with various kinds of pollution, as well as climate change. Such top-level support is necessary for a policy as comprehensive as ETS to be implemented.

Furthermore, utilizing a market mechanism to improve energy intensity was seen as a policy tool consistent with China's development stage, called 'The New Normal' – a new governing philosophy introduced by President Xi Jinping in 2014 to describe the changed socioeconomic situation of slower economic growth, improved economic structure and more innovation-promoted development than previous decades. After President Xi's announcement of a 2017 start for the national market, the political bargaining on whether to implement a national market was put to rest. When launched, the national ETS in China will be one of a range of policy tools for dealing with GHG emissions, in addition to industrial and economic restructuring, low-carbon development, energy efficiency and renewable energy (Qian and Chen 2015: 14; State Council 2016). Linking with other policy processes like the trading of rights to use energy would be highly relevant. Building and improving market mechanisms are mentioned in the 13th Five-Year Plan's Comprehensive Work Plan for Energy-Saving and Emissions Reduction, not only for carbon emissions, but also for energy use and pollution rights (Government of China 2016: ch.9.34). To achieve an emissions peak by 2030, industry will have to peak in 2020 (ERI et al. 2016: 14, 34–35).

As mentioned, the idea behind the pilot projects was to try out various design features on a smaller scale before making decisions for the whole country – a deliberate *internal learning* process. After the seven pilots were approved, other jurisdictions expressed interest in ETS pilots or starting with carbon market–related policies: these included Anhui province, Jinchang and Jiuquan, cities in Gansu province, Qingdao city in Shandong province and Hangzhou city in Zhejiang province (Reklev 2015a). Moreover, the seven official pilots had applied to the NDRC and gained approval – rather than the NDRC choosing and emplacing responsibilities on the jurisdictions. Such interest from local jurisdictions illustrates several features of Chinese politics today. First, local leaders are now performance evaluated on economic growth and on ecological measures. The ETS is

Table 11.1 Pilots design

	Beijing	*Shenzhen*	*Shanghai*	*Tianjin*	*Chongqing*	*Hubei*	*Guangdong*
Type of system and start date	Cap and trade 28 November 2013.	Cap and trade 18 June 2013.	Cap and trade 26 November 2013.	Cap and trade 26 December 2013.	Cap and trade 19 June 2014.	Cap and trade 2 April 2014.	Cap and trade 19 December 2013.
Economy-wide ambition level 1	Carbon-intensity target 2011–15: 18% 2016–20: 20.5%.	Carbon-intensity target 2011–15: 21% By 2020: 50% from 2005.[2]	Carbon-intensity target 2011–15: 19% 2016–20: 20.5%.	Carbon-intensity target 2011–15: 19% 2016–20: 20.5%.	Carbon-intensity target 2011–15: 17% 2016–20: 19.5%.	Carbon-intensity target 2011–15: 17% 2016–20: 19.5%.	Carbon-intensity target 2011–15: 19.5% 2016–20: 20.5%.
Coverage	CO_2. Electric power, heat, cement, petrochemical and the service sector during 2013–15, and transportation added in 2016. During 2013–15: fixed installations with annual emissions of at least 10,000 tons of CO_2; in 2016, fixed installations, urban rail transit operating units and public electric passenger transportation units with annual emissions of at least 5,000 tons of CO_2.	CO_2. Power, water supply, manufacturing sectors, buildings, public transportation. Emissions of at least 3,000t CO_2e/year for enterprises; 10,000m^2 for buildings.	CO_2. Iron and steel, petrochemicals, chemicals, non-ferrous metals, electric power, building materials, textiles, papermaking, rubber; non-industrial sectors including chemical fibre, civil aviation, ports, airports, railways, business, hotels and finance during 2013–15. Shipping included since 2016. For power and industry: 20,000t CO_2/year (before 2015), 10,000t CO_2/year (2016); For non-industry: 10,000t CO_2/year.	CO_2. Heat and electricity production, iron and steel, petrochemicals, chemicals, exploration of oil and gas. Entities with annual CO_2 emissions equal to or more than 20,000 tons since 2009.	CO_2, CH_4, N_2O, HFCs, PFCs, SF_6. Power, electrolytic aluminium, ferroalloys, calcium carbide, cement, caustic soda and iron and steel. Annual emissions reaching 20,000 CO_2e tons during any year between 2008 and 2012.	CO_2. Electric power and heat, automobiles and other equipment manufacturing, non-ferrous metals and other metal products, iron and steel, glass and other building materials, cement, chemicals, petrochemicals, food and beverage, chemical fibre, papermaking and medicine in 2014. Cogeneration and ceramic manufacturing, general equipment manufacturing added in 2015.	CO_2. Energy, iron and steel, cement, petrochemicals during 2013–15, and paper and pulp and civil aviation added in 2016. Enterprises with annual CO_2 emissions of 20,000 tons or more (or energy consumption if 10,000 tons of standard coal equivalents [tce]) in 2011 or 2012; new projects with annual CO_2 emissions of 20,000 tons or above (or energy consumption of 10,000 tce) during 2013–15 and in the 13th FYP period.
Allocation mechanism	Free allocation and auctions.	Free allocation and auctions.	Free allocation and auctions.	Free allocation.	Free allocation.	Free allocation and auctions.	Free allocation and auctions.
Offsetting	Offsetting credits limited to 5% of the annual free allowances. CCERs issued, carbon emission reductions from energy-saving projects and forest carbon sink projects. CCERs from projects outside Beijing can be used up to 2.5% of the annual allowances.	CCERs limited to 10% of the annual compliance obligation. Credits from hydro projects not eligible.	CCERs limited to 5% of the annual free allowances. Credits for reductions that were realized before January 2013 cannot be used for compliance.	CCERs limited to 10% of the annual compliance obligation. Credits must stem from CO_2 reduction projects, excluding hydro, and have to be realized after 2013.	CCERs limited to 8% of the compliance obligation. Credits from hydro projects not allowed. Reductions have to be achieved after 2010; carbon sink projects excepted.	CCERs limited to 10% of the annual allowances allocated at beginning of compliance period; from Hubei. Credits from large and medium hydro not	CCERs limited to 10% of the annual compliance obligation. Half have to be from CO_2 or CH_4 reduction projects; 70% from Guangdong.

	Credits from hydropower, HFC, PFC, N_2O and SF_6 projects not eligible; reductions must be achieved after beginning of 2013.						
MRV and enforcement	Annual reporting of CO_2. Third-party verification required. Penalties exist for non-compliance (can result in fines) and for failure to surrender sufficient allowances to match emissions.	Annual reporting of CO_2 emissions with a tier approach taking into account the size of the company. Third-party verification is required. Penalties exist for failure to submit emissions/ verification report on time/ providing fake information/ disturbing the market.	Annual reporting of CO_2 emissions. Verification: Third-party verification is required. Penalties exist for failure to submit emissions/ verification report on time and for fraudulent information.	Annual reporting of CO_2 emissions. Third-party verification required. No financial penalties; non-compliant companies are disqualified for financial support for three years.	Annual reporting of GHG emissions. Third-party verification required. No financial penalties for non-compliance. The punishments may include media reporting and public exposure of the non-compliance.	Annual reporting of CO_2 emissions. Third-party verification required. Penalties for failing to submit an emissions or verification report on time.	Annual reporting of CO_2 emissions. Third-party verification required. Penalties for failing to submit an emissions or verification report on time and for failure surrender sufficient allowances to match emissions
Price/ quantity management	Development and Reform Commission (DRC) can organize temporary auction/ buy in case of market fluctuations.	DRC: sell extra allowances from a reserve at fixed price in case of market fluctuations.	Shanghai Environment and Energy Exchange: price stabilization measures/ suspend trading in case of 10% variations in one day.	Tianjin DRC: organize temporary buy/sell.	Chongqing Carbon Emissions Exchange: price stabilization measures. Compliance entities must not sell more than 50% of their free allocation.	DRC with advisory committee (can buy or sell allowances in order to stabilize the market.	Auction floor price.
Revenue earmarking	Open Market Operation Fund.	N/A.	N/A.	N/A.	N/A.	Carbon Mitigation Fund.	Guangdong Low Carbon Development Fund.

Sources: State Council (2016); ICAP 2016; Tao and Duan (2016).

[1]13th FYP goal aims to reduce national GDP CO_2 intensity by 18% below 2015 levels by 2020. The work plan of the FYP allocates specific carbon-intensity goals to the pilots indicated in the table.

[2]Shenzhen intends to peak its carbon emissions by 2020, and rather than a carbon-intensity target between 2016 and 2020, it has set its target from the year 2005 (Shenzhen DRC 2016b: ch.2.2).

seen as a policy which caters to both. Second, some interviewees explained that local leaders want to be the first to implement a new mechanism in order to be able to host exchanges and obtain a first-mover advantage.

Explaining the specific design of the pilots

We first present the different design elements and the reasons for these choices (see Table 11.1). Then we move into a section discussing more overall tendencies of drivers for design.

Type of system and ambition level: supporting the carbon-intensity targets

The pilots first set out on annual compliance periods from 2013/14 to 2015, with varying absolute caps and intensity targets. In Guangdong, the government announced a cap for 2013 equalling 350 million tons of CO_2, whereas in Shenzhen there was a cap on absolute emissions between 2013 and 2015, in combination with individual carbon-intensity targets for the compliance units covered (Munnings et al. 2014: 17–18). The pilot projects varied in how much information of the calculations and caps was made public (Carbon Pulse 2016). All pilots were cap and trade. Ambition levels varied according to the jurisdictions' carbon-intensity targets within the 12th FYP period – ranging from a 17 per cent reduction for Chongqing and Hubei to 21 per cent for Shenzhen (Government of China 2011; Shenzhen Government 2013a).

The ambition levels of the pilot caps were calculated and determined by domestic reasons. The pilot markets supported achieving pilots' carbon-intensity targets in the 12th FYP period (Duan et al. 2014: 529). Cap calculations included local growth rate, carbon intensity and energy figures in 2010 and 2015 projections; emissions were also divided into sectors covered by the pilot and the part of the economy not included (Duan et al. 2014: 530; Carbon Pulse 2016).

Allocation method: avoiding EU mistakes

All pilots except Guangdong allocated allowances for free in the first compliance cycles. Guangdong decided on free allocation for 97 per cent of the compliance entities' allowances and mandatory auctioning of the remaining 3 per cent. In 2015, the share of free allocations and voluntarily auctioned allowances in Guangdong was changed to 90 per cent and 10 per cent, respectively (Munnings et al. 2014: 21; Carbon Pulse 2016). Whereas most pilots allocated every year, in the Shanghai pilot allowances were allocated for the first three cycles (2013, 20014, 2105) at the same time (Zhang et al. 2014: 12).

The pilots tended to us a combination of benchmarking and grandfathering in allocating. However, in Shenzhen the very first round of allocation for 2013 was conducted according to game theory, in particular the Shapley value:[4] each compliance unit was offered a certain amount of allowances. If they accepted the offer, that was it and they exited the game. For those who did not accept the allocation offer in the first round, there was a second offer – but, as more companies accepted offered allowances, the allowance pool would be correspondingly reduced, leaving fewer allowances for the later rounds of the allowance game. This provided an incentive for companies to accept the first offer. However, this procedure was followed only once. Later regulations allowed a mix of grandfathering and benchmarking in allocating allowances (Shenzhen DRC 2016).

In order to understand this picture we find the diffusion mechanism *learning* helpful, leading to divergence in designs. Allocation difficulties experienced in the EU ETS, and that uncertainties about future economic growth may create over-allocation, were lessons which China noticed. The pilot projects sought to address this challenge in their allocation choices by choosing designs different from the EU ETS and more in line with their own situations. Nevertheless, they did not manage to solve the problem of over-allocation fully (China Carbon Forum 2016: 4). Giving priority to letting companies get accustomed to the system over deep emissions cuts in the beginning contributed to over-allocation in the pilots.

Furthermore, the different pilot Development and Reform Commissions (DRCs) also had different opinions of the best allocation method for their own jurisdictions. In Guangdong the DRC wanted to obtain revenues from the pilot and decided to auction parts of the allowances. Shenzhen's first allocation according to game theory and the Shapley value is an example of one individual's influence on design. This choice came about as a result of the vice-mayor, who was also a professor of economy. He took a special interest in the pilot and recommended using this allocation method. Additionally, the benchmarking approach was largely informed by the experience of the EU ETS. Two types of benchmarking were used in the pilots: historical or current production. Some applied the same approach as in EU ETS: Guangdong used historical production-based benchmarking in the first year, but abandoned this from the second year (Duan et al. 2014).

There were also local drivers for the choices of allocation approaches. Some pilot governments conferred with local industry, businesses and stakeholders. The industry wanted free allocation to help the transition into the carbon market (Wu et al. 2014: 1, 13). In Beijing, one month was set aside for soliciting stakeholder feedback, and in Shanghai, local industries and companies were consulted (Shanghai DRC 2015: 21). To some extent, companies and industries were consulted prior to the decision on allocation methods. From our interviews we learned that companies, especially from coal industry and the power association, signalled that they were not pleased with the new policy. They felt that they were already subjected to enough taxes and burdens. Other companies were more positive towards participation and eager to understand how a carbon market would affect their business.

The pilot governments accommodated their concerns to some extent. In Shanghai, local companies had some sway over allocation regulations. Companies with rapid growth asked to have their situation taken into consideration in the allocation process. Others that had already implemented energy-saving measures did not want their early actions to be forgotten; they preferred benchmarking, seeing this as a more just allocation method. To a certain extent, these views were heeded; allocations for the power sector were based on benchmarking, whereas allocations for airlines, ports and airports were based on historical emissions intensities. There were also provisions in the pilot regulations for changing allocated allowances on grounds of energy-saving projects conducted from 2006–11. Paying attention to the complying companies and incorporating their wishes when possible were important for the Shanghai government, which recognized that in the end it was the companies that would have to abide by the pilot regulations (Stensdal 2016: 12–13).

Sector, gases and emissions covered: local economic situations and the national power sector

All pilots all covered CO_2, but Chongqing included the other GHGs as well: CH_4, N_2O, HFCs, PFCs, SF_6 (Carbon Pulse 2016). Commonly covered were the power sector, iron and steel sector, cement sector and chemical and petrochemical sectors, but there were also some differences. Shanghai was the only pilot to include domestic civil aviation, for example (Duan et al. 2014: 531). Entry thresholds ranged from emissions as low as 3,000 tons CO_2 annually for enterprises in the Shenzhen pilot to energy consumption higher than 60,000 tons of coal equivalents for enterprises in the Hubei pilot (Carbon Pulse 2016). (See Table 11.1 for details.) Emissions coverage ranged from an estimated 33 per cent of emissions in Hubei to 60 per cent in Shanghai (Zhang et al. 2014: 12).

When it became clear that there would also be a phase 2 of the pilots, from 2016, many pilots added new sectors: for instance, Guangdong added aviation for 2016; Shanghai added a few more sectors, including shipping; and Shenzhen added transportation companies (Guangdong DRC 2016; Shanghai DRC 2016; Shenzhen DRC 2016a).

As to which sectors to include, the pilots largely chose sectors on the basis of local economic, emission and energy conditions. The inclusion of aviation in Shanghai, for example, was decided after a city-wide economic survey, where the pilot government examined mitigation potential and feasibility. The choice of 20,000 tons of CO_2 as the entry threshold in Chongqing, Guangdong, Shanghai and Tianjin might indicate *simple emulation*: the 2003 EU ETS Directive set the entry threshold for combustion installations at 20 MW, and the choice of the figure 20,000 might have been inspired by this (EU 2003: Annex 1).

All pilots covered both direct and indirect emissions. Indirect emissions are emissions, for example, from electricity used in production of goods imported into the pilot area (Zhang et al. 2014: 12). This is quite unique to China: most schemes cover only direct emissions because including indirect emissions entails the risk of double counting emissions.

Indirect emissions were included because they constitute a large share of emissions in many provinces. It is not a very complicated to measure indirect emissions from electricity generation flow. Furthermore, China has an electricity sector with fixed and regulated prices, so costs cannot be transferred to the consumers.

Including indirect emissions would also be an incentive to industry to reduce electricity consumption (Zhang et al. 2014: 12).

Offsets, price management and revenue earmarking: testing different approaches

All pilot projects allowed the use of CCERs, but with maximum percentages ranging from 5 to 10 per cent in the period from 2013–15. Pilots also had restrictions regarding the location of CCERs' origin and time of production. In Guangdong, at least 70 per cent of the CCERs used had to originate from the province, and no pre-CDM credits were accepted. Beijing, Chongqing, Guangdong, Hubei, Shenzhen and Tianjin did not allow offsets from hydro projects (ICAP 2016).

All pilots project had wording that allowed the pilot government to intervene in case of price fluctuations or if deemed necessary, but they varied in their rules for regulating prices. Guangdong, for example, operated with a price floor (Munnings et al. 2014: 28; ICAP 2016). Changes to the rules were also made during time of operation. In June 2015 Shanghai's pilot government changed the price rules, narrowing range of price movements from one day to another from 30 per cent to 10 per cent for transactions traded on the exchange (Reklev 2015b).

Some pilots also allocated a certain amount of allowances to form a reserve. In Guangdong the pilot was set up with an allowance reserve intended for use in case of market intervention or to enable allocations to new entrants (Guangdong Provincial Government 2014: ch.3.11). Shenzhen maintained a reserve of 2 per cent of the allocated allowances for price-regulation use (Munnings et al. 2014: 28). As to revenue earmarking, in Guangdong the authorities created a fund that included revenues from allowance auctioning. In October 2015 this fund was reportedly around 100 million RMB, expected to increase sixfold in the coming years (Carbon Pulse 2016).

These design aspects can be seen as results of the pilot projects testing out different approaches. As they all had some wording on price management in their regulations, it is plausible to assume that this was a result of *learning* from the EU ETS experience with price problems. Concerning offset regulations, all designs attempted to restrict the amount of offsets in the markets. Several interviewees explained that the restrictions on time and type were meant to ensure the quality of eligible offsets and limit their quantity, to avoid possible flooding of the market by offsets – a lesson learned from the EU ETS. The wording of price regulations was not equally specific in all pilots, and some rules were created along the way in response to *ad hoc* situations. For example, Shanghai restricted the scope of price fluctuations as a response to price shocks where allowance prices had fallen by 30 per cent from one day to the next (Reklev 2015b).

MRV and enforcement: initial lessons from the EU and easing into the system

For monitoring, reporting and verification (MRV), the pilot projects each had unique methodologies for their sectors. All pilots required third-party verification (ICAP 2016), but the regulations on penalties varied significantly. There were no direct economic penalties in the Chongqing and Tianjin pilots (Chongqing Trading Center 2014; Dong et al. 2016: 8). However, in Hubei the penalties for various kinds of offenses ranged between 3,000 and 150,000 RMB, and from 10,000 to 100,000 RMB in Shanghai (ICAP 2016). The pilots operated with various types of legal basis. Only Beijing and Shenzhen had their People's Congresses pass legislation enabling these two pilots to issue higher fines for non-compliance than the local DRCs could do without such a legal basis. In Beijing, the rules allowed the government, in cases where compliance entities did not surrender allowances, to issue fines equal to three to five times the worth of the allowances not submitted (ICAP 2016).

For MRV, lessons from the EU were important. To facilitate study, the EU rules for measuring and reporting were translated into Chinese. As the EU rules were important in the initial studies, we may assume that *sophisticated learning* occurred as domestic and local conditions were considered in the design choices. It is hard to delimit the influence of the two, however. Customary domestic practices influenced design choices. In the EU, installations are the compliance units, whereas in the Chinese markets the compliance units are enterprises. Legal companies/enterprises are compliance units because this is the common unit for similar regulations in China, such as energy-intensity, energy-efficiency and energy-conservation regulations. Pre-existing data were by legal company unit, not by installation. The logic behind many design choices in the pilots was the aim of getting the stakeholders used to the new mechanism, rather than trying to achieve major emissions cuts immediately. Compliance units are allowed to 'ease' into the system in the first few years. As an extension of this logic, the Chongqing and Tianjin pilots had no direct economic penalties (Dong et al. 2016: 8).

Discussion

In 2011, the pilot projects began preparing their markets. NDRC supervised the work, giving guidance when asked, but the pilots were free to design their markets as they saw fit. This entailed a steep learning curve: the go-ahead was given in late 2011, and they started in 2013/14. In preparing the projects, the pilot governments first needed to understand the basic cogs and wheels of a carbon market. This they did by studying existing markets such as the EU and Californian markets. The EU ETS was the most important model for China in the beginning. China has also participated in the Asia Pacific Carbon Market Roundtable (APCMR) since its inception in 2011, with the other jurisdictions California, Chile, Indonesia, Japan, Korea, New Zealand, the North American Regional Greenhouse Gas Initiative,

Singapore and Thailand (Hill 2016: 317). Several countries and organizations collaborated with the pilot governments on training and capacity-building projects, such as the UK's training for Guangdong, Hubei and Shenzhen and the Asian Development Bank's Advancing Shanghai Carbon Market through Emissions Trading (ADB 2016b).

In most cases, however, the domestic conditions and local circumstances were the decisive element in design specifics, as with intensity targets leading the climate policy ambition, and the economic and industrial mix guiding which sectors to include. There were differences in actual design, but the factors shaping the decisions were generally similar. Local economic, emission and energy conditions were important in most design choices and later changes, but the process started with studies of other markets. That contributed to *sophisticated learning,* taking lessons as to what to do and what to avoid and making design choices suited to local and domestic conditions.

As to local drivers, the economic and energy circumstances influenced many design details, particularly in choices on sector coverage. Further, the opinions of local stakeholders were sought before decisions were made: several pilot governments invited industry and stakeholders to comment. Additionally, a few months before the adoption of the main regulation document, comments from the public were welcomed in both Shanghai and Shenzhen (Shenzhen Government 2013b; Shanghai DRC 2015: 21).

The conditions for diffusion were inherently different before and after China's 2011 decision to implement an ETS was made, however. Prior to 2011, *learning* influenced the decision to adopt the policy. That policy decision can be seen as a tipping point that opened the way to further actions and possibilities for diffusion on the various design aspects that needed to be decided. From when the work on pilots began, where studying previous market mechanisms was a first step, diffusion continued, mostly as *learning.* First, the focus was on understanding the basic mechanisms; then as the pilot governments gained knowledge and came to decide on design elements, it was important to avoid previous mistakes, such as the over-allocation that had plagued the EU ETS.

Explaining the national market

In September 2015, in connection with President Xi's state visit to the US, the two countries issued a joint statement on climate change. President Xi also confirmed a starting date for China's national market: in 2017 (White House 2015). For the national market to be governed effectively, China must have firm legal backing. The NDRC has sent a text proposal to the State Council, and such legislation was on the priority list of the State Council's work plan for 2016. However, that proposal has been in a queue behind some 80 other issues that the State Council must handle first (China Carbon Forum 2016: 4; Idea Carbon 2016). At time of writing (October 2017) the State Council has yet to adopt any legislation, so the regulations issued by the NDRC are what currently regulate the national market. In

Table 11.2 National system design

	National system
Type of system and start date	Cap and trade 2017
Economy-wide ambition level	Carbon-intensity target 2011–15: 17% 2016–20: 18%
Coverage	CO_2 1. Petrochemical industry (crude oil processing, ethylene) 2. Chemical industry (calcium carbide, synthetic ammonia, methanol) 3. Building construction and materials (cement clinker and plate glass) 4. Iron and steel 5. Non-ferrous metals (electrolytic aluminium, copper smelting) 6. Pulp and papermaking (pulp manufacturing, machine-made paper and paperboard) 7. Power (generation, cogeneration, power grids) 8. Aviation (civil passenger transport, cargo, airports)
Allocation mechanism	Free allocation as the major approach in the beginning, auctions will also be introduced
Offsetting	Offsetting rules not issued at time of writing (October 2017)
MRV and enforcement	Annual reporting of CO_2 emissions Third-party verification required Penalties for non-compliance suggested by NDRC: 3–5 times of average market value in the previous year of the outstanding allowances (specific rules not issued at time of writing, October 2017)
Price/Quantity Management	A reserve of allowances for market adjustments and new entrants likely (rules not issued at time of writing, October 2017)
Revenue Earmarking	The revenues from bought allowances to be used towards carbon reductions and capacity building (rules not issued at time of writing, October 2017)

Sources: Carbon Pulse 2016; Idea Carbon 2016; NDRC 2014, 2016.

December 2014, the NDRC issued the Interim Management Rules on Emissions Trading, providing a temporary design for the national market (NDRC 2014). The presentation in Table 11.2 is thus not complete on the eight design dimensions, but it shows the specific details known so far and the shaping factors we are aware of.

Type of system and ambition level

The national system will be a cap-and-trade system like the pilot projects. At present, there is no official pre-determined absolute cap (Carbon Pulse 2016), and for the first few years of the national scheme (up to 2020) the cap is not expected to be very stringent (China Carbon Forum 2016: 5). The cap consists of free allowances, allowances for auctioning and market intervention. The amount of free allowances will be determined by allocation approaches directly related to the actual production of the enterprises covered. As production varies from year to year, the cap will vary every year (Pang and Duan 2016: 818). NDRC has also signalled that the first years of the national market up to 2020 will be regarded as a learning period for the national market.

Allocation: first for free, as in the pilots

According to the 2014 interim measures, allocations will mainly be free, with an unspecified gradual increase of payment for the allowances (NDRC 2014: ch.2.9). Gathering historical data including emissions data, in order to allocate for the national market, is already underway. Already in 2015, the provinces started the process of accounting, reporting and verification of historical data. Third-party verifiers were commissioned by the provincial authorities to verify emissions, with recommendations from the NDRC as to eligibility requirements and technical guidelines for verification. The 2014 measures made the central government responsible for formulating unified rules and put the provincial governments in charge of implementation of the rules, including allocation within their jurisdictions, also allowing local governments to stipulate more stringent allocation rules than the national system regulations (NDRC 2014: ch.2.12–13).

Allocations for free might be a lesson from the pilot projects: in order to get companies to join the national market, one should not burden them with heavy expenses in the beginning. In its proposal to the State Council, the NDRC suggested starting with allocations for free and increasing the payment for allowances as time progresses, as is also stipulated in the 2014 interim rules (Idea Carbon 2016: ch.2.8). Moreover, the national ETS will draw upon the benchmarking practices and experiences from the pilots. According to the document on allocation and cap setting approved by the state, allocation approaches to be used in China's national system will include a combination of benchmarking and historical intensity-based and absolute emission-based grandfathering ones, depending on the subsectors (Swartz 2016: 17).

Sector, gases and emissions covered: aviation coerced into the national system?

It is expected that the national system in the first few years will cover CO_2 only, involving some 10,000 entities emitting an estimated three to four billion tons of CO_2 (Carbon Pulse 2016). In January 2016, the NDRC issued a notice specifying eight sectors and 18 subsectors for purposes of historical data collection which may be included in the national market in the first years, but not necessarily all upon commencement:

1 Petrochemical industry (crude oil processing, ethylene)
2 Chemical industry (calcium carbide, synthetic ammonia, methanol)
3 Building materials (cement clinker and plate glass)

4 Iron and steel
5 Non-ferrous metals (electrolytic aluminium, copper smelting)
6 Pulp and papermaking (pulp manufacturing, machine-made paper and paperboard)
7 Power (generation, cogeneration, power grids)
8 Aviation (civil passenger transport, cargo, airports)

(NDRC 2016: Appendix 1).

As for sector coverage, the inclusion of the aviation sector has *competitive* aspects attached to it. In 2011 it became known that, starting from 1 January 2012, the EU Commission would require all airlines flying to Europe to be included in the EU ETS, which would mean they would have to purchase carbon permits once a given cap had been exceeded. China's Civil Aviation Administration (CAAC) was fiercely opposed to that rule, claiming it would cost Chinese airlines USD 123 million in 2012, trebling by 2020. Although there were fears of trade conflict and retaliatory measures among the European industry, the EU conveyed the message to Chinese airlines that if China regulated aviation itself, Chinese airlines would be exempt from EU ETS participation (Harrison 2011). This was described by some of our interviewees as a decision made on *competitive* grounds: China would rather include aviation in its own market than have the EU manage it and therefore 'ratcheted up' its own design to be on par with the EU ETS. This was also supported domestically: the CAAC saw inclusion of aviation in the national system as a competitive advantage. CAAC expected the International Civil Aviation Organization (ICAO) to regulate aviation in the future and saw it as an advantage for Chinese airlines to engage ahead of the international regulations. By adhering to high standards domestically, Chinese airlines would be at the forefront internationally as well. As CAAC expected, ICAO member countries reached an agreement in October 2016, and the Carbon Offsetting and Reduction Scheme for International Aviation (CORSIA) was adopted, although negotiations on details are set to continue in the coming years (Chen et al. 2016).

Offsets and linking: recycling CDM methodologies; linking after 2020

The specific rules for the national market have yet to be issued as of the time of writing (October 2017) and are not seen as priorities during the stage of preparing for the national system. According to the interim measures, additional requirements will be established, and statements from the NDRC have signalled that there will be tight restrictions on what kinds of projects will be eligible and a limit for how large a share will be permitted (Reklev 2016b). The EU's offsetting rules were studied for Chinese offsetting rules. National CCER rules were issued in 2012 (NDRC 2012), but most CCER methodologies were based on the CDM methodologies (Yin 2013). This simple emulation was because the CDM methodologies were deemed a sufficient, cost-effective and quick starting point, whereas developing new methodologies is resource demanding. As such, the reason was not a fully uncritical embrace, but was also connected with time and resource constraints. Linking to other carbon markets is another aspect which has attracted considerable international interest and anticipation. However, such linking designs will probably be in focus only after 2020, when China's national market has been operating for some years (Garside 2015; Reklev 2016c).

MRV and enforcement: adjusting EU rules to national conditions, and State Council regulation needed

MRV lessons from abroad, in particular the EU ETS, have been important for China. Measuring and registry is similar to the EU compliance cycle, but in creating MRV routines the capacity challenges have to be taken into account. Both the NDRC and several local DRCs are understaffed when it comes to ETS (Swartz 2016: 18). The suggested solution is for the central government to formulate regulations, leaving implementation to the province-level governments (NDRC 2014: ch.2.12–13). The national ETS will be built upon 24 sectoral guidelines for accounting, reporting and verification that are based on both international standards and pilot-project experiences, including accreditation rules for independent verifiers (Roldao 2016: 27). Only Chinese verification companies were allowed in the pilots (Swartz 2016: 15).

The interim measures do not give the NDRC much room for forcing companies to comply or penalizing them. Non-compliant companies can be put on a blacklist, but that is not seen as effective in ensuring compliance. In the NDRC proposal to the State Council, it is suggested that fines for violating MRV regulations and other illegal activities should range from CNY 100,000 to 1 million (Idea Carbon 2016: ch.6.31). Fines in the same size range are proposed for verifiers and exchanges for violating rules or illegal activity (Idea Carbon 2016: ch.6.33–34). If a company fails to surrender allowances by the deadline for compliance, it is suggested that the province-level government should allow issuing a fine equivalent to three to five times the average market price of the non-surrendered allowances and should deduct the allowances against the following allocation period (Idea Carbon 2016: ch.6.32).

Price management and revenue earmarking

The 2014 interim measures prescribed that in the national system there would be a reserve of allowances for market adjustments (NDRC 2014: ch.2.11). Revenues from allowances purchased should also be used towards carbon reduction and capacity building (NDRC 2014: ch.2.11). There are no further details on these points at the time of writing. In its proposal to the State Council, the NDRC proposed setting aside a part of the allocations for future management of the market or to allow for new entrants. The reasoning is that it is more in line with a market logic to intervene in the market to adjust prices, instead of having a price floor (Idea Carbon 2016: ch.2.7).

There are still design elements of the national market which will need to be clarified, such as further price management and offset rules. With annual allocations, the scheme is designed to allow for continuous adjustments – different from, for instance, the EU approach.

Discussion

With the design of China's national market, diffusion occurred mainly in the form of learning as regards the various design aspects. While such learning was significant for gaining an understanding of the cogs and wheels of emissions trading schemes, the design choices relate largely to domestic concerns and conditions. The inclusion of aviation in the national system is probably an exception, due to competitive concerns. Interestingly, domestic lessons have played an important role in the preparation of the national system design. Pilot projects have given feedback to the NDRC on the national market. The NDRC has learned from these experiences, applying these lessons when designing the national market. The importance of drawing on pilot lessons has been stressed by higher levels within the NDRC. Further, the first years of the national market up to 2020 are regarded as a 'learning-by-doing' period. Hence, substantial internal learning has taken place.

International collaborations and the UNFCCC process have been significant in the development of China's emission market. China is dedicated to incorporating and applying the lessons from the EU–China ETS project in managing its own national ETS (China Carbon Forum 2016: 3). Province-level leaders and industry representatives have received training in China and on study tours to Europe. To maximize outreach, there have been sessions to train the trainers so they can take the knowledge back to their provinces and teach stakeholders there. The topics of bilateral talks and workshops have progressed from the broad European experience to a greater focus on details and technicalities. In the beginning of EU–China training, Chinese participants learned from the EU experience, but as the Chinese pilot projects have taken shape, there has been mutual learning on market management and regulation (China Carbon Forum 2016: 2). Of other collaborations, MRV training built on capacity-building projects funded by Norway, Australia, Germany, the World Bank and the Asian Development Bank (ADB) (World Bank 2013; ADB 2016a; China Carbon Forum 2016: 3; GIZ 2016). As to the UNFCCC negotiation processes, the 2015 Paris meeting (COP21) was an international milestone. China's preparation and submission of Intended Nationally Determined Contributions (INDC) to this meeting further propelled work on the national market, as the INDC lists the national market as one of China's policies for addressing climate change.

As to domestic politics, the NDRC has conferred with other parts of bureaucracy such as the ministries of science and technology, environmental protection, housing and construction, industry and information technology, transportation and agriculture. They have also consulted the Forestry Bureau, Civil Aviation Administration and local governments (Idea Carbon 2016: Addendum 5.2). In July 2015, the NDRC's Climate Department held a hearing on the draft national market-management regulations it later submitted to the State Council for legislation. Invited representatives included the pilot governments, the World Bank, China Electric Power Enterprise Association, UNDP, China Standardization Research Institute, large emitters such as State Grid, Sinopec, China National Offshore Oil Corporation (CNOOC), Shenhua Group and Shougang Group, as well as certification and third-party verifiers such as China Quality Certification Centre (CQC) (Idea Carbon 2016: Addendum 6; NDRC 2015). This shows that the NDRC has solicited feedback and comments from a range of invited stakeholders and contributors. Which suggestions to take to heart was, however, up to the NDRC to decide. The China Securities Regulatory Commission (CSRC), a financial regulation agency, requested the removal of references to futures trading. The NDRC did not heed this, and the proposal to the State Council contains such references (Reklev 2016a). The proposal that the NDRC sent to the State Council also indicates that some suggestions from the pilot projects were incorporated (Idea Carbon 2016). The various provinces and localities have argued for market designs which reflect their specific situations. The central government is considering fairness between provinces, in view of the differing energy situations and levels of development. Domestic equity here somewhat resembles the EU burden sharing. The NDRC has also stated that it is taking the regional differences into consideration (Idea Carbon 2016: Addendum 5.3). The pilot governments have become stakeholders advocating for retention of their own unique regulations also within the upcoming national market.

Conclusions

China will soon launch its national trading system. This launch has been preceded by intense preparations, involving collaboration with other governments and international organizations, trial periods in seven pilots and engaging and training local governments and stakeholders all over China. Domestic conditions and concerns have been the basis throughout the process, from before the 2011 decision to establish a carbon market and up to the latest publications of design rules. A complex set of reasons and drivers has determined actual policy choices and design options for the ETS. We have seen that diffusion has occurred mostly as learning – with a few exceptions such as for aviation, perhaps due to competitive concerns. Learning has largely been used as a first step on the path to making suitable choices for local, then national, conditions. A unique feature is the prominence of internal learning. Testing out a new mechanism or policy on a smaller scale before adopting it nationwide is a common feature of Chinese politics, a 'crossing the river by feeling the stones' tradition. For the ETS, the internal learning process also created considerable interest in this new policy tool, leading other non-pilots to start ahead of the national market schedule.

Our case study also supports Inderberg et al.'s (2017) finding that the temporal aspect is important for gaining a comprehensive understanding of how diffusion mechanisms and domestic conditions interact. In our case, diffusion was triggered by *ideational impact* before the 2011 decision to implement an ETS in China. The conditions for diffusion were inherently different before the decision was made and afterwards. The decision functioned as a tipping point, enabling further actions and possibilities for diffusion on the various design aspects. In this period, diffusion occurred mainly as *learning*. Then, as the pilot projects were prepared and commenced operation, the diffusion conditions changed, with the addition of feedback from the pilot projects to national market preparations – or *internal learning*.

Moreover, the UNFCCC negotiation process has been important for China in developing an ETS. The years of negotiations and UNFCCC activities fostered a better grasp of market mechanisms. Additionally, the CDM experience brought understanding of the benefits of a trading mechanism, and the process and objectives of its INDCs in 2015 submitted before the Paris meeting provided incentive for China to consolidate its plans for a carbon market.

The ETS has support from the highest level of Chinese government, and considerable funding and prestige have been invested. The development of the national market concerns more than China alone: as China is the world's largest market, it is likely to influence the reactions and evaluations of such a policy tool in other parts of the world as well. This case also gives rise to the question of how much 'collaboration' or lobbying one country can receive before this can be seen as intentional lobbying and not the diffusion mechanism of *learning*. China is of course not the only country to receive support and training from foreign organizations, but the degree to which international organizations and countries have been ready to collaborate with and support China in its ETS development presents a unique situation. Foreign partners have spent resources and hosted training sessions on a wide range of aspects in the process leading up to China's decision to go for an ETS – and creating a successful ETS in China is important also for these countries and international organizations. As some our interviewees noted, ETS success in China is important for the European Commission. Should China succeed, that will be advantageous for proponents of the EU ETS. Conversely, if the Chinese national market flops, that might give disgruntled stakeholders in the EU scheme clout behind their misgivings and complaints. Some interviewees also indicated that the ultimate goal for the European Commission is for China's national market to be in harmony with the EU ETS on elements such as accreditation for third-party verifiers, monitoring plans and financial products. From the EU side, the strategy has been not to tell China what to do, but to enable the Chinese to decide on the appropriate choice themselves, perhaps trying to nudge the Chinese towards what the EU sees as the right choices. In any case, the decisions have remained with the Chinese government and the pilot governments. Although influenced by the *learning* from pre-existing markets, and the EU ETS in particular, design specifics seem to be have determined largely on the basis of domestic needs and conditions.

As the national scheme is rolled out and starts operation, there is no shortage of challenges for the future. Many interviewees noted the need for transparency for the national scheme to function properly. This is related to another challenge mentioned several times: the need for good data. High-quality data is the foundation for proper allocation and compliance, and market data beyond the aggregated volumes and prices traded are essential for compliance companies to make informed market decisions. Furthermore, as experience from the pilot projects has shown, it takes some time for the companies involved to become familiar with the market mechanism.

Importantly, the Chinese government and experts have expressed the need for a strong legal basis for the ETS, to enable effective implementation and potential punishment of non-compliance. Enforcing the surrender of allowances by the enterprises covered is crucial, and pilot experiences have shown that this might prove difficult in the national system, requiring significant administrative resources.

The NDRC is well aware of such challenges ahead. Precisely because beginner's problems are expected, the first few years of the national scheme are to be a national trial period, so that the NDRC may continue work on correcting anticipated and unanticipated challenges.

An emerging perception that market mechanisms could be a lower-cost solution for curbing carbon emissions in China contributed to China's decision to commence building a national market. After the decision was made, *learning* has been China's main strategy: first through bilateral and international cooperation, then by creating a round of *internal learning* with seven pilot projects and, finally, by designating the first years of the national market up to 2020 as a learning period for the national market. Constructing an ETS is indeed no easy matter. As China has understood, in order to be in it to win it, it must first be in it to learn it.

Notes

1 Danish Minister for Environment (2004) and Minister for Climate and Energy (2007–9), planner and host of the 2009 Copenhagen climate summit, and European Commissioner for Climate Action (2010–14).

2 Directive 2009/29/EC amending Article 11a of Directive 2003/87/EC. For definitions of least developed countries see: http://ec.europa.eu/clima/policies/ets/markets/docs/def_ldc_en.pdf (accessed 10 November 2016).

3 Just as the Chinese CDM-CERs were mostly renewable, more than 70 per cent of China's certified emissions reductions (CCERs) are projects of renewable energy. Energy-saving projects constitute the second-largest type of projects, with more than 12 per cent (NDRC Climate Change Department 2016).

4 The Shapley value, presented by Lloyd Shapley in 1953, is part of cooperative game theory. It holds that numerically evaluating the value of playing a game is possible (Roth 1988: 1).

References

12th Five-Year Plan. 2011. 中华人民共和国国民经济和社会发展第十二个五年规划纲要 [The People's Republic of China's 12th Five-Year Plan for National Economic and Social Development]. http://ghs.ndrc.gov.cn/ghwb/gjwngh/201109/P020110919590835399263.pdf accessed 6 May 2012.

13th Five-Year Plan. 2016. 中华人民共和国国民经济和社会发展第十三个五年规划纲要 [The People's Republic of China's 13th Five-Year Plan for National Economic and Social Development]. www.sdpc.gov.cn/fzgggz/fzgh/ghwb/gjjh/201605/P020160516532684519514.pdf accessed 4 December 2016.

ADB (Asian Development Bank). 2016a. *Developing Tianjin Emission Trading System*. www.adb.org/projects/45038-001/main#project-pds accessed 9 November 2016.

ADB (Asian Development Bank). 2016b. *Advancing Shanghai Carbon Market through Emissions Trading*. www.adb.org/projects/46054-001/main#project-pds accessed 9 November 2016.

Andrews-Speed, P. 2012. *The Governance of Energy in China: Transition to a Low-Carbon Economy*. London: Palgrave Macmillan.

Buhr, K., P. Thörn and M. Hjerpe. 2012. The clean development mechanism in China: Institutional perspectives on governance. *Environmental Policy and Governance* 22 (2), 77–89 (doi: 10.1002/eet.597).

Carbon Pulse. 2016. *DOSSIER: China's Emissions Markets*. http://carbon-pulse.com/18865/ accessed 6 October 2016.

Chen, K., S. Reklev, B. Garside and M Szabo. 2016. EXCLUSIVE: Is China backtracking on UN aviation carbon market deal? *Carbon Pulse*. 7 October. http://carbon-pulse.com/27942/ accessed 19 December 2016.

Cheng, C. and Z. Xu. 2011. A study on the construction of China's Carbon Emissions Trading System. *Energy Procedia* 5, 1037–1043 (doi: 10.1016/j.egypro.2011.03.183).

China Carbon Forum. 2016. *China's National Emission Trading Scheme and the European Perspective – What to Expect from 2017?* Discussion records from meeting, 26 April 2016. www.chinacarbon.info/wp-content/uploads/2016/07/Executive-Summary-Chinas-National-ETS-20160427.pdf accessed 7 October2016.

Chongqing Trading Center. 2014. 重庆市碳排放权交易管理暂行办法 [Chongqing Interim Management Measures for Carbon Emissions Trading], 7 May. http://222.178.87.205/news/objects/76.html accessed 8 November 2016.

Donald, S. H. and R. Benewick. 2005. *The State of China Atlas*. Berkeley: University of California Press.

Dong, J., Y. Ma and H. Sun. 2016. From pilot to the National Emissions Trading Scheme in China: International practice and domestic experiences. *Sustainability* 8 (6), 1–17 (doi: 10.3390/su8060522).

Duan, M., T. Pang and X. Zhang. 2014. Review of carbon emissions trading pilots in China. *Energy & Environment* 25 (3), 527–550 (doi: 10.1260/0958–305X.25.3–4.527).

ERI (Energy Research Institute), Rocky Mountain Institute, Lawrence Berkeley National Laboratory, and Energy Foundation China. 2016. *Reinventing Fire China: A Roadmap for China's Revolution of Energy, Production and Consumption to 2050*. September 2016. https://rmi.org/Content/Files/RFChina_Execsummary_Final.pdf accessed 6 March 2017.

EU. 2003. *DIRECTIVE 2003/87/EC of the European Parliament and of the Council of 13 October 2003*. http://eur-lex.europa.eu/legal-content/EN/TXT/PDF/?uri=CELEX:32003L0087&from=EN accessed 14 July 2016.

Garside, B. 2015. China's Xie Touts Prospect of China – Korea ETS link. *Carbon Pulse*. 6 December. http://carbon-pulse.com/12922/ accessed 10 October 2016.

GIZ. 2016. *Capacity Building for the Establishment of Emissions Trading Schemes in China*. http://ets-china.org/ accessed 9 November 2016.

Government of China. 2011. 国发 〔2011〕 41 号, 国务院关于印发十二五控制温室气体排放工作方案的通知 [*Notice of the State Council on Issuing the Work Plan for Greenhouse Gas Emission Control During the 12th Five-Year Plan Period, State*

Council Notice number 41, 2011]. www.gov.cn/zwgk/2012-01/13/content_2043645.htm accessed 6 November 2016.

Government of China. 2016. 国发〔2016〕74号，国务院关于印发十三五节能减排综合工作方案的通知 [*Notice of the State Council on Issuing the Comprehensive Working Plan for '13–5' Energy-Saving and Emission-Reduction, State Council Notice Number 74, 2016*]. www.gov.cn/zhengce/content/2017-01/05/content_5156789.htm accessed 12 March 2017.

Guangdong DRC. 2016. 粤发改气候[2016] 430 号，广东省发展改革委关于印发广东省2016年度碳排放配额分配实施方案的通知 [Notice of the Guangdong Provincial Development and Reform Commission on Issuing the Implementation Plan for the 2016 Annual Carbon Emission Allowance Allocation in Guangdong Province, Guangdong DRC Notice number 430, 2016]. *NDRC*. http://dtfz.ccchina.gov.cn/archiver/LowCD/UpFile/Files/Default/20160714093558793864.pdf accessed 7 October 2016.

Guangdong Provincial Government. 2014. 广东省人民政府令第197号 [Decree no. 197 of Guangdong Provincial Government]. http://zwgk.gd.gov.cn/006939748/201401/t20140117_462131.html accessed 7 October 2016.

Harrison, P. 2011. EU must be firm in aviation CO2 dispute with China. *Reuters*. 5 June. www.reuters.com/article/us-airlines-emissions-europe-idUSTRE7540T020110605 accessed 13 October 2016.

Hart, C. and Z. Ma. 2014. China's regional carbon trading experiment and the development of a national market: lessons from China's SO2 Trading Programme. *Energy & Environment* 25 (3 and 4), 577–592 (doi: 10.1260/0958–305X.25.3–4.577).

Heggelund, G. and I. F. Buan. 2009. China in the Asia – Pacific Partnership: Consequences for UN climate change mitigation efforts? *International Environmental Agreements: Politics, Law and Economics* 9 (3), 301–317 (doi: 10.1007/s10784-009-9099-5).

Heggelund, G. and R. Nadin. 2017. Climate change policy and governance. In *Routledge Handbook of Environmental Policy in China*, edited by E. Sternfeld, 97–112. New York: Routledge.

Heggelund, G., S. Andresen and I. F. Buan. 2010. Chinese climate policy: Domestic priorities, foreign policy and emerging implementation. In *Global Commons, Domestic Decisions: The Comparative Politics of Climate Change*, edited by K. Harrison and L. McIntosh Sundstrom, 229–259. Cambridge MA: MIT Press.

Hill, D. 2016. Regional cooperation and Asia's low carbon economy transition: The case of New Zealand. In *Investing on Low-Carbon Energy Systems Implications for Regional Economic Cooperation*, edited by V. Anbumozhi, K. Kalirajan, F. Kimura and Yao, Xianbin, 309–326. Singapore: Springer.

Hübler, M., S. Voigt and A. Löschel. 2014. Designing an emissions trading scheme for China: An up-to-date climate policy assessment. *Energy Policy* 75, 57–72 (doi: 10.2139/ssrn.2411970).

ICAP. 2016. *ICAP ETS Map* https://icapcarbonaction.com/en/ets-map accessed 13 October 2016.

Idea Carbon. 2016. 《全国碳排放权交易管理条例》（送审稿 [National Carbon Emissions Trading Management Regulations (Submitted Draft)]. *Idea Carbon*. 29 March. www.ideacarbon.org/archives/31714 accessed 7 October 2016.

Inderberg, T. H. J., I. Bailey and N. Harmer. 2017. Designing New Zealand's emissions trading scheme. *Global Environmental Politics* 17 (3), 31–50 (doi: 10.1162/GLEP_a_00414).

Jiang, J., D. Xie, B. Ye, B. Shen and Z. Chen. 2016. Research on China's cap-and-trade carbon Emission Trading Scheme: Overview and outlook. *Applied Energy* 178 (15 September 2016), 902–917 (doi: 10.1016/j.apenergy.2016.06.100).

Kinkead, B. 2012. *Harnessing Market Mechanisms to Promote Sustainable Development: Lessons from China*. London: Climate and Development Knowledge Network. http://cdkn.org/wp-content/uploads/2012/09/China-InsideStory_final_WEB.pdf accessed 15 May 2017.

Le Quéré, C., R. M. Andrew, J. G. Canadell, S. Sitch, J. I. Korsbakken, G. P. Peters, A. C. Manning et al. 2016. Global Carbon Budget 2016. *Earth System Science Data* 8, 605–649 (doi: 10.5194/essd-8–605–2016).

Liu, L. 2011. *Understanding China's Climate Change Mitigation Policy Development: Structures, Processes and Outcomes*. Ph.D. dissertation, Florida International University.

Liu, L., C. Chen, Y. Zhao and E. Zhao. 2015. China's carbon-emissions trading: Overview, challenges and future. *Renewable and Sustainable Energy Reviews* 49 (September 2015), 254–266 (doi: 10.1016/j.rser.2015.04.076).

Munnings, C., R. Morgenstern, Z. Wang and X. Liu. 2014. *Assessing the Design of Three Pilot Programs for Carbon Trading in China*. Washington, DC: Resources for the Future. www.rff.org/files/sharepoint/WorkImages/Download/RFF-DP-14-36.pdf accessed 15 May 2017.

NBS (National Bureau of Statistics of China). 2016. *China Yearbook 2016*. Beijing: China Statistics Press.

NDRC (National Development and Reform Commission). 2011. 发改办气候 [2011] 2601 号. 国家发展改革委办公厅关于开展碳排放权交易试点工作的通知 [Notice on Carrying out Carbon Emissions Trading Pilots, NDRC's Climate department notice [2011] no.2601]. www.sdpc.gov.cn/zcfb/zcfbtz/201201/t20120113_456506.html accessed 13 July 2016.

NDRC (National Development and Reform Commission). 2012. 发改气候[2012] 1668 号 国家发展改革委关于印发 温室气体自愿减排交易管理暂行办法的通知 [NDRC Climate Department Notice [2012] no.1668. Notification of NDRC's Publication of Interim Measures of Managing the Voluntary Emissions Trading]. http://cdm.ccchina.gov.cn/WebSite/CDM/UpFile/File2894.pdf accessed 6 October 2016.

NDRC (National Development and Reform Commission). 2014. 中华人民共和国国家发展和改革委员会令 第17号 [The People's Republic of China National Development and Reform Commission Decree No. 17]. http://qhs.ndrc.gov.cn/zcfg/201412/t20141212_652007.html accessed 15 July 2016.

NDRC (National Development and Reform Commission). 2015. 气候司就《全国碳排放权交易管理条例（草案）》涉及行政许可问题举行听证会 [Climate Department holds hearing on National Carbon Emissions Trading Management Ordinance (Draft) Involving Administrative Licensing Issues]. 10 August. www.sdpc.gov.cn/gzdt/201508/t20150810_744890.html accessed 7 October 2016.

NDRC (National Development and Reform Commission). 2016. 发改办气候[2016]57号. 国家发展改革委办公厅关于切实做好全国碳排放权交易市场启动重点工作的通知 [NDRC Climate department notice [2016] no.57. NDRC General Office's notification regarding the start of key work on effective implementation of the national carbon emission trading market]. www.sdpc.gov.cn/zcfb/zcfbtz/201601/t20160122_772123.html accessed 6 October 2016.

NDRC (National Development and Reform Commission), Climate Change Department. 2016. *Approved Projects by Scope*. http://cdm-en.ccchina.gov.cn/NewItemTable7.aspx accessed 14 March 2017.

Pang, T. and Duan, M. 2016. Cap setting and allowance allocation in China's emissions trading pilot programmes: Special issues and innovative solutions. *Climate Policy* 16 (7), 815–835 (doi: 10.1080/14693062.2015.1052956).

PBL (Netherlands Environmental Assessment Agency). 2007. *China Now No.1 in CO2 Emissions: USA in Second Position*. www.pbl.nl/node/47363 accessed 7 October 2016.

Qian, G. and Z. Chen. 2015. Emissions trading in China, progress on the path towards a unified national system. In *Emissions Trading Worldwide: International Carbon Action Partnership (ICAP) Status Report 2015*, edited by C. Serre, M. Santikarn, K. Stelmakh, A. Eden, M. Frerk, A. Kachi, C. Unger et al., 14–15. Berlin: International Carbon Action Partnership. https://icapcarbonaction.com/images/StatusReport2015/ICAP_Report_2015_02_10_online_version.pdf accessed 15 May 2017.

Qiu, J. 2011. China announces energy-saving plans. *Nature*. 4 March. www.nature.com/news/2011/110304/full/news.2011.137.html accessed 7 October 2016.

Reklev, S. 2015a. Gansu cities to pilot carbon trading ahead of China's National ETS. *Carbon Pulse*. 16 March. http://carbon-pulse.com/gansu-cities-to-pilot-carbon-trading-ahead-of-chinas-national-ets/ accessed 7 October 2016.

Reklev, S. 2015b. Shanghai changes CO2 market rules in wake of price crash. *Carbon Pulse*. 15 June. http://carbon-pulse.com/5044/ accessed 6 November 2016.

Reklev, S. 2016a. China's NDRC passes emissions trading bill to State Council. *Carbon Pulse*. 4 April. http://carbon-pulse.com/17641/ accessed 6 November 2016.

Reklev, S. 2016b. Official warns of tight offset limit in China ETS. *Carbon Pulse*. 28 October. http://carbon-pulse.com/26028/ accessed 3 November 2016.

Reklev, S. 2016c. UK envoy talks up EU – China carbon market link – media. *Carbon Pulse*. 26 January. http://carbon-pulse.com/14705/ accessed 10 October 2016.

Reuters. 2009. Q+A – What Is China's 'carbon intensity' target? *Reuters*. 26 November. www.reuters.com/article/idUSPEK12370 accessed 3 March 2017.

Roldao, R. 2016. China's National ETS: 'It's not how it starts, but how it ends. In *Bridging the Emissions Gap, the Rise, Reach and Power of Carbon Markets: IETA GHG: Greenhouse Gas 2016/17 Market Report*, edited by A. Vitelli, 26–27. Geneva: International Emissions Trading Association. www.ieta.org/resources/Resources/GHG_Report/2016/IETA_GHG_Report_2016_web.pdf accessed 15 May 2017.

Roth, A. E. 1988. Introduction to the Shapley Value. In *The Shapley Value*, edited by A. E. Roth, 1–30. New York: Cambridge University Press.

Saich, T. 2015. *Governance and Politics of China*, 4th ed. Basingstoke: Palgrave Macmillan.

Shanghai DRC. 2015. 上海碳市场报告 *（2013－2014）[Shanghai Carbon Market Annual Report (2013–2014)]*. Shanghai: Shanghai DRC.

Shanghai DRC. 2016. 关于印发《上海市碳排放交易纳入配额管理的单位名单（2016版）》的通知 [Notice on Issuing the Unit List of Shanghai Carbon Emission-Trading Entering Allowance Management (2016 edition)]. www.shdrc.gov.cn/gk/xxgkml/zcwj/zgjjl/23039.htm accessed 10 July 2016.

Shenzhen DRC. 2016a. 深圳市发展和改革委员会关于开展2016年度碳排放权交易工作的通知 [Notice About Shenzhen DRC's Launch of the 2016 Work on Carbon Emissions Trading]. www.szpb.gov.cn/xxgk/qt/tzgg/201609/t20160918_4938028.htm accessed 13 October 2016.

Shenzhen DRC. 2016b. 深圳市应对气候变化十三五规划[Shenzhen City's Plan for Addressing Climate Change in the 13th Five-Year Plan period]. www.szpb.gov.cn/xxgk/ghjh/zxgh/201612/t20161213_5677847.htm accessed 17 December 2016.

Shenzhen Government. 2013a. 深圳市碳排放权交易启动工作发布会 [Meeting on the Occasion of Shenzhen Carbon Trading's Start]. www.sz.gov.cn/cn/xxgk/xwfyr/wqhg/20130521/ accessed 6 November 2016.

Shenzhen Government. 2013b. 《深圳市碳排放权交易管理暂行办法（征求意见稿）》征集市民意见 [Solicitation for Public Opinions on Interim Measures for the

Administration of Carbon Emissions Trading in Shenzhen (Draft for Comments)]. www.sz.gov.cn/rmzffzbgs/qt/tzgg/201311/t20131106_2233320.htm accessed 19 December 2016.

State Council. 2016. 国务院关于印发“十三五”控制温室气体排放工作方案的通知 [State Council Notice on the Work Plan for Controlling GHG Emissions in the 13th Five-Year Plan]. *Government of China*, 27 October. www.gov.cn/zhengce/content/2016-11/04/content_5128619.htm accessed 4 November 2016.

State Council Office. 2016. 国务院办公厅关于印发 国务院2016年立法工作计划的通知 国办发〔2016〕16号 [State Council Office Notice on Issuing Legislative Work Plans for 2016] Sate Council General Office Notice no.16, 2016. *Government of China*. www.gov.cn/zhengce/content/2016-04/13/content_5063670.htm accessed 12 November 2016.

Stensdal, I. 2014. Chinese climate-change policy, 1988–2013: Moving on up. *Asian Perspective* 38 (1), 111–135 (doi: 10.5555/0258–9184–38.1.111).

Stensdal, I. 2015. China: Every day is a winding road. In *The Domestic Politics of Global Climate Change*, edited by G. Bang, A. Underdal and S. Andresen, 49–70. Cheltenham: Edward Elgar.

Stensdal, I. 2016. *New Policy, Old Institutions? The Establishment and Enforcement of Shanghai's Emission-Trading Scheme Pilot*. Paper presented at International Studies Association Convention, Atlanta, GA, 16 March.

Swartz, J. 2016. *China's National Emissions Trading System: Implications for Carbon Markets and Trade*. ICTSD Global Platform on Climate Change, Trade and Sustainable Energy, Climate Change Architecture Series, Issue Paper No. 6. Geneva: International Centre for Trade and Sustainable Development. www.ieta.org/resources/China/Chinas_National_ETS_Implications_for_Carbon_Markets_and_Trade_ICTSD_March2016_Jeff_Swartz.pdf accessed 15 May 2017.

Tung, C. 2015. Reflections on the Chinese carbon market. In *Research Handbook on Climate Change Mitigation Law*, edited by G. Van Calster, W. Vandenberghe and L. Reins, 86–100. Cheltenham: Edward Elgar.

UNDP. 2012. *Climate Change and Development in China: Three Decades of Support*. Beijing: UNDP. www.undp.org/content/dam/china/docs/Publications/UNDP-CH-EE-Publications-Climate-Change-and-Development-in-China.pdf accessed 15 May 2017.

White House. 2015. *FACT SHEET: The United States and China Issue Joint Presidential Statement on Climate Change with New Domestic Policy Commitments and a Common Vision for an Ambitious Global Climate Agreement in Paris*, 25 September. www.whitehouse.gov/the-press-office/2015/09/25/fact-sheet-united-states-and-china-issue-joint-presidential-statement accessed 7 October 2016.

World Bank. 2013. *Partnership for Market Readiness (PMR), China Final Market Readiness Proposal*, 11 March. www.thepmr.org/system/files/documents/PA5_China_Final_MRP__presentation.pdf accessed 8 November 2016.

World Bank. 2016. *World Bank Indicators*. http://data.worldbank.org accessed 7 October 2016.

Wu, Q., M. Neelis and C. Casanova. 2014. Chinese Emission Trading Schemes: Initial assessment on allocation. *Ecofys*. 7 April. www.ecofys.com/files/files/ecofys-2014-industry-view-chinese-ets-allocations-english.pdf accessed 7 October 2016.

Yin, D. 2013. China's carbon emissions: Traders await offset demand. *Ecosystem Marketplace*. 9 July. www.ecosystemmarketplace.com/articles/china-s-carbon-emissions-br-traders-await-offset-demand/ accessed 6 November 2016.

Zhang, B., H. Fei, P. He, Y. Xu, Z. Dong and O. R. Young. 2016. The indecisive role of the market in China's SO2 and COD emissions trading. *Environmental Politics* 25 (5), 875–898 (doi: 10.1080/09644016.2016.1165951).

Zhang, D., V. Karplus, C. l. Cassisa and X. Zhang. 2014. Emissions trading in China: Progress and prospects. *Energy Policy* 75, 9–16 (doi: 10.1016/j.enpol.2014.01.022).

Zhang, Z. 2015. Carbon emissions trading in China: The evolution from pilots to a nationwide scheme. *Climate Policy* 15 (supplement 1): S104–S126 (doi: 10.1080/14693062.2015.1096231).

12 ETS design and potential effects in China

Comparison with the EU

Christoph Böhringer, Knut Einar Rosendahl and Tang Weiqi

Introduction

Previous chapters have discussed the evolution of emissions trading systems (ETSs) for different countries or regions, and eight central design properties have been considered for each of these ETSs. Whereas the preceding chapters have focused on the role of diffusion in shaping these design properties, this chapter quantifies the potential effects of ETS design with respect to effectiveness (reductions in CO_2 emissions) and economic efficiency (economic welfare costs of emission reductions). We focus on the upcoming national ETS in China (see Chapter 11 of this book) and four of the eight design properties discussed in preceding chapters: ambition level, sector coverage, allocation of allowances and access to offsets. We are particularly interested in the potential effects on emissions, at the national and the sectoral levels, as well as carbon prices and the economic costs of reducing emissions.

Further, we compare the effects of ETS design in China with corresponding effects in the EU. One key question is how expanding the Chinese ETS to cover more sectors may affect Chinese emissions – and how this compares with similar expansion of the EU ETS. Once the Chinese ETS becomes operative (probably in late 2017), the Chinese ETS and the EU ETS will be the world's largest emissions trading systems in terms of regulated emissions. Here we explore similarities and differences between the two jurisdictions as regards potential effects and important design properties.

For our quantitative assessment, we use a standard simulation model for economy-wide analysis – a multi-region, multi-sector computable general equilibrium (CGE) model. In the model, the world is divided into 13 regions, each with 17 sectors producing specific goods (e.g. five distinct energy sectors). These goods are sold either on the domestic market (to consumers or to other producers) or exported. A (quota) price on emissions makes it more expensive to produce emissions-intensive goods, thereby incentivizing producers to switch towards less emission-intensive inputs (for instance, from coal to gas or renewable energy). The model is described in further detail in the 'Model summary' section that follows.

Chinese emissions currently constitute between 25 and 30 per cent of global greenhouse gas (GHG), and CO_2, emissions, whereas EU emissions constitute around 10 per cent. Therefore, China's and the EU's policies to reduce emissions can be expected to have non-negligible effects on the global economy, especially with respect to trade in energy and energy-intensive goods – which makes an international perspective indispensable for an appropriate assessment. As the practicability of model-based analysis hinges on simplifying assumptions, the results should be viewed with some caution. Nevertheless, we believe they can provide policy-relevant insights into the importance of the various design properties for China, as well as how it compares with the EU.

As the discussions in Chapters 3 and 11 have shown, there are both similarities and differences between the EU ETS and the Chinese ETS as regards the four design properties in focus in this chapter. First, the level of ambition, as reflected in realized and expected CO_2 prices, is quite moderate in both the EU and China but could be strengthened towards 2030. Second, the two ETSs cover almost the same set of sectors, such as electricity generation, manufacturing industry and aviation (see e.g. Table 11.2 in Chapter 11). Third, as in the EU, the Chinese ETS will initially rely heavily on free allocation of emissions allowances, gradually moving towards auctioning. Whereas the EU, in the case of energy-intensive industries, has moved from mostly grandfathering (based on historic emissions) towards benchmarking (based on production output), a mixture of the two allocation methods is likely in China's national ETS. Fourth, access to external offsets such as the Clean Development Mechanism (CDM) has been an important ingredient in the initial phases of the EU ETS; the Chinese ETS will also allow the use of offsets – but these will be domestic and not foreign offsets. The offset rules for the national ETS in China have not yet been determined (see Chapter 11 regarding experience with offsets in Chinese pilot projects).

There is a sizable literature on the effects of the EU ETS on, for instance, emissions and costs of emission reductions. Although historic emission and GDP levels are known, it is difficult to indicate how large emissions and GDP would have been without the EU ETS, and thus how much the ETS has contributed to emission reductions and changes in GDP (or other measures of welfare costs). To analyse this issue, one can either use economic modelling tools (e.g. CGE models, as in this chapter) or perform statistical analyses. Various economic modelling studies have used CGE models (for a cross-model meta-analysis, see Böhringer et al. 2009), but there have been relatively few statistical studies (two examples are Klemetsen et al. 2016, and Martin et al. 2016).

There are also some CGE modelling studies that analyse the potential effects on emissions and costs of emission reductions of a Chinese ETS. Hübler et al. (2014) investigate the effects of a possible linkage with the EU ETS, considering, among other things, the competitiveness effects of energy-intensive trade-exposed (EITE) sectors. Similarly, Xu et al. (2017) examine the implications of an integrated ETS with several countries/regions (China, US, Europe, Japan, Korea and Australia). Zhang et al. (2016) incorporate regional details for China, quantifying the distributional impacts of Chinese ETS designs across provinces.

A main conclusion from our model simulations is that a Chinese ETS may induce relatively stronger emission reductions than the EU ETS, provided that the emission prices are approximately the same in the two systems. Or: if the percentage emission reduction is the same, a lower emission price can be expected in China than in the EU. There are two main reasons for this. First, China has a large share of coal-powered generation which can be replaced by less carbon-intensive power generation at relatively low cost. Second, the potential for energy-efficiency improvements is greater in China than in the EU. A major qualification, however, is that regulated electricity prices in China be adjusted to reflect the ETS price. Furthermore, expanding the ETS to cover more sectors than the current coverage will lead to quite modest additional emission reductions in the two jurisdictions. Third, if benchmarking is implemented, there will be lower emission reductions for a given ETS price (or the ETS price will be higher for a given cap). However, the differences are rather small, unless benchmarking is used for the Chinese electricity sector *and* the electricity market is liberalized. Fourth, moderate access to domestic offsets seems sufficient to realize most of the potential cost savings from offsets, both in China and in the EU. Cost savings from using offsets are significant only if the ambition levels are high.

ETS design properties

Table 12.1 lists the ETS design properties to be considered. The first two – ambition level and sector coverage – are fundamental to the significance of the system. The other two – allocation mechanism and offset rules – have been shown to be important in theoretical and quantitative economic studies of ETSs (see e.g. Böhringer and Lange 2005; Golombek et al. 2013; Rosendahl and Strand 2015). We restrict the time horizon of our analysis to the year 2020 in order to reduce uncertainty regarding future economic and technological development. However, the results should provide more general insights regarding the consequences of climate policy design also in the subsequent decade to 2030.

Ambition level may be defined as the level of the emission cap and emissions cut aimed for within a given period (see Chapter 2 of this book). Here we employ a slightly different interpretation, as we consider various CO_2 prices instead (see Table 12.1). However, since there is a one-to-one relationship in our model between the CO_2 price and the emission cut for a given country, the analysis implicitly shows the potential effects of different emission caps as well.[1] The EU ETS price has been below EUR 10 since 2012 – substantially under the price levels deemed consistent with achieving the 2°C target (see IPCC 2014). The China ETS price is expected to be slightly below USD 10 in 2020, but, according to the National Development and Reform Commission's preliminary estimate, a carbon price of RMB 300 (USD 40–50) will be needed in the long run to guide the shift to a low-carbon, green economy (Environomist 2017). Our analysis operates with CO_2 prices up to USD 100 per ton of CO_2, with USD 10 and USD 50 as the default prices for low and high ambition levels when the other design properties are taken into consideration.

The second design property concerns the *coverage* of the ETS: which sectors are included in the system. Here we explore the importance of sector

Table 12.1 ETS design properties considered

Design property	*Description*
Ambition level	CO_2 prices varying between USD 0 and USD 100 per ton of CO_2
Sector coverage	Sequential addition of sectors
Allocation mechanism*	No free allocation (only auctioning)
	Benchmarking to energy-intensive trade-exposed sectors
	Benchmarking to the electricity sector
	Benchmarking to all sectors
Offsets	Varying the percentage share of domestic offsets allowed

* Auctioning and unconditional grandfathering would have equivalent effects in our analysis, as long as we do not focus on distributional effects (between the government and firm owners) or recycling of auction revenues.

coverage in the two jurisdictions, starting with only one sector (electricity generation) and then adding one sector at a time into the ETS. This model exercise will show how important it may be, as regards emission reductions and mitigation costs, to expand the coverage of the emissions trading systems. Note that in our scenarios, non-ETS sectors are not regulated by any CO_2 price (or other climate policies), as we want to focus on the effects of the ETS. The default assumption here is shown in Table 12.2: that the ETS includes the sectors expected to be part of the Chinese ETS (see also Table 11.2 in Chapter 11 of this book).[2]

The third design property is *allocation of allowances*. One important distinction is between auctioning and free allocation. If allowances are handed out for free, in perpetuity, without any conditions related to, for instance, sustained activity, the only difference between this and auctioning is the distributional effect (between firm owners and the government).[3] Our analysis distinguishes auctioning from benchmarking (also referred to as 'output-based allocation', see e.g. Böhringer et al. 2014), meaning that firms receive allowances in proportion to their production output. An alternative allocation mechanism, which we do not model, is grandfathering, where firms receive allowances on the basis of past emissions. The effects of such a scheme will depend on to what degree current and future allocation is conditioned on firms' activity (see e.g. Böhringer and Lange 2005). In the EU ETS, a variant of benchmarking has been used since 2013 for the EITE industries, as they are considered to be exposed to carbon leakage, whereas most electricity producers no longer receive free allowances (see Chapter 3 of this book). On the other hand, in the Chinese pilots, benchmarking has been quite common for the electricity sector. The precise allocation mechanisms for the Chinese national ETS are not yet clear, and both benchmarking and grandfathering could be chosen (see Chapter 11 of this book). As shown in Table 12.1, we will consider four alternatives with respect to which sectors are entitled to benchmarking (with the remaining sectors then receiving no free allowances), with full auctioning as the default assumption.

The fourth design property is *access to external offsets*: regulated firms may, to varying degrees, pay for emissions reductions outside the ETS, to replace their own emissions reductions (or instead of buying allowances from other ETS firms). In the EU ETS, access to offsets or credits from the CDM under the Kyoto Protocol has been an important initial provision for accommodating cost savings through greater 'where' flexibility in emissions abatement. The total amount of CDM credits used in the EU ETS has been high and may partly explain the low ETS prices (see Chapter 3 of this book). After 2020, however, access to foreign offsets will no longer be permitted. The Chinese ETS will allow a limited use of offsets, but these will be domestic rather than foreign offsets, as in the pilots where the maximum use of offsets has been set to 5–10 per cent of total allowances (see Table 11.1 in Chapter 11). Our analysis considers only the use of domestic offsets, varying the upper limit on this use. We assume that the cheapest abatement options in non-ETS sectors are then utilized, which probably means that we overestimate the cost reductions of using offsets.[4] The default assumption here is *no use* of offsets.

Model summary

In order to quantify the potential effects of emissions trading and ETS design in China, and compare with corresponding effects in the EU, we apply a multi-region, multi-sector CGE model of global trade and energy intended for the analysis of carbon emission control strategies (for an appraisal of CGE models for environmental impact assessments, see Böhringer and Löschel 2006).[5] We consider economic effects at the economy-wide and sector levels as well as the environmental effects in terms of changes in CO_2 emissions. The model is calibrated to empirical data from the Global Trade, Assistance and Production (GTAP version 9) project, which provides detailed national accounts of production and consumption (input–output tables) together with bilateral trade flows and CO_2 emissions for the year 2011 (Narayanan et al. 2015). As explained, our analysis focuses on potential effects of ETS design in the year 2020. We first develop a reference scenario for 2020, incorporating business-as-usual (BaU) assumptions on economic growth, energy demands and international fuel prices provided by the US Energy Information Agency in its International Energy Outlook (EIA 2013). Then we implement emission trading in either China or the EU in the model to assess the potential effects in 2020 of different ETS design properties in the two jurisdictions. Since we treat ETS design in the same manner for China and the EU, any differences that emerge in the results will be due to differences between the Chinese economy and that of the EU – sectoral composition, energy use, efficiency, etc.

Table 12.2 gives a summary of the sectoral and regional disaggregation of the GTAP data for our model application. As to sectoral disaggregation, we have deliberately included in our composite dataset various primary and

Table 12.2 Sectors and regions in the model

Sectors and commodities	*Countries and regions*
Energy sectors:	China (CHN)
Coal (COA)	EU-28 + EFTA (EUR)
Crude oil (CRU)	Japan (JPN)
Natural gas (GAS)	India (IND)
Refined oil products (OIL) [a,b]	South Korea (KOR)
Electricity (ELE) [a]	Australia and New Zealand (ANZ)
Other sectors:	United States of America (USA)
Chemical products (CRP) [a,b]	Russian Federation (RUS)
Iron and steel (I_S) [a,b]	Brazil (BRA)
Non-ferrous metals (NFM) [a,b]	Rest of East Asia (REA)
Non-metallic minerals (NMM) [a,b]	Rest of OECD (ROE)
Paper and pulp (PPP) [a,b]	OPEC Countries (OPC)
Air transport (ATP) [a]	Rest of the World (ROW)
Water transport (WTP)	
Other transport (OTP)	
Motor vehicles (MVH)	
Agricultural energy-intensive trade-exposed goods (AIC)	
Other energy-intensive trade-exposed goods (OIC)	
All other manufactures and services (AOG)	

[a] Regulated by the ETS in the main scenarios.
[b] Energy-intensive and trade-exposed industries regulated by the ETS.

secondary energy carriers: coal, crude oil, natural gas, refined oil products and electricity.[6] This disaggregation is essential in order to distinguish energy goods by CO_2 intensity and the degree of substitutability. In addition, we separate the main EITE industries (chemical products, iron and steel products, non-ferrous metals, non-metallic minerals and paper and pulp). Other EITE industries are grouped into three sectors: motor vehicles[7] and two composite sectors distinguishing between agricultural goods and other goods. The remaining industries covered in our dataset are three transport sectors (air transport, water transport and other transport), as well as a composite sector of all remaining manufacturers and services.

Regarding regional disaggregation, China and the EU are obviously separate regions in the model. Since energy and energy-intensive goods are much traded internationally, it is important to account for international trade in the model: therefore, the model includes the rest of the world, divided into 11 regions. We single out large countries in the Asia-Pacific area (Japan, India, South Korea and Australia/New Zealand), which are all major trading partners for China, as well as some other geopolitically important countries or regions (US, Russia and Brazil). The three composite regions reflect geographic proximity to China, advanced economic development and importance of fossil-fuel exports: Rest of Asia, Rest of OECD (Organisation for Economic Co-operation and Development) and OPEC (Organization of Petroleum Exporting Countries) countries. All remaining countries in the GTAP dataset are aggregated into a residual composite labelled Rest of the World.

Our analysis disregards climate policies in other regions. Although there will probably be some carbon pricing in other regions in 2020 (see e.g. ICAP 2016; World Bank Group 2016), it is difficult to anticipate the exact level of these prices. Furthermore, the effects of ETS in China and the EU investigated in this chapter will be affected by moderate carbon pricing in other regions only slightly. We also disregard other climate and energy policies in China and the EU than emissions trading, as we want to focus on the effects of the ETS and ETS design; however, other climate-related policies implemented in parallel with the ETS will of course influence the effects of the ETS (see e.g. Böhringer and Rosendahl 2010).[8]

Quantitative model results

Business-as-usual scenario

Before investigating the potential effects of emissions trading and ETS design on emission cuts and mitigation costs, it is useful to take a closer look at the business-as-usual – our hypothetical reference scenario without any explicit climate policy. Figure 12.1 shows the projected BaU level of GDP and CO_2 emissions in 2020 for the 13 regions, based on the Energy Information Administration (EIA 2013) forecast.[9] China accounts for 14 per cent of global GDP and 29 per cent of global emissions. Together with Russia and India, China has the highest CO_2 intensity (CO_2 emissions per GDP) in the BaU scenario for 2020 – about two times higher than the world average and more than four times higher than the EU, Japan and Brazil. This indicates that the potential for emissions reductions is greater in China than in the EU. China's high emissions intensity is due largely to the considerable share of coal in its primary energy demand – almost 80 per cent of fossil-based CO_2 emissions in China stem from coal combustion in 2020.[10]

Figure 12.2 shows how Chinese and EU emissions are distributed across sectors, as well as the CO_2 intensities of each sector calculated as emissions divided by the gross production value of the sector. Sectors are shown in descending order with respect to emissions in the Chinese sectors. We see that the electricity sector (ELE), mostly coal-power plants, accounts for a very large share of China's emissions: 54 per cent of the country's total emissions in our BaU scenario for 2020. The sector also has much higher emissions intensity than any other sector. Energy-intensive trade-exposed industries like non-metal minerals (NMM), iron and steel (I_S) and chemical products (CRP) are other

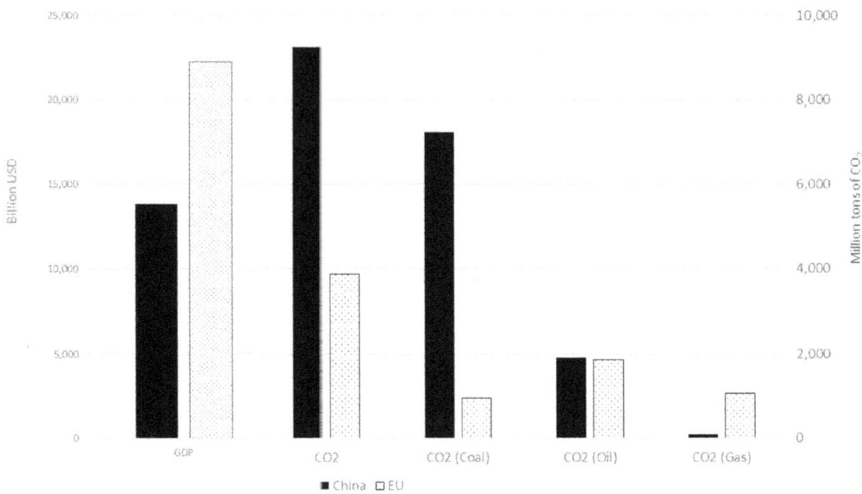

Figure 12.1 GDP level (billion USD) and CO_2 emissions (million tons), BaU 2020 scenario

Note: All monetary values are measured in USD, as the model is calibrated to data for the year 2011.

large sectors as regards China's emissions, in total accounting for around 20 per cent of domestic emissions. Other transport (OTP) (mostly road transport), water transport (WTP), coal extraction (COL) and refined oil products (OIL) are also sectors with substantial emissions. Coal extraction has the highest emissions intensity of the non-electricity sectors. Taken together, the sectors to be covered by the Chinese ETS account for some 75 per cent of the country's emissions in 2020.[11]

The electricity sector is also the biggest emission sector in the EU, but it accounts for a much lower share than in China, 32 per cent. Further, transport sectors have higher emissions shares in the EU than in China, with other transport (OTP), air transport (ATP) and water transport (WTP) ranking second, fourth and fifth, respectively. Together, these sectors account for 27 per cent of EU's total emissions, whereas in China the corresponding share is 8 per cent. On the other hand, the EITE sectors (see Table 12.2 for definition) jointly account for 11 per cent in the EU, compared to 22 per cent in China. As the ETS in both jurisdictions mainly regulates the EITE sectors in addition to the electricity sector, the EU ETS covers a much lower share of overall emissions than the Chinese ETS – around 50 per cent, as against 75 per cent. Finally, we see that CO_2 intensity is generally higher in the Chinese sectors than in the corresponding EU ones – especially in electricity, due to the high share of coal power in China, but also in the EITE sectors.[12]

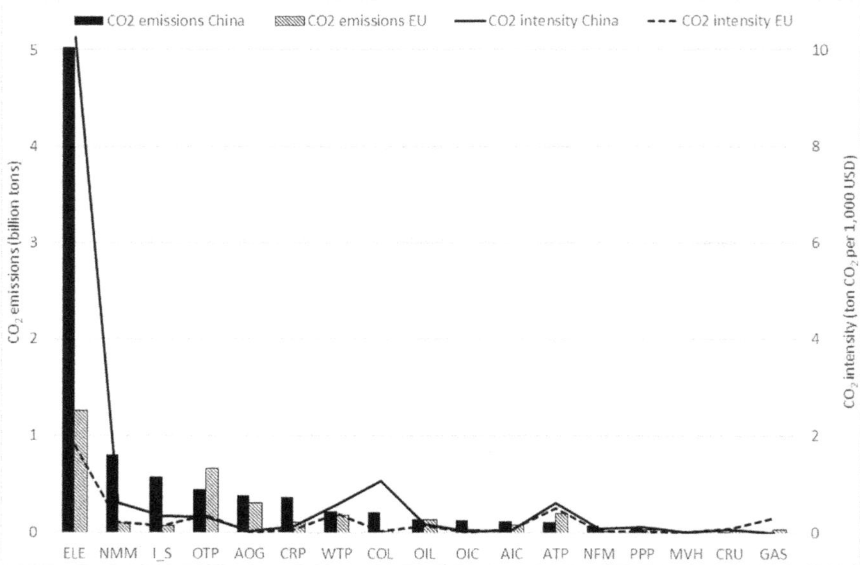

Figure 12.2 CO_2 emissions (billion tons) and CO_2 intensity (ton CO_2 per 1,000 USD) across sectors in China and the EU, BaU 2020 scenario

Note: ELE: electricity, NMM: non-metallic minerals, I_S: iron and steel, OTP: other transport, AOG: all other manufactures and services, CRP: chemical products, WTP: water transport, COL: coal, OIL: refined oil products, OIC: other energy-intensive trade-exposed goods, AIC: agricultural energy-intensive trade-exposed goods, ATP: air transport, NFM: non-ferrous metals, PPP: paper and pulp, MVH: motor vehicles, CRU: crude oil. Final demand, accounting for respectively 0.5 and 0.7 billion tons of CO2 in China and the EU (6 per cent and 17 per cent of domestic emissions), is not included in the figure.

Effects of emissions trading in China and the EU

Ambition level

We now turn to the potential effects of emissions trading and the effects of the different ETS designs in Table 12.1. We start by considering the level of ambition, examining the effects of different CO_2 prices (keeping other factors constant). Figure 12.3 shows the effects on emissions in the two jurisdictions, measured as percentage reductions from the BaU emission levels. The figure shows effects on total emissions as well as effects on emissions in the sectors regulated by the ETS. We see that a given CO_2 price leads to much greater emissions reductions in China than in the EU, particularly as regards total domestic emissions. For instance, at an ETS price of USD 20 per ton CO_2, Chinese emissions are reduced by 17 per cent, whereas EU emissions are reduced by only 6 per cent.

There are two main reasons for this difference. First, as noted, the Chinese ETS regulates a greater share of the country's emissions than does the EU ETS.

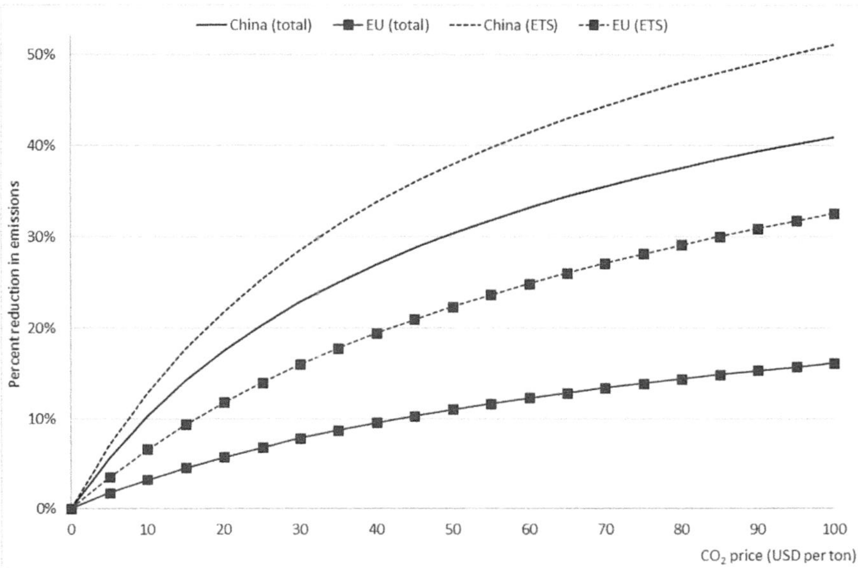

Figure 12.3 Effects on domestic CO_2 emissions of differing emission prices in China and the EU, percentage reductions relative to the 2020 BaU scenario

Hence, an ETS price of USD 20 per ton CO_2 will affect relatively more emission sources in China than in the EU. To indicate the importance of this, the figure also shows relative emission reductions within the ETS sectors. The differences between China and the EU are then reduced: with USD 20 per ton CO_2, emission reductions in the Chinese and EU ETSs are 22 per cent and 12 per cent, respectively.

Second, ease of abatement is higher in China than in the EU – especially in the electricity sector, where coal can be replaced by gas, nuclear or renewable power. As China has a very high share of coal power in its electricity sector, there is more room for utilizing less carbon-intensive or carbon-free abatement options than in the EU. In addition, the much lower energy efficiency in China than in the EU implies that Chinese emissions can more readily be reduced by installing more energy-efficient equipment. Our model accounts for all these changes.

For both China and the EU, the curves are concave: if the emissions price is doubled, the emissions reduction achieved is less than doubled. Or: if the emissions reduction target is doubled, the emissions price will need to be more than doubled. For instance, if the target for emissions reductions in the ETS sectors is raised from 10 per cent to 20 per cent, the necessary ETS price will rise from USD 7.5 to USD 18 in China, and from USD 17 to USD 42 in the EU.

Figure 12.4 shows the economic welfare costs for China and the EU of implementing an emissions trading system, assuming different ambition levels represented by different ETS prices. By 'welfare costs' we mean losses in real income

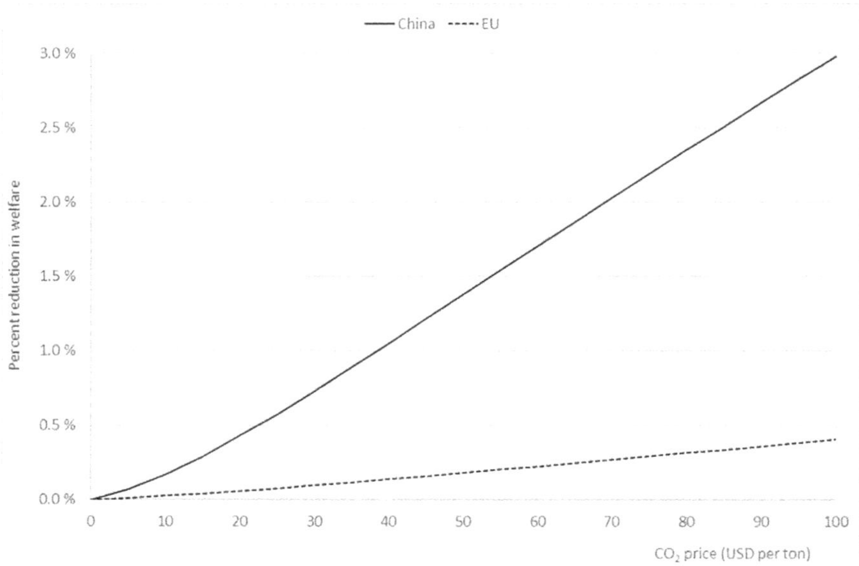

Figure 12.4 Economic welfare effects of differing emissions prices in China and the EU, percentage welfare reductions relative to the BaU 2020 scenario

for the country in question. Moderate prices in the range of USD 10–20 per ton CO_2 have small welfare costs in both jurisdictions, in other words, less than 0.5 per cent of the BaU welfare level. With high ETS prices in the range of USD 50–100, welfare costs become more sizeable in China – 1.5–3 per cent – but remain low in the EU (still less than 0.5 per cent).

There are several reasons for this difference. First, as noted, a given CO_2 price will lead to much higher emissions reductions in China than in the EU – and more emissions reductions typically mean higher welfare costs. A second reason for the cost difference, and in particular the quite low welfare costs in the EU, is related to terms of trade effects (changes in import and export prices). For the EU, these effects go in an advantageous direction: when the EU implements climate policies, the price of imported goods like fossil fuels tends to fall, due to lower demand, and the import bill decreases. Also, China imports fossil fuels, but to a lesser extent than the EU when measured as share of domestic fossil-fuel consumption. Further, the EU is a net exporter of EITE goods, whereas China is a net importer, as measured in value of net trade. As the ETS tends to increase the prices of EITE goods (due to higher costs), the terms-of-trade effects again go in a positive direction for the EU, but in a disadvantageous direction for China as regards EITE goods in aggregate.

Sector coverage

Prior, we assumed that the ETS coverage is quite consistent with the coverage in the upcoming Chinese ETS (see Table 12.2, as well as Table 11.2 in Chapter 11 of this book), as well as in the EU ETS. Now we turn to how expansion of the ETS coverage affects domestic emissions and economic welfare. To investigate the implications of ETS sector coverage, we start from a situation with no ETS and then add one sector at a time to the ETS. The sequence of the sectors is based on their relative importance for CO_2 emissions in China (in descending order – see Figure 12.2). First, we add sectors that are/will be ETS regulated in both the EU and China. Second, we add the motor vehicles sector, which may be partly included in the Chinese ETS already from the start. Third, we add the three fossil-fuel extraction sectors already regulated by the EU ETS. Next, we add the remaining individual sectors, then we add composite sectors and, sixth, we add final demand. We perform simulations for two quite different ETS prices – USD 10 and USD 50 per ton CO_2 – which might be considered as candidates for low and high price expectations over the next decade.

Figure 12.5 shows the outcome of this sector expansion with respect to emissions reductions. We see that an ETS covering only the electricity sector already leads to substantial emission reductions – at least two times higher than the additional emission reductions obtained by regulating all sectors.[13] This is the case for both China and the EU, irrespective of the two emission prices. The reason is partly that the electricity sector accounts for large shares of emissions in China and the EU: slightly more than one-half and around one-third, respectively. In addition, ease of abatement is significantly higher in the electricity sector than in most other sectors – involving, for instance, replacing coal power with gas, nuclear or renewable power. This simulation also shows that if the regulated

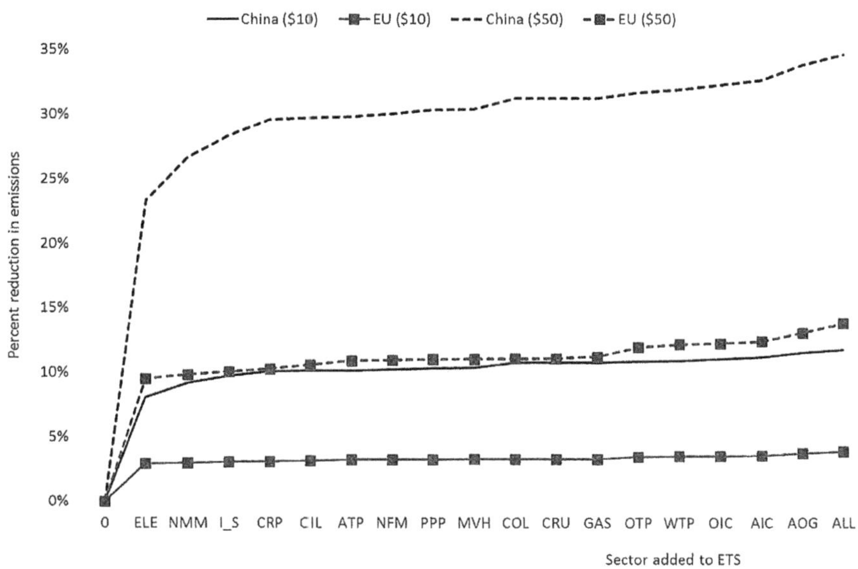

Figure 12.5 Effects on domestic CO_2 emissions of adding sectors to the ETS in China and the EU, percentage reductions relative to the 2020 BaU scenario

electricity sector in China fails to respond to the ETS (for instance, by not adjusting the regulated electricity prices), the emissions trading system will have substantially less effect on Chinese emissions.

Next, we see that adding the EITE sectors has greater effects on domestic emissions in China than in the EU. This is due to the higher share of coal as well as the lower energy efficiency in the Chinese sectors. Together this makes CO_2 intensity in the Chinese sectors higher than in the corresponding EU sectors (see Figure 12.2, notes a and b), providing greater scope for emissions reductions. In particular, adding the non-metallic minerals sector (like cement) reduces emissions notably in China, but also with the sectors iron/steel and chemical products. Expanding the ETS to include motor vehicles has negligible effects on domestic emissions, due to its low share of emissions. By contrast, including the fossil-fuel extraction industries (already regulated by the EU ETS) has noticeable effects – at least, adding coal extraction to the Chinese ETS. Simulations show that this reduces Chinese emissions by 0.4–0.8 per cent, depending on the ETS price. Including other transport sectors than air transport (already regulated) in the ETS yields relatively modest additional emission reductions in China, but has somewhat higher effects in the EU, where transport sectors account for a greater share of domestic emissions (see Figure 12.2). In China, all transport sectors together account for 8 per cent of domestic emissions in 2020. Finally, including all sectors, also those that are not emissions intensive, as well as final demand in the ETS, yields non-negligible emissions reductions.

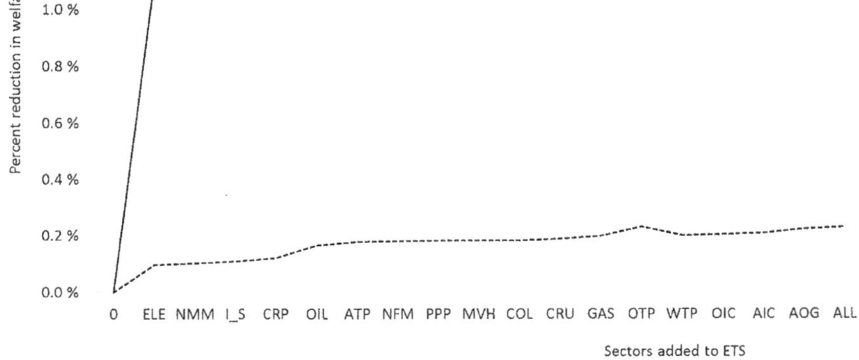

Figure 12.6 Effects on domestic welfare of adding sectors to the ETS (price: USD 50 per ton CO_2) in China and the EU, percentage reductions relative to the 2020 BaU scenario

Figure 12.6 shows the welfare costs of adding more sectors to the ETS in the case of a CO_2 price of USD 50 per ton CO_2. To a considerable extent, the welfare costs follow the emission reductions shown in Figure 12.5. Note that the environmental benefits of lower emissions are not accounted for in this figure. These benefits are partly related to lower CO_2 emissions, but also to co-benefits from decreased urban air pollution due to lower emissions from, for example, diesel cars and nearby electricity and industrial plants.

Obviously, the higher welfare costs of expanding the coverage of the ETS go along with greater domestic emission reductions. Thus, we could also ask how welfare costs are affected by adding more sectors to the ETS, while domestic emissions reduction is kept fixed. We return to this in the following in discussing access to offsets.

Allocation mechanism

The third design property concerns the allocation of emission allowances. Thus far, we have assumed full auctioning, or (equivalent) allocation of allowances that do not affect firms' behaviour (see discussion in 'ETS design properties' prior). We now turn to the consequences of implementing benchmarking (output-based allocation) to some or all sectors that are regulated by the ETS. Benchmarking is likely to be implemented in some sectors of the China ETS (see Chapter 11 of this book) and has already been used in the Chinese pilots as well as in the EU ETS. As shown by, for example, Böhringer and Lange (2005), such an allocation mechanism will tend to stimulate production, as firms then receive more valuable allowances for free – in other words, it functions similarly to a production subsidy. For a given ETS price, we should therefore expect less emissions reductions in sectors where benchmarking is implemented.

Figure 12.7 shows the effects on emissions of alternative assumptions about benchmarking. We see that implementing benchmarking to the EITE industries has little effect on overall emission reductions in both the EU and China, partly because these industries account for only around one-quarter of total ETS emissions (in the BaU scenario). More importantly, however, the EITE industries do not expand their production much in response to benchmarking, especially in the low-price scenarios (USD 10 per ton CO_2) where the implicit subsidy (which is proportional to the emission price and the carbon intensity of the industry) is quite small. In the scenarios with high price and auctioning (USD 50 per ton CO_2), total EITE production drops by 3.1 per cent and 1.6 per cent, respectively, in China and in the EU (vis-à-vis BaU). With benchmarking, output reductions become 1.7 per cent and 0.7 per cent.

Implementing benchmarking in the electricity sector has greater effects on emissions in the case of EU as well as China: total abatement drops by about 20 per cent. This reflects the very large share of ETS emissions from the electricity sector (70 per cent in China and 66 per cent in the EU in the BaU). Electricity producers react more strongly to benchmarking than, for instance, EITE producers simply because the carbon intensity of production is higher, making the implicit subsidy rate of benchmarking higher. For instance, whereas electricity generation in China drops by 17 per cent in the high emission-price scenario (USD 50 per ton CO_2) under auctioning, it drops by only 2 per cent with benchmarking. This indicates a potential

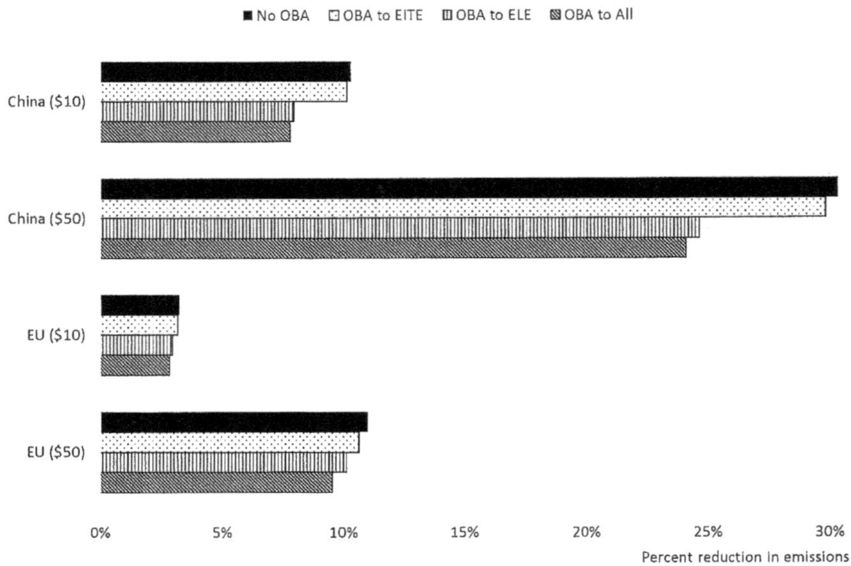

Figure 12.7 Effects on domestic CO_2 emissions of benchmarking to various sectors in China and the EU, percentage reductions relative to the 2020 BaU scenario

benefit of choosing auctioning rather than benchmarking for the electricity sector. In the EU, the corresponding figures are −4 per cent and −0.6 per cent. If benchmarking is implemented in all sectors, emissions reductions are further decreased, but not much more than in the scenarios with benchmarking to the electricity sector.

The welfare costs of reducing CO_2 emissions decline when benchmarking is implemented. This is the case in both China and the EU, and irrespective of whether benchmarking is implemented in the electricity sector, the EITE sectors or all sectors. However, since the emissions reduction is also smaller, implementing benchmarking is not necessarily advantageous from an economy-wide cost-effectiveness perspective. A complete evaluation of benchmarking would require taking into account the effects on carbon leakage as well. However, carbon leakage from China to other countries is very low, according to our simulations.[14] Without leakage, benchmarking will typically increase the costs of reducing emissions, as it stimulates the production of energy-intensive goods.

Offsets

Finally, we consider access to domestic offsets: whether and to what degree the regulated firms can pay for emission reductions in non-regulated firms instead of reducing their own emissions or buying allowances from other regulated firms. Thus far we have assumed no access to offsets: now we examine the effects of allowing some limited access to domestic offsets. The Chinese ETS will allow this, whereas the EU ETS has allowed the use of foreign offsets (i.e. CDM credits), but not after 2020. In investigating the effects of offsets, we keep the domestic emission reduction fixed and examine the effects on the emission price (Figure 12.8) and the welfare costs (Figure 12.9) of achieving the same target with (limited) access to offsets. Access to offsets is limited to either 10 per cent, 25 per cent or 50 per cent of the emission reduction realized in the scenario without access to offsets.

Our modelling of offsets is quite simplistic, as we allow any emission reductions that would be realized with an emissions price equal to the ETS price imposed in the non-regulated sectors. Moreover, we disregard transaction costs. Hence, the modelling results overestimate the potential for offsets – because we omit transaction costs, and because several types of emission reductions cannot be realized through an offset scheme (for instance, less use of private cars).

We find that allowing a limited 10 per cent share of offsets brings down the costs of reaching the same emission target by up to 11 per cent (see Figure 12.9), while the necessary emissions price drops by up to 24 per cent (see Figure 12.8). The effects are greater in China than in the EU – probably because the Chinese ETS yields larger emissions reductions than the EU ETS (as a share of the country's emissions), making access to offsets more important. Moreover, the effects are greater for high than for low emission prices. Allowing up to 25 per cent offsets has only small additional effects, and allowing 50 per cent offsets has no further effects. Thus, even rather restricted access to offsets seems sufficient to achieve a markedly more cost-effective emission reduction in China and in the EU. Given other problematic issues related to offsets, such as the additionality problem and transaction

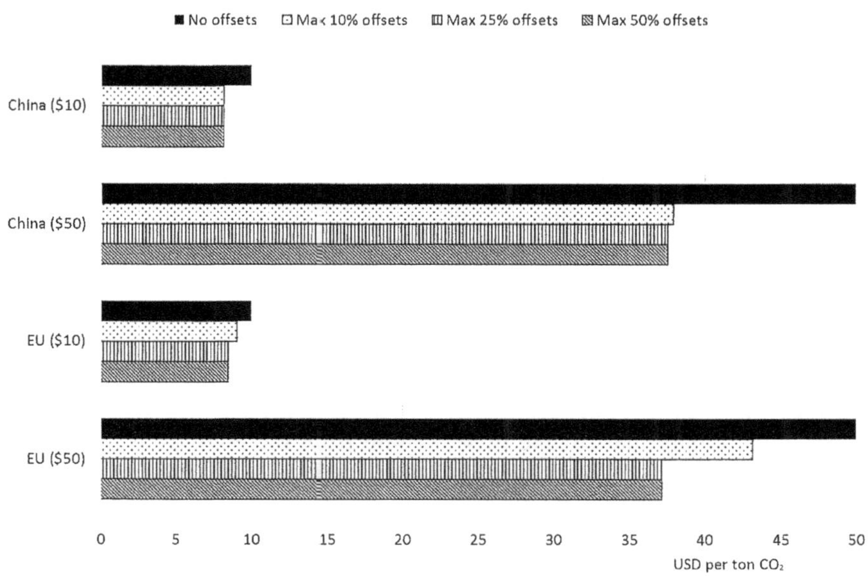

Figure 12.8 CO_2 emission prices in China and the EU under differing assumptions of access to domestic offsets, USD per ton CO_2.

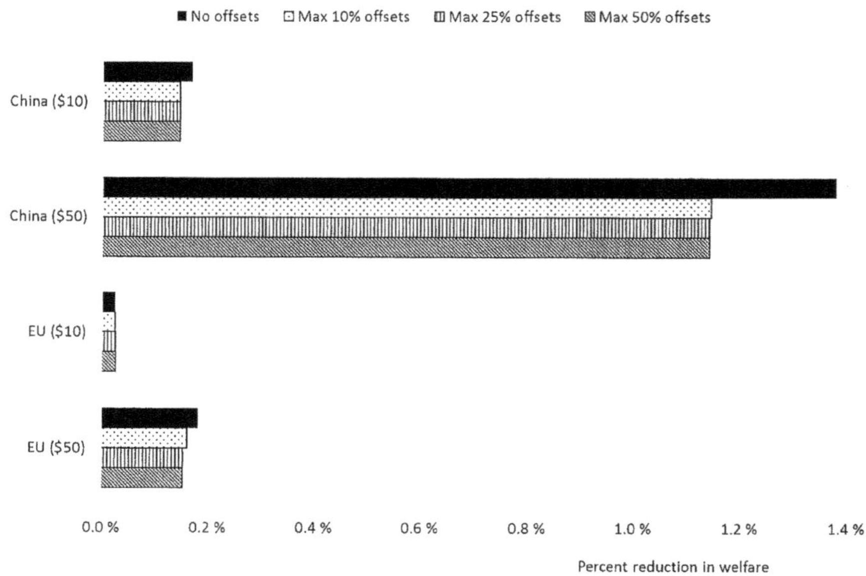

Figure 12.9 Domestic welfare effects in China and the EU under differing assumptions of access to domestic offsets, percentage reductions relative to the 2020 BaU scenario

costs (which are disregarded in our analysis), allowing a share of access higher than 10 per cent might prove counter-productive. If we also take into account that the model overestimates the potential for offsets, the upper limit on offsets could probably be set even lower than 10 per cent without reducing cost-effectiveness notably.

One reason why as little as 10 per cent use of offsets seems sufficient to induce cost-effective domestic abatement is that most of the cheap abatement options are found in the ETS sectors, especially the electricity sector. In China, three quarters of BaU emissions are regulated by the ETS, so it is not surprising that only a smaller share of emission reductions should take place outside the ETS sectors in a cost-effective solution. In the EU, half of the BaU emissions are regulated by the ETS. Of the non-ETS emissions, one-third are in the 'other transport' sector (mostly road transport), whereas another third are in final demand, which are both emission sources with relatively high abatement costs.

In China, around half of the offsets come from the composite sector 'all other manufactures and services' and 'final demand'. In addition, there is notable use of offsets from 'other transport' and the two composite EITE sectors not regulated by the ETS (AIC and OIC). In the EU, more than half of the offsets come from 'other transport', 'all other manufactures and services' and 'final demand'.

Conclusions

China is set to establish a national ETS in late 2017, after a few years' experience with seven pilots (regional ETSs) (see Chapter 11 of this book). In this chapter we have used a multi-region, multi-sector CGE model of the world economy for quantitative analysis of the potential effects of ETS design in China and comparison with corresponding effects in the EU. Four important ETS design properties have been examined. From our quantitative simulations we can draw the following key conclusions:

- For a given emission price, a Chinese ETS has the potential to provide substantial emissions reductions – probably greater reductions than the EU ETS, due to China's large initial share of coal-power generation, which can be replaced by less carbon-intensive power generation at relatively low cost. China also has a considerable potential for energy-efficiency improvements. Further, our analysis indicates that the welfare costs of ETS will not be excessive in China, or in the EU, even with rather high levels of ambition.
- Expanding the ETS to include more sectors will bring additional emissions reductions, but the benefits will be moderate in China as well as in the EU (for a given ETS price). One reason is that reducing emissions in non-ETS sectors (e.g. road transport) is generally more expensive than within the ETS. In addition, the ETS already includes a large share of domestic emissions – our simulations have assumed that the Chinese ETS will include around three-quarters of CO2 emissions, which is in the upper range of current expectations. In fact, our analysis showed that an ETS which covered only the electricity sector would bring about two-thirds of the emissions reductions that would be achieved if the whole economy were regulated by the ETS. This applies both for China and the EU.
- If allowances are given out for free to the regulated firms in proportion to their production level (benchmarking or output-based allocation), the realized emission reductions will be lower for a given emission price. In other words, for a given emission cap, the ETS price will be higher. This is especially the case if the electricity sector in China is given free allowances in this way.
- Access to domestic offsets can reduce the economic welfare costs of the ETS, especially in China, if the ambition level is high. However, even a rather moderate share of offsets is sufficient to realize most of the cost savings.

Our quantitative analysis relies on some assumptions that could be discussed and may warrant more refined follow-up assessments.

First, we have modelled the electricity sector in China like any other market-based sector, even though electricity prices in China are regulated (Reklev 2016b). Thus, our analysis implicitly assumes that the regulated prices are adjusted to fully reflect the costs of CO_2 emissions as represented by the ETS price. If, however, electricity prices are not adjusted, upstream or downstream, emission reductions will not be realized in this sector. Given the huge importance of this sector in China, the Chinese ETS will then have much less effect on domestic emissions.

Including indirect emissions in the ETS, as in the Chinese pilots (see Chapter 11 of this book), could remedy some of this shortcoming.

Second, our model captures the medium- to long-term effects of policy changes. In the short run, the effects on emissions (for a given emission price) are likely to be more moderate than our results indicate, as it takes time to change machineries, technologies, etc. Moreover, the costs of reducing emissions by a certain amount are likely to be higher in the short run than in the longer run. Our results may therefore be more relevant for the years closer to 2030 than for the year 2020 which we have analysed here.

Third, we have disregarded climate policies in other parts of the world. Obviously, other countries will implement policies for reducing CO_2 emissions in the coming years. Nevertheless, moderate climate policies elsewhere are likely to have only a minor impact on the effects of emissions trading in China as well as in the EU.

Fourth, in considering allocation mechanisms and access to offsets, we have operated with some simplifying assumptions. In practice, benchmarking is often based on previous output (and not current output), which may dampen the effects of such allocation. Further, the potential for offsets is lower than what we implicitly assume, and we have disregarded the problematic issue of additionality of offsets. Thus, our analysis should be seen as indicating an upper limit of the effects of benchmarking and offsets.

Nevertheless, our main conclusion remains: emissions trading in China as well as in the EU can provide substantial emissions reductions at moderate welfare costs, irrespective of further expansion, allocation of allowances and/or access to offsets.

Notes

1 One reason for focusing on emissions prices instead of emissions cuts is that the overall emissions cap in the Chinese ETS has not been set yet (see Chapter 11 of this book). Furthermore, there will be market adjustment mechanisms, such as allocation reserves that can be used to intervene in the market to adjust the price, and annual allocation allowing for continuous adjustment of the cap if the price becomes too low or too high (see e.g. Wang et al. 2017). In the EU ETS, a Market Stability Reserve has been adopted because of the increasing surplus of allowances and low prices (see Chapter 3 of this book).

2 The only main difference between the sector coverage in the EU ETS and the Chinese ETS, with regard to the sector aggregation in our model, is that fossil-fuel extraction is covered by the EU ETS but not the Chinese ETS.

3 If auction revenues are used to reduce existing taxes, there are economy-wide impacts from revenue recycling. Revenue earmarking is one of the eight design properties considered in this book but is not included in our analysis.

4 We disregard that some cheap abatement options are difficult (or even impossible) to realize through an offset mechanism, and also that there may be significant transaction costs related to using offsets. We also disregard the additionality problem, i.e., the risk that some of the offsets accepted for use in an ETS may be related to projects that would have taken place also in the absence of offsets (see e.g. Zhang and Wang 2011).

5 For a detailed algebraic model description, see e.g. Böhringer et al. (2014).

6 Whereas all energy sectors are included in the EU ETS, only the secondary energy sectors (refined oil and electricity) are included in the Chinese ETS. Our default is to follow the Chinese ETS, but we also analyse the effects of sector coverage.

7 Automakers have been among the candidates for inclusion in the Chinese ETS, but could be administered separately from the ETS: China Climate Change Info-Net, Government set to roll out carbon credit scheme, 15 August 2016, http://en.ccchina.gov.cn/Detail.aspx?newsId=62988&TId=96.

8 For instance, in China the five-year plans (FYP) are important. One of the targets in the 13th FYP for 2016–20 is to reduce the share of coal in electricity production to about 57 per cent, as against 66 per cent in 2015. The plan also includes a binding goal of 58 per cent for the share of coal consumption in total energy consumption, as well as an indicative coal consumption cap of 4.1 billion tons by 2020.

9 Given the slowdown in Chinese GDP growth, coal consumption and CO2 emissions since the 2013 EIA projections (Cheng and Eikeland 2015; Green and Stern 2016), the BaU scenario may possibly overestimate both GDP and CO2 emissions levels for China in 2020. However, this will not alter our conclusions significantly, as we do not incorporate a specific absolute cap for Chinese CO2 emissions.

10 Market exchange rates (MER) are used in comparing GDP across countries. An alternative metric could be Purchasing Power Parity (PPP), whereby Chinese GDP would increase when compared to the EU. In turn, the difference in emissions intensity (emissions per GDP) between China and the EU would decline, indicating that the potential for lowering emissions intensity in China may not be as great as indicated by Figure 12.1.

11 Estimates differs as to the size of the upcoming Chinese ETS. While government officials have indicated that the ETS will regulate 3–4 billion tons of CO2 (see Chapter 11 of this book), the analyst company ICIS holds the actual amount could be as high as 6.5 billion tons (Reklev 2016a). The latter figure is in the same range as in our simulations.

12 China's higher CO2 intensity is due not only to higher emissions from producing one unit of electricity, steel or cement, but also to the lower market value of the produced output (electricity, steel, cement, etc.).

13 Note that the relative contribution of the different sectors is not path independent: if we changed the sequencing, the relative contributions would also change somewhat. Nevertheless, there can be no doubt as to the massive importance of the electricity sector.

14 In the case of USD 10 per ton CO2, the leakage rate is 2 per cent without benchmarking, falling to 1 per cent with benchmarking to all sectors in China. In the EU, the corresponding leakage rates are 14 per cent and 8 per cent.

References

Böhringer, C. and A. Lange. 2005. On the design of optimal grandfathering schemes for emission allowances. *European Economic Review* 49, 2041–2055.

Böhringer, C. and A. Löschel. 2006. Computable general equilibrium models for sustainability impact assessment: Status quo and prospects. *Ecological Economics* 60, 49–64.

Böhringer, C., C. Fischer and K. E. Rosendahl. 2014. Cost-effective unilateral climate policy design: Size matters. *Journal of Environmental Economics and Management* 67, 318–339.

Böhringer, C. and K. E. Rosendahl. 2010. Green serves the dirtiest: On the interaction between black and green quotas. *Journal of Regulatory Economics* 37, 316–325.

Böhringer, C., R. S. J. Tol and T. F. Rutherford. 2009. The EU 20/20/2020 targets: An overview of the EMF22 Assessment. *Energy Economics* 31 (2), 268–273.

Cheng, H. and P. O. Eikeland. 2015. *China's Political Economy of Coal: Drivers and Challenges to Restructuring China's Energy System, FNI Report 10/2015*. Lysaker: Fridtjof Nansen Institute.

EIA. 2013. *International Energy Outlook 2013, U.S. Energy Information Administration.* www.eia.gov/forecasts/ieo/ accessed 15 May 2017.

Environomist. 2017. *Environomist China Carbon Market Research Report 2017*. www.cn.undp.org/content/dam/china/docs/Publications/UNDP-CH-Environomist%20China%20Carbon%20Market%20Report%202017_En.pdf? accessed 15 May 2017.

Golombek, R., S. A. C. Kittelsen and K. E. Rosendahl. 2013. Price and welfare effects of emission quota allocation. *Energy Economics* 36, 568–580.

Green, F. and N. Stern. 2016. *China's Changing Economy: Implications for Its Carbon Dioxide Emissions, Working Paper No. 228*. London: Grantham Research Institute on Climate Change and the Environment.

Hübler, M., S. Voigt and A. Löschel. 2014. Designing an emissions trading scheme for China: An up-to-date climate policy assessment. *Energy Policy* 75, 57–72.

ICAP. 2016. *Emissions Trading Worldwide: Status Report 2016*. Berlin: International Carbon Action Partnership (ICAP).

IPCC. 2014. *Climate Change 2014: Mitigation of Climate Change, Contribution of Working Group III to the Fifth Assessment Report of the Intergovernmental Panel on Climate Change*. Cambridge: Cambridge University Press.

Klemetsen, M. E., K. E. Rosendahl and A. L. Jakobsen. 2016. *The Impacts of the EU ETS on Norwegian Plants' Environmental and Economic Performance, Working Paper 3 / 2016*. Norwegian University of Life Sciences, School of Economics and Business.

Martin, R., M. Muûls and U. J. Wagner. 2016. The impact of the European Union Emissions Trading Scheme on regulated firms: What is the evidence after ten years? *Review of Environmental Economics and Policy* 10, 129–148.

Narayanan, B. G., A. Aguiar and R. McDougall (eds.). 2015. *Global Trade, Assistance, and Production: The GTAP 9 Data Base*. Lafayette, IN: Center for Global Trade Analysis, Purdue University. www.gtap.agecon.purdue.edu/databases/v9/v9_doco.asp accessed 15 May 2017.

Reklev, S. 2016a. China ETS could regulate twice as much CO2 as previously estimated – analysts. *Carbon Pulse*. 28 October. http://carbon-pulse.com/26024/ accessed 15 May 2017.

Reklev, S. 2016b. Power supply spat hints at obstacles for China's carbon market. *Carbon Pulse*. 16 February. http://carbon-pulse.com/15663/ accessed 15 May 2017.

Rosendahl, K. E. and J. Strand. 2015. Emissions trading with offset narkets and free quota allocations. *Environmental and Resource Economics* 61, 243–271.

Wang, B., F. Jotzo and S. Qi. 2017. Ex-post cap adjustment for China's ETS: An applicable indexation rule, simulating the Hubei ETS, and implications for a national scheme. *Climate Policy* (doi: 10.1080/14693062.2016.1277684).

World Bank Group. 2016. *State and Trends of Carbon Pricing, October*. Washington, DC: World Bank Group. http://documents.worldbank.org/curated/en/598811476464765822/State-and-trends-of-carbon-pricing accessed 15 May 2017.

Xu, Z., Q. Tian-yu, O. Xun-min and Z. Xi-liang. 2017. The role of multi-region integrated emissions trading scheme: A computable general equilibrium analysis. *Applied Energy* 185, 1860–1868.

Zhang, D., M. Springmann and V. J. Karplus. 2016. Equity and emissions trading in China. *Climatic Change* 134, 131–146.

Zhang, J. and C. Wang. 2011. Co-benefits and additionality of the clean development mechanism: An empirical analysis. *Journal of Environmental Economics and Management* 62, 140–154.

13 Comparative analysis and conclusions

Jørgen Wettestad, Lars H. Gulbrandsen, David G. Victor and Arild Underdal

Introduction

In recent years, carbon emissions trading programmes have emerged at many levels – from the subnational to the regional – across Europe, North America and the Asia-Pacific. These schemes allow firms to buy and sell emissions allowances in an effort to find the least costly ways to control emissions. Launched in 2005, the EU Emissions Trading System (EU ETS) was the first major scheme in the world. It remains by far the largest, covering more than 11,000 factories, power stations and other installations in all 28 EU member-states, as well as Norway, Iceland and Lichtenstein.

But China is poised to take over the ETS leadership mantle. Having tested seven pilot provincial projects from 2013 and 2014 onwards, China is launching a national ETS in 2017, covering up to 10,000 companies and eventually a market twice the size of the EU ETS. While these will be the largest programmes, there are many other important efforts underway. The Regional Greenhouse Gas Initiative (RGGI), established as a cooperative effort among north-eastern states in the United States, became effective at the start of 2009. It was the first mandatory market-based carbon reduction programme in the US. California created its own programme shortly after RGGI – a programme that covers nearly all emissions in the state (the world's seventh-largest economy) and is now managed in tandem with a carbon market in the Canadian province of Quebec. Across the Pacific Ocean, New Zealand has launched a national ETS as a cornerstone in its climate mitigation policy, although Australia has repealed its scheme. Programmes have emerged elsewhere as well, with Kazakhstan, South Korea and Tokyo as key examples.

What is striking about this experience is that the original logic for emissions trading was arguably anchored in the idea that all countries would adopt similar systems and a global market would emerge rather quickly. Learning and diffusion would help accelerate that process. Instead, significant diversity has prevailed. This book set out to explain that outcome by offering insights that are important not just to understand how the world has arrived at today's position, but also for the future.

Other chapters in this book have introduced our expectations, methods and case studies. In this chapter we take stock of what we have learned. We begin by exploring why jurisdictions chose trading – instead of (or, usually, in tandem with) carbon taxes. Then we proceed with an examination of the main similarities and differences across systems and their design properties. For each focused design feature, we discuss the extent to which and how policy diffusion can explain the similarities and differences observed. Then follows a discussion of specific questions and expectations about policy diffusion outlined in Chapter 2, not least the role of networks and domestic politics as mediating factors and actors. We wind up the chapter with some concluding reflections on the challenges and opportunities for future research on the politics of emissions trading and the prospects ahead for carbon markets and their role in the implementation of the Paris Agreement.

Why did jurisdictions turn to emissions trading?

The initiation of the EU ETS took place against the backdrop of a failed effort to agree on a carbon tax. Industry and member-states such as the UK had fought intensely against such a tax, the adoption of which would require unanimity. Hence, in 1998 the EU was in desperate need of a common policy instrument that could be welcomed by industry and key member-states and be adopted as a common EU policy. But the EU was also inspired by the experiences of others, particularly the US and the perceived success of sulphur emissions trading. Furthermore, the adoption of the flexibility instruments under the Kyoto Protocol provided an additional incentive for the EU to get more acquainted with the emissions trading instrument.

Much of the same dynamic was found in New Zealand, where a failed carbon tax proposal contributed significantly to the ETS emerging as the main candidate policy for meeting the country's Kyoto Protocol obligations. Indeed, the failure of the carbon tax proposal in New Zealand is a clear example of a policy failure that encouraged deeper consideration of an ETS approach. In Australia, initial work on developing an ETS began shortly after the conclusion of the Kyoto Protocol in 1997, when the government began work on how to meet Australia's Kyoto target. Although government support for an ETS dissipated when Prime Minister John Howard announced in 2002 that he would not ratify Kyoto, design activity continued at both the state and national levels and accelerated following the change of government in 2007. Interestingly, the subsequent failure of one ETS proposal in Australia led to revising the idea rather than walking away from it, because it was still seen as the preferred policy instrument by the government. What was needed, according to the government, was to iron out design (and hence political) problems rather than introducing another policy instrument.

In California and RGGI in the United States, the lack of federal climate action – which would have been a nationwide cap-and-trade system, but that plan failed in 2009 – was an important trigger for the inception of regional ETS. These actors initially focused on knowledge acquired from emissions trading experience gleaned within the EU, at first glance reaffirming our expectation that an important source of motivation is found in what policy-makers perceive to be a well-functioning ETS in one or more other jurisdictions. An important part of the explanation is probably that in the mid-2000s there were not many other real-world models to offer inspiration. Policy-makers in California (and many other places) quickly realized that the EU ETS was *not* very well-functioning and in important respects chose somewhat different designs – a topic we examine in more detail in the following.

In China, as well, an important contributing factor in the choice of emission trading was ineffective command-and-control efforts to improve energy intensity. Other important drivers also included rapid economic development (and thus higher emissions) coupled with heightened awareness of climate change's negative impacts on the country. That the country was also active as the largest host for Clean Development Mechanism (CDM) projects was also a factor that predisposed Chinese policy-makers to consider trading. The choice of trading diffused to China, as well, when the EU and US, along with other governments, international organizations and non-governmental organizations (NGOs), lobbied the country actively and offered policy design support.

In South Korea, rapid economic growth and related greenhouse gas (GHG) emissions were not matched by effective climate policies. But possibly even more important was that establishing an ETS fit well with former president Lee Myung-bak's Low Carbon, Green Growth Strategy as a way to seize the economic opportunities arising from the low-carbon transition globally. In addition, somewhat similar to the case of China, CDM experiences played a role, as did international normative pressure from the global climate regime. There were contacts with the EU and others, but ETS policy diffusion entered more strongly in the more specific design phase.

In Tokyo, previous non-binding targets in the early 2000s had produced only minor emissions reductions. This led to the establishment of more ambitious climate-change strategies, plans and targets (including a target of 25 per cent reductions below 2000 levels by 2020), which in turn led to the creation of the Tokyo ETS. This was also motivated by the absence of a nationwide ETS and the wish of the then governor of the Tokyo Metropolitan Government to exert leadership by example. Policy diffusion played no role in Tokyo's turn to emissions trading.

In some instances, failure of other policies has not triggered the adoption of ETS – notably in countries and regions that appear to have opted for emissions trading primarily through *emulation* of more prestigious peers. In the case of Kazakhstan, the more general wish to develop closer political relations with the EU must be recognized as an important driver for the adoption of emissions trading. This reminds us that 'technical' ETS policies are sometimes woven into political high-level diplomacy games.

The role of policy diffusion in shaping ETS designs

Now we turn to the central question in this book – what has been the role of policy diffusion in shaping the design of trading systems? A quick design overview is presented in the Annex to this chapter. Basically, despite some obvious similarities in the design properties we have examined, there are several important differences in their more specific elaborations, as shown here.

Type of system: similarities influenced by policy diffusion; differences mainly domestically shaped

With the qualified exception of New Zealand, which has a national carbon trading scheme but no national cap, all the systems examined in this book can be classified as cap-and-trade systems. However, the types of cap and the ambition levels differ substantially. With the exception of Kazakhstan, all systems studied here allow banking, although with certain differences in the details. The possibility for banking has been identified as one of the major design properties influencing carbon prices (see e.g. Zaklan et al. 2015; Schmalensee et al. 2017). As to borrowing, the picture is more varied, with the New Zealand and planned Australian systems (and to some extent California and South Korea) more open to it, whereas borrowing is not allowed in the other systems.

There are also differences as to other basic system features, such as division into phases and length of trading periods. The EU ETS has been a frontrunner in introducing increasingly longer periods, going from the 3-year pilot phase to the 10-year fourth phase. In addition, the 'Linear Reduction Factor' operating from 2013 on and reducing the cap each year by 1.74 per cent with no specific end-point gives the EU ETS a unique long-range character matched by no other system internationally. Most of the other systems have shorter trading periods: California, South Korea and Tokyo have three 5-year periods. The initial test phase of China's national ETS is planned to last for 3 years (2017–20).

Most systems examined in this book have included an initial phase defined as a pilot phase – reflecting the acknowledgement that emissions trading is a new and largely untried instrument which requires a pilot phase for necessary adjustment, based on lessons learned from experience (see Chapters 3, 9 and 11 here).

What then is the role of policy diffusion? We have noted convergence around the choice of cap-and-trade, although that cannot in itself be regarded as evidence of learning and emulation of the merits of this basic design. However, the case-study evidence seems quite robust, so we can safely assume learning to have been a major mechanism. New Zealand's somewhat different type of system must be seen as partly 'internationally inspired' (as the design was linked to New Zealand's Kyoto commitments), but also due to perceived flaws in the EU ETS model. Thus, in the case of New Zealand we see that learning may lead to divergence.

Furthermore, we have found substantial similarity in the choice of not allowing inter-phase borrowing. In part, this can be attributed to learning between systems: in almost all cases in this volume, the authorities studied the EU ETS model in their initial ETS design discussions. But we cannot exclude some 'parallel play' here – that is, the possibility that in the absence of policy diffusion, rational actors facing similar problems end up with similar solutions. System administrators might simply have realized that inter-phase borrowing would create too much flexibility, obstructing the manageability of the system.

We have noted similar choices across systems in the embrace of banking, which it seems reasonable to see as the result of both learning and some parallel play (as to the former, recall the cases of South Korea and Kazakhstan). System administrators seem to agree that such banking is an important safety valve against excessive carbon price variations. Tellingly, in the pilot phase of the EU ETS, which did *not* include a banking option, the carbon price hit rock bottom in 2007, when excess allowances flooded the market.

Ambition level: divergence due to domestic concerns; similar international pressure effects

Some systems seem to rely heavily on emissions trading to achieve reductions, as in the case of New Zealand. Other systems include looser references to contributing to overall GHG emissions reductions in the jurisdiction target. The systems in South Korea and Tokyo stand out as the only ones with specific sectoral caps. Certainly striking is the considerable variation regarding the level of the cap and emissions cuts. This variation is also reflected in differing carbon prices (although the latter are influenced by a range of factors), as shown in Table 13.1.

The concept of *policy diffusion* does not seem to shed much light on the level of ambition adopted in the various cases. This is not surprising, since a great many factors go into how each jurisdiction determines its level of ambition and the role of ETS in concert with other instruments. An illustrative example is the EU ETS. Its targets have been derived from overall EU emissions reductions targets. The ETS has been (at least rhetorically) established as a cornerstone of EU climate policy, and the reduction targets of the ETS sector have in several rounds been more ambitious than the non-ETS sector, based on the assumption that the former has better possibilities to cut emissions in the established time periods. Most importantly, the ETS ambition is 'baked' into the overall ambitions of EU climate policy and must be understood in this broader context.

The California ETS has been given a less prominent place in the overall climate policy mix, in practice functioning more as a 'backstop policy' than a climate policy cornerstone, with no specific targets explicitly communicated for the ETS

Table 13.1 Allowance prices 2016/17 (in EUR; rough figures)

	EU ETS	*RGGI*	*CA*	*Tokyo*	*NZ*	*AUS*	*S. Korea*	*Kazak.*	*China pilots*
Price	5	4	12	12 (but huge fluctuations)	10.6	ETS halted	25 (2016 peak)	Between 0.1 to 3.6 in 2013–16 ETS now on hold	Variation from Chongqing (0.1) to Beijing (6.6)

sector. China has not adopted any 'regular' emissions reductions targets at all: the Chinese pilot systems operate in relation to intensity reduction targets. Perhaps with the exception of New Zealand, none of the cases studied here can reveal a jurisdiction that has relied mainly on ETS to achieve reductions – a striking finding, when contrasted with the core logic of using market instruments to allow the market to discover least-cost strategies for emissions control.

Most of the governments in the systems examined here have placed the ambitions of their ETS in an international context, seeking to influence others or being influenced by, for instance, the Kyoto Protocol. This may have a 'ratcheting up' effect, with, for instance, the EU seeking to nudge others to adopt similarly ambitious targets as itself. South Korea's GHG emissions reduction target was in part a response to international developments and pressure. Given its rapid economic development and steep rise in GHG emissions, South Korea could no longer claim that it was a developing country of which no climate mitigation action could be required.

But we also observe a 'race to the bottom' effect that has influenced most governments: they are reluctant to regulate their industries more strictly than their economic competitors. This concern for the competitiveness of domestic industries is reflected in volatile and, with the exception of Tokyo (and for a short period also South Korea), rather low carbon prices all over the world (see Table 13.1). The lesson learned is that governments will need to ramp up their ambitions significantly in order to make emissions trading a major driver of the low-carbon transition (Schjolset 2017).

Allowance allocation: much similarity; significantly shaped by diffusion

All systems started out with a mix dominated by free allocation, with auctioning becoming stronger over time. Among the systems examined, only RGGI introduced full auctioning almost from the very beginning.

Learning and in some cases emulation can explain these patterns of allocation. In both South Korea and Kazakhstan, as well as in some of the Chinese pilots, we find clear evidence of diffusion by emulation, copying from the EU ETS in particular. With California, it is interesting to note that policy-makers there claim to have learned from the EU case that free allocation has its drawbacks. They have periodically stated their intention to reduce free allocation – partly because funds raised from auctioned permits are used for politically popular activities – but the degree of auctioning introduced in the Californian system thus far is rather modest (10 per cent), and the further increase is planned to happen gradually (reaching 25 per cent by 2020). With its perennial budget problems, California also learned that the ETS could be a major source of revenues if auctioning of permits were required.

Further, differences in the design of ETS schemes also had considerable impact on the extent to which policy-makers were concerned about (and responded to) how limits on emissions would affect economic competitiveness. In the case of the EU ETS, we noted a significant *general* economic competition concern. But this did not really fit into the policy diffusion category as we have defined it. The choice of handing out allowances for free was partly motivated by significant uncertainty and reluctance among energy-intensive industries regarding the emissions trading instrument. These industries are, to varying degrees, exposed to global competition; distributing generous amounts of allowances for free was a key response from policy-makers to the widespread reluctance. Perceptions among European industries of an uneven global climate policy playing field, where competitors faced no or more lenient regulations, have lingered on, influencing the choice of maintaining a significant share of free allowances right up to the present negotiations on the 2030 ETS framework.

How, then, can the divergent design choice in the case of RGGI be explained? It seems that this system quickly landed on full auctioning not only because other systems were experiencing windfall profits problems related to free allocation, but also because its narrow sectoral coverage made such a design choice less controversial. RGGI covers only power producers (who can pass on ETS costs to consumers far more easily than can energy-intensive industries that are more exposed to outside competition), and the utility sector came to include industry players that did not oppose auctioning.

Coverage: both similarities and differences; much shaped by diffusion

All systems examined here cover the large and relatively easily monitored emissions from the power sector. Beyond that, we find substantial variation. In the EU ETS, coverage includes power producers and energy-intensive industries such as steel, cement and pulp and paper – as in China's pilot systems and its forthcoming national ETS. Interestingly, the Chinese pilot systems have sought to cover electricity consumption and hence 'indirect emissions'. In addition, the South Korean system includes such indirect emissions. This is related to the highly regulated power sectors in these jurisdictions, where utilities have limited possibilities for passing costs on to consumers (and hence for carbon pricing to influence consumers in such indirect ways). RGGI stands out as having particularly narrow coverage: the system applies solely to CO_2 emissions from utilities.

Regarding other sectors, aviation is in various ways included in the EU, South Korea, Shanghai pilot and coming national Chinese ETSs. Other transport emissions are covered in systems such as Beijing and South Korea, and to some extent California, which has the broadest coverage within the energy system. The NZ ETS is unique in its inclusion of forestry; Tokyo is unique in its focus on large-scale office buildings. With regard to gases, CO_2 is covered by all. Four systems stand out as having very wide coverage in this respect (five or more GHGs): California, China's Chongqing pilot system, New Zealand and South Korea. Here we can note a development over time: moving from the pilot phase to subsequent phases, most systems have gradually expanded their coverage of sectors and industries.

Some of these similarities and differences can be explained by international policy diffusion. Regarding the similarities, we see evidence of learning and, in cases such as Kazakhstan and South Korea, directly copying from the EU ETS model. However, there has also been some 'parallel play': the power sector is a key emitter in most of the jurisdictions and is comparatively easy to monitor, so it stands out as a central target group to include in an ETS. We have noted some divergence in the role of the transport sector, aviation in particular. Here, closer scrutiny of available evidence about 'late adopters' like the Shanghai pilot system points mainly to domestic drivers, not inspiration from the 'aviation frontrunner' EU ETS.

In sum, then, policy diffusion cannot explain *all* the variation we have found regarding coverage. The inclusion of forestry in the New Zealand ETS is rooted in domestic sectoral characteristics, with significant emissions from the forestry sector. A particularly noteworthy aspect of both the South Korean ETS and the Chinese pilot systems is that they seek to cover electricity consumption and 'indirect emissions'. As indicated, this is clearly related to the highly regulated power sectors in these jurisdictions and the limited possibilities for utilities to pass on the costs to electricity consumers.

Offsets and linking: divergence primarily due to domestic concerns

All the systems examined provide access to some types of credits to cover obligations, although quantitative and qualitative restrictions on their use vary significantly. For example, quantitative restrictions differ across trading systems, with the Californian system having relatively strict quantitative restrictions for the use of credits to cover obligations. In addition, qualitative restrictions differ across the systems examined here. For example, the EU ETS allows for only very limited use of credits from land use, land-use change and forestry; by contrast, California, Australia and New Zealand allow for the use of credits generated by forest and land-use projects. In Kazakhstan – unlike, for instance, the EU ETS, which currently applies only to CO_2 projects – projects which reduce emissions of any greenhouse gas can be implemented as domestic offset projects.

In principle, nearly all these systems are designed to allow international linkages. For instance, the EU ETS has been positive to linking with Kyoto Protocol ratifiers; in 2009, the EU launched a vision of an Organisation for Economic Co-operation and Development (OECD)-wide carbon market by 2015. California has allowed formal linkage from the beginning, although the rules that would make that possible were implemented very narrowly. The original vision for the California system was that many western US states would be involved – something that, so far, has not happened. Kazakhstan has had a very explicit vision of linking up to the EU ETS.

Not so surprisingly, the variation observed in offset rules cannot be explained by international policy diffusion. However, some basic learning has certainly taken place as actors have learned from each other about the benefits of opening systems up for some sort of offsetting, particularly about the need to provide industrial actors with additional safety valves against excessive price fluctuations and skyrocketing prices. In the EU ETS, for example, we know that such considerations played a role when the system was being established. And policy-makers interviewed in California mentioned negative EU experiences as one of the shaping factors for the more restrictive implementation of their offset regime. Formally, the 8 per cent capping of each entity's allowed use of offsets is not so different from the rough initial 10 per cent cap in the EU system; in practice, however, the California rules have been more restrictive.

To conclude, offsetting rules have generally been shaped by differing internal and domestic considerations in the various jurisdictions. For instance, in New Zealand, the very open access to offsetting before 2015 must be understood in the context of the perceived lack of technically feasible/affordable domestic abatement options in agriculture. With China, the access to 'repurposed CDMs' (Chinese certified emission reductions, CCERs) has its roots in China's earlier dominant position as a CDM credit provider; the Chinese authorities wished to uphold some use for these activities and the credits created in a situation where external demand (from the EU in particular) was decreasing markedly.

Monitoring, reporting and verification (MRV) and enforcement: substantial convergence; much shaped by diffusion

All systems examined have established procedures for MRV and enforcement. Most trading schemes have established emissions trading registries to enable monitoring of trade in allowances and have introduced third-party verification and enforcement mechanisms. Indeed, only one ETS to date, that in Kazakhstan, was introduced without any systems in place for MRV and enforcement. However, regarding penalties and responses to non-compliance, we find significant variation among the systems, with very little common ground.

Policy diffusion by learning and emulation holds significant explanatory power for the observed convergence in these aspects of ETS design. Evidence from several cases points to substantial copying of EU ETS procedures – as in South Korea, the Chinese pilot schemes, Kazakhstan and to some extent Tokyo. Even if the EU system has experienced some problems with fraud and double counting, these have not significantly weakened the position of the EU ETS as a role model. As to the EU ETS itself, we note that the initial MRV and compliance regime learned from the US SO_2/NOx trading experiences.

That Kazakhstan initially had no MRV system in place can be explained by domestic factors, particularly the fast-tracked nature of the Kazakh ETS implementation process as a result of high-level political pressure from the government. Kazakhstan was more interested in opening possibilities for linking with the EU than in exactly how that link should be designed. The subsequent MRV development borrowed much from the EU ETS.

The substantial differences in penalties systems must be understood in light of jurisdictional and regulatory traditions in each of the jurisdictions. Moreover, whereas MRV has been regarded as rather technical and hence uncontroversial to copy, penalties raise more fundamental concerns which require responses tailored to the specific legal and societal context.

Price and quantity management: both convergence and divergence partly shaped by learning

Initially, the frontrunner EU ETS had no price- or quantity-management mechanisms. By contrast, several other jurisdictions have introduced a price floor or ceiling. Both RGGI and California have quite complex arrangements, with both a price floor and a sort of ceiling – for example, the Allowance Price Containment Reserve in the case of California and the auction reserve prices in both systems. Some of the Chinese pilots have included price-floor mechanisms, as well as other mechanisms for price management.

The first phase of Australia's Carbon Pricing Mechanism was based on a fixed price. The intention was to replace the fixed price with a price ceiling in the second phase, which would have been removed in the third phase. Hence, the Australian ETS would have gradually allowed greater volatility in the carbon price through the removal of price-management mechanisms. Similarly, New Zealand introduced a price ceiling as part of its 2009 reform. South Korea and China (that is, some of the pilots and the coming national system) have centrally steered quantity-adjustment systems.

Convergence in the creation of price floors can be attributed to considerable policy diffusion, mainly in the form of avoidance learning. 'Follower' jurisdictions observed price volatility and related problems in the EU ETS and wanted to avoid them. This was explicitly mentioned by policy-makers in several of the systems studied here, including California, RGGI, Australia and some Chinese pilots. However, domestic concerns pulled in the same direction as avoidance learning as regards ensuring price predictability in several of these jurisdictions, such as Australia.

Within this broader picture of convergence around the choice of price floor designs, there are many variations in the details. One example is the *level* of price floors, with the RGGI one as low as USD 2, while the California price floor stands at around USD 14. These variations can be explained by domestic political and economic factors. For instance, in California the specific design of the price-control mechanism was based partly on advice from a committee consisting of economists from California's top universities. An important underlying concern was to find the right place for the ETS in California's climate policy package because central political players were opposed to any use of market forces at all. They held that direct regulation would better ensure environmental outcomes and environmental justice and worried that trading would lead to pollution hotspots. Thus, from the beginning, California designed a climate policy that would use markets alongside other traditional regulatory policies. An additional concern was the goal of contributing to a predictable investment horizon for key industrial stakeholders – the experts on the design committee were aware of those concerns and aware from theory (and practice as revealed in the EU ETS) that a price floor would help create a more predictable price environment for long-term investments.

Domestic factors must also be taken into account in order to understand the central steering mechanisms adopted in South Korea and in the Chinese pilots. In these systems, more centralized decision-making procedures remain in place (and in China, those planning systems operate at the province and local levels as well), and trading systems have been layered on top. In effect, then, price and quantity decisions are not purely (or even mainly) the result of market choices: they are the result of these other administrative processes.

Revenue earmarking: not much of it, and primarily shaped by parallel play

We find significant variation in the recommendations and requirements for revenue earmarking across the systems examined. A few systems have earmarked proceeds from allowance auctions to greenhouse gas reduction funds (as in RGGI and California). But most of these systems have been designed with more diffuse and non-binding rules. For instance, for the EU ETS phase 3 (2013–20) there is a recommendation to use a certain proportion of auctioning revenues for climate-change mitigation and adaptation measures. In the first two phases of the EU ETS, allowances were mostly handed out for free, making the question of revenue earmarking from auctions largely irrelevant.

The main shaping factors here have clearly been domestic political and economic ones. As a general rule, finance ministries across the globe are reluctant to allow revenue earmarking; they prefer to retain the option of spending revenues (whether from permit auctions or other sources, such as taxes) according to shifting economic and political priorities. This is reflected in the fact that the obligation adopted in the EU ETS is a non-binding recommendation. A common feature of the rules and mechanisms in the other systems with some revenue earmarking is also that these rules are rather diffuse, consisting more of good intentions than specified and binding requirements.

One exception is California, where the earmarking of revenues for the Greenhouse Gas Reduction Fund, and hence economic redistribution, must be seen as part of a general effort to increase ETS acceptance among key stakeholders. Another exception is Australia, where earmarked revenues were intended to provide targeted assistance and support for transitions to harder-hit industries (like coal and power generators), but also more generally to offset the costs of the Carbon Pricing Mechanism (CPM) to consumers via the introduction of the Household Assistance Package.

Although these instances generally had very little to do with reducing emissions, they still represent specific earmarking of revenues from an ETS for issues related to or created by the ETS. These cases show that, politically, it is useful to distinguish between earmarking measures to support emissions reductions – addressing effectiveness issues – and earmarking measures more broadly to ease the financial pain of an ETS – speaking more to the economic efficiency of the policy instrument overall.

Assessing the specific expectations about diffusion and design

In Chapter 2, we formulated five expectations about policy diffusion and design outcomes. Those expectations were broad, organizing hypotheses that helped guide the empirical research presented in this book. Here we evaluate the expectations against what we found.

Why did the emissions trading idea catch the interest of decision-makes?

We expected that interest in emissions trading would increase when the policy instruments in use were considered insufficient or ineffective and emissions trading in other jurisdictions was deemed successful. Our examination of the turn to emissions trading across jurisdictions broadly supports that expectation.

Which design properties are most likely to diffuse across systems?

We suggested that general principles and operational technicalities would diffuse with fewer and less radical adjustment than would main policy components. Our case studies broadly support that expectation. We consider factors such as MRV procedures and enforcement rules as important examples of operational technicalities. Our case studies find significant similarities in such operational technicalities across systems and conclude that these similarities are to a significant extent due to learning and even outright copying between jurisdictions. Examples that stand out here are Kazakhstan, South Korea and some Chinese pilot projects. Another example is New Zealand's adoption of some ETS features already introduced by Australia.

We consider ambition level, allocation mechanisms, offset rules and price/quantity mechanisms as main policy elements – that is, elements of the design that have the greatest implications for the level and variation in carbon price. Consistent with our expectations, we find large variation in these main policy factors across systems for emissions trading. All these principal policy components seem to undergo significant changes/adaptations as domestic stakeholders seek to protect and advance their interests, mediated by relevant domestic institutions, during the process of policy design and implementation.

In California, for example, evidence indicates that the EU experience did not play a prominent role in the political discourse about emissions trading – whether or not the EU ETS existed, California policy-makers and experts knew that emission trading was a major policy option – but the EU ETS seems to have influenced more technical discussions on certain design properties. The EU ETS is cited both as a positive example from which to draw lessons, and as a negative case that enabled lesson-drawing from mistakes made, particularly in the first phase of the

EU ETS when policy experts sought to promote the ETS through various direct contacts with North American actors.

Evidence of jurisdictions scrutinizing what others are doing, leading to the adoption or avoidance of certain design features, seems most pronounced during the early stages when the intellectual foundations for ETS design are being laid. Without their own experience to draw on, countries look to what others have been doing, to see what is technically and politically feasible before commencing the political process of seeking stakeholder cooperation and legislative approval.

How do different design properties diffuse (if they do diffuse)?

We expected that general principles and operational technicalities would spread primarily through learning or emulation, whereas main policy components would be designed mainly in response to competition in international or domestic markets. If we view ambition level, allocation mechanisms, offset rules and price/quantity mechanisms as principal elements, our expectation seems to be partly supported. For ambition level and offset rules at least, the mechanisms of learning and emulation do not appear to have played any noteworthy role. The design of these policy components was generally shaped by a mixture of domestic concerns and concerns for international competitiveness.

Learning seems to play a more important role with regard to allocation mechanisms and price/quantity mechanisms. One instance is the case of the Chinese pilots – which led to *divergence*. We also note that the design of MRV and enforcement in the Chinese pilots was influenced by learning from the EU ETS model – but here it led to *convergence*. Both observations lend some support to our expectation that learning and emulation may be most important for the diffusion of operational technicalities. However, the cases do not provide conclusive evidence in support of that expectation. In fact, in several instances it was hard to determine whether and how a specific diffusion mechanism influenced a specific design feature. These observations indicate that more work is required to further refine our research design.

Who are the main agents driving diffusion processes?

We expected that, when learning is the main mechanism of diffusion, expert networks found in research institutions, governments, environmental non-governmental organizations (ENGOs), industry/business and broader 'epistemic communities' would be important, particularly during the initial policy-making phases. Further, we expected that when the process reaches the stage of competitive bargaining over the main policy components of an ETS, policy-makers and industry/business stakeholders would play more prominent roles, some as drivers and others as blockers.

The studies presented in this book generally support that expectation. Experts and broader epistemic communities seem to have played important roles in the early stages of policy initiation, in all cases examined. As the policy process moved from the agenda-setting stage to the policy adoption and implementation stages, industry/business stakeholders and political actors become more involved, gaining increasing influence over the main policy components of an ETS. But we also find evidence of expert networks continuing to influence ETS design in the adoption and implementation stages, not least the operational technicalities, as we expected.

How do different diffusion mechanisms affect outcomes?

We expected that emulation would lead to upwards convergence, with a more advanced system being copied; that learning would lead to more effective and efficient design but not necessarily to convergence; and that competition might generate a race to the bottom or to the top, depending on the circumstances. A first observation after reviewing all the case-study evidence is that no clear pattern emerges. Evidence from our case studies indicates that learning in many cases resulted in divergent designs, with jurisdictions learning from the mistakes made by others. However, we cannot conclude that such avoidance learning generally resulted in more effective or efficient design. The case-study evidence also indicates that competition as a diffusion mechanism can indeed result in both upwards and downwards change, but the data available do not enable us to distinguish reliably the conditions that lead to change upwards from those leading to downwards change.

The more general question of whether we see upwards or downwards change as systems diffuse calls for attention to changes within as well as across systems. With regard to *intra-system* change, we have substantial evidence to conclude that most of the systems examined here have become more ambitious, thereby changing upwards over time. For instance, most systems have adopted timetables for periodic review in order to ensure some upward change. However, there is also substantial variation, with the EU ETS being an example of a system with relatively strong mechanisms for upwards change – not least with its Linear Reduction Factor, which was adopted in 2008 and started functioning from 2013 on (i.e. that the cap is reduced by 1.74 per cent each year). The Linear Reduction Factor does not have a specific end-point in time. No other system examined has a comparable long-term reduction mechanism.

The evidence is inconclusive as to whether there is upwards or downwards change as systems diffuse *across* jurisdictions. The clearest case of emulation in this book is that of Kazakhstan, which copied several design elements from the EU ETS in developing its national system. However, we find no clear evidence of a general upward change as a result of copying the EU ETS: what we see are schemes with some design features stronger and other design features less stringent than the EU model.

Concluding reflections

Let us end this volume by briefly reflecting on some of the implications of this work, along two dimensions. One dimension is future research on theory as well as empirical investigations into emission trading systems (the first subsection here). We explore whether and how the theoretical foundation and conceptual tools adopted in this book project have proven useful for identifying the main mechanisms at work and for predicting/explaining outcomes. We also explore how our case study approach can help fill the remaining gaps. The second dimension concerns politics and policy (addressed in the second subsection). While this study is academic in design and purpose, our findings – in particular, about the divergence of important design and policy choices across existing trading systems – have important implications for how trading may unfold as a policy instrument in the future.

Theoretical foundations and empirical findings

Most theory-oriented research on (international) policy diffusion assumes that the actors involved – not only governments but also firms, industries and other stakeholders – are boundedly rational in the sense of focusing attention on options likely to meet their own general ambitions and specific targets. In developing policies for climate-change mitigation, these will be options that meet mitigation targets at politically acceptable costs. In searching for such acceptable systems, actors are likely to explore arrangements adopted by others, especially schemes developed and implemented by more prestigious peers. Interest in how others go about achieving effective low-cost cuts in emissions can best be understood as engagement in learning.

Our case studies indicate that learning is particularly important at two stages. In the first stage, decision-makers begin taking a serious interest in introducing a particular policy instrument – in this setting, a *market* mechanism: trading – to supplement other and more conventional modes of regulation. When the basic decision to introduce trading of emission permits has been made, various more technical questions arise in the second stage – for example, how to design and implement procedures for monitoring and reporting performance. These second-stage questions concern design aspects where lessons learned by others may enable the newcomer to avoid beginners' mistakes. At both these stages diffusion of ideas will be driven largely by newcomer interest; the more advanced front-runners seem willing to share with interested newcomers information about the strengths and weaknesses of their own systems.

When attention turns to the policy decisions most critical to domestic stakeholders – including overall ambition level, activities to be included in the scheme and methods for allocating permits – *adaptation* seems to take over as the main design strategy. Adaptation is often used to defend one's own industries and business against 'distortion' in domestic and international markets caused by other actors, but it can also be used as a cooperative response. In the former scenario, the parties involved risk generating a 'race to the bottom'; in the latter scenario, mutual positive responses may generate a 'race to the top'.

Most formal rational choice models assume that, faced with the same set of options, actors will make identical (or very similar) choices. When we embarked upon this project we realized that the landscape to be studied was considerably more diverse than formal models acknowledge and would require substantial amounts of in-depth empirical research. We nevertheless expected to find that diffusion – to the extent it actually occurred – would lead more often to convergence in the design of emission trading systems than to divergence.

That expectation came in part from theory – when policy-makers in different jurisdictions designed trading systems, they were assumed to look to frontrunners and learn the 'right' lessons about what actually works. It was bolstered by considerable previous empirical work that reported evidence of convergence (e.g. Elkins and Simmons 2005). In financial accounting, for example, national bureaucrats and officials have made extensive efforts to compare best practices (and codify some of them in international standards), leading to convergence (e.g. Büthe and Mattli 2011). In environmental regulation, learning and diffusion leading to convergence has been evident, for example, in the rapid adoption of concepts like the precautionary principle as well as the diffusion of more detailed European and Californian standards on clean fuels and air quality (e.g. Vogel 1997). In short, the standard view emerging from diffusion research was that when policy-makers pay close attention to what is happening in frontrunner jurisdictions, they tend to go for similar although not necessarily identical arrangements.

As shown prior, our case studies provide only limited support for that expectation. Instead, they indicate (a) that policy-makers quite often respond differently to what appear to be quite similar challenges, because the learning and adaptation process is heavily influenced by local political interests and institutions; and (b) that they often learn at least as much from the failures of others as from their success stories.

We believe that these findings reflect an important advantage of empirical case research over stringent rational choice formulas: the ability to *contextualize* more broadly, and thereby better understand actors' reasoning and behaviour. Researchers engaged in empirical case studies have the advantage of 'getting closer' to the problem diagnoses and preferences of the decision-makers involved. This can position them better for discovery and taking into account concerns that are missed (or misinterpreted) in models narrowly focused on the costs and benefits directly related to climate-change mitigation.

In democracies, governments often depend heavily on electoral support from particular groups of voters concerned primarily with activities that stand to lose from ambitious policies for mitigating climate change and its effects. In such cases, a government concerned with its own prestige and survival can be expected to search for solutions that will not (significantly) alienate these groups. Such solutions may be weaker in delivering mitigation; however, in some instances, a government may be able to 'purchase' group acceptance of a more ambitious mitigation programme by offering side-payments in domains particularly important to these groups. Similar – although often more brutal – mechanisms can be found in authoritarian states. The main message seems to be that – at least in the field of climate-change mitigation – we can improve our understanding of international diffusion (and co-evolution) of ETS designs by further developing the interplay between theoretical foundations and conceptual tools on one hand, and in-depth empirical research on the other.

Because this project was designed to contextualize our understanding of national and regional trading systems, the case studies presented here find far greater divergence than might be expected from conventional theory approaches. In the prior we have unpacked these findings in various ways. Here we summarize the four core explanations for this observed pattern of divergence:

- *The diversity of local politics*. No country adopts limits on emissions solely for the purpose of contributing to solving a global commons problem. To varying degrees, the mission of decarbonization is pursued alongside other, usually related, policy goals. In some jurisdictions, the global goals may appear relatively weak and fleeting, whereas local goals – such as tackling local air pollution or enhancing energy security – are much stronger.
- *The diversity of design features*. Some design features are more adaptable to local political contexts than others. This means that divergence on some measures is not really meaningful because they must be the same in each venue (e.g. carbon must be accounted for), whereas we do see divergence on other design features (like offsetting rules) even when the general idea of carbon markets is adopted.
- *Learning what not to do*. Several instances of learning reported in our case studies have aimed at not replicating certain earlier designs. The EU ETS was the first major carbon trading system, and its sheer size and relevance eclipsed earlier emissions trading systems as 'models' for learning, such as the US sulphur trading programme. Had the EU ETS been an undisputed success, we might have seen more active efforts to follow and converge on the EU model. But the price crash and suspicions that the EU's offsets programme (via the CDM) was not robust led other policy-makers to focus on how not to replicate what had happened in the EU case. Learning focused on avoidance, not convergence.
- *Lack of relevant international standards*. Often, the process of diffusion and convergence is assisted by international standards that create focal points, mechanisms for coordination and a backstop against extreme divergence. The convergence around financial standards and accounting, for example, displays interplay between bureaucratic processes inside countries and international pressures for convergence conveyed through standards (e.g. Büthe and Mattli 2011). In emissions trading – perhaps partly because of the difficulties with the EU ETS – no such single set of standards has emerged, although work on carbon accounting standards set in motion by the Paris Agreement is a promising development (Jevnaker and Wettestad 2016).

What does all this mean for future research? First and foremost, the diversity of local politics means that researchers must contend with the fact that there are many complex domestic processes and mechanisms to uncover and understand. There is clearly a need for more research on how design choices are rooted in local conditions – and to search for patterns in how those local factors shape outcomes. Our book makes important contributions here, but much remains to be done, not least regarding the interactions between ETS and other policies – notably those outside the strict domain of climate and energy policy.

A second front for new research is to investigate whether one of our central findings – design divergence rather than convergence – holds for cases not analysed in this book, like the emerging systems in countries such as Thailand, Vietnam and South Africa. Or perhaps these new cases can reveal new modes of diffusion that might be replacing the 'wave of divergence' observed in this book, with convergence around a better design model that has been refined through more experience. New research should investigate whether the age of the policy reforms affects the patterns of convergence and divergence. Particularly useful would be to examine other areas where divergence has been observed, to see whether earlier research on policy diffusion (which tended to show convergence) may have been biased by focusing on areas like financial regulation, where convergence was easier and there were stronger incentives for convergence.

Third, additional research is needed to know more about the implications of divergent design choices for the functioning of systems. Do the more recent systems function better than the frontrunners, for example? Are policy-makers finding that divergent systems create difficulties in linking different systems, thereby perhaps undermining one of the chief supposed economic advantages of trading systems?

Implications for carbon-market politics and policy

Our finding of divergence has sobering implications for the vision of a global carbon market that many policy-makers think could help integrate different national efforts into a common planet-wide effort. Bold visions for carbon markets have been offered, and large trading companies have been created around that vision (Rosenzweig 2016). The Kyoto Protocol seemed to affirm that vision through the creation of a market in offsets that could be used in any of the advanced industrialized countries. By this logic, a common core market could create incentives for jurisdictions to link their efforts, and there have been many bold plans for doing just that – such as linkages between the EU and Australia and other markets. Apart from the EU linking up to European Economic Area (EEA) members Norway, Iceland and Lichtenstein, none of those linkages have materialized, although two markets (California and Quebec) now operate in parallel with common auction rules.

The studies presented in this book help explain why linkage has been slow. In effect, divergence has created various different 'currencies' that are regulated by 'central bankers' who respond to different rules (Victor et al. 2005). Unfettered linkage between these markets would not create incentives for divergence – instead, it would create currency and capital flows. Policy-makers who have overseen this divergence – who have deliberately chosen rules that diverge – know that unfettered linkage would give them less control over local outcomes (see Green et al. 2014; Wettestad and Jevnaker 2014).

In the 1990s, markets were seen as a means of creating systems for convergence and deeper cooperation. Today, that mechanism is much weaker than originally expected, and may even be a source of divergence. In the 1990s, it was possible to imagine a set of 'first best' mechanisms for promoting global cooperation; today, the world is a realm of the 'second best' (Barrett and Stavins 2003). It seems more likely that effective cooperation will emerge through bottom-up processes and in smaller groups where it is easier to work out deals and monitor behaviour (Victor 2011). Indeed, that vision is reflected in the Paris Agreement, which provides a global umbrella over a host of bottom-up processes, national pledges and club-based cooperation (Victor 2015; Bodansky 2016).

In the future, the role of carbon markets is likely to be different. Such markets can be envisioned as operating at the 'seams' between different national efforts. The core of these national and other policy efforts will reflect local political and administrative realities. They will reflect how different jurisdictions see market instruments serving different functions – for some (like California), the market is a backstop; for others (like the EU) the market plays a more central role. Still others (like China) see the market more as a mechanism for promoting experimentation. In most cases, emissions trading will not be the core mechanism affecting emissions – a host of other regulatory measures will have greater impacts, and trading will backstop and optimize the residual. Given this diversity in goals and administration, it is hardly surprising that unfettered interconnection of markets across borders – which would create the equivalent of a single common currency and would force some homogeneity in price and effort – has remained elusive.

For some analysts who image a world of global trading, this is a bleak picture, far removed from their 'first best' vision of what should be done. For students of politics and public administration, it is much more rooted in reality. In this world of divergence, far more attention will be needed to the mechanisms for linking different carbon markets – not unfettered linkages, but careful links that can be managed to prevent excessive capital flows and linkages that create incentives for convergence in trading rules over time (see also Lazarus et al. 2015; Green 2017). That process will be slow, since it must confront the need not just to learn the right lessons but also to rewire local politics and administrative procedures around common standards and expectations.

While the overall finding of divergence was unexpected and perhaps disturbing for visions of global trading quickly leading to global cooperation, the studies in this book do indicate some areas where there are some elements of convergence. Lessons are being learned – from failures, and from successes. For example, efforts in many jurisdictions to avoid the price volatility seen in the EU has led to more widespread use of price floors – so that emission trading systems, in effect, mimic carbon taxes. In some jurisdictions, including the EU, that lesson is known but is impractical to implement – because tax/price-focused measures face higher political hurdles to adoption. Instead, the EU has adopted a quantity-based mechanism, which could be of interest to other jurisdictions with similar political hurdles (Jevnaker and Wettestad 2017). The national system in China aims at dealing with this challenge by allocating allowances annually.

In addition, there is much more widespread agreement today on the need for market measures to play a role in emissions policy – a lesson that the firms most exposed to the cost of emission controls are themselves keen to promote, as shown by discussions at the 2017 Davos summit (Carbon Pulse 2017). The world may be on the cusp of another major push to using market instruments – this time, guided by greater technical and political awareness of exactly where and how such instruments can function and how they can be linked across borders.

References

Barrett, S, and R.N. Stavins. 2003. Increasing participation and compliance in international climate change agreements. *International Environmental Agreements: Politics, Law and Economics* (3), 349–376.

Bodansky, D. 2016. The Paris Climate Change Agreement: A new hope? *The American Journal of International Law* 110 (2), 288–319.

Büthe, T. and W. Mattli. 2011. *The New Global Rulers: The Privatization of Regulation in the World Economy*. Princeton: Princeton University Press.

Carbon Pulse. 2017. Davos: World needs $50–100 CO2 price, non-elite 'ambassadors' to relay that message to a distrusting public. 19 January.

Elkins, Z. and B. Simmons. 2005. On waves, clusters and diffusion: A conceptual framework. *Annals of the American Academy of Political and Social Science* 598, 33–51.

Green, J. 2017. Comment: Don't link carbon markets. *Foreign Affairs*. 22 March. http://foreignaffairs.co.nz/2017/03/22/comment-dont-link-carbon-markets/ accessed 25 May 2017.

Green, J., T. Sterner and G. Wagner. 2014. A balance of 'bottom – up' and 'top – down' in linking climate policies. *Nature Climate Change* 12 (4), 1064–1067.

Jevnaker, T. and J. Wettestad. 2016. Linked carbon markets: Silver bullet or castle in the air? *Climate Law* 6 (1–2), 142–151.

Jevnaker, T. and J. Wettestad. 2017. Ratcheting up carbon trade: The politics of reforming EU emissions trading. *Global Environmental Politics* 17, 105–124.

Lazarus, M., L. Schneider, C. Lee and H. van Asselt. 2015. *Options and Issues for Restricted Linking of Emissions Trading Systems*. Berlin, Germany: ICAP, September 2015.

Rosenzweig, R. H. 2016. *Global Climate Change Policy and Carbon Markets – Transition to a New Era*. London: Palgrave Macmillan.

Schmalensee, R. and R. Stavins. 2017. Lessons learned from three decades of experience with cap and trade. *Review of Environmental Economics and Policy* 11 (1), 59–79.

Schjolset, S. 2017. Emissions trading: time to make it work. *Energy Post*, 31 January.

Victor, D. G. 2011. *Global Warming Gridlock: Creating More Effective Strategies for Protecting the Planet*. Cambridge: Cambridge University Press.

Victor, D. G. 2015. Why Paris worked: A different approach to climate diplomacy. *Yale Environment 360*. 15 December. http://e360.yale.edu/features/why_paris_worked_a_different_approach_to_climate_diplomacy accessed 29 May 2017.

Victor, D. G., J. C. House and S. Joy. 2005. A Madisonian approach to climate policy. *Science* 309 (5742), 1820–1821.

Vogel, D. 1997. Trading up and governing across: Transnational governance and enviromental protection. *Journal of European Public Policy* 4 (4), 556–571.

Wettestad, J. and T. Jevnaker. 2014. The EU's quest for linked carbon markets: Turbulence and headwind. In *Toward a New Climate Agreement: Conflict, Resolution and Governance*, edited by T. L. Cherry, J. Hovi and D. M. McEvoy, 266–279. London: Routledge.

Zaklan, A., D. Ellerman and V. Valero. 2015. *An Analysis of Allowance Banking in the EU ETS*. Beiträge zur Jahrestagung des Vereins für Socialpolitik 2015: Ökonomische Entwicklung – Theorie und Politik – Session: Environmental Economics III, No. C13-V1.

Annex

Table 13.2 Design overview

	EU ETS	*Tokyo*	*RGGI*	*California*	*New Zealand*	*Australia*	*China*	*South Korea*	*Kazakhstan*
Type of system	Cap and trade Phase 1: 2005–7 Phase 2: 2008–12 Phase 3: 2013–20 Phase 4: 2021–30 Banking allowed from Phase II on	Cap and trade Phase 1: 2010–14 Phase 2: 2015–19 Phase 3: 2020–22 Banking allowed	Cap and trade Phase 1: 2009–11 Phase 2: 2012–14 Phase 3: 2015–20 Banking but not borrowing	Cap and trade Phase 1: 2013–14 Phase 2: 2015–17 Phase 3: 2018–20 Banking allowed – and some borrowing	Trading, but no cap Banking and borrowing	Planned transition to cap and trade from 2015 Some banking and borrowing to be allowed	Cap and trade pilot systems 2013–17 Eight pilot systems, with differing designs Combination of absolute caps and intensity targets	Cap and trade Phase 1: 2015–17; Phase 2: 2018–20; Phase 3: 2021–26 Banking allowed, but not borrowing between phases	Cap and trade Phase 1: 2013 Phase 2: 2014– Banking not allowed; borrowing only within phases
Ambition level	Initially no common cap 2013–20: 21% reduction by 2020 (2005)	25% reduction by 2020 (2000)	Caps through emission budgets for each phase	Help meet ambition to stabilize state emissions at 1990 levels by 2020	Low and unspecified; aligned with Kyoto target	Contribute to achieve 5% reductions by 2020 Target to reduce emissions by 80% below 2000 levels by 2050	Intensity targets converge around a 17–21% band	29% reduction by 2020 (BaU)	Phase 1 (pilot phase): allocation equal to 100% of the non-verified emissions (2010) Phase 2: 1.5% reduction in emissions by the end of 2015 compared to a company's average emission level 2011–12 Phase 3: Emissions to be kept at 2013–14 levels until 2020
Coverage	Power producers and a number of energy-intensive industries – airlines from 2012 Upstream focus ('direct' emissions) CO_2; also nitrous oxide and perfluorocarbons	CO_2 emissions from offices, commercial and public buildings, district heating and industrial facilities Around 1,300 facilities	Electricity generators larger than 25 MW in nine states Only CO_2	Broad coverage of energy suppliers and industries – also imported electrical cars from 2015 Seven GHGs Around 450	Gradual phasing in of sectors: forestry, liquid fossil fuels, stationary energy and industrial processes, waste	Energy generation, energy-intensive industries, fugitive emissions and waste – but also fuel-related transport	Mainly power producers and energy-intensive industries – but also aviation (Shanghai) Both direct and indirect	Five sectors; 23 industries Power producers, industries, aviation Six GHGs 525 large emitters	Three sectors: 1. Energy (electricity and heat production) 2. Industry (mainly non-ferrous metals) 3. Coal mining, oil and gas extraction Only CO_2 166 companies

	Around 11,000 installations				Six GHGs Totally around 2,300 entities	CO_2 and three other GHGs Around 260 entities and around 60% of CO_2 emissions	Most pilots only CO_2 – but Chonquing six GHGs		
Allocation mechanisms	Initially mainly free allocation From 2013 on, ca 40% auctioning, to increase	Free allocation	Almost 100% auctioning	Initially 90% free allocation	Free allocation	Combination of free allocation and auctioning	Mainly free allocation Some experiments with auctioning	Initially 100% free allocation Gradually a limited auctioning and phased-in benchmarking from 2018	Free allocation
Offsetting and linking	Initially rough 10% CDM/JI limit Certain credits / projects banned from 2013	Four types of domestic offsets allowed: 1. Small- and Medium-sized Facility Credits 2. Outside-Tokyo Credits 3. Renewable Energy Credits 4. Saitama Credits	Max 3.3% domestic offsets for each installation	Max 8% for each company Various offsets in US, Canada and Mexico Parallel operation with Quebec ETS from 2014	Open access to international credits (until 2015)	Liberal domestic and international offsets rules International allowances only permitted after the fixed-price period	Chinese 'repurposed' CDM credits (CCERs) Differing restrictions	Max 10% domestic offsets No international credits	Domestic offsets
MRV	Annual reports from installations, verified by third part Initially EUR 40 penalty for non-compliance; then 100	Annual reports from installations, verified by third part Penalty: shortfall multiplied by 1.3	Yearly reports through EPA system Penalty provisions in two stages	Annual reports to CARB	Annual reports to NZ EPA, with some audits	Oversight by Clean Energy Regulator Strategic guidance by independent Climate Change Authority	Non-harmonized MRV protocols Differing penalty systems	Annual reports, verified by a third-party governmental register	Annual, verified reports No penalties initially

(*Continued*)

Table 13.2 (Continued)

	EU ETS	*Tokyo*	*RGGI*	*California*	*New Zealand*	*Australia*	*China*	*South Korea*	*Kazakhstan*
Price and quantity management	Initially nothing, then rule about two years of high price in 2009 Market Stability Reserve adopted in 2015, to function from 2019 on	No price controls by the Tokyo Metropolitan Government (TMG) In a case of excessive price evolution, the TMG may increase the supply of credits	Price floor and ceiling	Price floor starting at $10 in 2012; increasing 5% annually Also soft ceiling	No mechanisms	Three phases: fixed (AUD 23 2012–13 with 2.5% real terms increase to 2015), flexible and floating	Guangdong has price floor; in most systems the DRC can intervene in case of market fluctuations	The Allocation Committee can increase quantity if 'too high' price and generally adjust system Also a low-end price threshold	No mechanisms
Revenue earmarking	From 2013, recommendation to use 50% of revenues for climate purposes	None	Revenues to support energy efficiency, renewable energy and direct bill assistance	Revenues go into Greenhouse Gas Reduction Fund	No specific earmarking	Some revenues for low-carbon technologies and extensive assistance to industry and households	Guangdong: Low Carbon/ Development Fund; Hubei: Carbon Mitigation Fund	Revenues to contribute to Low Carbon Green Fund (being established)	None

Index

Page numbers in italic indicate a figure and page numbers in bold indicate a table on the corresponding page.

For Product Safety Concerns and Information please contact our EU representative GPSR@taylorandfrancis.com
Taylor & Francis Verlag GmbH, Kaufingerstraße 24, 80331 München, Germany

www.ingramcontent.com/pod-product-compliance
Ingram Content Group UK Ltd.
Pitfield, Milton Keynes, MK11 3LW, UK
UKHW010958180926
475701UK00004B/436
9780367264468